This book takes as its starting-point Plato's incorporation of specific genres of poetry and rhetoric into his dialogues. The author analyzes the intertextuality in Plato's dialogues in the context of both literary and social history, arguing in particular that Plato's "dialogues" with traditional genres are part and parcel of his effort to define "philosophy." Before Plato, "philosophy" denoted "intellectual cultivation" in the broadest sense. When Plato appropriated the term for his own intellectual project, he created a new and specialized discipline. In order to define and legitimize "philosophy," Plato had to match it against genres of discourse that had authority and currency in democratic Athens. By incorporating the text or discourse of another genre into his own dialogues, Plato "defines" his new brand of wisdom in opposition to traditional modes of thinking and speaking. By targeting individual genres of discourse, each of which had a specific audience and performative context, Plato marks the boundaries of "philosophy" as a discursive and as a social practice.

Genres in dialogue

Genres in dialogue

Plato and the construct of philosophy

Andrea Wilson Nightingale

Assistant Professor of Classics, Stanford University

CAMBRIDGE
UNIVERSITY PRESS

Published by the Press Syndicate of the University of Cambridge
The Pitt Building, Trumpington Street, Cambridge CB2 1RP
40 West 20th Street, New York, NY 10011-4211, USA
10 Stamford Road, Oakleigh, Melbourne 3166, Australia

First published 1995

Transferred to digital printing 1997

Printed in Great Britain by Biddles Short Run Books

A catalogue record for this book is available from the British Library

Library of Congress cataloguing in publication data

Nightingale, Andrea Wilson.
    Genres in dialogue : Plato and the construct of philosophy /
Andrea Wilson Nightingale.
        p. cm.
    Includes bibliographical references and index.
    ISBN 0 521 48264 X
    1. Plato.   2. Greek literature – History and criticism.
3. Literary form.   4. Rhetoric, Ancient.   I. Title.
B395.N54   1996
184 – dc20   95-5879
                                                                     CIP

ISBN 0 521 48264 X hardback

AO

For Douglas and Diana Wilson

Contents

Acknowledgments

My scholarly and personal debts are many, and none are more pressing than those owed to teachers. It is a great pleasure to thank Rachel Jacoff, who first guided me to Plato, via Dante. Without Rachel's generosity of mind and of spirit, I could not have completed this arduous pilgrimage. I owe a special debt to Oliver Taplin, who mentored me for two years at Oxford. More than he will ever realize, Oliver made it possible for me to envision and execute this project. Finally, I am deeply grateful to Tony Long, who has labored over several versions of the manuscript; his inspirational teaching and expert criticism have contributed to what is best in this book.

I would also like to thank my colleagues at Stanford for criticism, counsel, and encouragement. I am especially grateful to Mark Edwards, who has been a vital interlocutor for many years; he read the entire manuscript in its first incarnation, and saved me from a number of errors. Susan Stephens has been an invaluable mentor and critic, and has continually challenged me to rethink my most basic intellectual assumptions. The Stanford Humanities Center provided the ideal intellectual atmosphere for writing this book; I am grateful to its directors and fellows for support and criticism, and most especially for an ongoing dialogue across the disciplines.

Many friends and scholars have helped to bring this book into the world. First and foremost, I want to thank Kathryn Morgan, a superb interlocutor and fierce critic; she has covered several versions of this book with acute comments, and has stimulated my thinking from beginning to end. I am indebted to the following scholars for vital dialogues and incisive criticisms: Martin Bloomer, Diskin Clay, Kenneth Dover, Mark Griffith, Steve Johnstone, Andrew Laird, Linda Lomperis, Lisa Maurizio, Marsh McCall, Ian Morris, Richard Patterson, Alice Raynor, Rush Rehm, Christopher Rowe, Richard Sorabji, and the late Gregory Vlastos. Thanks are also owed to the two anonymous readers at Cambridge University Press, who rescued me from numerous errors and infelicities, and to my editor, Pauline Hire, for her efficiency and expertise. I am fully aware that I have not met all objections and criticisms; the errors which remain are my own.

This book is lovingly dedicated to Douglas and Diana Wilson, whom I am privileged to call my parents. As scholars and as human beings, they have informed every aspect of my work. This book is but a small tribute to these lifelong and lifegiving interlocutors. Finally, I would like to express my special gratitude to Tom Gregory, Spook Nightingale, and the North Yuba River, for constancy and surprise; and to my beloved husband Steven, for the ineffable and the unmentionable.

Versions of several portions of this book have appeared in print: "Generic transformation in Plato's *Gorgias*," *Classical Antiquity* 11 (1992), and "The folly of praise: Plato's critique of encomiastic discourse in the *Lysis* and *Symposium*," *Classical Quarterly* 43 (1993). Permission to reprint is gratefully acknowledged.

Abbreviations and texts

AJP	*American Journal of Philology*
BICS	*Bulletin of the Institute of Classical Studies* (London)
CA	*Classical Antiquity*
CM	*Classica et Mediaevalia*
CP	*Classical Philology*
CQ	*Classical Quarterly*
CR	*Classical Review*
CSCA	*California Studies in Classical Antiquity*
DK	*Die Fragmente der Vorsokratiker*, edd. H. Diels and W. Kranz, 6th ed., 3 vols. (Berlin 1951–2)
FGrH	*Die Fragmente der griechischen Historiker*, ed. F. Jacoby, 15 vols. (Berlin and Leiden 1923–58)
G & R	*Greece and Rome*
GRBS	*Greek, Roman, and Byzantine Studies*
HSCP	*Harvard Studies in Classical Philology*
JHS	*Journal of Hellenic Studies*
K	*L'Antiope d'Euripide*, ed. J. Kambitsis (Athens 1972)
PLF	*Poetarum Lesbiorum Fragmenta*, edd. E. Lobel and D. Page (Oxford 1955)
N	*Tragicorum Graecorum Fragmenta*, ed. A. Nauck with a supplement by B. Snell (Hildesheim 1964)
OSAPh	*Oxford Studies in Ancient Philosophy*
PCG	*Poetae Comici Graeci*, edd. R. Kassel and C. Austin, vols. 2, 3.2, 4, 5, 7 (Berlin 1983–?)
PCPS	*Proceedings of the Cambridge Philological Society*
PhR	*Philosophical Review*
PMG	*Poetae Melici Graeci*, ed. D. Page (Oxford 1962)
QUCC	*Quaderni Urbinati di Cultura Classica*
TAPA	*Transactions of the American Philological Association*

Texts

The works of Plato are quoted according to Burnet's Oxford text. For Isocrates, I have used the Teubner edition. Other writers are quoted according to the Oxford Classical Texts. Where there is no OCT edition, the text used will be cited in the footnotes. Unless otherwise noted, all translations of Greek are my own; although I have aimed for literal rather than literary renderings, I have occasionally opted for freer translations in an effort to avoid stilted and artificial English.

Introduction

Clov: What is there to keep me here?
Hamm: The dialogue.

Beckett, Endgame

The fact is that every writer *creates* his own precursors. His work modifies our conception of the past, as it will modify the future.

Borges, "Kafka and his Precursors"

In book three of the *Laws*, in an account of the deterioration of Athens from the time of the Persian wars, Plato ascribes the city's increasing anarchy to the mixture of traditional genres of music and poetry (698a–701c). As the Athenian Stranger says at 700d–e,

After [the Persian wars], as time passed, there arose as leaders of an unmusical lawlessness poets who, though artistic by nature, had no knowledge of what is just and lawful in the domain of the Muses. These people, frenzied as bacchantes and possessed by pleasure beyond what is right, blended together (κεραννύντες) dirges with hymns and paeans with dithyrambs and imitated songs for the flute in cithara-tunes and mixed (συνάγοντες) all the genres with one another. On account of their ignorance, these men unwittingly slandered art, saying that it does not have any standard of correctness, and that it is judged correctly by the pleasure of the auditor, regardless of whether he is a good or a bad man. Having created artistic compositions of this nature and added words that were similar in kind, these poets engendered in the populace a contempt for artistic norms and the bold conceit that they were capable of judging these things.

This intermingling of musical and poetic kinds, the Athenian explains, led to the violation of law not only in the realm of the arts but also in the domain of politics and government; generic mixture is thus directly responsible for the lawlessness that now characterizes the democracy. In order to avoid this degeneration into *anomia*, the Athenian recommends that the lawgiver take his cue from the Egyptians: he should legislate – and, indeed, "consecrate" (καθιεροῦν) – the correct genres of music and literature to ensure that there will be no "alteration or innovation" in the established forms (656d–657b).[1]

---

[1] I follow England's emendation of θαρροῦντα at 657a7 to καθιεροῦν τά. The context of the passage, first of all, strongly suggests that the Athenian is urging that the genres of music

1

This plea for generic purity – which has been championed and contested repeatedly in Western *belles lettres* since the time of Plato – has come under especially heavy fire by scholars and theorists in recent decades. As Ralph Cohen remarks,

Postmodern critics have sought to do without a genre theory. Terms like "text" and "écriture" deliberately avoid generic classifications. And the reasons for this are efforts to abolish the hierarchies that genres introduce, to avoid the assumed fixity of genres and the social as well as literary authority such limits exert, and to reject the social and subjective elements in classification.[2]

These theorists have suggested that "postmodern" or "metafictional" writing – writing that "blurs genres, transgresses them, or unfixes boundaries that conceal domination and authority" – should not be classified or interpreted by reference to genre.[3] The category of "postmodern" writing, of course, itself lacks firm boundaries: as scholars have often observed, many texts written long before the advent of postmodernism – texts such as *Don Quixote, Joseph Andrews*, or *Tristram Shandy* – display precisely those features that are now referred to as "postmodern." While Plato is often scripted as a villain by theorists of postmodernism, it is noteworthy that the same man who voices such a ringing condemnation of generic impurity in the *Laws* exhibits a positive hankering for the hybrid in so many of his texts: again and again, Plato mixes traditional genres of discourse into his dialogues and disrupts the generic boundaries of both his own texts and the texts that he targets. Indeed, Plato explicitly thematizes this disruption in a number of dialogues: in the *Symposium* (223d), Socrates insists the same person should be able to write both comedy and tragedy (an artistic feat not attempted by ancient Greek writers); in the *Phaedo*, a recurrent dream telling Socrates to "make music" prompts him to dress the prosaic fables of Aesop in the dignified garb of verse (60d–61b); and in the *Phaedrus*, Socrates observes with mock horror that his speech of invective has stolen into the lofty realm of epic discourse (241e).[4]

and poetry be given the sanction of religion. Second, as England 1921.I: 286–7 points out, καθιεροῦν is bolstered by its occurrence at 657b6 and 813a1; note also 799a4, where the Athenian once again recommends that the Magnesians adopt the Egyptian practice of "consecrating (καθιερῶσαι) all forms of dance and music."
[2] R. Cohen 1989: 13.
[3] R. Cohen 1989: 11.
[4] Socrates' first speech in the *Phaedrus*, of course, was meant to be an encomium of the non-lover. The speech, however, is unfinished, and never achieves the form of an encomium. As it stands, the speech deals only with the lover, who is attacked in a lengthy stream of invective. Note that Socrates himself identifies this speech as an invective twice in the dialogue (241e, ψέγων; 265c, ψέγειν).

This study takes as its starting-point the incorporation of the genres of Greek poetry and rhetoric into the Platonic dialogues. To cite a few of the most obvious examples: the Simonides poem in the *Protagoras*, the funeral oration in the *Menexenus*, the prose eulogies in the *Symposium*, the mock encomium of "Lysias" in the *Phaedrus*. To be sure, Plato explicitly defines the mode of discourse used by the philosopher ("dialectic") in opposition to the seductive language of poetry and rhetoric; but his dialogues never confine themselves to dialectic. In fact, the dialectical conversations of the interlocutors (which have been the focus of the great majority of Platonic scholars) are only one aspect of the Platonic dialogue. For many of Plato's texts are also constituted by the dialogues they conduct with other genres of discourse. In order to grasp the nature of this "conversation" with other genres, we must first address the notion of genre. As Conte has suggested,

genre must be thought of as a discursive form capable of constructing a coherent model of the world in its own image. It is a language, that is, a lexicon and a style, but it is also a system of the imagination and a grammar of things. Genres are the expressive codification of a culture's models; indeed, they are those very models subjected to a process of stylization and formalization which gives them a literary voice.[5]

If genres are not merely artistic forms but *forms of thought*, each of which is adapted to representing and conceptualizing some aspects of experience better than others, then an encounter between two genres within a single text is itself a kind of dialogue.[6] A dialogue of this kind, in fact, can have an extremely broad range, encompassing ethics, politics, and epistemology as well as language and literature. When Plato incorporates the text or discourse of another genre into a philosophical dialogue, he stages a scene in which the genre both speaks and is spoken to: it is this intergeneric "dialogue" that I want to investigate in this book.

How, then, does intertextuality operate in the Platonic dialogues and why does Plato enter into the "mixed" mode? Let me begin with some

---

[5] Conte [1991]/1994: 132 (see also 1986 passim).

[6] This conception of genre was first developed by Bakhtin and his circle (see, e.g., Bakhtin/ Medvedev 1985: especially ch. 7, Bakhtin 1981: especially 3–40, 259–422, and 1984: especially ch. 4, cf. 1986: 60–102; for a discussion of the ways in which Bakhtin's views on genre evolved and changed, see Morson and Emerson 1990: ch. 7). Todorov [1978]/1990 has a similar theory of genre; as he states: "In a given society, the recurrence of certain discursive properties is institutionalized, and individual texts are produced and perceived in relation to the norm constituted by that codification. Any genre, whether literary or not, is nothing other than the codification of discursive properties" (pp. 17–18). As Bakhtin and Todorov emphasize, genres/texts must be interpreted within their socio-political (as well as their literary) contexts. There is, of course, no single way to perform a historicized reading of a literary text or genre. The approach I use in this book is therefore eclectic.

reflections on the genre of the *Sōkratikoi logoi* (as Aristotle called them[7]). This genre, of course, had its origin in the late fifth century, just before Plato began writing. Although a great many of Socrates' associates were the authors of *Sōkratikoi logoi*, all that remains of this vital genre is some few fragments of Aeschines and the Socratic dialogues of the fourth-century writers Xenophon and Plato.[8] It is therefore impossible to ascertain the conventions of the early stages of the genre. But the ample corpus of Xenophon's Socratic writings provides an important comparandum for Plato's work. In a recent article on the origins of the Socratic dialogue, Diskin Clay acknowledges the dialogue's affiliation with the genres of mime and biography, but places special emphasis on its interaction with comedy and tragedy.[9] The Socratic dialogue, of course, resembles drama in its mimesis of people in conversation and in action; it is in comedy, after all, that Socrates makes his first appearance as a literary character. According to Clay, comedy provided both a model and a target for early Socratic writings, whereas tragedy offered itself as a paradigm after Socrates' execution turned him into a famous (or infamous) historical figure. As Clay remarks:

if the comic poets of Athens offered models for the literary Socratics while Socrates was alive, the tragic poets of Athens offered models for the dramatic representation of Socrates once he was dead. In dealing with history, the literary Socratics who wrote after Socrates' death could exploit a resource available to both the tragedian and the historian; the actors in the events they narrate or dramatize were unaware of the full implications of their words and actions.[10]

This theory is provocative and compelling. But it should be noted that Xenophon's Socrates bears little or no relation to either comic or tragic heroes; nor does Xenophon borrow or imitate structural, stylistic, or thematic elements of the genres of comedy and tragedy. It is only in Plato that we find the imprint of comedy and tragedy. As Clay himself observes, it is Plato who exploits the technique of tragic irony; and it is Plato who "reflect[s] within his Socratic dialogues on the established literary genres in terms of which his dialogues were to be understood and against which they were to stand in contrast."[11]

[7] *Poetics* 1447b11; cf. *Rhetoric* 1417a21.
[8] For discussions of the characteristics and evolution of the genre of the Socratic dialogue (as well as the many writers who composed *Sōkratikoi logoi*), see Hirzel 1895: especially 1–274, Field 1930: chs. 10–12, and, more recently, Cherniss 1977, Havelock 1983a, and Clay 1994. On the extant fragments of Aeschines (the date of whose writings is uncertain), see A. Taylor 1934, Dittmar 1912, and Kahn 1994.
[9] Clay 1994. The genre of biography and its relation to the Socratic writings is analyzed by Momigliano [1971]/1993: 46–64 and Gera 1993: 2–13. As Dover [1986]/1988 suggests, Ion of Chios' *Epidēmiai* may also be a generic predecessor of the Socratic dialogue.
[10] Clay 1994: 45–6.
[11] Clay 1994: especially 46.

Plato diverges from Xenophon, finally, by authoring "mixed" dialogues. For Plato not only offers "reflections" on the established literary genres but actually incorporates both the *topoi* and the texts of these genres into his dialogues.[12] Are Plato's deviations from Xenophon also deviations from the traditional form of the Socratic dialogue? Since we lack the writings of other Socratics, it is impossible to assess the extent to which Plato was innovating. It is at least possible that it was Xenophon who was deviating from previous generic practices; certainly he could have inherited a genre characterized by mixed texts and turned it into something more simple. But it is much more reasonable to suppose that Plato took a simple genre characterized by recorded or dramatized conversations and transformed it into a multi-generic hybrid.[13]

Why did Plato opt for the intertextual mode? And what is distinctive about Plato's use of intertextuality? First of all, Plato regularly chooses to interact with the texts of genres other than his own. His target, moreover, is never simply an individual author or text. For, when he incorporates a particular work of poetry or rhetoric into a dialogue, he invariably treats it synecdochically – i.e. as the representative of a genre. In fact, the incorporated texts are often composed by Plato himself: take, for example, the funeral oration in the *Menexenus*, or the encomiastic speeches in the *Symposium*. Since Plato is concerned not so much with a specific author or text as with the genre as a whole, it makes little difference whether the subtext is written by Plato or by someone else. It should be emphasized that Plato targets genres that have currency in classical Athens – genres which make some claim to wisdom or authority. Not surprisingly, then, when Plato engages with a given genre of discourse, his stance is usually adversarial. As I will argue, Plato uses intertextuality as a vehicle for criticizing traditional genres of discourse and, what is more important, for introducing and defining a radically different discursive practice, which he calls "philosophy."

Let me briefly outline the formal structures and operations of Platonic intertextuality.[14] Plato "incorporates" other texts and genres into his dialogues in a number of different ways. He can, first of all, borrow or

---

[12] As Gera 1993 has recently shown, Xenophon's *Cyropaedia* is a multi-generic text. It is possible that the mixed form of this late work by Xenophon (Gera 1993: 25 dates it in the 360s) was directly influenced by Plato's polyphony.

[13] For several different answers to the question of how "Socratic" Plato's early dialogues are, compare Kahn 1981, Vlastos 1991: especially chs. 2–3, Penner 1992, and Stokes 1992. Sider 1980b argues that Plato may have written dialogues before the death of Socrates.

[14] Contemporary investigations of intertextuality are plentiful. I have found especially useful Bakhtin 1981 and 1984, Stewart 1978, M. Rose 1979, Riffaterre 1978 and [1979]/1983, Kristeva 1980, Todorov [1981]/1984 and [1978]/1990, Genette 1982, and Conte 1986 and [1991]/1994.

compose a complete text from a given genre and transplant it *in toto* in his own composition: an example of this approach is the funeral oration in the *Menexenus*, which is a finished text that faithfully represents the genre of the *epitaphios*. Alternatively, a text (and, thereby, the genre that it represents) can be incorporated by way of allusion: the numerous allusions to Euripides' *Antiope* in the *Gorgias*, for example, conjure up the themes and structure of that play together with the genre of tragedy as a whole. Finally, Plato can target a genre by incorporating the discourse, *topoi*, or themes that are peculiar to it and readily identified as such: when Callias' slave slams the door in Socrates' face at the opening of the *Protagoras*, for example, we are confronted with a *topos* from the genre of comedy.

When one genre enters into the text of another genre, it both acts and is acted upon. In this encounter, the targeted genre may be granted more or less authority. A useful discussion of this complex phenomenon is found in Bakhtin's analysis of intertextuality or "hybridization" in the genre of the novel.[15] According to Bakhtin, the author of a "hybrid" text

make[s] use of someone else's discourse for his own purposes, by inserting a new semantic direction into a discourse which already has, and which retains, an intention of its own. Such a discourse ... must be perceived as belonging to someone else. In one discourse, two semantic intentions appear, two voices.[16]

In such cases, then, the audience or reader "is meant to hear both a version of the original utterance as the embodiment of its speaker's point of view (or 'semantic position') *and* the second speaker's evaluation of that utterance from a different point of view."[17] Given that Bakhtin considered the Socratic dialogue a "precursor" to the dialogic novel, it comes as no surprise that so many of Plato's texts meet Bakhtin's criteria for the "novelistic hybrid": "*an artistically organized system for bringing different discourses in contact with one another*, a system having as its goal the illumination of one discourse by means of another ..." (his italics).[18]

There is, of course, a very wide range of possible relations between a primary text and the genre or text that is targeted. How, then, should Plato's hybrids be analyzed? Bakhtin's distinction between parodic and

---

[15] Bakhtin 1981: 358–66 and passim, and 1984: 181–203 and passim.
[16] Bakhtin 1984: 189 (note that Bakhtin, whose terminology is more fluid than fixed, often uses the words "voice" and "genre" interchangeably; as Hirschkop 1989 demonstrates, this can lead to conceptual confusion).
[17] As Morson 1989: 65 summarizes Bakhtin's position.
[18] Bakhtin 1981: 361; Bakhtin identifies the Socratic dialogue as a predecessor of the dialogic novel in 1981: 22 and 1984: 106, 109, 112.

non-parodic "double-voicing" provides a good starting-point for such an analysis.[19] In the case of parody, Bakhtin claims, the text will criticize, subvert, or co-opt the genre that it represents. When the targeted genre is denied authority, parody may decrease the "dialogism" in the text. Non-parodic hybrids which grant the targeted genre full semantic autonomy, by contrast, have a greater degree of "dialogism."[20] As I have suggested, Plato's relation to the genres he targets is generally adversarial (though there are important exceptions to this rule, which will be discussed below); in different ways and for different reasons, he forces poetic and rhetorical subtexts to serve his own purposes. His use of intertextuality should thus be analyzed as a species of parody.

Although parody is traditionally associated with comic ridicule, a number of contemporary theorists argue that this complex mode has a much broader scope. Linda Hutcheon, for example, who defines parody as "repetition with critical difference," suggests that "[t]here are as many possible techniques [of parody] as there are possible kinds of inter-relationships of repetition with differentiation."[21] Gary Morson, whose study of parody is modelled on Bakhtin's, argues along similar lines:

Parody recontextualizes its object so as to make it serve tasks contrary to its original tasks, but this functional shift need not be in the direction of humor. As negation can be on an indefinitely large number of grounds, parody can, in prin-ciple, adopt an indefinitely large number of tones. The direction and tone of the parody will depend on the nature of the parodist's disagreement with or disapproval of the original and the point of view from which he disagrees or disapproves.[22]

---

[19] Bakhtin's technical terms for these notions are "passive double-voiced discourse" (to which parody belongs) and "active double-voiced discourse" (which I am calling "non-parodic"). Although Bakhtin usually celebrates parody as dialogical, the use of parody to claim higher authority is not. I have chosen to avoid this terminology because I find it cumbersome and, for my purposes, over-complicated.

[20] Bakhtin 1981: 361–4 and passim, and 1984: 189–99 and passim. Note that, as Morson and Emerson observe (1990: 142–52), Bakhtin has several quite different notions of dia-logism. I am concerned with the dialogism that occurs when a text or utterance "actually contains mixed within it two utterances, two speech manners, two styles, two 'languages,' two semantic and axiological belief systems" (Bakhtin 1981: 305). As Mecke 1990: 202 reminds us, "dialogism" must be distinguished from "dialogue" (in the ordinary sense of a conversation between two or more speakers): "the existence of several participants in communication does not guarantee its dialogic character ... [for] one voice or subject may be disseminated through different individuals having the same opinions, sharing the same value system and the same language. Even though all external premises for dialogue are fulfilled, the internal condition, the tension between two or more semantic contextures, is completely missing." For discussions of Bakhtin's conceptions of dialogism, see Todorov [1981]/1984: especially chs. 4–5, Stewart 1986, Pechey 1989, Holquist 1990: especially chs. 3–4, Morson and Emerson 1990: especially chs. 6–8, Mecke 1990.

[21] Hutcheon 1985: 20, 25.

[22] Morson 1989: 69; cf. Rose 1979: 59, who defines parody as "the critical quotation of preformed literary language with comic effect."

Both Hutcheon and Morson stipulate that the "repetition" or "recontextualization" must be intended by the author, and that the parodic text must claim for itself a "higher semantic authority" than is granted to the target.[23] But, in spite of the parodist's criticism of his/her target, there is a fundamental ambivalence in the parodic mode: it can be both "conservative *and* transformative" since it affirms similarity and continuity even as it rebels against its predecessors.[24]

To interpret the parodies of Plato, then, one must first of all identify those passages in which a given genre of discourse is incorporated as a subtext. While there are numerous quotations from poets and other "wise men" in the dialogues, these may or may not signal an intergeneric encounter. As I have indicated, one of the following discursive structures must be present in a dialogue: an entire text from a given genre; a cluster of allusions to a specific text from a given genre; or the sustained use of the discourse, *topoi*, themes, or structural characteristics of a given genre. Once a specific subtext has been identified, the interpreter must determine the grounds on which the target is parodied. In particular, both the nature and the degree of Plato's opposition to the genre in question must be analyzed and assessed. Given that a parody may criticize its target on many different grounds, however, there is no single recipe for interpreting a parodic text. This is especially true in the case of Plato, whose parodies range into so many different territories: language and literature; ethics and politics; psychology, epistemology, and ontology. Each instance of intertextuality in Plato, then, will confront the reader with a unique set of issues and problems.

In this book, I offer detailed analyses of a representative sample of intertextual engagements in Plato's dialogues.[25] In each case, I will consider what a given genre's collision or collusion with Plato's enterprise tells us about the nature of philosophy as Plato conceived it. As I will suggest,

---

[23] Hutcheon 1985: 22–3, 37–8 (note that Hutcheon qualifies the latter of these two points on pp. 50–2) and Morson 1989: 67. Cf. Kristeva 1980: especially chs. 3 and 7, and Genette 1982, who analyze intertextuality as a purely formal category of textual interaction. See also Conte 1986: 26–31 and passim, who warns against "fall[ing] into the common philological trap of seeing all textual resemblances as produced by the intentionality of a literary subject whose only desire is to emulate. The philologist who seeks at all costs to read intention into imitation will inevitably fall into a psychological reconstruction of motive ..." (p. 27). Though Conte's attempt to "purge any excess of intentionalism from the concept of 'imitatio'" (p. 28) is methodologically compelling, I believe that Plato's use of intertextuality is intentional insofar as it is part of a deliberate and, often, explicit effort to define philosophy and devalue its rivals. This does not mean, of course, that every element of Platonic intertextuality is consciously deployed.

[24] As Hutcheon suggests (1985: 101 and 1989: 100–2); see also Kristeva 1980: 71.

[25] I have not attempted to discuss every instance of Platonic intertextuality: this study is meant to be suggestive rather than comprehensive.

Plato engages with the genres of poetry and rhetoric on two quite distinct levels. On the one hand, he approaches a given genre as the conveyor of a certain set of ideas by means of a specific discursive style and structure. But his critique invariably goes beyond the level of discourse and ideas. For he is always aware of a genre's context of performance and the ways in which it is implicated in the social and political institutions of the Athenian democracy. In order to comprehend fully Plato's interrogation of a given genre, then, the interpreter must first analyze the genre as a literary form grounded in a specific socio-political context. Fortunately, a good deal of recent scholarship in the field of Greek literature has set out to recontextualize various genres of poetry and rhetoric, focussing in particular on their specific performative contexts as well as the ways in which they reflect the social, political, and economic practices of their (respective) cultures.[26] In the case of most of the subtexts dealt with in this book, then, I will not conduct an extensive investigation of the genres that Plato is targeting. In those cases where the scholarship is insufficient, however, I have found it necessary to offer my own analysis of a genre.

If the genres that Plato targets function both as literary texts and as discursive practices embedded in various ways in the socio-political institutions of democratic Athens, what about the genre to which Plato's writings belong? The texts in this genre, of course, circulated in written form and thus reached a (relatively) small audience. But this does not mean that they were not implicated in the broader culture. As many contemporary scholars have indicated, philosophical texts, even those whose discourse is highly abstract, should not be abstracted from their social context.[27] In addition to looking at Plato's dialogues in the context of intellectual history, then, we need to interpret them in the context of social history. Considering the extraordinary changes that took place in the social, political, and economic structures of democratic Athens (and, indeed, in Greece as a whole) during the course of Plato's lifetime, this is an immense task. By focussing on the intergeneric engagements in the Platonic dialogues, I hope to make some small sallies into this territory.

While different intertextual passages will usher us into different aspects

---

[26] The following are representative of this broad trend. Homer and archaic: Herington 1985, Gentili [1985]/1988, R. Martin 1989, Nagy 1990a and 1990b, Kurke 1991; tragedy: Vernant and Vidal-Naquet 1988, Winkler 1985, Segal 1986, Goldhill 1986, 1990, Zeitlin 1990, Ober and Strauss 1990; comedy: Henderson 1990, Loraux [1984]/1993: ch. 4, Taplin 1993, Bowie 1993; funeral oration: Loraux [1981]/1986; forensic oratory: Ober 1989.

[27] Note in particular Lloyd (1966, 1979, 1987, 1990: chs. 1–2), whose approach to Greek science and philosophy has greatly influenced my own effort. For some recent investigations of ancient Greek philosophical thinkers/ideas within their (respective) socio-political contexts, see Gernet [1945]/1981, Vlastos [1964]/1981, Vernant [1962]/1982 and [1965]/1983: ch. 15, Detienne 1967 and [1981]/1986, Vidal-Naquet [1967]/1986, Humphreys 1978: ch. 9, Hahn 1987, P. Rose 1992: ch. 6, R. Martin 1993.

of Athenian culture, there is one historical thread that runs through my entire investigation. Plato was born into a culture which had no distinct concept of "philosophy," in spite of the fact that various kinds of abstract and analytic thinking had been and were being developed by the Presocratics, the mathematicians, different kinds of scientists, and the sophists. Previous to Plato, these intellectuals, together with poets, lawgivers, and other men of skill or wisdom, were grouped together under the headings of *"sophoi"* and *"sophistai."*[28] The word φιλοσοφεῖν and its cognates, in fact, rarely if ever occurs until the late fifth century and even then is used to designate intellectual cultivation in the most general sense. Indeed, as a careful analysis of the terminology will attest, φιλοσοφεῖν does not take on a specialized and technical meaning until Plato appropriates the term for his own enterprise.[29] When Plato set forth a specific and quite narrow definition of this term, I will suggest, he created a new and specialized discipline. In fact, "philosophy" as Plato conceived it comprised not just an analytic inquiry into certain types of subjects but a unique set of ethical and metaphysical commitments that demanded a whole new way of living.[30] It is for this reason that, in spite of his ongoing engagement with the ideas of many Presocratic thinkers, Plato's definition of the "philosopher" actually excluded these intellectuals.

I am not concerned, then, with Plato's methods and doctrines or, indeed, with his development and practice of analytic thinking. Rather, I want to analyze how Plato defines and characterizes the activity he calls "philosophy."[31] In order to create the specialized discipline of philoso-

---

[28] As Lloyd demonstrates (1987: 92–4 with notes 152–3), from Hesiod down through the fourth century, the words σοφίζεσθαι and σοφιστής are often used in a non-pejorative sense to designate a wide array of poets and sages.

[29] I will discuss this point at length in chapter 1.

[30] Note that our modern conception of philosophy derives from Plato's but also deviates from it in fundamental ways: for we see philosophy as the investigation of certain sets of issues by way of certain methods of analysis, but we do not believe that this investigation must be accompanied by a specific set of ethical and metaphysical values. While Plato did develop and practice specific modes of inquiry and analysis, and while he did address almost every major area of inquiry now associated with philosophy, his concept of philosophy was not encompassed by these intellectual activities.

[31] Cf. Kraut who, in the introduction to the *Cambridge Companion to Plato* (1992: 1), states that Plato is "the first Western thinker to produce a body of writing that touches upon the wide range of topics that are still discussed by philosophers today under such headings as metaphysics, epistemology, ethics, political theory, language, art, love, mathematics, science, and religion. He may in this sense be said to have invented philosophy as a distinct subject, for although all of these topics were, of course, discussed by his intellectual predecessors and contemporaries, he was the first to bring them together by giving them a unitary treatment. He conceives of philosophy as a discipline with a distinctive intellectual method, and he makes radical claims for its position in human life and the political community." Whereas Kraut focusses on Plato's invention of what *we* recognize as "philosophy" (so also Charlton 1985), my investigation deals with what *Plato says about*

phy, Plato had to distinguish what he was doing from all other discursive practices that laid claim to wisdom. It is for this reason that, in dialogue after dialogue, Plato deliberately set out to define and defend a new and quite peculiar mode of living and of thinking. This alone, he claimed, deserved the title of "philosophy." It should be emphasized that gestures of opposition and exclusion play a crucial role in Plato's many attempts to mark the boundaries of "philosophy." Indeed, it is precisely by designating certain modes of discourse and spheres of activity as "anti-philosophical" that Plato was able to create a separate identity for "philosophy." This was a bold and difficult enterprise whose success was by no means guaranteed: because history has conferred upon the discipline of philosophy the legitimacy and the high status that Plato claimed for it, we moderns tend to overlook the effort it took to bring this about.

In order to explicate the contention that Plato created the specialized discipline of philosophy, I have devoted the first chapter of this book to an intertextual reading in which Plato's writings form the subtext. This chapter takes as its starting-point Isocrates' *Antidosis*, a late speech in which the author attempts to define "philosophy" in the face of Plato's repeated attempts to appropriate the term for his own peculiar ideals and pursuits. The *Antidosis* alludes not only to Plato's portrait of Socrates in the *Apology*, but to the explicit definitions of the "philosopher" offered in the *Gorgias*, *Republic*, and *Theaetetus*. In particular, Isocrates' speech invites us to compare the way that each thinker defines and positions his "philosopher" in relation to the Athenian democracy. By analyzing the ways in which these definitions respond to the ideology of the democracy, we can better comprehend Plato's creation of "philosophy" in the context of fourth-century Athenian culture. In addition, the explicit claims that these thinkers make about philosophy can serve to guide our readings of Plato's intertextual engagements with traditional genres of literature, where the attempt to define and legitimize philosophy is (for the most part) implicit.

In the explicit definitions of "philosophy" analyzed in the first chapter, Plato proceeds by contrasting the philosopher to all other claimants to wisdom. The former, he urges, is true coin and the latter counterfeit: difference is coded as opposition. In the remaining chapters of this book, I will examine Plato's attempts to legitimize philosophy by way of intertextual encounters with other genres of discourse: chapter 2 deals with the *Gorgias'* rescripting of a Euripidean tragedy; chapter 3 with Plato's parodic handling of the discourse of eulogy in the *Symposium*; chapter 4 with

what he is doing – with his explicit and deliberate attempts to define and defend his own peculiar way of thinking and living in the context of a culture which had no distinct concept of "philosophy."

the many genres that function as "alien voices" in the *Phaedrus*; and chapter 5 with Plato's borrowings from the genre of comedy. Although Plato's parodies do not always include explicit statements about philosophy, they offer a definition and defense of philosophy that is no less distinct. As we will see, in most of Plato's "mixed" texts, traditional discursive practices are scripted as foils for philosophy – as antithetical to, rather than different from, philosophical discourse and praxis. Not surprisingly, these intertextual encounters evince the same gestures of opposition and exclusion that are found in the explicit definitions of philosophy. In the intertextual mode, then, Plato found a vehicle for criticizing traditional genres on a number of specific grounds and for defining a new kind of wisdom in opposition to the varieties on offer.

In most of his intertextual engagements, Plato employs parody as a strategy for marking the boundaries of philosophy. But there are important exceptions to this rule – passages or texts in which Plato affirms the positive potential of a genre of poetry or rhetoric. In addition to the parodic texts, then, we need to analyze Plato's rare but pointed alliances with traditional genres of discourse. As these instances reveal, in addition to his revolt against prior discursive practices, Plato also sensed the need for continuity. In the non-parodic passages, Plato remains open to the possibility that a genre may in fact make a positive contribution to the philosopher's enterprise. Instead of rejecting traditional genres out of hand, Plato opts to explore the potentialities as well as the liabilities of these discursive practices. In these cases where he eschews parody, I will suggest, Plato actually blurs the boundaries that he took such pains to create. As this ambivalence reveals, Plato did not fix the boundaries of philosophy once and for all. Perhaps he sensed that philosophy is not well served by a permanent and closed border.

By entering into the mode of intertextuality, Plato transgresses the boundaries of both his own genre and the genres that he targets. Plato's use of intertextuality, in fact, is *about* boundaries. Or, to be more precise, intertextuality allows Plato to explore the boundaries of this new activity he calls "philosophy" – the boundaries of a unique way of living and of thinking. By foregrounding this intergeneric aspect of Platonic texts, I will argue, we can reassess Plato's quarrel with poetry and rhetoric as well as the debt he owes to these "unphilosophical" adversaries. In addition, by interpreting Plato's "dialogue" with literary and rhetorical genres within the socio-political context of classical Athens, we can better comprehend both the specificity and the historicity of Plato's creation of "philosophy."

1 Plato, Isocrates, and the property of philosophy

I am prepared for a demand for money and he wants – truth. Truth! And wants it like that – so bare, so blank, as though truth were coin! ... However, such modern coin that is only made by stamp, that one needs only to count upon the counting board – that is not truth by any means. Like money into the bag, should one be able to sweep truth into the head?

Lessing, *Nathan the Wise*

Slow Gold – but Everlasting –
The Bullion of Today –
Contrasted with the Currency
Of Immortality –

A Beggar – Here and There –
Is gifted to discern
Beyond the Broker's insight –
One's – Money – One's – the Mine –

Emily Dickinson

In his *Lectures on the History of Philosophy*, Hegel explains that there is a paradox inherent in the very notion of a "history of philosophy." As he states in the introduction,

The thought which may first occur to us in the history of Philosophy, is that the subject itself contains a contradiction. For Philosophy aims at understanding what is unchangeable, eternal, in and for itself: its end is Truth. But history tells us of that which has at one time existed, at another time has vanished, having been expelled by something else. Truth is eternal; it does not fall within the sphere of the transient, and has no history.[1]

Although few scholars would now endorse Hegel's solution to the problem of "how it happens that Philosophy appears to be a development in time and has a history,"[2] the tension between philosophy and history still remains. For, if the notion of an atemporal and transhistorical truth is no

[1] Hegel 1892: 7–8.
[2] Hegel 1892: 32.

longer in vogue, the discipline that we have come to call the "history of
philosophy" is nonetheless constituted by the documentation and analysis
of a given set of ideas or doctrines that is, for the most part, abstracted
from its cultural context. While I do not wish to challenge the validity and
importance of this enterprise, my aim in this chapter is to approach the
history of philosophy from a different angle. In brief, my concern is not
with the history of philosophical ideas but rather the history of the idea
– and, indeed, the foundational ideology – of philosophy. In particular, I
will argue, the construction of the discipline of philosophy needs to be
analyzed as a historical event located in a particular socio-political
context.

The discipline of philosophy emerged at a certain moment in history. It
was not born, like a natural organism. Rather, it was an artificial construct that had to be invented and legitimized as a new and unique cultural practice. This took place in Athens in the fourth century BCE, when
Plato appropriated the term "philosophy" for a new and specialized
discipline – a discipline that was constructed in opposition to the many
varieties of *sophia* or "wisdom" recognized by Plato's predecessors and
contemporaries. Philosophy as Plato conceived it was a very exclusive
vocation. Indeed, it was precisely by designating certain modes of discourse and spheres of activity as anti-philosophical that Plato was able to
create a separate identity for "philosophy." In this chapter, I will take as
my focus the "definitions" of philosophy offered by Plato and (after him)
Isocrates. The intertextual relationship between Isocrates' *Antidosis* and
Platonic texts such as the *Apology*, *Gorgias*, *Republic*, and *Theaetetus* invites us to explore what was at stake in the initial construction of the
discipline of philosophy. In particular, I want to examine the rhetorical
strategies that each writer used to differentiate the "philosopher" from his
rivals and to position this new sage in relation to the social and political
economy of fourth-century Athens.

Before I turn to Plato and Isocrates, let me briefly discuss the history of
the word "philosophy." First of all, φιλοσοφεῖν and its cognates were not
often used before the fourth century, and they certainly did not have a
technical sense that indicated a specific group of thinkers practicing a
distinct discipline or profession.[3] When it did appear, the term was used

[3] The following is a list of the occurrences of the word φιλοσοφεῖν and its cognates through
the end of the fifth century (see also Überweg 1871: 1–4, Havelock 1963: 280–1 with notes,
and 1983b: 56–7). According to Cicero (*Tusc.* 5.3) and Diogenes Laertius (1.12 and 8.8),
Pythagoras was the first to call himself a "philosopher"; Diogenes cites as evidence a dialogue of Heraclides of Pontus, a member of Plato's Academy (for discussions of the validity of this claim, see Jaeger 1948: 432–3, 455–9, Burkert 1960, and Guthrie 1962: 164–6,
204–5). Even if we accept Heraclides' rather dubious claim, there is no evidence that
Pythagoras initiated a technical use of this term. Likewise, Heraclitus' statement, if it is

to designate "intellectual cultivation" in a broad and unspecified sense. While Pericles' famous "φιλοσοφοῦμεν ἄνευ μαλακίας" suggests that virtually all Athenians were practicing "philosophy" (Thucydides 2.40.1), the term is generally used to designate a smaller group of individuals, namely, people who have the time and the inclination to engage in intellectual pursuits as young men and adults. The narrowest application of the word in this period, in fact, is found in Gorgias' *Encomium of Helen* (DK B11.13), where those people who make a practice of verbal disputation (φιλοσόφων λόγων ἁμίλλας) are distinguished from both astronomers and rhetoricians.[4] Perhaps the most important indication of the valence of this term in late fifth-century Athens, however, is its absence from the texts of Old Comedy. Although the fragments of Old Comedy as well as the plays of Aristophanes contain a number of attacks on intellectuals, they have nothing to say about "philosophers."[5] Before the fourth century, then, there was no special subgroup of intellectuals that had appropriated the title of *"philosophoi."*

Although the "philosophy" word-group continued to be used throughout the fourth century to signify "intellectual cultivation" in general, it is in this period that we find the first attempts to assign the words a specific and technical meaning.[6] According to Überweg, it was not Socrates him-

genuine (see Kahn 1979: 105), that "men who love wisdom (φιλοσόφους ἄνδρας) must be good inquirers into many things" (DK B35) does not point to any specific group of professional thinkers. Even in the late fifth century, the word-group is rare. Herodotus 1.30.11 describes Solon as "philosophizing"; the late fifth-century historian Herodorus of Heracleia asserts that Heracles "philosophized right up to his death" (*FGrH* 31F14); Thucydides 2.40.1 is quoted in the text above, as is Gorgias' *Encomium of Helen* 11.13; Prodicus is said to have separated the field of "philosophy" from that of "politics" (DK B6); Critias refers to the generous friendship of "philosophers" (DK B20); and the two uses of the word-group in the *Dissoi Logoi* (1.1; 9.1), as T. Robinson observes (1984: 238), do not refer to "philosophical specialists" but to "education" in general.

[4] Cf. Hippocrates' *Ancient Medicine* 20 (generally dated *circa* 400 BCE), where the author suggests that the study of the nature of man is the province of "philosophy" and not medicine. He goes on to cite Empedocles and others "writing on *phusis*" as examples of thinkers who have studied the nature of man, but he also says that "doctors and sophists" investigate *phusis*.

[5] The single use of a "philosophy" word in Aristophanes is found in a play written in the early fourth century, the *Ecclesiazusae* (571), where "φιλόσοφον" modifies a "thought" rather than a person or activity. I will discuss the attacks on intellectuals in comedy in chapter 2. Kerferd, who notes that the word σοφία was not a regular Attic prose word in the late fifth century, points out that this word, and its cognates, occurs 30 times in Aristophanes' *Clouds*; it would appear that Aristophanes is making fun of the pretentiousness of this "newish term" (1976: 22).

[6] For examples of the use of the word-group in the sense of "intellectual cultivation" in the fourth century, see Isocrates, *Panegyricus* 47; Plato, *Charmides* 153d, *Gorg.* 485a, *Symp.* 218b; Xenophon, *Mem.* 4.2.23, *Symp.* 4.62, *Cyrop.* 6.1.41; Ps.-Demosthenes, *Erotic Essay* 44 (Blass 1907.III.1: 406–8 denies the authenticity of this speech, basing his argument on its style. He finds no fault with the idiom, however, which would suggest that the speech was written in the fourth century).

self but the "disciples of Socrates" who first used the "philosophy" words as a technical designation.[7] Minus Plato's dialogues, however, the writings of Socrates' followers offer little if any support for this claim. To be sure, there are only minute remains of these writings if one leaves out Xenophon. But the ample corpus of Xenophon provides important evidence for this inquiry. Surprisingly, a mere sixteen instances of the word φιλοσοφεῖν and its cognates are found in Xenophon's writings, and only ten of these are found in the "Socratic" treatises. Of these ten instances, moreover, eight are clearly used in the broad sense of "intellectual culture" outlined above.[8] There are, then, only two passages in Xenophon's Socratic treatises where one finds the suggestion that "philosophy" is a term that describes some intellectuals rather than others. At *Memorabilia* 1.2.19, in the course of his own defense of Socrates' activities, Xenophon says:

Perhaps many of those who allege that they are philosophizing (πολλοὶ τῶν φασκόντων φιλοσοφεῖν) will say that a just man can never become unjust or a temperate man intemperate, nor can a person who has learned something ever become ignorant of any of the things that he has learned. But I think differently about these things.

Here, Xenophon implies that people who hold these views are not really philosophizing. But this tells us almost nothing about what distinguishes philosophers from imposters aside from the fact that philosophers are right and the others wrong on this particular subject. The second instance is found in the *Symposium* (1.5–6), where Socrates calls himself and his companions αὐτουργούς τινας τῆς φιλοσοφίας in contrast with Callias, who has paid a great deal of money for wisdom. Here, Socrates indicates that he and his associates are but humble and self-employed laborers in the fields of philosophy whereas Callias can afford to employ others to work for him. Though Socrates does not explicitly deny that Callias is practicing philosophy, he does invite the reader to acknowledge two quite different approaches to the cultivation of the intellect. As in the first passage, however, very little is offered here which might serve to distinguish

---

[7] Überweg 1871: 3.

[8] These eight passages are as follows: *Mem.* 4.2.23, where Euthydemus calls his own intellectual activities "philosophy" (note that the phrase φιλοσοφεῖν φιλοσοφίαν found here counts as two instances); *Mem.* 1.2.31, where Critias is said to have attacked Socrates with the slander commonly used against "philosophers"; *Mem.* 1.6.2 (two instances), where Antiphon says that, while "people who philosophize must necessarily become happier," Socrates' "philosophy" has had the opposite effect; *Symp.* 4.62, where Socrates says that Callias is "in love with philosophy"; *Symp.* 8.39, where Solon is described as "philosophizing" (8.39); *Oec.* 16.9, where Socrates tells Ischomachus that it is "characteristic of the philosopher" to enjoy learning. The six instances in the non-Socratic treatises are: *Anab.* 2.1.13, *Cyrop.* 6.1.41, *Poroi* 5.4, *Cyneg.* 13.6, 13.9 (twice).

one form of intellectual cultivation from others. Nowhere in Xenophon's Socratic writings, in sum, is Socrates (or anyone else) singled out as the proper claimant to the title of "philosopher."[9]

How, then, do we arrive at the idea that philosophy is a specific kind of pursuit practiced by a distinct kind of person? Havelock suggests that

> any assiduous search for usage in the fifth century is in danger of missing the main point, which is that the clues to the history of the word "philosopher", and therefore to a history of the idea of philosophy, are first fully supplied in the *Republic* itself, where the type of person symbolized by this word is identified simply as the man who is prepared to challenge the hold of the concrete over our consciousness, and to substitute the abstract. It is treated as a word which needs definition.[10]

Havelock is right to focus on the *Republic*, since it contains the most explicit and detailed definition of "philosophy" in the Platonic corpus. Indeed it is not until the middle dialogues of Plato that we find any attempt to appropriate or to define the term "philosophy."[11] The definition offered in the *Republic* begins towards the end of book 5, when Socrates suggests that philosophers should be rulers and rulers philosophers (473c–d). The term "philosopher" does indeed cry out for definition, as Havelock suggests. And Plato duly complies by describing the "philosopher" in detail and at length.[12]

The "definition" of philosophy found in the *Republic* does not, how-

---

[9] Interestingly, it is in a non-Socratic treatise that we find Xenophon's single attempt to exclude a group of intellectuals from the realms of philosophy. In the *Cynegeticus*, Xenophon attacks intellectuals who are "sophists and not philosophers" (τοὺς νῦν σοφιστὰς καὶ οὐ τοὺς φιλοσόφους, 13.6). Their crimes are as follows: they falsely profess to teach the young virtue (13.1); they have written books on trivial subjects (1–2); their language contains no "maxims" (*gnōmai*) which lead the young to virtue (3–4); they speak with the aim of deceiving and write in order to profit themselves (8); they are not wise (8); and they are willing to be called "sophists" even though this is a term of reproach among intelligent people (8–9); finally, "the sophists hunt the rich and the young, but the philosophers are available and friendly to all alike, and they neither honor nor dishonor the fortunes of men" (9). Note that the passage offers no solid criteria for distinguishing the two kinds of thinkers, although the final tag may be taken to indicate that sophists take fees whereas philosophers do not.

[10] Havelock 1963: 281.

[11] In the early dialogues, Plato uses the "philosophy" word-group only in the general sense of "intellectual cultivation" outlined above; nowhere does he suggest that the title of "philosophy" should be given only to Socrates and his circle. Indeed, it is in the *Gorgias*, which is generally thought to come at the end of the early period, where we find the first attempt to define "philosophy"; even here the "definition" is less than explicit (I will analyze this definition in chapter 2). Note also that the pseudo-Platonic *Erastai* explicitly addresses the question "what is philosophy?" But, quite apart from the question of the authorship and date of this dialogue, its thrust is negative rather than positive: we learn only what philosophy is not, and are left to ponder what exactly it is.

[12] The "definition" runs at least until bk. 7, 521b, though one could argue that it terminates at the end of bk. 7.

ever, offer a "simple" identification of the philosopher.[13] To be sure, Socrates has a good deal to say about the epistemic aspects of philosophy. In particular, he indicates, the true philosopher will develop the rational part of his soul in order to make the journey from appearance to reality, from opinion to knowledge, from the physical world of particulars to the immaterial realm of the Forms. But this is just the tip of the iceberg; for the "definition" articulated in books 5–7 is a rhetorical *tour de force* which ranges far beyond the intellectual activities that characterize philosophy. Recall, for example, the "monstrous" *eikōn* of the wise man on a ship with a purblind captain and savage crew, which is expressly designed to allegorize the relations of the true philosopher to the democratic city (488a–489a); the account of the desertion of philosophy by gifted people who have been seduced by honor and power, and the rush of unworthy suitors that ensues; the description of the victor in this contest as a baldheaded metalworker recently freed from slavery who puts on his best clothes and comes to marry the abandoned bride (494a–496a); the image of the true philosopher's precarious habitation among the "beasts" that govern the city, and his sheltering behind a wall to avoid the storm that surrounds him (496d–e); or, finally, the allegory of the cave, which returns to the theme of the dangerous position of the philosopher within the democratic polis. The list could go on. But enough has been said to demonstrate that this is very far from a neutral definition of philosophy as the practice of a certain kind of thinking.

One should note, too, that Plato makes no mention of philosophic predecessors in the *Republic*: his definition is exclusive, not inclusive.[14] Indeed, "philosophy" as he describes it is not something with a development or a history. On the contrary, Socrates insists that the group of true philosophers is positively minute (496a–c; cf. 490e):

There is some tiny (πάνσμικρον) group remaining which consists of those who consort with philosophy worthily, whether it be a noble and well-born character constrained by exile who, in the absence of people who would corrupt him, re-

---

[13] As Havelock suggests in the passage quoted above. Havelock is wrong to claim that Plato was simply giving a name to a "movement, a current of effort which involved all who had need of a conceptual language in which to describe phenomena whether human or natural" (1963: 280). While *we* may see Plato as part of a movement characterized by the development of certain kinds of analytic thinking, this is not the way that he conceived of his "philosophers." By claiming that Plato defines philosophy in a "simple" and neutral fashion, Havelock ignores the extraordinary rhetoric that surrounds all of Plato's "definitions."

[14] I am not suggesting that Plato was not influenced by or responding to the Presocratics and sophists in his own philosophy. My point is simply that, in spite of his deep engagement with the ideas of many of these thinkers, Plato did not consider them to be "philosophers" in his sense of the term. It was Aristotle, not Plato, who conceived of philosophy as a certain brand of thinking/ideas that had a determinate history.

mains true to [philosophy] in accordance with its nature, or when a great soul who is born in a small town disregards and disdains the affairs of the city. And perhaps some small group of an excellent nature might turn to philosophy from another art, which they justly look down on. And the bridle of our companion Theages may provide a restraint. For all the other conditions for falling away from philosophy were at hand in the case of Theages, but his sickly constitution restrained him by keeping him out of politics. My own situation – the divine sign – is not worth mentioning, since it has probably happened to few if any people before me.

This is the only passage in the entire definition where Socrates refers to a *group* of philosophers, and it is noteworthy that the defining criterion is political orientation rather than method or doctrine.[15] Contrast the "Anthology" of "related ideas" written by the sophist Hippias in the later fifth century, which placed different sages under the heading of one or another distinctive idea (such as "all things are one").[16] Although the "Anthology" falls far short of a developmental account of the history of ideas (this must wait for Aristotle and Theophrastus), it does offer Plato a model for linking himself up with earlier thinkers – for identifying his "philosophers" with a group of sages who had developed certain doctrines and/or methods of analysis.[17] Plato, however, chooses to present philosophy as a quite new discipline – a discipline whose practitioner is unique both as a rational and as a political animal.

I have foregrounded the "definition" explicated in the *Republic* because it well illustrates the complexity of Plato's effort to put "philosophy" on the map. But while the *Republic* offers the most detailed definition of the "true" philosopher, one should not forget that the nature of philosophy and the philosopher is addressed (be it implicitly or explicitly) in the great majority of the middle and late dialogues.[18] Plato's construction of philosophy, in fact, has many different facets, and can hardly be handled

---

[15] It is only in the brief mention in book 10 of the "ancient quarrel" between poetry and philosophy that Plato seems to indicate that "philosophy" has a history (though note that no "philosophers" are actually named). As I will suggest in my discussion of this passage in chapter 2, the reference to this quarrel should be interpreted in its immediate context rather than as a serious attempt at historical reportage.

[16] This treatise is briefly described in DK 86B6; as Snell [1944]/1966, Mansfeld [1983]/1990 and [1986]/1990, and Patzer 1986 demonstrate, Hippias proceeded by identifying important ideas articulated by poets and prose writers alike; each idea formed the heading under which a given set of sages was grouped.

[17] On Aristotle's "history" of philosophy, see Cherniss [1953]/1977 and Mansfeld [1985]/1990.

[18] Note that "philosophy" in Plato is sometimes defined as an everlasting *pursuit* of the Forms (like that of Eros in the *Symposium*) and at other times by the *knowledge achieved as a result of this pursuit* (such as in the *Republic*, where the philosophers' claim to rule is based on comprehensive knowledge). Since my investigation in this chapter centers on the positioning of philosophy / the philosopher vis-à-vis the polis, it makes little difference which of the two definitions Plato subscribes to in a given text.

in a short investigation. I will not attempt, then, to offer a comprehensive account of Plato's attempts to define and legitimize what he calls "philosophy." Rather, I want to investigate those issues raised by Isocrates' polemical response to Plato's appropriation of this title. In particular, I will take as my focus the rhetoric of negotiation and exchange that both Plato and Isocrates use to position the philosopher in relation to the social and political transactions that characterized the Athenian democracy. Each thinker, as I will argue, conceived of philosophy as a certain type of intellectual property which served as a counter in specific kinds of exchange.

As G. E. R. Lloyd has observed in his analysis of the writings of early Greek scientists,

One recurrent phenomenon, not just in medicine, but also in philosophy and even in mathematics, is the attempt at explicit self-definition, the concern to state what, in the eyes of the authors in question, marks out *their techne* (art, craft or science) from others, or *their* approach to that *techne* from other approaches.[19]

This self-definition, according to Lloyd, is not put forth by way of a neutral description of a given activity; rather, it depends on "the development of a discourse, or one might say a rhetoric, of legitimation."[20] It is this explicit attempt at self-definition that distinguishes Plato and Isocrates from their "philosophical" predecessors and contemporaries – i.e. the Greek writers and thinkers that are now (anachronistically) called "philosophers."[21] For Plato and Isocrates both offer detailed descriptions of the program of study and education which constitutes "true" philosophy, and they both reject all other activities as "false" or "counterfeit" philosophy. It should go without saying that these "definitions" of philosophy contain as much rhetoric as they do description. For the mere description of a given programme of study cannot, by itself, provide a

---

[19] Lloyd 1990: 57.
[20] Lloyd 1990: 43.
[21] To be sure, many Presocratics did seek to distinguish themselves from other "wise men," be they poets or prose writers (one thinks especially of Xenophanes' rejection of Homer's and Hesiod's portrayals of the gods, and Heraclitus' attacks on Homer, Hesiod, Pythagoras, and Hecataeus). But these attacks were invariably *ad hominem*, and they should not be mistaken for the *explicit and systematic differentiation of a new genre of discourse/ thought from other genres of discourse/thought*. Although we do see in the Presocratics the development of the modes and topics of inquiry which we now recognize as "philosophical," these thinkers did not articulate the criteria that distinguished their intellectual endeavors from those of others. It is significant, of course, that some opted for prose over verse, and that some repudiated "mythic" modes of wisdom, but this is very far from explicitly defining a new discipline. For several recent analyses of the attempts by certain preplatonic writers (including poets and historians) to repudiate "mythic" modes of thought and/or discourse, see Detienne [1981]/1986, Lloyd 1987: ch. 4 and passim, and Morgan forthcoming. I will discuss the preplatonic attacks on poets and other rivals in chapter 2.

rationale for laying claim to the title of "true" philosophy. Both Plato and Isocrates "define" philosophy, first of all, by explicitly excluding a variety of "imposters" on a number of grounds; in particular, these imposters are identified by their alleged ignorance and/or bad influence. But this is only part of the story. For "philosophy," as Plato and Isocrates conceive it, is not just a mode of discourse or a program of study but rather a way of living and thinking that is based on a specific set of social and political values. A crucial aspect of the "definitions" of philosophy offered by these thinkers is the attempt to articulate the relation of this new cultural practice to the political and social institutions of the Athenian democracy. Each offers a definition that cannot be fully understood outside of the culture of democratic Athens.

II

A brief discussion of the position of the intellectual in classical Athens will set the context for Plato's invention of "philosophy."[22] Let me begin with Humphreys' description of the intellectual's orientation towards his community in the archaic and classical periods:

The change in Greek politics brought about first by tyranny, and then by the increased formalization of political procedures which followed it, was decisive for the independent stance of the intellectual. From the late sixth century onwards the ambiguities surrounding the position of the charismatic sage and of the poet – mediators between nobles and *dēmos*, between past and future – begin to dissolve. One might almost say that the intellectuals, from being middlemen, move into the position of outsiders. They are outside city politics and comment on them from every point of view which an outsider can take....[23]

Democratic Athens, of course, offered rich opportunities for intellectuals of various stripes; at the same time, however, the political and ideological structures of the democracy rendered the position of "outsiders" who offered opinions on political and social issues uncomfortable if not precarious. As Dover has suggested,

the Athenians had very good reason for thinking of the typical intellectual as a visiting foreigner dependent on the patronage, hospitality and generosity of a small number of rich and distinguished families ... And we should consider the probability that foreign intellectuals were widely regarded as exercising, through their wealthy Athenian patrons, great influence over Athenian policy, while not

---

[22] For several detailed analyses of intellectual freedom in classical Athens, see Dover [1976]/ 1988 and Wallace 1994.
[23] Humphreys 1978: 263. For more detailed examinations of the positioning of the archaic poet vis-à-vis the community or city, see Detienne 1967, Nagy 1990b: 36–82 and passim, Kurke 1991, and R. Martin 1992.

themselves accountable for the execution of policy. As foreigners, they could be regarded as not owing their primary loyalty to the Athenian *dēmos* ... It is even possible that an Athenian, such as Damon or Socrates, who gained a reputation as "teacher" of wealthy and powerful men, incurred special odium inasmuch as he was felt to have alienated himself from the community by choosing a foreigner's role...[24]

Consider first the intellectuals who were foreigners to Athens: the sophists. As foreigners, the sophists were by definition engaging in transactions that were not embedded in Athenian social and political relationships.[25] An excellent (if somewhat extreme) example of what I mean by the disembedded status of the sophist is found in Isocrates' description of Gorgias in the *Antidosis*:

This man spent time among the Thessalians when these people were the wealthiest of the Greeks; he lived a long life and was devoted to making money; he had no fixed dwelling in any city and therefore did not spend money for the benefit of the public and was not compelled to pay any taxes; in addition, he did not take a wife or beget children and was not taxed by this, the most ongoing and expensive of services ... (155–6)[26]

Gorgias, this passage suggests, was not only foreign from the perspective of the Athenians, but had managed to become a foreigner (as it were) in his own homeland insofar as he had rejected all those things that connect a person to a given society: wife, children, a home, and the participation in the civic life of a polis. An interesting reformulation of this phenom-

---

[24] Dover [1976]/88: 155–6. For a useful indicator of Athenian hostility towards foreigners, see Lysias' *Against the Grain Dealers*. For attitudes to foreigners in Attic comedy, see Ehrenberg 1962: ch. 6.

[25] I refer here to Polanyi's claim that, in pre-market economies, economic transactions are "embedded" in the social system, whereas in the modern market economy, transactions are "disembedded" from the social structure and thus operate in a separate sphere which is not subject to social control (1957: 68 and passim; for an analysis of Polanyi's thesis and its impact upon the modern debates about the economy of ancient Greece, see Humphreys 1978: ch. 2). Many scholars claim that (at least) the beginnings of a disembedded economy are discernible in fourth-century Athens (Humphreys 1978: chs. 6 and 7, Thompson 1982, Osborne 1991, Burke 1992, E. Cohen 1992: 4–5 and passim; but cf. Rostovtzeff 1941: 100–1, Polanyi 1957, Finley 1970, Austin and Vidal-Naquet 1977: 147–52). It should be emphasized that the development of a disembedded economy need not destroy or replace the previously existing embedded economy. Millet, who offers an important modification of the Polanyi/Finley position (1990, 1991), rightly observes that gift-exchange and market exchange (together with the ideologies that attend them) can coexist in a single city or state, and did so in fourth-century Athens (1990: 171).

[26] This description, of course, is not entirely accurate: Gorgias is known to have come to Athens as an envoy for his own city of Leontini. Other sophists, too, would no doubt have closer ties to their own native cities than Isocrates attributes to Gorgias. But, whether or not the sophists were enmeshed in the social and political structures and transactions of their own cities, they were by definition disembedded from the civic and political life of Athens.

enon is found in Plato's *Protagoras*, where Hippias places the sophists'
rootlessness in a more positive light: "you men who are present, I consider
you all to be relatives and family and fellow-citizens by nature, not by
convention" (337c–d). Or, as Aristippus proclaims in Xenophon's *Memorabilia* (2.1.13–14), "I do not shut myself up in a civic community but
am a stranger everywhere." This (implicit) rejection of the traditional ties
of family and city, of course, would have confirmed the average Athenian's worst fears. How could a foreigner who had cut himself off from
family and civic connections and therefore owed no allegiance to anybody
but himself offer an education that was beneficial to Athenian citizens
and, indeed, to Athens herself? Protagoras adverts quite explicitly to the
precariousness of this enterprise in Plato's *Protagoras*: "A foreign man
who goes into powerful cities and persuades the most talented young
men there to abandon their association with other people – relative and
acquaintance, young and old – and to spend time with him in order that
they will be made better by this association, needs to be on his guard"
(316c–d). Finally, as Socrates says in Plato's *Timaeus*, "inasmuch as they
are wanderers from one city to another and have no settled abodes of
their own," the sophists are in no position to offer sage opinions on
political issues (19e).[27]

A more detailed (and also more hostile) rendering of the disembedded
transactions of the sophist is found in Plato's *Sophist*. At 222e–223a, the
Stranger begins by distinguishing the sophist from the parasite: the latter
offers flattery in exchange for food, whereas the former "professes to be
forming associations for the sake of virtue and exacts money as his
wage." Next, the sophists' activities are located in that branch of the
"acquisitive art" (τῆς κτητικῆς τέχνης) which deals with "exchange" (τὸ
δὲ ἀλλακτικόν, 223c). The exchange that the sophists engage in, however,
is not that which deals with "gift-giving" but rather with "buying and
selling" (ἀγοραστικόν, 223c). This category is itself divided into "local
trading" (καπηλική) and "mercantile exchange" (ἐμπορική, 223d): in the
former case, the *kapēlos* or local trader (often a retailer) sells the goods he
buys from producers in the marketplace of the city/town in which he
dwells; in the case of "mercantile exchange," the *emporos* or merchant
makes a living by traveling from one city to another, buying and selling
goods in each polis.[28] Not surprisingly, Plato's depiction of the sophist

[27] The passages from Plato, though not all equally hostile, are generally much more critical
of the sophists than Isocrates is. Note that Isocrates' description of Gorgias' activities in
the *Antidosis* is not particularly derogatory; in fact, it is designed to serve his argument
that the profession of sophistry is not as lucrative as people think.
[28] Finley 1935 discusses the distinctions between the *emporos*, the *nauklēros*, and the *kapēlos*.
For Athenian prejudices against traders, see Ehrenberg 1962: ch. 5, Dover 1974: 40–1,

centers on the merchant or *emporos*.[29] Just as there are merchants of food
for the body, says the Stranger, so also are there merchants of food for the
soul (223e–224b). Of this latter group – for whom Plato coins the wonderful title "ἡ ψυχεμπορική" ("the art of marketing the goods of the
soul," 224b4) – the sophists form that subset which "deals with *logoi* and
the teaching of virtue" (224d1).

Plato's comparison of the sophist to the *emporos* must be understood in
the context of the economic and political practices of ancient Athens. In
Athens of the classical era, the majority of merchants were non-Athe-
nians. Although Hasebroek's contention that there were no citizen traders
of any kind in classical Athens is clearly untenable, it is generally agreed
that metics and foreigners dominated this sector of the Athenian economy.[30] This indicates that the business of trade and marketing was carried out by one group of people and the business of politics by (for the
most part) another. In fact, trade and marketing were generally considered to be incompatible with whole-hearted participation in social and
political life; for an interaction "in which each party was expected to
consider only his own immediate economic advantage was a flagrant
contradiction of every conception of social life: *the man who lived by such
transactions could only be an outsider.*"[31] To be sure, economic practices
in fourth-century Athens fell short of the ideal of a complete division

Mossé 1983: 58–9, McKechnie 1989: 178–88, Millett 1990: 184–5, Connor [1971]/1992:
154 n. 39. As Millett remarks (1990: 185), "The healthy suspicion with which market
traders were regarded in Athens should not be confused with the downright hostility and
even contempt they meet with in the pages of Plato and Aristotle." Note also Demosthenes 57.30–1, where Euxitheus refers to laws "which order that anyone who re-
proaches either a male or a female citizen for doing business in the market-place is liable
for slander"; this would suggest that insults against traders in Athens were common
enough to require legislation.

[29] Though the Stranger adds, almost as an afterthought, that sophists can also serve as *kapēloi* provided that they settle down in a city and sell wares that they themselves have
produced (*Sophist* 224d). For Socrates' claim in the *Protagoras* that the sophist is a
"merchant or a local trader of the goods by which the soul is nourished" (313c), see section V of this chapter.

[30] Hasebroek 1933: 22–43. Critiques and revisions of Hasebroek's position are found in
Hansen (in Isager and Hansen 1975: especially 64–74), Whitehead 1977: 116–21, Thompson
1982, Mossé 1983, Millett 1983, 1990, and 1991: passim, Osborne 1991, E. Cohen 1992:
passim. Millett 1991: 220 suggests that "impersonal credit relations were concentrated
in the sphere of trade and typically involved non-citizens. Although essential to the
survival of the Athenian state, trade and traders were seen as external to the *polis* in its
sense of a *koinōnia* or community of citizens." Hansen (Isager and Hansen 1975: 72),
who is much more critical of Hasebroek's thesis, nonetheless concludes that "metics
and aliens were perhaps in the majority among *nauklēroi* and *emporoi*, but they certainly did not dominate Athenian foreign trade completely." In contrast with the *emporoi*, the local traders or *kapēloi* would have included a much larger group of citizens
in Athens, although metics and slaves may still have outnumbered citizens in this sector
of the economy.

[31] Humphreys 1978: 144.

of labor according to political status; for my purposes, however, the ideology is more important than the factual details.[32]

By comparing the sophists to merchants, Plato highlights their status as foreigners. But, given that the Athenians experienced the assembly and the marketplace "as separate social contexts with sharply differentiated norms of behaviour,"[33] the comparison cuts much deeper. For when Plato locates the sophists in the context of the marketplace and its norms of behavior, he indicates that the ethos and, indeed, the interests of the sophists were fundamentally opposed to those of the Athenian citizen participating in the civic and political life of the city.[34] Yet it is precisely this latter – civic and political activity – that the sophists professed to teach. The trouble, therefore, is not so much that the sophists behave like merchants; this, in itself, is not out of the ordinary. The problem arises when the private and mercantile activities of the sophist insinuate themselves into the alien sphere of Athenian politics.

What, then, of the Athenian intellectuals? Since the sophists, as foreigners, really were "outsiders" in Athens, their position needs to be distinguished from that of Athenian citizens who occupied – or were perceived as occupying – the position of "outside" critic and advisor described by Humphreys. Unlike the sophist, an Athenian intellectual ran the risk of being perceived as an insider behaving like an outsider. As Humphreys observes,

The question of the role of the intellectual in the city therefore affected Athenian intellectuals particularly closely, both because they had to face the question of the justice of Athens' policies and because their audience was made up of fellow citizens. Democratic Athens expected participation and comment from its citizens. It was a society in which books had a wide circulation, but public oral communication was still the essence of communal life. The dominant contexts of communication, assembly, law courts, and theater, were all forms of drama; in each of them a small number of protagonists performed before a mass audience of judges.[35]

Obviously, those intellectuals who chose to address themselves to the

---

[32] As Hansen observes in his book on democracy in the age of Demosthenes (1991: 120), in spite of the fact that Athenian citizens did participate in trade and marketing, "the Athenians would have preferred things to be as Plato outlines them in his utopia [i.e. the *Laws*, where all artisans and traders are denied citizenship]. We meet at every turn the idea that to occupy oneself in trade and manufacturing is demeaning, and that agriculture is the only respectable way for a citizen to earn his living."

[33] Humphreys 1978: 172.

[34] Appadurai 1986: 33 suggests that this tension is present in capitalist as well as precapitalist economies: "whereas merchants tend to be the social representatives of unfettered equivalence, new commodities, and strange tastes, political elites tend to be the custodians of restricted exchange, fixed commodity systems, and established tastes and sumptuary customs."

[35] Humphreys 1978: 228.

"mass audience of judges" in the "dominant contexts of communication" were acting as insiders. It was only when an intellectual did not
address the mass audience and avoided these contexts of communication that he would have been perceived as an insider behaving like an
outsider.

For different reasons and with differing results, Plato and Isocrates
chose not to subject themselves to the mass audience of judges: both offered their ideas in written texts which circulated, for the most part,
among elite audiences;[36] both were unwilling to play a direct role in the
political machinery of Athens. As Athenian citizens, these men were (at
least in principle) answerable to the city for their doings. As wealthy
members of the elite who refused to participate directly in Athenian politics, their activities were likely to come under special scrutiny. Although it
is difficult to gauge the extent to which these men felt pressured to account
for themselves, the fact is that each offered an explicit description and
definition of his activities as a "philosopher"; each positioned the philosopher in a specific relation to democratic Athens.

III

In the *Panathenaicus* 19, a rival is quoted as saying that Isocrates "would
destroy all of the philosophies and teachings of others, [since he] says that
all men are talking nonsense except for those who partake in [his] own
course of study." Although Isocrates denies this charge,[37] the explicit
definition he offers of "philosophy" in the *Antidosis* shows that his accuser is not far wrong.[38] This begins at sections 170–7, where Isocrates
suggests that philosophy has been unjustly slandered because its de-
tractors are not aware of its true nature and have confused it with other

[36] On the extent of literacy in classical Athens and the ways in which writing was used in this
period, see Turner 1952, B. Knox 1968, Harris 1989: ch. 4, Thomas 1989: ch. 1 and 1992:
ch. 7.

[37] Isocrates' argument against this accusation is that he is only "waging war on the false
pretenders" (τοῖς ἀλαζονευομένοις πολεμῶν, 20). But this can hardly be said to invalidate
the charges!

[38] In the extant part of his treatise *Against the Sophists*, which was written at the beginning of his career (*circa* 390), Isocrates does not offer a definition of "philosophy."
Rather, he attacks the principles and practices of three groups of intellectuals: "teachers
of disputation" (τῶν περὶ τὰς ἔριδας διατριβόντων, 1), which clearly includes the Socratics;
"professors of political discourse"; and the "older sophists" who wrote "the treatises that
are called *technai*" (19). In section 11, Isocrates claims that he wishes that "philosophy"
could do all the miraculous things that his rivals claim it does; the specious claims made
by these thinkers, he adds, bring slander not only upon them but upon "all the others who
are in the same profession." Isocrates does not here suggest that his rivals are in a different profession from philosophers, but he may have qualified this point in the part of the
treatise that is lost.

intellectual pursuits.[39] Practitioners of these other pursuits are identified
as "those who are skilled in disputation and those who are engaged in
astronomy and geometry and studies such as these" (τοὺς ἐν τοῖς ἐριστικοῖς
λόγοις δυναστεύοντας καὶ τοὺς περὶ τὴν ἀστρολογίαν καὶ τὴν γεωμετρίαν
καὶ τὰ τοιαῦτα τῶν μαθημάτων διατρίβοντας, 261). Isocrates grants that
these various courses of study offer some small benefit to students, but he
insists that "these disciplines are different in nature from the other ones
which we teach" (ταῦτα τὰ μαθήματα τὴν φύσιν οὐδὲν ὁμοίαν ἔχει τοῖς
ἄλλοις οἷς διδασκόμεθα, 263–4). The criterion of differentiation is as follows: "the latter [i.e. Isocrates' education] benefits us when we have achieved knowledge, but the former can be of no benefit to people after they
have mastered them (except for those who choose to make a living from
this source), but only aid people when they are in the process of learning"
(264). The disciplines of Isocrates' rivals, in short, serve only to exercise
and sharpen people's minds; they do not produce a body of knowledge
that is, like Isocrates' teachings, useful and beneficial in speech and
action.

Having indicated that these disciplines are different from his in kind,
Isocrates proceeds to draw the obvious conclusion: "I do not think that it
is right to confer the title of 'philosophy' on something that is of no benefit to us in the present either in regard to speech or to action; rather, I call
this course of study a gymnastic of the mind and a preparation for philosophy" (266). Isocrates acknowledges quite explicitly that he is dealing
at the level of "words" – specifically, the words "wisdom" and "philosophy" (270) – and he even defends the need for an excursion into seman-
tics: "since I deny that the thing called 'philosophy' by certain people is in
fact philosophy, it is fitting that I define and make clear to you what it is
that is justly called by this name" (270–1). In fact, it is precisely because
people are not using the word "according to nature" (κατὰ φύσιν, 283)
that Isocrates is compelled to articulate the true meaning of "philosophy." On the one hand, he registers total disagreement with his rivals:

They say that the people who pay no heed to things that are necessary but enjoy
the outlandish discourses of the ancient sophists are philosophers, but that the
people who are learning and practicing the things which will enable them to
manage wisely both their private households and the commonwealth of the city
are not. (285)

[39] Isocrates, of course, was competing for students and for prestige with a number of different intellectuals (on Isocrates' rivals, see Wilcox 1943; Lynch 1972: ch. 2 discusses the
different schools of higher learning that were instituted in this period). Alcidamas' *On the
Sophists* well exemplifies the kind of infighting that was going on in intellectual circles in
this period. We need to distinguish, however, these general polemics among intellectuals
from Plato's and Isocrates' appropriations of the title of "philosophy," which constituted
a specific and quite distinct battle.

His own position, as he articulates it, is just the opposite:

Since it is not in the nature of man to attain a scientific knowledge (ἐπιστήμην) by which, once we possess it, we would know what to do or say, I consider those men wise who are able by means of conjecture (ταῖς δόξαις) to hit upon, for the most part, what is best; and I call those men "philosophers" who are engaged in the studies from which they will most quickly achieve this kind of wisdom. (271)[40]

Knowing what to do and to say and learning how best to manage the affairs of one's household and city: this is the task of philosophy according to Isocrates.

In his explicit definition of philosophy in the *Antidosis*, then, Isocrates attempts to exclude other claimants to the title of "philosopher" by differentiating his pedagogic and epistemic principles from theirs. But, by itself, this does not suffice to gain for philosophy the legitimacy and importance that Isocrates claims for it. Even more important than these explicit statements of principle is Isocrates' attempt to position the philosopher within the democratic city. This "rhetoric of legitimation" is harder to identify than the explicit definition of philosophy, for it runs through the entire speech and cannot be articulated merely by reference to the practices and principles of other "philosophers." Whereas Isocrates' explicit definition of philosophy is readily grasped in the context of an intellectual polemic, his positioning of the philosopher can only be understood in the socio-political context of classical Athens.

Let me turn, then, from principles to positioning, from polemics to politics. Isocrates' *Antidosis* is a peculiar document, not least because of its form. Isocrates states at the opening of his speech that he had recently been challenged to an "exchange of property" (*antidosis*); a trial ensued in which Isocrates was the loser, and he was therefore compelled to fund a trierarchy. Incensed at his loss in this trial over property, Isocrates admits quite frankly his grief and surprise at the discovery that the Athenian public holds him in so little esteem. A defense is in order; but what kind of a defense? Isocrates announces that he has composed a speech which "pretends" (προσποιουμένην, 13) that he is on trial for corrupting the

---

[40] Cf. 183–4: "those who are engaged in philosophy offer to their students a detailed analysis of all the forms in which language is used. And, when they have made them familiar with these things and gone through them in minute detail, they turn the students back to their exercises, they habituate them in hard work, and they compel them to bring together the individual things they have learned, in order that they may grasp them more securely and that they may get closer to the proper measure and moment for action by means of conjecture (ταῖς δόξαις). For it is not possible to get hold of these things by way of scientific knowledge (τῷ ... εἰδέναι), since in all cases they elude scientific knowledge (τὰς ἐπιστήμας)." Plato and his circle are clearly targeted in these passages. On Plato's and Isocrates' polemic over the proper principles of a "philosophic" education, see J. Cooper 1986 and Batstone 1986 (responding to Cooper).

young by teaching them to "make the worse argument appear the better" (15). Isocrates pretends, in short, that he is Socrates defending his life before a jury of Athenians. Although he does not mention Socrates by name, the frequent allusions to Plato's *Apology* leave no doubt about his intentions.[41]

This instance of intertextuality, I will argue, deserves serious investigation, for the Socratic subtext is part of a literary strategy that has important socio-political ramifications. I begin with the most obvious question: why should a person who wants to defend his life in the wake of a damaging property trial turn to the *Apology* for a subtext? Norlin suggests that this evinces Isocrates' "warm feeling" and "high regard" for Socrates.[42] But if Isocrates did indeed want to express his high regard, why would he yoke Socrates' extraordinary trial and death to his own situation, which is trivial by comparison? Jaeger takes a different tack, suggesting that Isocrates was impressed by the "autobiographical" possibilities of the genre of the *apologia*; according to Jaeger, Isocrates "clearly felt that his position was closely similar to Socrates', for he took every opportunity to remind the reader of it by verbal imitations of Plato's words and of the accusation aimed at Socrates."[43] Jaeger is surely right to stress the attractions offered by the "autobiographical" genre of the apology. But why the "autobiography" of *Plato's* Socrates? Surely it was open to Isocrates to avoid referring to a specific text within the genre or to target some other subtext, such as Gorgias' *Defense of Palamedes*.[44] In short, he did not have to drag Socrates into his speech at all. Given the repeated allusions to Plato's *Apology*, it seems reasonable to suggest that Isocrates was deliberately juxtaposing himself not just to Socrates but to Plato's Socrates. As I see it, Isocrates is inviting his readers to attend to the differences as well as the similarities between himself and Plato's philosopher. This is bolstered by the fact that Isocrates offers in the *Antidosis* a lengthy definition of the philosopher that is clearly aimed at the definitions of philosophy put forward by Plato in the *Gorgias*, the middle books of the *Republic* (473b–521b), and the "digression" in the *Theaetetus* (172c–176d).[45] The imitation of the *Apology*, then, is part of Isocrates' attack on *Plato's* portrayal of the philosopher.

---

[41] 15–16, 21, 26–7, 33, 89, 95, 100, 145, 154, 179, 240, 321.

[42] Norlin 1980: xvii.

[43] Jaeger 1944: 133. See also Momigliano [1971]/1993: 59–60 on Isocrates' transformation of Plato's "pseudo-autobiography" of Socrates into an "authentic autobiography."

[44] See Coulter 1964, Feaver and Hare 1981, and Seeskin 1982 for analyses of the intertextual relationship between Plato's *Apology* and Gorgias' *Defense of Palamedes*.

[45] In addition to the allusions to Plato that I will discuss in this chapter, note the following parallels: the *topos* of the "usefulness" of the philosopher, found at, e.g., *Gorg.* 484d–e, 485d–486c, 521d–522a, *Rep.* 487d–e, 489b, and *Theaet.* 173c–176d, esp. 174a–b and

Plato's *Apology*, however, is not the only generic subtext in Isocrates' speech. For the *Antidosis* is also informed by a genre of discourse which operated in a forensic context quite different from that of Socrates' trial, namely, the kind of speech used in the court case that followed a challenge to an *antidosis*.[46] What was the nature of the *antidosis* challenge?[47] This arose when an Athenian who was assigned to perform a compulsory public service or "liturgy" sought exemption on the grounds that another individual was wealthier than he and should shoulder the financial burden in his stead. The person assigned the liturgy would proceed by challenging this wealthy individual either to meet the expense of the liturgy or to accept an exchange of property. If this individual refused both of these injunctions, a formal adjudication took place to determine which of the two was better able to finance the liturgy. The speeches made at such a trial, then, focussed primarily on questions concerning property. As Gabrielsen observes about the *antidosis* process,

> if a challenger and challengee tried to settle their dispute through a law-court appeal (a διαδικασία hearing), each of them had to prove that the other's property was the largest and thus the one better able to sustain liturgical expenditure. However, the few cases we know of show the virtual inability of the contestants to furnish such a proof; and this notwithstanding the fact that each of them was obliged to submit "a right and just" inventory of his property. More important still, at the ensuing trial each party sought to inflate the value of the opponent's property by mobilizing a host of arguments designed to demonstrate that, besides his φανερὰ οὐσία (visible wealth), the latter owned a sizable amount of ἀφανὴς οὐσία (invisible wealth).[48]

A defendant at a such a trial was required by law "to make visible (ἀποφαίνειν) his wealth in a right and just manner."[49] But he would also have to convince the jury that he was not "hiding" any wealth. It is im-

---

176d, is picked up by Isocrates at *Antidosis* 261–2, 269; the suggestion that philosophy has been unjustly slandered, which is illustrated in detail in the *Gorgias* and *Theaetetus* and explicated in the *Republic* (489c–d, 491a), is explicitly sounded at *Antidosis* 170–8; and Plato's identification of *pleonexia* as a fundamentally anti-philosophical activity (see, e.g., *Gorg.* 483c, 490d–e, 491a, 508a, *Rep.* 343e–344a, 349b–c, 349e–350c, 359c, 362a–c, 365d) is directly contradicted by Isocrates' defense of *pleonexia* at *Antidosis* 281–5.

[46] Isocrates makes this explicit when he says that some portions of his speech are "fit to be spoken in a courtroom," whereas others involve "frank discussions of philosophy" (10). It is the presence of these two kinds of discourse that makes the speech a "mixed *logos*" (12).

[47] On the *antidosis* challenge and the legal suit that followed, see MacDowell 1978: 162–4, Gabrielsen 1987, Christ 1990.

[48] Gabrielsen 1986: 100–1. On the notion of visible/invisible property, see also Finley 1952: 53–6, Kurke 1991: ch. 9, E. Cohen 1992: especially 191–206. Gernet [1968]/1981: ch. 16 discusses the way in which the philosophic distinction between the "visible" and the "invisible" relates to the dichotomy between visible and invisible property in the economic sphere.

[49] This law is mentioned at Demosthenes 42.11 and 18.

portant to emphasize that, although cash and other forms of movable
wealth lent themselves most readily to concealment, the terms "visible"
and "invisible" property cannot be connected with one or another form of
wealth; as Gabrielsen suggests, "Acknowledgement of ownership (for-
mally an ὁμολογία or δήλωσις) is the fundamental and necessary step for
converting property into visible [wealth]; failure to do so, as a rule, allows
the property to remain in the area of the invisible and marks the act of
concealment (ἀπόκρυψις οὐσίας)."[50] Strictly speaking, then, the material
possessions that a person claims as his own are "visible property" and
those which he disclaims (or neglects to claim) are "invisible property."

In the opening sections of the *Antidosis*, after describing his loss in the
property trial, Isocrates announces his intention to set the record straight
by setting forth the truth about his activities and transactions. But he then
proceeds to invent a fictional trial in which he is accused of harming the
city by offering the youth an education in corruption. The two trials seem
completely disparate, yet Isocrates claims that his accuser in the fictional
trial will "use the same slanders that were enunciated in the suit concerning the exchange of property" (8). The real trial, then, does not simply
serve as a convenient pretext for the defense offered in the fictional trial;
rather, the arguments made in the property trial will subtend and inform
Isocrates' defense of his activities as an educator in the fictional trial. Two
different modes of discourse issuing from two quite different spheres of
activity – that of material possessions on the one hand and of educational
transactions on the other – are thus intertwined.

This intertwining produces an interesting result: Isocrates' fictional
"Socratic" defense is fueled by the discourse of "visible wealth." It is not
so much that Isocrates discusses his material possessions in his fictional
defense. Although he does address himself to this issue (146–7, 155–160),
his primary effort is to lay bare the wealth (so to speak) of his wisdom and
teaching.[51] The discourse of visible and invisible property, in short, is
applied to the immaterial realm of wisdom and its transmission rather
than to the material realm of money and property. Take, for example,
Isocrates' claim in section 44:

[50] Gabrielsen 1986: 104.
[51] Isocrates' notion of wisdom as "intellectual property" must be distinguished from the
legally recognized forms of intellectual property found in modern western culture. The
former can only be understood in the context of the systems of exchange – social, political, and economic – operating in democratic Athens. See Harrison 1992, who analyzes
intellectual property in economies where "the circulation of goods creates social relationships between the transactors, rather than impersonal relations of price between the
objects transacted" (p. 234). Note also Bourdieu's analysis of the circulation of "symbolic
capital" as a disguised form of economic exchange ([1972]/1989: esp. 171–83), as well as
his discussion of education *qua* "symbolic capital" in contemporary French culture
([1979]/1984: ch. 1 and passim).

For I would be ashamed before my students if, having often stated that I would be happy to have all of the citizens know about the life that I live and the discourses that I am engaged in, I were not ready now to make them visible to you (δηλοίην ὑμῖν) and appeared rather to be hiding (ἀποκρυπτόμενος) these things.

Isocrates had thought, he says with exasperation, that he had "made it manifest" (πεποιηκέναι φανερόν, 3) that his writing and teaching dealt with lofty political themes rather than with petty forensic rhetoric, but the jurors at his trial were evidently fooled (3–4). It is slander (διαβολή), he says in section 18, that has "made the truth completely invisible" (ὅλως δὲ τὴν μὲν ἀλήθειαν ἀφανίζει). Isocrates is thus compelled to "make manifest the truth about myself" (περὶ ἐμοῦ δηλῶσαι τὴν ἀλήθειαν, 13). In fact, he says later in the speech, he has been advised not to tell the whole truth lest he should create even greater misunderstanding and enmity; nonetheless, he continues, he will "lay bare" (δηλωτέον) his views and he will not "hide" (ἀποκρύψομαι) any of them (140–1).

The vocabulary derived from the property trial that pervades the speech, then, is consistently applied to Isocrates' efforts to "make visible" his possession and transmission of knowledge.[52] But how does one make this kind of possession visible? Isocrates' first strategy is to avail himself of the written word:[53]

If, then, I were on trial for some criminal activities, I would not be able to furnish these actions for you to see (οὐκ ἂν οἷός τ' ἦν ἰδεῖν ὑμῖν αὐτὰς παρασχεῖν); instead, it would have been necessary for you, forming conjectures on the basis of the things that were spoken, to reach whatever judgment you reached. But since I am accused over my discourses, I think that I will be better able to make visible (ἐμφανιεῖν) the truth. For I will place before your eyes (ὑμῖν δείξω) the discourses that I have spoken and written ... (53–4)

Isocrates proceeds to quote lengthy passages from three of his speeches: the *Panegyricus* 51–99 (*Antid.* 59), *On the Peace* 25–56, 132-end (*Antid.* 66), and *Ad Nicoclem* 14–39 (*Antid.* 73).[54] To a certain extent, these extracts resemble the written testimony of witnesses made compulsory in the Athenian courts (*circa* 378/7);[55] they can thus be seen as witnesses to the wisdom of his beliefs and activities. But the writings make Isocrates' intellectual wealth visible not simply because they are *inscribed logoi* but

---

[52] See, e.g., 6, 13, 18, 44, 52–3, 67, 69–70, 76, 98, 140–1.

[53] As Gabrielsen 1986: 105 observes, written documents of a given transaction keep a person's property visible: "Written documents, made up in connection with transactions involving landed holdings as well as statements of a similar nature made in the presence of witnesses, carried the validity of juridical proof against which little could be done by individuals seeking to conceal their property." Isocrates' display of his writings, then, may also function to remind the jury that he is not trying to conceal anything.

[54] A passage from *Against the Sophists* (14–18) is also included later in the speech (194).

[55] Calhoun 1919, Humphreys 1985: 316–21, Thomas 1989: 42–4.

because they are Isocrates' *own logoi*. For this reason, they are more than just outside witnesses to his "wealth"; they both contain and embody Isocrates' wisdom. They are, one might say, the visible vessels of his property.

Isocrates' second strategy for evincing his intellectual wealth is to trundle out his students:

I will now reveal (δηλώσω) the men who have associated with me from youth to old age, and I will also furnish as witnesses to the things that I say men from your ranks who are members of my generation. (93)

Isocrates proceeds to name a number of his pupils who were crowned by the city with golden wreaths because they were good men and had spent large sums of their own money for the benefit of Athens (93–4). These men are not called on to speak on his behalf; rather, the manifest beneficence of these individuals and the high honors they have received from the city is itself evidence of the high quality of the teacher. Having named and claimed this group of students, moreover, Isocrates addresses himself to his opponents' suggestion that he is keeping some of his products out of sight: they will argue, he says, "that many other men – meddlesome ones – are my students, and that I am hiding (ἀποκρύπτομαι) them from you" (98). Once again, Isocrates vigorously denies that he is hiding some portion of his "property."

As in the case of his writings, then, Isocrates offers his students as embodiments of his intellectual wealth. They are not just external witnesses; they are the products as well as the keepers of his wisdom. It is for this reason that Isocrates insists on his readiness to take complete responsibility for his students; as he puts it at section 104,

It is fitting for a private individual to speak in defense of his own actions and then to step down (lest he appear to be going too far), but for those who are considered to be counsellors and teachers it is necessary to offer a defense of their associates as well as of themselves.

The language and deeds of the students, Isocrates indicates, directly reflect those of the teacher. In fact, Isocrates even goes so far as to indicate that he has singlehandedly produced numerous benefactors for the city and that he is "co-responsible" (συναίτιος, 96) for their good deeds:

For if you accept that I was their counsellor and teacher, it would be just for you to feel greater gratitude to me than to those who are fed in the prytaneum on account of their excellence. For each of these men has furnished himself alone as a benefactor, but I have furnished all those whom I have just now named. (95–6)

In the context of classical Athens, of course, there would be nothing odd about a teacher taking so much credit for the activities and productions of his students. As Dover observes, the Athenians of the fifth century were accustomed to regard the relation between teacher and pupil or between master and apprentice as the transmission of techniques, not as the development of abilities which might issue in independent critical thought. It was therefore assumed that the principles and attitudes of the teacher were embodied in the pupil; this, after all, was the purpose of traditional Athenian education.[56]

The transmission of *logoi* and *aretē*, however, presented a special case; indeed, the validity of this novel kind of education was a hotly debated issue in Athens of the late fifth and early fourth centuries. Isocrates' position on this issue is instructive:

in the case of all arts and crafts we regard as the most skilled those men who produce pupils whose craftsmanship is as similar to one another as possible. This also turns out to be the case in philosophy. For all those who have happened upon a true and intelligent guide will be found to possess a style of speaking that is so similar that it is manifest (φανερόν) to everyone that they have shared the same training. In fact, if no common regime and technical training had fallen to their lot, it is impossible that they would have achieved this similarity. (205–6)

Here, Isocrates claims that the "true" philosophical teacher, like the teachers in the arts and crafts, produces a distinct and recognizable product. In other words, the teacher's knowledge and skill is the kind of thing that can be directly transmitted to the student. The intellectual wealth of the teacher, in sum, manifests itself in his students just as it does in his writings.

I would argue, then, that the intertwining in the *Antidosis* of two different genres of rhetorical discourse – the one deriving from a private suit dealing with property and the other from a public suit dealing with education – invites us to look at Isocrates' activity as an educator from a particular angle. The educator, as I have tried to show, is figured as a person in possession of intellectual wealth that can be owned and disowned in the same way as material wealth. It is a possession that can be offered up for public scrutiny or hidden away so as to benefit only the teacher and his associates. Let me emphasize that this is not just an interesting metaphor. Rather, Isocrates' insistence that he is not "hiding" his intellectual wealth has important political implications. As Kurke suggests,

in the term *invisible property* we can see an embedded economy trying to put a name to the process of its own *disembedding*, for invisible property is the product of those who privilege pure economic considerations over the social and political embedding of property. Thus the motive of such men is strictly economic and the

[56] Dover [1976]/1988: 155.

result of making their property invisible is that they are themselves disembedded from the social fabric of their community.[57]

In this passage, Kurke recalls Polanyi's distinction between pre-market economies, in which economic relations are "embedded" in the social system, and the modern market economy, which is "disembedded" from the social structure and operates in an independent sphere not subject to social control.[58] It is widely agreed that Finley's "substantivist" position, according to which "ancient economic activity was controlled by a complex of social and political institutions and practices, with economic behavior shaped by familial, religious, and sociopolitical values," offers an accurate description of Athens up to (at least) the late fifth century.[59] But in fourth-century Athens, as many scholars have argued, the onset of a disembedded economy is discernible.[60]

We can infer, then, that when Isocrates manifests his "visible wealth" in the *Antidosis* and denies that he is hiding anything, he is effectively claiming to be embedded in the social fabric of the community. He is not laying claim to intellectual wealth in some abstract sense; rather, he repeatedly indicates that his transactions as a teacher of philosophy are embedded in the social and political structures of the Athenian polis. Again and again, Isocrates entreats the Athenians to recognize him as a responsible and beneficial "insider" rather than as a citizen who is playing a suspiciously alien role. What exactly is this alien role? Recall, for a

[57] Kurke 1991: 227. Of course, in Athens of the fourth century, a single individual could possess both visible and invisible property: the two are not mutually exclusive (as Kurke appears to suggest). E. Cohen 1992: 190–206 and passim builds a powerful case for an extensive "invisible economy" in fourth-century Athens.

[58] On Polanyi's thesis, see note 25 above.

[59] Finley 1981 and 1985 clearly set forth the "substantivist" position. The quote is from Burke's summary of Finley's argument (1992: 199). For an analysis of Finley's contribution to ancient economic history, see the "Editors' introduction" to Finley 1981, written by B. D. Shaw and R. P. Saller. Morris (forthcoming) rightly reminds us that Finley's "substantivist" approach to the ancient economy should not be conflated with the "primitivist" approach, which argued (*contra* the "modernists") that the ancient economy was a household economy (i.e. at the opposite end of the spectrum from the modern capitalist economies).

[60] Arguments for the growth of a disembedded economy in fourth-century Athens are cited above, in note 25. Not coincidentally, references to visible/invisible property are found almost exclusively in fourth-century texts (although, as Gabrielsen 1986: 104–5 observes, the notion is found in several late Aristophanic comedies). Note also the distinction that Aristotle draws in the *Politics* between "wealth that is in accordance with nature" (ὁ πλοῦτος ὁ κατὰ φύσιν, 1257b19–20) and "wealth-getting that is unnecessary" (τῆς τε μὴ ἀναγκαίας χρηματιστικῆς, 1258a14–15), which seems to point to a sphere of activity where economic motives are more or less free from social control. There is a good deal of debate about this passage from Aristotle: see, e.g., Polanyi 1957, Finley 1970, Meikle 1979 (*contra* Polanyi and Finley). By itself, of course, it does not offer objective or even accurate evidence for new economic trends; if does, however, represent a (rare) attempt to analyze and classify commodity relations in this period.

moment, Isocrates' description of Gorgias' lifestyle: he devoted himself to making money; he sojourned in Thessaly when they were the wealthiest of the Greeks; he had no permanent home and thus paid no money in taxes or in public benefactions; and he had neither wife nor children to support and look after (155–6). Although Isocrates does not explicitly differentiate himself from Gorgias in this passage, the contrast emerges elsewhere in the speech: unlike Gorgias, we are reminded, Isocrates dwells in Athens with his family and son (145); like his father before him (161), he has spent a good deal of money on liturgies and other public benefactions (145); he entered the profession of teacher not in order to get rich but rather to repair his patrimony, which was lost in the war (161–2).

Why, then, does Isocrates worry that he will be subjected to the "common slanders used against sophists" (168–9)? Consider the statement of an unnamed associate whom Isocrates quotes in the *Antidosis*: "what judgment do you expect such people to reach, when the life and activities that you are describing are not even a tiny bit similar to theirs ...?" (143). Isocrates' life and activities are suspicious because they do not fit the ordinary codes of behavior. On the one hand (as he himself admits), Isocrates has opted out of a wide array of civic affairs: he has never brought anyone to trial or stood trial (up until the *antidosis* proceeding), nor has he appeared as a counsel or witness for anyone else; he has avoided those activities "in which all those who are involved in the political life of the city are engaged," and he has held aloof from public offices and the benefits that accrue from these (144–5). On the other hand, he has set himself up as a teacher of rhetoric whose pupils are "not only private people ... but also orators and generals and kings and tyrants" (30). This latter is problematic on two counts. First, Isocrates' dealings with Athenian orators and generals could be seen as an attempt to influence civic and political issues from behind the scenes. And, second, the fact that he was in the pay of kings and tyrants – i.e. wealthy and powerful foreigners – might call into question Isocrates' allegiance to Athens.

Isocrates responds to this suspicion by describing, again and again, the benefactions that he has conferred on Athens. This rhetorical strategy, as Ober demonstrates, was commonly used by aristocratic Athenians as a way of gaining public approval for their possession of "elite assets" such as noble birth, wealth, and higher education. For the secure possession of these assets "was made contingent upon continuing mass approval. That approval was given only on the condition that elite assets were shared with the masses and so were demonstrably a benefit to the citizen body as a whole."[61] Isocrates is quick to recall the liturgies and other

61 Ober 1989: 291–2.

material favors he has conferred on the city (145, 150–1), and he even
congratulates himself for benefiting the city with money that comes from
foreigners rather than from Athenians (164–5). But most of his efforts are
aimed at showing the ways in which his intellectual "wealth" has served
the good of Athens. Take, for example, the suggestion – made not once
but twice in the speech – that, as an intellectual and an educator, Isocrates
has done more for the city than victorious athletes and other public benefactors who are awarded meals in the prytaneum (95–6; 301–2).[62] Kurke
points out that

> victory at the games can be located within the public sphere of *megaloprepeia*, as a
> common benefaction bestowed on the city by the victor. Clear evidence for the
> latter perception is the custom, attested in Athens and elsewhere, of feasting ath-
> letic victors at public expense at the prytaneum or civic hearth, for this honor was
> conferred only on those who were considered benefactors (εὐεργέτεις) of the city.[63]

Isocrates indicates, then, that his own activities as an intellectual and educator are, like the benefactions conferred on the city by its victorious
athletes, a kind of *megaloprepeia* or private expenditure for the public
good.

Isocrates is careful to spell out the ways in which his activities have
benefited the city. We have already seen that he takes partial credit for his
students' contributions to the democracy. But his own direct contributions receive special emphasis. First, Isocrates points to the many eulogies
that he has written for Athens (166), an example of which is offered in the
lengthy passage quoted from the *Panegyricus*. As he says in his summary
of this speech,

> First of all, what kind of discourse could be more pious and just than one which
> praises our ancestors in a manner that is worthy of their virtue and of the deeds
> which they accomplished? And what could be more appropriate for a citizen and
> fitting for the city than one which shows that the hegemony belongs to us rather
> than the Lacedaemonians by virtue of our exploits in war and our other good
> deeds? (76–7)

But Isocrates' efforts on behalf of the city are not confined to praise: he
has also served the city by criticizing her when she has gone wrong and
offering intelligent counsel. As he describes his speech *On the Peace*: "I
exhort [Athens] towards justice, I chastise those who have erred and I give
counsel for future policy" (65). In democratic Athens, as Ober suggests,
"the good orator not only praised the people, he also criticized and op-

---

[62] These passages clearly recall Socrates' statement in Plato's *Apology* that his "penalty"
should be to receive meals in the prytaneum (36d). I will deal with Socrates' version of this
topos below.

[63] Kurke 1991: 170.

posed them; orator and audience alike recognized that criticism and opposition to the will of the masses were central to the orator's political
function."[64] In the *Antidosis*, Isocrates claims for himself a function
similar to that of the orator: the wise counsellor to the city of Athens.[65]
Isocrates, of course, has also been offering counsel to people outside of
Athens. But even these efforts, he claims, are "useful and advantageous"
to the city (78). In fact, he has included a lengthy excerpt from his *Ad
Nicoclem* precisely that he may show

in what fashion I am accustomed to dealing with private men and with princes; for
I will be seen to speak with Nicocles as a free man and as an Athenian should
(ἐλευθέρως καὶ τῆς πόλεως ἀξίως), not paying court to his wealth and his power but
coming to the aid of his subjects and trying my hardest to procure for them the
mildest possible government. And since I have spoken on behalf of the *dēmos* in
my converse with a king, surely I would be zealous in urging those who live in a
democracy to pay court to the majority. (69–71)

Even when addressing foreigners, then, Isocrates speaks as an Athenian
and for the benefit of Athens and her ideals. Indeed, he even suggests at
the end of the speech that, as a teacher of rhetoric, he contributes to the
very thing that is most distinctive and characteristic of the city: Athenians
are considered the "best educated in thought and in speech" of all the
Greeks (294) and the city as a whole is looked upon as the "school" for all
students of rhetoric (295). Since excellence in thinking and speaking is an
Athenian prerogative, then Isocrates' activities must necessarily reflect
and, indeed, augment the special wisdom of the city. So far from behaving
like an outsider, Isocrates establishes himself as the insider *par excellence*.

In the *Antidosis*, then, Isocrates demands that his own activities be
accorded a place in the social and political transactions of the city of
Athens. He has conferred numerous benefactions on the city, and he explicitly asks for recompense. Pindar, he reminds the jury, was rewarded
with both honor and money for composing but one short eulogy of Athens (166). His own benefactions, he suggests, should also be given their

---

[64] Ober 1989: 323. See also Dover 1974: 23–5.
[65] Isocrates takes pains to show that his panhellenic sympathies do not call his allegiance to
Athens into question. He says at 79–80, "if you obey my counsel, you will direct the
whole of Hellas in a way that is honorable, just, and advantageous to the city. It is proper
for men of intelligence to concern themselves with both of these things, but of these two
that which is greater and worthier deserves preference ... " What Isocrates says here is not
that Athenians should consider the good of Hellas as more important than their own
interests, but rather that *Athens should direct Hellas* by considering the greater good.
Athens' role as leader is asserted even as she is exhorted to consider the common good. As
Isocrates puts it at section 85, "I attempt to persuade the entire city to pursue a policy
from which the Athenians themselves will be prosperous and will release the other Greeks
from their present evils." Once again, Athens is seen as the leader and author of the
common good.

proper due. What sort of recompense does he have in mind? Isocrates says repeatedly and emphatically that the Athenians owe "praise" and "honor" to him and to people like him (36, 141, 152–3, 162–3, 226, 301–2, 309). But perhaps even more pointed is his claim to the *charis* of the Athenians. As he says at 60–1,

> Consider well whether I seem to be corrupting the youth with my discourse and if I am not, on the contrary, exhorting them to a life of virtuous activity and of dangers undertaken on behalf of the city; and consider whether it is just that I should pay a penalty for the words that have been spoken or whether, on the contrary, I should not receive the greatest gratitude (χάριν) from you ...

This appeal to *charis*, which is reiterated elsewhere in the speech,[66] has a specific valence in political discourse of fourth-century Athens. As Ober reminds us,

> In classical Athens, the interaction between giver and recipient never developed into a formal system of patronage on the Roman model, but the Athenian relationship based on *charis* was overt nonetheless. The individual who had received a gift owed his benefactor not mere thanks but a favor in return. The benefactor could legitimately demand that the return favor be rendered. With the institutionalization at a national level of the *charis* relationship into the system of liturgies there were some changes; especially important was the introduction of the idea that the corporate recipients had the right to judge the spirit in which the gift was given. Yet the essential concept of the recipient's duty to repay the donor was retained. Thus, litigants who had performed remarkable liturgies could not merely request but also demand the jurors' sympathy.[67]

When Isocrates asks the jury for *charis*, then, he is demanding a specific favor in return for the services he has rendered the city. But Isocrates' plea is unusual because the benefactions for which he asks a return were brought about (for the most part) by the expenditure of intellectual rather than material wealth. In other words, he asks that his activities as a writer and educator be acknowledged and rewarded as a new kind of liturgy or expenditure on the city's behalf.

[66] See, e.g., 95, 144, 287; cf. 99 and 106, where Isocrates asks that the jurors give *charis* to his students rather than to him if they have turned out well, but to put the blame on him if they have turned out badly. Here, Isocrates' paradoxical refusal to accept *charis* only underlines how much he deserves it.

[67] Ober 1989: 229 (see also 226–36 and passim). Davies 1981: 88–105 offers a useful analysis of the notion of *charis* in classical Athens (see also Davies 1971: xvii–xviii and passim, Dover 1974: 293–5). As Davies 1981: 92–3 observes, "The form of *charis* most prevalent by the fourth century is forensic, as a claim, on the grounds of civic, and particularly liturgical, virtue, for favourable treatment from a jury if the individual investor came to be involved in a law-suit. Examples of such a claim are so numerous and so unambiguous as to leave no doubt of the way in which the investment was expected to pay dividends." Strauss 1986: 13 claims that "munificence was still of considerable political, and not solely forensic importance in postwar Athens."

It is important to emphasize that Isocrates does not deny that his profession takes the form of a private business transaction and that it enriches him personally. His point is that this transaction is itself situated in a larger arena of exchange, namely, the social and political institutions and practices of the Athenian polis. Isocrates' intellectual property, in short, can and should be measured in monetary terms – as a commodity that can be exchanged for money. But it must also be measured in symbolic terms – as something that deserves public credit, whether it be in the form of honor, power, or other civic favors.[68] These two kinds of exchange, Isocrates suggests, are not antithetical; on the contrary, the material worth of his wisdom is solid evidence of its high value in the symbolic realm.[69] The wisdom and teaching of Isocrates' philosopher, in sum, should be given a place in the social economy of Athens, where it can be used for the public good and where it can enact and enhance that glorious thing known as Athenian wisdom.[70]

IV

Isocrates' *Antidosis*, of course, was written after Plato's many discussions of the nature of "philosophy." I have chosen to analyze the Isocratean material first because it helps both to focus and to contextualize Plato's creation of "philosophy." As my analysis of the *Antidosis* has shown, Isocrates foregrounds the socio-political aspects of the new cultural practice that he calls "philosophy." The fact that the *Antidosis* has little to say about the intellectual or epistemic aspects of philosophy is usually interpreted as a sign of Isocrates' mediocrity as a thinker. But we need to attend to what Isocrates' definition of philosophy includes as well as what it excludes. If we take the *Antidosis* on its own terms, it becomes clear that Isocrates' primary concern was to negotiate a place for philosophy in the

[68] As Bourdieu [1972]/1989: 181 suggests, "symbolic capital is always *credit*, in the widest sense of the word, i.e. a sort of advance which the group alone can grant those who give it the best material and *symbolic* guarantees ..." (his italics).

[69] Note that Isocrates does not apologize for or defend his acceptance of money for teaching. Although he does suggest that he is not like other sophists (147–8), he clearly categorizes himself as a sophist in his discussion of Gorgias (155–8). The only time that Isocrates defends himself from the charge of ill-gained profit is at 36–7, where he insists that he has no dealings with "speeches for the courts." Clearly, he is more concerned with being labelled a logographer than with being called a sophist.

[70] Isocrates' negotiation with the jury of Athenians is, of course, a fiction (the actual audience for his speech is that elite group of people who had the leisure and the inclination to read such a speech or to attend the various gatherings where these kinds of written texts were read aloud – an activity that is described at *Panathenaicus* 233). But, as we have seen, Isocrates uses the same kinds of arguments on the fictional *dēmos* that Athenian orators and litigants used on the real *dēmos*: his definition and positioning of the philosopher is thus best understood in relation to the democracy and its institutions.

social and political practices of the Athenian democracy; it is for this reason that the "rhetoric of legitimation" is far more prominent in the speech than an explication of philosophical principles. Given that Isocrates' definition was deliberately forged in opposition to that of Plato, the Isocratean material invites us to examine the ways in which Plato positions his philosopher in relation to the social and political economy of classical Athens.

As I have suggested, the *Antidosis* is (among other things) a polemical attack on the definitions of philosophy put forward by Plato in a number of dialogues. Let me begin with the *Apology*, which is the most obvious target of Isocrates' speech in spite of the fact that it does not attempt to appropriate the term "philosopher" for its extraordinary hero. Like Isocrates after him, Plato's Socrates claims to be a benefactor to Athens (30a; 30d–31b; 36d). As we saw in the *Antidosis*, Isocrates claims that his intellectual property and its beneficial expenditure is demonstrable: it is a new kind of liturgy that deserves appropriate compensation. What, then, is the benefaction that Socrates has bestowed upon the city? According to the account in Plato's *Apology*, Socrates has exposed the citizens' pretensions to knowledge and has exhorted them to value their souls over their bodies and possessions (29d–30b). It should go without saying that these activities are not benefactions in the Athenians' eyes, and could easily be interpreted as a hostile attack on the citizenry if not the democracy as a whole.[71] But Socrates gives no currency to Athenian values, and thus refuses to negotiate on their terms. Consider, for example, Socrates' suggestion at the end of the speech that he deserves free meals at the prytaneum. As he says at 36d–e,

What, then, is fitting for a poor man who is a benefactor to the city and who needs leisure to exhort you? There is nothing more fitting for such an individual than to be given his meals in the prytaneum, and much more so than for a person who has won a victory in the horse-races at the Olympian games with a pair or a team of four. For he makes you seem to be happy, whereas I make you truly happy, and he is in no need of food, whereas I am needy.[72]

Compare this claim to that of Isocrates at *Antidosis* 95–6:

For if you accept that I was their counsellor and teacher, it would be just for you to offer greater *charis* to me than to those who are fed in the prytaneum on account of their excellence. For each of these men has furnished himself alone as a benefactor, but I have furnished all those whom I have just now named.

Isocrates assimilates his own benefactions to those recognized and re-

---

[71] See, e.g., Stokes 1992: 66–7.
[72] Cf. Xenophanes fr. 2, where the author claims that "wisdom" rather than physical strength or victory in the games is what benefits the city.

warded by the Athenians: his are similar to the others in kind but greater in degree. Socrates, on the other hand, makes it clear that his benefaction is qualitatively different from those of other "benefactors." Hence the claim that he bestows real blessings whereas the others offer "seeming" blessings: if he is a benefactor, then the others are counterfeiters. But if the others are counterfeiters, then the Athenians are to be blamed for their ignorance of what constitutes a benefaction. As Socrates puts it in the *Gorgias* (a dialogue which clearly glosses the *Apology*),

I know that I would have such an experience [i.e. the experience of *aporia*] if I were brought into court. For I would not be able to tell them about the pleasures (ἡδονάς) which I procured for them, which they call benefactions and useful services (εὐεργεσίας καὶ ὠφελείας); and I do not envy either those who procure these things or those for whom they are procured. (522b)

By requesting meals in the prytaneum, then, Socrates is not asking to be admitted into the social and political economy of Athens. On the contrary, he is calling this economy into question.

Socrates does of course suggest that he deserves something good (36d), but he cashes this out in his own terms: he does not need glory or some political favor, but food. Note that Isocrates does not ask specifically for meals in the prytaneum, but rather for *charis* – a *charis* that will match the value of his contributions. Socrates, on the other hand, has no interest in *charis*. In fact, he is quite emphatic that he is not asking for any favors; as he says at 35b–c,

it does not seem to me to be just to plead with the judge or to gain acquittal by begging, but rather to teach and to convince. For the judge does not sit here in order to grant favors (καταχαρίζεσθαι) in matters of justice, but to judge them. And he has sworn not to offer favors (χαριεῖσθαι) to whomever he likes, but to judge according to the laws.

When Socrates suggests that he be awarded meals in the prytaneum, then, he is not entering into the discourse of *charis* that is so common in Attic oratory. In fact, Socrates only brings up the notion of recompense after the jury has voted: it forms no part of his defense. Next to Isocrates' attempt to embed his philosophic property within the social and political economy of Athens, Socrates' behavior at his trial emerges clearly as a refusal to negotiate with the Athenians. Indeed, it is precisely his positioning outside of the transactions of the Athenian democracy that makes him a true philosopher in Plato's eyes. As Socrates says in the *Republic*, the group of true philosophers is πάνσμικρον insofar as it is extremely rare that a person with the right qualifications *is excluded from the power and honor of his homeland* by the lucky happpenstance that he has been exiled, or has come from a small town whose seductions are easy to resist, or has been prevented from participating in civic life because of physical impairment or disease (496a–c). Plato's philosopher, in short, is by definition a kind of outsider.

What is the nature of this new brand of alien? As I will argue, one of the most prominent aspects of Plato's definition of the philosopher is the opposition he forges between the philosophic "outsider" and the various types of people who made it their business to traffic in wisdom.[73] Let me illustrate what I mean by the "traffic in wisdom" by examining what is perhaps the clearest and most explicit enunciation of this phenomenon in the Platonic corpus: the *Symposium*'s handling of the exchange of "virtue" for sexual favors. In his speech on Eros, Pausanias attempts to draw a distinction between a "heavenly" or good kind of love and a "popular" or bad kind of love. Since Socrates articulates a very different distinction between good and bad love later in the dialogue, we are clearly meant to see Pausanias' categories as unsound. Pausanias' speech is largely concerned with defining the proper kind of sexual exchange – the heavenly kind that he claims has "no share in *hubris*" (181c). Interestingly, he begins by criticizing countries in which sex is given no currency as a token of exchange. In Elis and Boeotia and other places where "the people have no skill in speaking," he claims, it is customary for the beloved simply to give the lover what he wants. The reason for this, he says contemptuously, is that the people in these cities are thereby spared the pain and difficulty of having to persuade the boys, "inasmuch as they are unable to speak" (ἅτε ἀδύνατοι λέγειν, 182b). In many parts of Ionia and in "barbarian" countries, on the other hand, young men are prohibited from gratifying their lovers under any circumstances. According to Pausanias, this is because despotic rulers want to rid their countries of "philosophy" (or "high thoughts") and "strong friendships," both of which are fostered by *erōs* (182b–c). In each case, sexual intercourse is kept separate from intercourse in language: sex and *logoi*, in short, are not interchanged.

Pausanias proceeds to describe the more complicated custom of the Athenians. On the one hand, they encourage the lover to pursue his beloved and they applaud him when he succeeds (182d–183b). In fact, Pausanias observes, if a person behaved as lovers do in any other sphere of activity – if, for example, he were after money or political office or any other kind of power – he would be accused of "flattery and servile behavior" (κολακείας καὶ ἀνελευθερίας, 183b1). A lover, in short, is not held to ordinary rules of behavior and can even break his vows with impunity (183a–b). The beloved, on the other hand, is positively discouraged from

---

[73] The phrase "traffic in wisdom" is explicitly used to describe the sophists in the *Sophist* (224b). As we will see, the notion also applies to other kinds of people who offer their "wisdom" to the people in exchange for some form of recompense.

gratifying a lover, and is guarded and watched over by family and friends alike. When, then, is it right for a beloved to surrender himself? Pausanias spells this out at 184b–c:

According to our custom, one path is left if the boy is going to gratify his lover in the proper fashion. For it is the custom with us that, just as the lover's willingness to endure any kind of slavery (δουλεύειν ἐθέλοντα ἡντινοῦν δουλείαν) for the beloved is not considered flattery or reprehensible behavior (μὴ κολακείαν εἶναι μηδὲ ἐπονείδιστον), so also there is one kind of willing slavery (δουλεία ἑκούσιος) that is left [to the beloved] that is not reprehensible. This is the slavery that concerns virtue. For it is our custom that if someone wishes to serve a person in the belief that he will become better by this association either in regard to wisdom or any other part of virtue, this willing slavery is considered neither shameful nor a form of flattery (αὕτη αὖ ἡ ἐθελοδουλεία οὐκ αἰσχρὰ εἶναι οὐδὲ κολακεία).

In sum, the lover may "serve" the boy "in any way whatsoever" (ὑπηρετῶν ὁτιοῦν) so long as he "contributes" (συμβάλλεσθαι) virtue, and the beloved may "serve" the lover "in any way whatsoever" (ὁτιοῦν ... ὑπουργῶν) so long as he is "acquiring" (κτᾶσθαι) wisdom and the other virtues (184d–e).

While Pausanias' portrayal of the homoerotic practices of wealthy and aristocratic Athenians is in many ways accurate,[74] his articulation of these practices is clearly meant to jar the reader. Take, for example, Pausanias' admission that both parties enter into a "willing slavery" that would, in any other context, be considered "flattery" and "servile behavior." Is this behavior, Plato's strong language prods us to inquire, consonant with an education in virtue? Should we really admire, as Pausanias says we should, a young man who is ready to "do anything for anyone for the sake of virtue and self-betterment" (185b)? Pausanias' portrayal of the slavish beloved conjures up the very sphere of activity that is meant to be excluded: the prostitute's traffic in sexual favors. As Dover observes,

There seems little doubt that in Greek eyes the male who breaks the "rules" of legitimate eros detaches himself from the ranks of male citizenry and classifies himself with women and foreigners; the prostitute is assumed to have broken the rules simply because his economic dependence on clients forces him to do what they want him to do; and conversely, *any male believed to have done whatever his senior homosexual partner(s) wanted him to do is assumed to have prostituted himself.*[75] (my italics)

---

[74] Dover 1964 shows that Aeschines' speech against Timarchus offers a picture of the homoerotic practices of the wealthy and aristocratic Athenians that is in fundamental accord with that of Pausanias. But Pausanias implies that the beloved may submit to penetration, which was clearly not condoned in these circles.

[75] Dover [1978]/1989: 103.

As Dover indicates, a young man who is not in the profession of prostitution may none the less be assimilated with "real" prostitutes if his behavior is overly servile. Plato's pointed portrayal of "heavenly love" in the Pausanias speech invites us to ponder the difference between selling oneself for money and selling oneself for virtue: how can one confidently draw the line between these two kinds of exchange? Is servicing someone sexually in exchange for virtue really so different from ordinary prostitution?[76]

The social and political ramifications of this question cannot be over-emphasized. For an Athenian citizen who was shown to have prostituted himself was punished by *atimia* – the loss of his "entitlement as a citizen to take part in the civic and religious life of Athens."[77] Halperin explains the logic of this punishment:

Anyone who prostituted himself, whether out of economic necessity or greed (sexual desire is never mentioned as a possible motive), indicated by that gesture that his autonomy was for sale to whoever wished to buy it. The city as a collective entity was supposedly vulnerable in the person of such a citizen – vulnerable to penetration by foreign influence or to corruption by private enterprise. No person who had prostituted himself could be allowed to speak before the people in the public assembly because his words might not be his own; he might have been hired to say them by someone else, someone whose interests did not coincide with those of Athens, or he might simply want to bring about a political change that would advance his private interests at the expense of the public good – servility and greed evidently being the dominant features of his personality.[78]

Plato's emphasis on the servile behavior of the beloved, then, is clearly meant to indicate his unfitness for political and civic life. So far from getting a training in *aretē* that will equip him to assume political and other civic duties, the beloved runs the risk of corruption and possible disenfranchisement. It should go without saying that Plato considers the lover at least as compromised as the beloved. For, even though the lover does not assimilate himself to women and foreigners by virtue of submitting to bodily penetration, his servile behavior and use of flattery are hardly worthy of a free citizen. In Plato's eyes, this person is nothing but a servile flatterer claiming that he possesses virtue; blinded by his desire for the boy, he is in no position to offer any real education.

What Plato indicates in the Pausanias speech, albeit in an indirect way, is that a truly good man would never offer to hand over virtue in exchange for sex, since the two are by nature incommensurable. This is

---

[76] Dover [1978]/1989: 106–7 notes that there was a fine line between legitimate *erōs* and prostitution – a line which was not precisely articulated by Athenian law.
[77] Halperin 1990: 94.
[78] Halperin 1990: 97–8.

made explicit later in the dialogue in the famous scene where Alcibiades recounts his attempt to seduce Socrates. Like Pausanias' beloved, Alcibiades seems quite sanguine about a sex-for-knowledge swap: "I believed that it was my marvelous good fortune that, if I gratified Socrates sexually, I could hear everything that he knew" (217a). As he says to Socrates at 218c–d, "I believe that it is pure folly to refuse to offer you sexual gratification or anything else that you want either of my property or that of my friends. For nothing is more important to me than to become the best man possible, and there is no-one more capable than you of being my accomplice in this regard." Alcibiades, then, considers not only sex but also material "goods" appropriate currency for purchasing Socrates' knowledge. Socrates' response to this proposition goes right to the point:

> if ... you are attempting to strike a bargain (κοινώσασθαι) and to exchange (ἀλ-λάξασθαι) [your] beauty for [my] beauty, you are clearly intending to get the better of me in no small way (οὐκ ὀλίγῳ μου πλεονεκτεῖν διανοῇ). For you are attempting to acquire true beauty in exchange for seeming beauty and, in truth, you are con-triving to exchange bronze for gold (ἀλλ' ἀντὶ δόξης ἀλήθειαν καλῶν κτᾶσθαι ἐπι-χειρεῖς καὶ τῷ ὄντι "χρύσεα χαλκείων" διαμείβεσθαι νοεῖς). (218e–219a)

Socrates' suggestion that Alcibiades is offering bronze in exchange for gold is, of course, an allusion to the famous scene in Homer's *Iliad*, where Glaucus gives Diomedes golden armor in exchange for bronze (6.232–6). In that scene, Homer indicates that the value of the two pieces of armor differs in degree rather than in kind: the bronze armor is worth nine oxen, whereas the gold is valued at one hundred oxen (τεύχε' ἄμειβε | χρύσεα χαλκείων, ἑκατόμβοι' ἐννεαβοίων, 235–6). In other words, the exchange could have been a fair one if Glaucus received (roughly) eleven times as much bronze as Diomedes in fact gave him. As in other gift economies, Glaucus and Diomedes' exchange operates according to a logic quite different from that in a monetary economy; as Morris observes about the workings of gift economies,

> Gift objects divide up into what we can call "spheres of exchange" with objects classified into a hierarchical sequence of ranks, and valued not cardinally but or-dinally ... In some cases, objects can never be exchanged between spheres, while in others cases it is possible to cross the boundaries, but only under exceptional circumstances.[79]

In the Homeric world, the "top rank" of objects are women, cattle, and finished objects of metal;[80] it is for this reason that bronze and gold can be exchanged and, indeed, made commensurable.

---

[79] Morris 1986: 8. For the notion of "spheres of exchange," see Firth [1965]/1975: 340–4.
[80] Morris 1986: 9.

It should be immediately clear that the exchange that Alcibiades proposes, at least as Socrates describes it, is not quite analogous to that of
Glaucus and Diomedes. For Socrates' claim that Alcibiades is attempting
to barter "seeming" for "true" beauty clearly indicates that the two items
in question are not in the same "sphere of exchange." On the contrary, no
amount of Alcibiades' physical beauty will add up to the "true" beauty of
Socrates. True beauty and seeming beauty, in short, can never be exchanged, since there is no way of making them commensurable. Pausanias' insistence that the interchange of sex and *logoi* – which he claims
distinguishes the cultured and "philosophical" Athenians from other
more boorish peoples – is thus subjected to a withering critique. The true
philosopher, Plato indicates, will refuse such an exchange on the grounds
that knowledge and virtue cannot be measured in terms of sex or any
other "good" that resides in the physical "sphere of exchange." As Socrates says at 175d, it would be wonderful if wisdom could be conveyed
from one person to another "like water, which flows from the fuller into
the emptier cup when you connect them with a piece of yarn." This
physicalist model of transferring goods from one person to another simply
does not apply to "goods" such as wisdom and virtue. These occupy a
sphere that can never be made commensurable with the "goods" that
occupy the physical world.

V

The notion of different and, indeed, incommensurable spheres of "goods"
is at the root of Plato's handling of other kinds of traffic in wisdom: that
of the sophist, the poet, and the politician. Let us consider, first, the
sophistic practice of selling wisdom for money. Socrates' claim in the
Apology that he has never accepted pay for his activities (31b–c), since he
is not in fact a teacher (33a–b) and does not possess true wisdom (21b), is
clearly meant to differentiate him from the sophists. Unlike the sophists
(and, indeed, Isocrates), Socrates has no intellectual property to give or to
sell. But what exactly is at stake in Plato's insistent reminders that Socrates does not take pay?[81] In a recent article, "Socratics versus Sophists
on payment for teaching," David Blank suggests that Xenophon and
Plato both associate Socrates' refusal of payment with his "desire to be
able to pick and choose his students."[82] While Xenophon places the emphasis on Socrates' choice of a "free" life over one in which he is obliged

---

[81] See Blank 1985: 7 on the evidence for Socrates' refusal of fees. For an excellent discussion
   of our access – or lack thereof – to the historical Socrates, see Stokes 1992. Forbes 1942:
   24 discusses the evidence for Plato's own refusal to take fees in the Academy.
[82] Blank 1985: 19.

to render services by taking fees, Blank argues, Plato stresses Socrates' "elitist desire not to speak to just anybody."[83] I agree that Plato criticizes the sophists for their willingness to speak to all and sundry, and that this reflects an elite bias. But his repudiation of the exchange of ethical knowledge for money goes much farther than Blank indicates. For, as I will suggest, it is part and parcel of Plato's attempt to define the philosopher by removing him from the systems of exchange – both material and symbolic – operating in the Athenian democracy.

One of Plato's most blunt statements on the subject of the exchange of wisdom for money is found in the *Hippias Major*, where Socrates contrasts the modern-day sophists with the ancient sages:

None of the ancients ever thought it right to exact money as a wage or to give displays of their wisdom in front of people of all kinds; they were so simpleminded that it escaped their notice that money is of great value. But each of these two men [i.e. Gorgias and Prodicus] earned more money from his wisdom than any other *dēmiourgos* from whatever art he practices. (282c–d)

Here, Socrates places the sophists in the category of artisans who exchange their products for money. As he puts it at 283b, "it is agreed by many that it is necessary for the wise man to be wise most of all for himself; and the measure of this is whoever makes the most money." The notion that wisdom is meant to benefit, first and foremost, its owner, highlights the commercial nature of the sophists' enterprise: the exchange is not embedded in political and social structures but is a mercantile transaction in which the sophist thinks only of maximizing his profits. This emphasis on commercialism resembles the passage from the *Sophist* quoted above, where the sophist is compared to a merchant. And the same image is used in the *Protagoras* (313c), where Socrates says that the sophist is a "merchant or a retailer of the goods by which the soul is nourished (ἔμπορός τις ἢ κάπηλος τῶν ἀγωγίμων, ἀφ' ὧν ψυχὴ τρέφεται)." In this passage, Socrates warns a young man named Hippocrates about the acquisition of sophistic wares:

For the danger involved in the purchasing of knowledge is in fact much greater than in the purchase of foods. For the person who buys food and drink can carry it away from the retailer or merchant in vessels, and before he accepts these things into his body by drinking or eating, he can store it in his house and call an expert in to advise him regarding what he ought and ought not to eat and drink, and how much and when. So the danger in the actual purchase (ἐν τῇ ὠνῇ) is not great. But it is not possible to carry away knowledge in a vessel; once a person pays the price he must necessarily accept the knowledge into his soul and, having learned it, be benefited or harmed accordingly. (314a–b)

---

[83] Blank 1985: 19 (and passim).

This passage is trickier than it might first appear. Note that Socrates says directly after this that he and Hippocrates should go and "hear" Protagoras (ἀκούσωμεν τοῦ ἀνδρός, 314b6–7) in an effort to determine whether his wares are in fact beneficial to the buyer. We can infer from this that merely listening to Protagoras is not, in itself, dangerous. But why should this be so? What does Socrates mean by saying that it is only when a person "pays the price" that the sophists' "wisdom" penetrates his soul?

Socrates does not explicate this point, but the gist of his reasoning is clear. The mere act of listening to a sophist differs from that of enlisting oneself as his student. It is only by paying a sophist that one sets him up as a teacher and authority. As Socrates suggests, the danger lies "in the actual purchase": when a person buys the sophist's wares, he has implicitly acknowledged that the sophist possesses wisdom and can hand it over just as a merchant hands over a material commodity. Part of Plato's point, of course, is that the sophists do not possess wisdom and are thus deceiving their customers; as Socrates says at 313d, the sophists praise all of their wares, regardless of whether they are good or bad. But this is not the whole story. For it is the notion of the interchangeability of wisdom and money that is at the root of the problem. Take the case of Protagoras, who proudly describes his unusual method of exacting payment: "for when someone learns from me, he pays the money which I charge, if he is willing; if he is not, he goes into a temple and states under oath how much he thinks the learning is worth, and he pays that amount" (328b–c). In this case, the customer is allowed to "listen" to the sophist *before* he pays. Does this mean that Protagoras' students can avoid being harmed? Clearly, Plato does not think so. In particular, while the student may differ about the price of the product, the *terms of the transaction* are not in question: the student accepts, at least in principle, that wisdom is a commodity that can be purchased with money; he wouldn't have sought the teaching of the sophist in the first place if he did not accept the terms of this exchange. The very transaction that the sophists offer, then, is evidence that they do not possess wisdom; if they did, Plato indicates, they would not consider it something that can be measured and valued in monetary terms. For wisdom and money, in Plato's view, operate in totally different spheres.

The incommensurability of wisdom and money is also discussed in the *Gorgias*. At 520c, Socrates claims that if the sophists were telling the truth when they claimed to teach *aretē*, then they would never have to worry about being cheated of their wages, since their students would necessarily behave justly upon completing their education. While this may sound like an assurance that a true education in *aretē* would guarantee recompense in the form of a monetary fee, the rest of the passage suggests otherwise:

to take a fee for giving advice in other spheres of activity, such as that of house-building or the other *technai*, is in no way disgraceful ... But when it comes to this sphere of activity, namely, how someone might become the best man possible and manage his own household and the city in the best fashion, it is considered shameful to refuse to give advice unless someone pays money for it ... And this is clearly the reason, that this is the only kind of service that makes the recipient eager to make a like return (ἀντ' εὖ ποιεῖν), so that it seems to be a good sign when someone who has rendered this favor is treated well in return. (520d–e)

As this passage shows, teaching *aretē* (if such a thing is possible) is not like other *technai*. For it is not a service for which one should charge money. Rather, the reward which the giver receives for such a service is nothing other than virtuous activity. The giver, in short, is paid back *in kind*; his service is not measured (or, indeed, measurable) in monetary terms but is accorded its proper value.

Thus far, I have been dealing with the exchange of knowledge for physical and material "goods" such as money and sex. But Plato is at least as concerned with the ways in which wisdom is exchanged for im-material "goods" such as honor and power as he is about its circulation in material transactions. The most important forum for the communication of "wisdom" in democratic Athens was, of course, the assembly (and, to some extent, the lawcourts), where orators and politicians undertook to advise the Athenian citizens regarding political and civic affairs. Plato's conception of the exchange that goes on in the assembly is vividly por-trayed in the *Gorgias*. Early in the dialogue, Socrates identifies rhetoric as a species of "flattery" (κολακεία, 463a–c), and he returns to this notion again and again. At 502d–e, for example, he says of "the rhetoric that is directed at the *dēmos*":

Do the orators appear to you to speak on every occasion with an eye to what is best, and to use their *logoi* for the purpose of making the citizens the best they can be, or are they impelled towards gratifying (χαρίζεσθαι) the citizens and do they ignore the common good for the sake of their own private interests (ἕνεκα τοῦ ἰδίου τοῦ αὐτῶν ὀλιγωροῦντες τοῦ κοινοῦ) ...?

Here, Socrates sets forth two kinds of speakers: the kind who aims at the common good and the kind who says what the people want to hear in exchange for the power and honor he will get in return. Throughout the dialogue, Socrates recurs to the problem inherent in the giving and getting of *charis*. Take, for example, his statement at 521d–e:

I think that I am among the few Athenians (not to say the only one) who is en-gaged in the true political art and, of men today, I am the only person practicing politics. Since I do not say the things that I say on each occasion in exchange for favor (πρὸς χάριν), but I aim at what is best, not at what is most pleasant.

Again, at 521a, Socrates says to Callicles,

Distinguish for me which of the two kinds of civic service you recommend for me: that of battling the Athenians like a doctor so that they will be the best men possible, or that of serving and consorting with them in exchange for favor (διακονήσοντα καὶ πρὸς χάριν ὁμιλήσοντα).

The language used in the assembly, as Plato sees it, offers a favor in exchange for a favor. Under the guise of communicating wise advice, the politician does nothing other than "flatter" the people in order to garner power and influence.[84]

The politician's traffic in wisdom is also foregrounded in the definition of philosophy offered in the "digression" in the *Theaetetus* (172c–176d). In this passage, the philosopher is explicitly defined in opposition to the man of politics. Whereas the philosopher has σχολή for conversation and thought, the politician can never think or speak freely:

His *logoi* always concern a fellow-slave and are directed towards a master who sits holding some suit or other in his hand; the contests, moreover, are never for some indifferent prize but they always concern the politician himself, and often the race is for life itself. As a result, these men become eager and shrewd. They know how to flatter the master with their words and fawn on him with their deeds, but they are small and crooked in their souls. (172e–173a)

The politician is a slave, a servile flatterer, a person who always acts out of self-interest. The philosopher, by contrast, is free. He avoids the marketplace, the lawcourts, the assembly, and every other public gathering, not because he is seeking honor or a good reputation (τοῦ εὐδοκιμεῖν χάριν, 173e2) but because his occupation is somewhere else; while his body dwells in the city, his mind is concerned with the nature of reality (173c–174a). It is important to stress that the philosopher is not simply pursuing theoretical knowledge.[85] Socrates makes it quite clear that the philosopher's wisdom is fundamentally concerned with *praxis*. For the philosopher not only inquires "about justice and injustice in themselves"

---

[84] Note that the language of "gratification" and "flattery" is identical to that which Plato uses to describe the lovers' exchange of sex and knowledge in the *Symposium*. This is no coincidence, since in both the political and the erotic scenarios, a person offers his "wisdom" in exchange for some form of personal gratification.

[85] Carter 1986: 178–9 overstates Plato's endorsement of a life of pure *theōria* in his depictions of the philosopher. Just because philosophy requires heavy doses of abstract thinking does not mean that Plato's philosopher lives a "theoretical life." As Jaeger 1948: especially 438 shows, for Plato metaphysics are inextricably bound up with ethics; it is Aristotle who, by separating these two fields, identifies and endorses the life of *theōria*. Annas 1981: 260–71 comes to the same conclusion in her analysis of the *Republic*: "Plato does not want to allow that practical and theoretical reasoning ... ever *could* conflict ... He would reject any distinction of practical and theoretical reasoning, and hence of the 'practical' and 'contemplative' conceptions of the philosopher ..." (p. 265).

but also "about kingship and human happiness and misery in general, what these things are and in what fashion it is fitting for human beings to acquire the one and avoid the other" (175c). The goal of philosophy, Socrates adds, is to "liken oneself to god" by becoming "as just as possible" (ὅτι δικαιότατος, 176c), for "the knowledge of this is wisdom and true virtue." The philosopher, in short, is not *uninterested* in practical affairs; rather, he approaches them from a position of impartiality or *disinterest*.

Before Plato, of course, we find numerous instances of orators and literary writers attacking certain politicians – especially those dubbed "demagogues" – on the grounds that they were acting out of self-interest rather than in the interests of the city. As Finley says in defense of the beleaguered demagogue,

Politicians regularly say that what they are advocating is in the best interests of the nation, and, what is much more important, they believe it. Often, too, they charge their opponents with sacrificing the national interest for special interests, and they believe that. I know of no evidence which warrants the view that Athenian politicians were somehow peculiar in this respect; *nor do I know any reason to hold that the argument is an essentially different (or better) one because it is put forth not by a politician but by Aristophanes or Thucydides or Plato.*[86] (my italics)

I would like to suggest that Plato's argument is in fact "essentially different" from those of both the politicians and the literary writers. For Plato does not merely attack one or another politician who is especially egregious. Rather, he suggests that all politicians are acting out of self-interest insofar as they have chosen to seek advancement within a democratic system which is designed to reward those leaders that please the *dēmos* with honor, power, and even money. According to Plato, the politicians and people who operate within this system simply cannot occupy a position of disinterest. The politician, in short, is inside the system, whereas the philosopher is an outsider. Only a person who is completely disembedded from the social and political economy of the city can act in a disinterested manner. I am not suggesting that Plato himself occupies this disinterested position. My point is that the criteria he sets up for "not acting out of self-interest" are different and, indeed, quite drastic.[87]

[86] Finley 1962: 18.
[87] Note that this is the first time in Western history that the *idea* of an impartial or disinterested agent is articulated and defended. Nowadays, it is commonly believed that a person can never be perfectly disinterested. But this in no way detracts from the significance of Plato's attempt to explicate the strange "outside" position that a person would have to occupy in order to act in a disinterested manner. When one considers that the most prominent ethical notion in Plato's day was that of "helping friends and harming enemies," the radicalism of Plato's new ethical platform stands out in bold relief. For an extensive discussion of the operations of the former notion in Athens in general and Sophoclean tragedy in particular, see Blundell 1989.

There is one more group which, according to Plato, traffics in wisdom: the poets.[88] Once again, Plato recurs to the theme of servile flattery. In the *Gorgias* 502b–d, for example, Socrates suggests that dramatic poetry is identical to political rhetoric insofar as it consists of "*logoi* spoken to large crowds and to the *dēmos*" (c9–10) which aim to "curry favor with" (χαρίζεσθαι, b3, c1) the audience; it is but one more kind of "flattery" (c2, d7). The analogy that Plato draws between rhetorical speeches and dramatic performances is, to be sure, simplistic and forced. But it is not completely off target. As Ober and Strauss suggest:

The seating in the theater was egalitarian, as it was in the Assembly and in the people's courts. In each case, the mass audience faced, listened to, and actively responded to, the public discourse of individual speakers. There were, of course, differences between the procedures of the theater and the more overtly political arenas of the Assembly and the courts – the playwright was not voted upon directly by his audience and did not face the audience in propria persona (although comic parabases could come close). But the congruity between the political and theatrical arenas meant that the responses of Athenian citizens as jurors and Assemblymen were inevitably influenced by the fact of their having been members of theatrical audiences, and vice versa.[89]

But, even if this congruity is granted, how can the poet be said to "curry favor with" the *dēmos* when it is not the *dēmos* as a whole that judges the artistic performances? In Plato's eyes, this is unimportant, since the judges are directly influenced by the audience. As the Athenian says in the *Laws*:

For the true judge must never give judgment according to the dictation of the audience, and he must not be driven out of his mind by the clamor of the crowd and by his own lack of education. Nor should he, when he knows the truth, lightly give judgment, speaking falsely out of the very same mouth with which he invoked the gods when he took his seat as a judge. For the judge, properly conceived, sits not as a student but as a teacher of the audience, in order that he might oppose those who give pleasure to the audience in a way that is not fitting or right. (659a–b)

In the Athenian democracy, according to Plato, the opposite takes place. As he goes on to say in book 3 of the *Laws*, the poets in Athens

instilled in the audiences a lawlessness and boldness in regard to artistic compositions, since they now thought that they were capable of judging the performances. Hence the spectators, who were once silent, became noisy, as though they understood what is good and bad in art, and in the place of an aristocracy in the artistic realm there came about a base theatocracy (θεατροκρατία). (700e–701a)[90]

---

[88] I will discuss "Plato and the poets" in detail in chapters 2 and 5.
[89] Ober and Strauss 1990: 238.
[90] For the "theatocracy" in Athens, see also *Rep.* 492b–d.

Plato's suggestion that poetry aims at pleasure is of course familiar to every reader of the *Republic*. But the notion that the pleasure is given not freely but for a price is often overlooked. When one considers that poetry was regularly performed in an agonistic context, the stakes in the contest are easy to see.[91] As Plato was well aware, the poets as a group (and especially those composing in "serious" genres such as epic and tragedy) were competing for no less a prize than honor, glory, and the reputation for wisdom – for inclusion among "les maîtres de vérité" (to borrow Detienne's phrase). As Socrates claims in the *Republic* 10, "if the poet is going to win the esteem of the many" (εἰ μέλλει εὐδοκιμήσειν ἐν τοῖς πολλοῖς), it is necessary that "his wisdom be packaged so as to please" (ἡ σοφία αὐτοῦ ... ἀρέσκειν πέπηγεν) the inferior part of the soul (605a; cf. 602b, 603a–b). In other words, Socrates says in the next section (605b–c), the poet must "curry favor with the mindless part of the soul" (τῷ ἀνοήτῳ αὐτῆς χαριζόμενον). Like the politician, then, the poet/performer gives *charis* in order to receive *charis*. As Ion puts it so bluntly in the *Ion*: "it is necessary for me to pay close attention to [the audience], for if I make them weep I myself will laugh when I get my money, but if I make them laugh I will weep because I have lost money" (535e).

In Plato's view, then, the sophists, the politicians and the poets resemble each other insofar as they traffic in wisdom. This point is driven home in the following passage from the definition of philosophy offered in the *Republic*. At 493a, Socrates says of the sophists: "each of these private wage-earners (μισθαρνούντων), whom the politicians call sophists and regard as their rivals, teaches nothing other than the opinions of the multitude – the opinions which are expressed when they are gathered together – and he calls this wisdom" (cf. *Theaetetus* 161e). Socrates illustrates this by portraying the sophist as the keeper of a huge beast who has learned to control the responses of the animal and has dubbed this mastery "wisdom" (493a–c). Having pictured the sophist as a "strange educator" (ἄτοπος ... παιδευτής, c7–8) who adopts the opinions of the multitude in the fashion of a good democrat, Socrates now brings both the poet and the politician onto the scene:

How, then, does the man who considers it wisdom to have learned the passions and pleasures of the variegated multitude when it is assembled – whether in the case of painting, or poetry, or, for that matter, politics (εἴτε δὴ ἐν πολιτικῇ) – differ from the sophist? For if a person associates with these people, exhibiting either his poetry or some other piece of craftsmanship or else his service to the city, and grants the multitude mastery over him (κυρίους αὐτοῦ ποιῶν τοὺς πολλούς) be-

---

[91] Osborne 1993 gives a useful survey of poetic (and athletic) competitions at festivals in the classical Athenian polis. For the agonistic aspect of early Greek poetry, see Griffith 1990.

yond what is necessary, the proverbial necessity of Diomedes will make him do the things which these people praise. (493c–d)

Like the sophists, poets and politicians presume to offer some form of wisdom to the people. They give the people what they want in order to acquire prestige and power for themselves. The poets resemble the politicians and both groups resemble the sophists: like these latter "wage-earners," the poets and politicians offer the public what it wants in return for a specific recompense.

VI

As this analysis has shown, part of Plato's strategy in defining the philosopher is the effacement of the boundaries between merchants, sophists, poets, and politicians – boundaries that are based on class and status. This effacement, I will argue, enables Plato to erect a new hierarchical system which places all people in one of two categories: that of the philosopher and that of the non-philosopher. Interestingly, Plato bolsters this new classification by exploiting and redirecting the rhetoric of *banausia* – rhetoric which was traditionally used by aristocrats to express their contempt for manual and/or servile labor. Take, for example, the claim found at *Symposium* 203a, where Socrates says:

God does not mix with man, but it is through this being [i.e. the intermediary called a *daimōn*] that all intercourse and conversation takes place between the gods and men, whether they are awake or sleeping. And the person who is wise in this regard is a daemonic man (δαιμόνιος ἀνήρ), *but the person who is wise in any other regard, whether in the realm of arts and sciences or manual labor, is banausic* (βάναυσος).[92] (my italics)

The dichotomy drawn here between the "daemonic man" (who is, of course, the philosopher) and the "banausic" individual recurs at *Theaetetus* 176b–d, where Socrates says:

God is in no way unjust, but is as just as it is possible to be, and there is nothing more similar to god than the man who becomes as just as possible. It is concerning this activity that a man is revealed as truly clever or else worthless and cowardly. For the knowledge of this is wisdom and virtue in the true sense, and the ignorance of it is manifest folly and viciousness. *All other things that appear to be cleverness and wisdom – whether their sphere is politics or the other arts – are vulgar or banausic* (βάναυσοι). (my italics)

---

[92] A comparable use of the rhetoric of βαναυσία is found at *Rep.* 495d–e (and cf. 522b); as Dover observes in his commentary on the *Symposium*, "In *Rep.* 495d–e Plato probably (though the interpretation is not certain) extends it [i.e. the word *banausos*] to the arts of the sophist and rhetorician, and that would accord with the sentiment given here to Diotima" (1980: 141).

By assimilating himself to god, Socrates indicates, the philosopher acquires the only kind of practical wisdom that is not vulgar or "banausic." What Plato suggests in these passages, then, is that all human wisdom that is not philosophic is "banausic." In other words, the varieties of human wisdom – together with their instantiations in one or another occupation or profession – are now recategorized as either "philosophic" or "banausic."

What is the valence of this rhetoric of "*banausia*"? In general, *banausia* is the label for people who earn their living by plying a "craft" that involves the use of the hands. But whose label is it? As Wood has argued, we need to separate the "disdain for dependent labour" which was probably a "universal cultural norm in Athens" from the "outright contempt for labour and labourers" exhibited by aristocratic writers such as Xenophon, Plato, and Aristotle.[93] It is noteworthy that the word *banausia*, and its cognates, is not found in oratory or comedy; in fact, in texts from the classical period, it is virtually monopolized by Xenophon, Plato, and Aristotle.[94] As Whitehead suggests, "The 'definition' of a *banausos*, it seems, can only be articulated by someone outside *banausia* ..."[95] In fact, it is precisely to define a group of people as "by nature" inferior and unfit for participating in politics that the term is commonly used. Aristotle, for example, places the "banausic" arts in the category of "wealth-getting that involves exchange" (*Politics* 1258b20–1): it is "labor for hire" (μισθαρνία b25), a designation that it shares with "unskilled workers useful only by

[93] Wood [1988]/1989: 139. As many scholars have observed (e.g. Connor [1971]/1992: 152–8, 171–5, Burford 1972: 156–7, Raaflaub 1983: 531–2), comic poets and orators (whose barbs are designed to be acceptable to a demotic audience) denigrate certain politicians by suggesting that they are employed in a craft-trade (the word "*banausia*" and its cognates, however, is not found in these writers). For example, Cleon is called a leather-seller (Aristophanes *Knights* 136), Hyperbolus a lamp-seller (Aristophanes, *Knights* 1315), Cephalus a potter (Aristophanes, *Eccles.* 252–3), and Cleophon a lyre-maker (Andocides 1.146, Aeschines 2.76). As Connor [1971]/1992: 171–2 argues, these authors are exploiting a general prejudice against these kinds of professions. On Greek attitudes towards labor and laborers, see Glotz [1926]/1987: 160–7, Mossé [1966]/1969: especially ch. 2, Burford 1972: 25–6, 184–218 and 1993: ch. 5, Rössler 1981: passim, Ste. Croix 1981: 179–204 and passim, Vernant [1965]/1983: chs. 10–11, and Wood [1988]/1989: 137–45 and passim.

[94] Exceptions are: Sophocles, *Ajax* 1121; Herodotus 2.165 (who says that *banausia* – which is later identified as *technē* (166) – is generally looked down upon by Greeks and barbarians alike); and Hippocrates, *de Morbo Sacro* 18 (Littré) and *de Decente Habitu* 2, 5 (if indeed this is a 4th-century text). For passages in Xenophon, Plato and Aristotle dealing with *banausia*, see Xenophon, *Oec.* 4.2–4.3, 6.5, *Symp.* 3.4, *Cyrop.* 5.3.47; Plato, *Alcib. 1* 131b, *Amat.* 137b, *Rep.* 522b, 590c, *Laws* 644a, 741e, 743d, *Epin.* 976d, Aristotle, *EE* 1215a, *NE* 1107b, 1122a, 1123a, *MM* 1205a, *Pol.* 1258b, 1260a–b, 1264b, 1277a–b, 1278a, 1289b, 1291a, 1296b, 1317a–b, 1319a, 1321a, 1326a, 1328b–1329a, 1331a, 1337b, 1338b, 1339b, 1340b–1342a, *Rhet.* 1367a, *Met.* 996a, *Oec*, 1343b. Rössler 1981: especially 203–5, 216–19, 226–31, and 241–3 offers a detailed survey of the notion of *banausia* in the fifth and fourth centuries.

[95] Whitehead 1977: 119.

virtue of their bodies."[96] According to Aristotle, a person who performs a banausic occupation should not be awarded citizenship and the political privileges that go with it; likewise, citizens and rulers should not be allowed to engage in *banausia*:

It is clear that [the citizens] should be taught the useful arts that are necessary, but not all of the arts, since liberal pursuits must be distinguished from illiberal pursuits. And it is clear that they should participate in those of the useful arts that will not make the participant banausic. One must consider a pursuit or a craft or a science banausic if it makes the body or soul or mind of a free man useless for the employments and activities of virtue. It is for this reason that we call "banausic" those crafts which damage the body and the occupations that involve wage-earning. For these make the mind unleisured and petty. (*Politics* 1337b)

It is important to note that, as Aristotle says more than once, the mere fact that a person engages in a craft does not make him banausic; rather, the defining criterion is the goal or end that he has in view. A person can escape becoming banausic if he takes up a craft or physical labor "on occasion, for his own private use (since this does not involve the relationship of master and slave)" (1277b5–7), or if he does it "for his own sake, for his friends, or for virtue" rather than "for other people" (1337b19–21; cf. 1341b8–15). It is the servile or wage-earning aspect of the activity, in short, that makes the *technē* and its practitioner banausic.

Banausia, then, is a loaded and highly derogatory term. Especially revealing, I believe, is Aristotle's suggestion at *Politics* 1278a that, in an oligarchy, while it is impossible for the *thētes* to be citizens since they are too poor to meet the property qualifications, the *banausoi* on the other hand will make the grade: "for the majority of the craftsmen (οἱ πολλοὶ τῶν τεχνιτῶν) are in fact rich" (1278a21–25). This is reinforced in the *Nicomachean Ethics*, where Aristotle identifies "vulgarity" (βαναυσία) and "paltriness" (μικροπρέπεια) as the two extremes of the mean that is "magnificence" (μεγαλοπρέπεια) (1107b; 1122a; 1123a). He glosses this at 1123a:

Such is the *megaloprepēs*. The person who exceeds this mean, the *banausos*, exceeds by virtue of spending beyond what is appropriate. In situations calling for small expenditures he spends a great deal and he makes himself conspicuous in a tasteless way, for example by feasting the members of his club in a manner suitable for a wedding or, when financing a comic chorus, by bringing them on in purple garments at the first entrance, as is done in Megara. And he will do all these things not out of goodness or nobility but in order to display his wealth, thinking that he is admired on account of these things, spending a little where he should spend a lot and spending a lot where he should spend a little.

[96] Lévy 1979 and Rössler 1981: 226–31 offer detailed analyses of Aristotle's conception of *banausia/banausos* in the *Politics*.

Although Aristotle is no doubt exaggerating the number of wealthy *banausoi*, it is clear that some *banausoi* were *nouveaux riches*, i.e. wealthy members of the non-aristocratic class.[97] The critics of *banausia*, we can infer, were at least as concerned with the upwardly mobile as they were with the poor: the fact that the *nouveaux riches* could acquire privileges and offices that were originally the prerogative of the aristocracy would suggest that these people in particular needed to be put in their place.

The rhetoric of *banausia*, then, serves an aristocratic ideology that seeks to mark off "true" rulers from "vulgar" rivals by casting the latter as "wage-earners."[98] Although Plato's deployment of this rhetoric in the *Laws* – a text that makes no attempt to define the philosopher – is in keeping with that of Xenophon and Aristotle, he makes a very different use of *"banausia"* in his definitions of philosophy.[99] As the passages from the *Symposium* and *Theaetetus* reveal, Plato directs the aristocratic rhetoric against the lower classes and the aristocrats alike: *everyone* is "banausic" except the true practitioner of philosophy. Upper-class citizens who are pursuing honor and power, in short, are no less banausic than the "servile" wage-earners. In the *Republic*, in fact, Socrates goes so far as to suggest that *banausia* is a servile condition of the soul rather than a matter of a person's trade:

Why is it, do you think, that *banausia* and working with one's hands is a matter of reproach? Shall we not say that it is because that part which is by nature the best in a man is weak, with the result that it is unable to rule the beasts within him, but serves them, and can learn nothing but the means of flattering them? (590c)[100]

---

[97] As Lévy 1979: 39–40 and Ste. Croix 1981: 271 observe, the evidence strongly indicates that the majority of *banausoi* were poor (or at least not rich).

[98] Raaflaub 1983 suggests that this rhetoric is part of a larger ideology constructed by oligarchs and their sympathizers in the later fifth and fourth centuries; in this period, Raaflaub argues, oligarchs "began to politicize the notion of *eleutherios* and develop the concept of the truly free citizen in order to bolster their aspirations to exclusive government and power in the polis" (p. 534). The "truly free citizen," as Raaflaub shows, is identified in part by the fact that he receives a "free" or "liberal" education.

[99] *Laws* 644a, 741e, 743d. Note that I am dealing with the *rhetoric* of *banausia* rather than with Plato's refusal to allow banausic and other hired laborers any political role in the ideal cities he constructs in the *Republic* and *Laws* (in the *Laws*, in fact, they are also barred from citizenship). While Plato's political constructs are in keeping with contemporary aristocratic ideology, the rhetoric of *banausia* that he uses to define the "philosopher" is directed against the aristocrats who are working inside the political system. For an interesting analysis of Plato's approach to *banausia* and banausic laborers, see Wood and Wood (1978: 143–64, esp. 158–60); their reading, which places Plato squarely within aristocratic ideology, does not account for his assimilation of certain aristocrats to banausic laborers in his definitions of "philosophy." For Plato's ambivalent views on the subject of craft (*technē*) and craftsmen, see Vidal-Naquet [1981]/1986: ch. 11, Bergren 1992: especially 262–9. Brumbaugh 1989: ch. 16 describes the surprising breadth and depth of Plato's knowledge of the crafts.

[100] As Rössler rightly observes (1981: 217–18), Plato's use of the discourse of *banausia* differs from that of other writers: "So sind die Bezeichnungen βάναυσος oder βαναυσία bei

It is the characteristic of "servility," in fact, that brings these disparate types of people under one heading. As Socrates observes in the *Gorgias* (517b–518c), the politicians are to the soul what "hucksters, merchants, and craftsmen" (κάπηλον ὄντα ἢ ἔμπορον ἢ δημιουργόν, 517d7) are to the body: practitioners of "slavish and servile and illiberal" (δουλοπρεπεῖς τε καὶ διακονικὰς καὶ ἀνελευθέρους, 518a2) professions.[101] The philosopher, by contrast, engages in an activity that is in fundamental opposition to the servile and the mercantile: he will not exchange his wisdom for material or symbolic capital. His wisdom is simply not negotiable.

Plato, in sum, suggests that the philosopher occupies a *disinterested* position, since his wisdom is by definition incommensurable with all other "goods." Unlike Isocrates, who firmly places himself and his philosophy within the social economy of Athens, Plato's philosopher is distinguished precisely by his willingness to remain outside of this economy. Hence Plato's insistence that the philosophic rulers in the *Republic* have neither nuclear families nor private property – nothing that could locate them inside the society. In fact, Adeimantus even compares them to "hired mercenaries" (ἐπίκουροι μισθωτοί, 419a) – as though they were working for a foreign city! Socrates' response is revealing: "yes, and what is more, they serve for food and receive no wage in addition, as other [mercenaries] do" (420a). But the notion of a mercenary who is not paid for his service is, quite simply, a paradox. The philosopher, as it seems, is a mercenary who is no mercenary: an outsider who serves the city free of charge.

Plato's notion of the philosopher as a disinterested outsider, of course, can and should be subjected to critical analysis. Likewise, I would urge, Isocrates' pleas for insider status should be given serious consideration. It is difficult to deny, however, that Isocrates' attempt to claim the title of "philosophy" for his own activities falls far short of Plato's both in scope and in force. Isocrates' effort to target the *Apology* and other Platonic definitions of philosophy in the *Antidosis*, in fact, might be seen as a sort of failed parody. For Isocrates' speech can neither contain nor control its complex and powerful subtexts. As I will attempt to show, Plato's definition and defense of philosophy goes far beyond the arguments analyzed in this chapter. His masterful use of parody as a device for defining and privileging his own pursuits will be the focus of the remaining chapters.

Platon nie – wie noch bei Herodot (2.165) oder später wieder bei Aristoteles – eindeutig auf eine bestimmte soziale Gruppe bezogen ... Für Platon ist βαναυσία eine Sache der Erziehung, gewissermassen der negative Gegenpol zu einem pädagogischen Ideal."

[101] In this passage, Plato uses the word διάκονος rather than βάναυσος to designate the servile trades plied by merchants, artisans, and politicians alike (see, e.g., 517b2–3; b3–4; d2; 518a2; c3).

2   Use and abuse of Athenian tragedy

> The Platonic dialogue was, as it were, the barge on which the ship-
> wrecked ancient poetry saved herself with all her children: crowded into
> a narrow space and timidly submitting to the single pilot, Socrates, they
> now sailed into a new world, which never tires of looking at the fantastic
> spectacle of this procession. Indeed, Plato has given to all posterity the
> model of a new art form, the model of the *novel* – which may be de-
> scribed as an infinitely enhanced Aesopian fable, in which poetry holds
> the same rank in relation to dialectical philosophy as this same philoso-
> phy held for many centuries in relation to theology: namely, the rank of
> *ancilla*.
>
> Nietzsche, *Birth of Tragedy*

There is perhaps no more famous formulation in the Platonic corpus than
Socrates' assertion in book 10 of the *Republic* that there is an "ancient
quarrel between philosophy and poetry" (607b). But "philosophy" was a
discipline that did not have an ancient pedigree: it is Plato who first uses
the term to designate a specific intellectual enterprise. In classical Athens,
the word "philosophy" signified "intellectual cultivation" in the broad
sense. In other words, a wide array of intellectuals – *including* many poets
– were described as practicing "philosophy."[1] It is Plato, in fact, who first
identifies "poetry" as an arch-enemy of this unfamiliar thing called
"philosophy." As I will argue, Plato's suggestion that there is an "ancient
quarrel" between these two genres should not be interpreted as true historical reportage; rather, it is part of a bold rhetorical strategy designed to
define philosophy and invest it with a near-timeless status. To people in
the fourth century BCE, the notion of a quarrel between philosophy and
poetry would have probably appeared rather ludicrous – an unknown
stripling brashly measuring himself against a venerable giant. Indeed,
philosophy was no real match for poetry in this period. For, in Plato's
day, poetry was addressed to large groups of people in a variety of oral/

---

[1] Note that Hippias included poets among the intellectuals who formulated the abstract
ideas contained in his "Anthology" (this treatise is described in chapter 1.I; see also Snell
[1944]/1966, Mansfeld [1983]/1990 and [1986]/1990, and Patzer 1986).

performative contexts, whereas philosophy reached a relatively tiny group of literate elites. The two contestants were thus not even playing in the same ballpark.[2]

As Adam observes in his commentary on the *Republic*, "There are few traces of this 'ancient feud' in the extant fragments of Greek poetry."[3] Socrates, of course, quotes four lines of poetry as evidence of this quarrel:

καὶ γὰρ ἡ "λακέρυζα πρὸς δεσπόταν κύων" ἐκείνη "κραυγάζουσα" καὶ "μέγας ἐν ἀφρόνων κενεαγορίαισι" καὶ ὁ "τῶν διασόφων ὄχλος κρατῶν" καὶ οἱ "λεπτῶς μερ-ιμνῶντες," ὅτι ἄρα "πένονται" ... (the "bitch yelping at its master" and "barking," and "great in the empty babbling of fools," and the "mob mastering those who are super-wise," and those "subtly reasoning" that in fact "they are poor") (607b–c)

The authors of these lines are unknown, but it is generally agreed that the first two are in lyric meters and the latter two in the iambic trimeters of comedy. Since we do not know the individuals at whom these jibes are aimed, or the contexts in which they are uttered, it is impossible to assess their import. We must therefore turn to the poetry that is extant. There is one preplatonic genre of poetry in which we find explicit criticisms of intellectuals: Old Comedy.[4]

Interestingly, very few individuals that are now known as philosophers get any press in Old Comedy. Socrates seems to have attracted the most attention (see Callias 15 *PCG*; Telecleides 41, 42 *PCG*; Eupolis 386, 395 *PCG*; Ameipsias 9 *PCG*; Aristophanes, *Clouds*, *Birds* 1280–3, 1553–8, *Frogs* 1491–9, and fr. 392 *PCG*). Socrates' companion, Chaerephon, is another popular butt (see Cratinus 215 *PCG*; Eupolis 180, 253 *PCG*; Aristophanes, *Clouds* passim, *Birds* 1562–4, and fr. 552 *PCG*). So also was Hippon, a "natural philosopher" who was accused of impiety in Cratinus' *See-alls* : one scholiast suggested that Aristophanes' handling of Socrates in the *Clouds* resembled Cratinus' portrayal of Hippon in important respects.[5] Finally, the astronomer and mathematician Meton makes a brief appearance in Aristophanes' *Birds* (992–1020), where he is dubbed an "imposter" (1016). Rather different are the references to Thales (*Clouds* 180, *Birds* 1009), who is treated as the prototype of the Greek sage; per-

---

[2] It is only when Greek poetry becomes "literature" (in the sense that it reaches its audience primarily through written texts) that the two parties in this "quarrel" can really be said to meet on equal ground.

[3] Adam 1902.II: 417.

[4] The poets of Middle Comedy, of course, also attacked intellectuals, but this "quarrel" is contemporary with Plato, and not "ancient." Brock 1990: 41 surveys the attacks in Middle Comedy. As he suggests, the poets of Middle Comedy refer to intellectuals with "increased accuracy." This accuracy, I would argue, is made possible by the intellectuals' explicit attempts to differentiate themselves from one another in the fourth century.

[5] For a discussion of this scholium, see R. Rosen 1988: 61–2.

haps this long-dead foreigner was not considered a good target for comic caricature or censure.

In addition to this tiny group of "philosophical" thinkers, one finds in Old Comedy a handful of references to the intellectuals now known as "sophists." Prodicus and Gorgias, for example, are each mentioned three times in Aristophanes (Prodicus: *Clouds* 361, *Birds* 692, fr. 506 *PCG*; Gorgias: *Wasps* 421, *Birds* 1701, *Thesm.* 1103–4), and Thrasymachus once (fr. 205 *PCG*). Protagoras plays the role of one of the "flatterers" of the rich Callias in Eupolis' *Flatterers* (frr. 157, 158 *PCG*). Two teachers of music (both of whom associated with Socrates) also draw fire: Connus, to whom Ameipsias devoted a play which seems to have included a chorus of intellectuals (*Connus*),[6] and Damon (Plato Comicus 207 *PCG*). Finally, Plato Comicus wrote a play entitled *Sophists* (dated *circa* 403 BCE).[7] It should be noted, however, that the references to Prodicus do not express hostility;[8] apparently some sophists did earn the respect of the Athenians.

The references to (what we now refer to as) philosophers and sophists in Old Comedy are not that numerous, and they hardly encourage the view that the comic playwrights had identified a large and cohesive group of thinkers as rivals of the poets. It seems reasonable to suppose that the comedians confined themselves to those thinkers who were notorious enough to evoke the laughter and/or anger of the *dēmos*; if extant comedy is at all representative, we can conclude that relatively few individuals fit in this category. One should emphasize, too, that the comic poets attacked many other types of intellectuals on exactly the same grounds as they did the philosophical thinkers.[9] Strattis, for example, wrote an entire play satirizing the impiety of Cinesias, a dithyrambic poet; and other comedians attacked Cinesias for the same crime (Pherecrates [155 *PCG*], Plato Comicus [200 *PCG*], and Aristophanes [*Ecclesiazusae* 330, *Birds* 1372–1409, *Frogs* 153, 366, 1437, and fr. 156 *PCG*]). Note also that the

---

[6] See Dover 1968a: l–li on Athenaeus' reference to the "*choros* of intellectuals" in the *Connus*.

[7] Note that Plato Comicus included among his sophists "Bacchylides the fluteplayer from Opus" (149 *PCG*). Clearly, the category of "sophist" was quite broad in the fifth century. Cf. Protagoras' claim in Plato's *Protagoras* 316d–e that "sophistry" was practiced (albeit in disguise) by "ancient" poets, healers, gymnastic trainers, and musicians.

[8] As Dover 1968a: lv observes.

[9] As Dover 1968a: liii–liv says of Aristophanes: "He drew one basic distinction, between the normal man and the abnormal man ... Ar. casts his net very wide in separating the abnormal and parasitic from the normal and essential; in *Nu.* 331ff. seers, medical writers, and lyric poets are included, under the general heading σοφισταί, as ἀργοί, and the parasitic philosopher, as typified by the comic Socrates, has obvious affinities with other parasitic types in comedy: the seer (*Pax* 1043ff.), the oracle-monger (*Av.* 959ff.), and the poet (*Av.* 904ff.)."

tragic poet Melanthius (to cite but one example from this popular target of comedy), who is lampooned by a great number of comic poets,[10] is accused of many of the same pernicious traits as the philosophers/ sophists were: gluttony (Pherecrates 148 *PCG*; Eupolis 43 and 178 *PCG*; Aristophanes, *Peace* 804–11, 1009–15; Leuco 3 *PCG*; Archippus 28 *PCG*; cf. Protagoras' eating habits in Eupolis 157 *PCG*); flattery (Eupolis 178 *PCG*; cf. Protagoras and Chaerephon as flatterers in Eupolis' *Flatterers* 157, 180 *PCG*); and idle babbling (Plato 140 *PCG*; cf. Socrates as babbler in Eupolis 386 *PCG*; Aristophanes, *Clouds* 505, 931, 1053, 1394, *Frogs* 1491–9, and fr. 392 *PCG*; and Prodicus as babbler in Aristophanes 506 *PCG*).

There can be no doubt that Old Comedy was quick to lampoon pretentious and trendy thinkers. But the comic playwrights did not attack these people as enemies of poetry. In fact, there were many *poets* that were identified as newfangled intellectuals (the most obvious example being Euripides). What we find in Old Comedy is a tendency to attack specific intellectuals of varying persuasions for being self-serving imposters who had a bad influence on society. Indeed, so far from distinguishing philosophers and poets, a number of comic playwrights yoke them together: Socrates and Euripides, for example, are regularly paired (Callias 15 *PCG*; Telecleides 41, 42 *PCG*; Aristophanes, *Frogs* 1491–9 and fr. 392 *PCG*). While Nietzsche took this coupling to mean that Euripides was destroying tragedy and the world-view that went with it, the poets of Old Comedy made no such global claim: they linked Euripides with Socrates because he was newfangled (Telecleides 41 *PCG*), a pretentious intellectual (Callias 15 *PCG*; Aristophanes, *Frogs* 1496), and full of stuff and nonsense (Aristophanes 392 *PCG*, *Frogs* 1496–7). A passage in Aristophanes' *Frogs* will help to illustrate this point. After Dionysus has proclaimed Aeschylus the winner in the poetry contest, the chorus reflects on Euripides' defeat:

It is not a fine thing to sit next to Socrates and babble (λαλεῖν), casting aside culture and neglecting the best elements of the tragic art (τά τε μέγιστα παραλιπόντα τῆς τραγῳδικῆς τέχνης). It is the foolish man who makes a lazy pastime out of pretentious language and nonsensical scratchings (ἐπὶ σεμνοῖσιν λόγοισι καὶ σκαριφησμοῖσι λήρων). (1491–9)

I cite this passage because it is the closest thing we find in preplatonic Greek poetry to the assertion that intellectualism is at odds with poetry. But Aristophanes stops short of making this claim, and indicates instead that Socrates has caused Euripides to write *bad* tragic poetry – poetry that

[10] See, e.g., Callias 14 *PCG*; Pherecrates 148 *PCG*; Eupolis 43, 178 *PCG*; Plato 140 *PCG*; Aristophanes, *Birds* 150–1, *Peace* 804, 1009–15; Leuco 3 *PCG*; Archippus 28 *PCG*.

"neglects the best elements of the tragic art." In short, a certain brand of intellectualism (i.e. that associated with Socrates) is antithetical to good tragic poetry since it substitutes pretentious nonsense for the noble and beneficial material that should characterize the genre.[11] This falls far short of the notion that poetry as a whole is battling some distinct intellectualist movement.

What, then, about the other half of the equation? Is there evidence that philosophers (as we now call them) were hostile to poetry? As Halliwell observes, "the main surviving cases of philosophical objections to poetry before Plato's time [are] Xenophanes frs. 1, 11–12, 14–16, ?34, Heraclitus A22–3, frs. 40, 42, 56–7, 104 DK."[12] But it should be emphasized that these fragments do not contain "objections to poetry" per se (Xenophanes, after all, was writing in verse), but rather quarrels with individual poetic and other intellectual practitioners, often on very specific grounds. As Adkins rightly reminds us,

Xenophanes attacks [Homer] as a purveyor of immoral and untrue stories about the gods. Heraclitus castigates Homer and Hesiod (B40, 42, 57, 106), apparently for their ignorance rather than their vocabulary; but he also castigates Xenophanes, Pythagoras, and the logographer Hecataeus, apparently on similar grounds. Havelock claims that Heraclitus' "Homer deserves to be expelled from the contests and clubbed: also Archilochus" (B42) demonstrates the philosopher's opposition to the competitive recitations and the culture which accompanies them; but Heraclitus does not argue that the contests should be abolished, merely that Homer and Archilochus are unworthy to compete in them.[13]

Several Presocratic thinkers, then, explicitly objected to certain individual claimants to wisdom and authority – a group which included poets and prose writers as well as thinkers such as Pythagoras. It was these individuals' reputation as "masters of truth" that prompted attacks from the margins: when Heraclitus complains, for example, that "the teacher of most is Hesiod (διδάσκαλος δὲ πλείστων Ἡσίοδος); it is him they know as knowing most ..." (DK B57), it is clear that he is attacking Hesiod as a false authority, not as a poet. While no one would deny that many of the Presocratics played an important role in developing a new type of prose literature and that this literature diverged in crucial ways from the oral-poetic tradition whose most prominent spokesmen were Homer and Hesiod, there is in fact no evidence in the Presocratics of an explicit repudiation of poetry as a whole.[14]

---

[11] See Dover 1993: 381 at 1491.
[12] Halliwell 1988: 154.
[13] Adkins 1983: 221. See also Nussbaum 1986: 123.
[14] The closest thing we find to an attack on poets is Heraclitus DK B104: "What wit or understanding do they have? They believe the poets of the people and take the mob as their

If this is on target, then the notion that "poetry" – as a mode of discourse that promulgates a certain set of values – is fundamentally opposed to "philosophy" (and vice versa) was not articulated before Plato. It is Plato's private quarrel, then, which is retrojected back onto the ancients in *Republic* 10 and thereby made to escape the contingency and specificity of Plato's own historical moment. The quarrel is thus made to appear natural rather than artificial, a historical fact rather than one of Plato's more powerful fictions.[15]

But why would Plato make such a move? Recall that in the definition of philosophy set forth in the middle books of the *Republic*, Socrates separates a large group of pretenders who court philosophy in spite of the fact that they are "unfit for education" from the tiny few who are true philosophers. As Socrates remarks in book 6:

There is some tiny (πάνσμικρον) group remaining which consists of those who consort with philosophy worthily, whether it be a noble and well-born character constrained by exile who, in the absence of people who would corrupt him, remains true to [philosophy] in accordance with its nature, or when a great soul who is born in a small town disregards and disdains the affairs of the city. And perhaps some small group of an excellent nature might turn to philosophy from another art, which it justly looks down on. And the bridle of our companion Theages may provide a restraint. For all the other conditions for falling away from philosophy were at hand in the case of Theages, but his sickly constitution restrained him by keeping him out of politics. My own situation – the divine sign – is not worth mentioning, since it has probably happened to few if any people before me. (496a–c)

When he mentions "philosophy" in book 10, however, Socrates seems to be referring to a much larger and more prominent group of intellectuals: a distinct and coherent movement important enough to have provoked the wrath of the poets. Is Plato now trying to suggest that there is a long tradition of thinkers who should in fact be called "philosophers" even if they did not use this term for themselves?

It should be emphasized that the reference to the ancient quarrel in book 10 occurs in the context of the long argument for the expulsion of the poets from Socrates' ideal city.[16] The passage is devoted entirely to

---

teacher (δήμων ἀοιδοῖσι πείθονται καὶ διδασκάλῳ χρείωνται ὁμίλῳ), not knowing that 'the many are worthless', good men are few" (all translations of Heraclitus are from Kahn 1979). As in the fragment on Hesiod (DK B57), Heraclitus is concerned with *popular* (and, therefore, ignorant) poets, not poetry *per se*.

[15] For several quite different readings of Plato's assertion of the quarrel between philosophy and poetry, see Gould 1990: especially 4-69 and S. Rosen 1993: especially ch. 1.

[16] On Plato's attacks on poetry in the *Republic* and other dialogues, see, e.g., Dalfen 1974, Gadamer 1980: ch. 3, Annas 1982b, Nehamas 1982, Woodruff 1982b, Belfiore 1983 and 1984b, Halliwell 1984a, Nussbaum 1986: ch. 7.3 and passim, and Ferrari 1989.

poetry; philosophy is not mentioned until the end of the argument, when Socrates announces the famous feud. Interestingly, Socrates does juxtapose the poets with a number of non-philosophical sages and benefactors. At 599b–600e, he observes that Homer, who has been identified as the "leader" of tragic poetry (598d8), was never the legislator for any city, as Lycurgus, Charondas, and Solon were, nor did he ever serve as a general or a counsellor in war. In addition, he has not left behind any "clever inventions relating to the arts or to other practical affairs" (a4–5), such as Thales and Anacharsis did. Finally, Homer has not educated men in the way that Pythagoras did, who had many disciples and whose legacy was a new mode of living; even Protagoras and Prodicus, Socrates adds, had flocks of admiring pupils. In this passage, Plato contrasts the poets not with philosophers but with legislators, generals, inventors, and educators. One would have expected philosophers to occupy the fourth category – that of the educator – but instead one finds Pythagoras grouped together with sophists such as Protagoras and Prodicus. To be sure, Socrates speaks with some irony about these latter, but he does not attempt to differentiate the true from the false educator, nor does he make any reference to the philosopher. Plato's point in this passage is that poets should not be grouped with wise men who bestowed real benefactions on humankind.

It comes as a surprise, then, when Socrates concludes his attack on the poets by announcing a quarrel between poetry and philosophy (607b–c). This abrupt claim cries out for elucidation, but aside from the four brief quotes from some unspecified poems, Socrates makes no effort to substantiate his assertion. As we have seen, the quotes themselves are vague and unhelpful; none refers to a distinct group of intellectuals, let alone a subgroup called "philosophers." All of them sound like comic attacks on modish intellectuals – intellectuals whom (with the exception of Socrates) we would expect Plato *to join in attacking*.[17] As Brock suggests, "the 'ancient quarrel between philosophy and poetry' is for Plato essentially a matter of comedy attacking philosophy."[18] But, as we have seen, the comedians were not even attacking a distinct movement or discipline. There is in fact no solid evidence for an ancient quarrel between comedy and philosophy, let alone between poetry and philosophy. Given

[17] If, as some scholars believe, the lyric as well as the iambic lines come from comedy, then an interesting paradox emerges: while Plato's attack in book 10 is devoted almost exclusively to "serious" poetry (comedy gets only the briefest of mentions at 606c), his only evidence of a quarrel with philosophy comes from comic texts. On the debate over the sources of the first two quotes, see Adam 1902.II: 417–18, Halliwell 1988: 155, and Brock 1990: 40–1. Note that the word κραυγάζουσα (in the first quote) is not found in epic or tragedy, and κενεαγορίαισι (in the second) is a neologism: both have a strong comic flavor.
[18] Brock 1990: 40.

the absence of any "ancient" antagonism between two distinct modes of thought and language, we can hardly interpret Plato's assertion of a quarrel between poetry and philosophy as a neutral piece of historical reportage. In particular, as I have suggested, this assertion actually contradicts the claims made in book 6, where philosophy is defined explicitly and in detail. If Plato were making a serious historical point in his mention of the "ancient quarrel" in book 10, in fact, he would be expanding the boundaries of philosophy to include the motley array of intellectuals who were excluded in his earlier definition.[19]

Clearly, this is not what Plato intends. Rather than foisting this overliteral reading on this passage, I would argue, we should interpret it as a rhetorical construct that has a specific function in its immediate context. Although Plato has not made any explicit reference to philosophy in his attack on poetry, his reference to the quarrel at the conclusion of this passage reminds the reader that the entire argument is in fact designed to differentiate philosophy from poetry. For if the poet is explicitly defined as ignorant of truth, as imitating appearances, as gratifying the multitude, as fostering the inferior part of the soul, then the philosopher is implicitly defined as the diametrical opposite. Philosophy is defined negatively, then, as the unmentioned opposite of poetry. By announcing a quarrel between philosophy and poetry, in short, Plato emphasizes that the discussion of poetry directly reflects upon the nature of philosophy. At the same time, he invests philosophy with an extraordinary status – a status that it certainly did not have in this period. For philosophy now emerges as the powerful adversary of the giant that is poetry. By picking a quarrel with poetry, in sum, Plato tries to have it both ways: although philosophers are a new and "tiny" group, they are engaged in an epic battle with the poets.

II

In this chapter, I would like to examine Plato's quarrel with one genre of poetry: Athenian tragedy.[20] As I will argue, Plato's quarrel with tragedy cannot be assessed merely by reference to the passages in which he explicitly denounces this genre. For we also need to attend to the incorporation of tragedy into the dialogues. What is the nature of Plato's

---

[19] At the very least, Plato would have to include the intellectuals who were attacked, along with Socrates, by the comic poets.

[20] I will not offer a full assessment of Plato's quarrel with the poets in this book. Rather, I have chosen to analyze Plato's engagements with a number of *specific genres of poetry*, both high and low; each genre, as I will argue, poses different problems for "philosophy" as Plato conceived it.

"inclusion" of tragic subtexts in the dialogues, and how does this reflect upon his attempt to define philosophy?

Recent scholarship on Greek tragedy has emphasized the importance of placing this genre in the socio-political context of classical Athens.[21] For Greek drama is not simply a literary phenomenon but a social institution that is implicated in various ways in the social, political, and religious practices of the Athenian democracy. As Vernant and Vidal-Naquet observe,

> Tragedy is not only an art form; it is also a social institution that the city, by establishing competitions in tragedies, set up alongside its political and legal institutions. The city established under the authority of the eponymous archon, in the same urban space and in accordance with the same institutional norms as the popular assemblies or courts, a spectacle open to all the citizens, directed, acted, and judged by the qualified representatives of the various tribes. In this way it turned itself into theater. Its subject, in a sense, was itself and it acted itself out before its public.[22]

As we saw in the first chapter, Plato conceives of tragedy as a kind of rhetoric performed before the Athenian *dēmos* – rhetoric designed to win favor by serving up discourse which is pleasing to its democratic audience. His engagement with the genre of tragedy, in short, goes well beyond a dispute about language or literature. Rather, Plato is concerned with, on the one hand, the false set of values that (he thinks) tragedy promulgates and, on the other hand, the way in which this value system reflects and reinforces the social and political practices of the Athenian democracy.[23]

Plato's famous diatribe in the *Republic* against tragedy in particular and poetry in general need not be rehearsed. But this is only part of the story about Plato's relationship with the genre of tragedy. For the trace of tragedy is visible in many of Plato's dialogues. Socrates' provocative claim in the *Symposium* that "the same man should know how to compose comedy and tragedy" (223d), of course, cleverly invites us to investigate Plato's affiliation with dramatic poetry. Many scholars, in fact, have teased tragic (and comic) elements out of the *Symposium* and other texts and analyzed the relation between the Platonic dialogue and Greek

---

[21] See, e.g., Vernant and Vidal-Naquet 1988, Foley 1985, Winkler 1985, Segal 1986: especially ch. 1, Goldhill 1990, Zeitlin 1990, Ober and Strauss 1990, Rehm 1994. For a similar approach to comedy, see Loraux [1984]/1993: ch. 4, J. Henderson 1990, Bowie 1993, and Taplin 1993. Easterling 1993 investigates the genre of tragedy in the early fourth century BCE.

[22] Vernant and Vidal-Naquet 1988: 32–3.

[23] Cf. Socrates' claim in the *Republic* (568c): "by going around the cities, collecting huge crowds, hiring powerful and persuasive voices, [the tragic poets] draw the governments towards tyrannies and democracies."

drama.[24] It is only in the *Gorgias*, however, that Plato uses an entire tragedy – the *Antiope* of Euripides – as the subtext for his philosophical drama.[25] By analyzing the incorporation of Euripides' tragedy into the *Gorgias*, I aim to approach Plato's quarrel with tragedy from a different angle. Rather than searching for tragic elements in – and tragic influence on – the dialogues, I will argue that Plato's detailed rescripting of a specific tragedy is a deliberate parody. This parodic critique of tragedy, in fact, is an important part of the *Gorgias'* attempt to define and delimit the discipline of philosophy.

The *Gorgias* signals its intertextual engagement with Euripides' *Antiope* in a number of passages. In the great *rhēsis* voiced by Socrates' opponent Callicles at 482c4–486d1, for example, no fewer than four passages from the *Antiope* are quoted almost verbatim.[26] Even more pointed is Callicles' explicit comparison of both himself and Socrates to the protagonists of that play, Antiope's sons Zethus and Amphion: "Socrates, I am quite friendly towards you. And I suppose I feel now what Zethus (whom I mentioned before) felt towards Amphion in Euripides. For I am moved to say the same things to you as he said to his brother" (485e). Socrates, on his part, accepts his role in the drama. As he says at 506b, he wants to "pay [Callicles] back with the speech of Amphion in return for that of Zethus."

As E. R. Dodds notes in his commentary on the *Gorgias*, the scene for which the *Antiope* was most remembered in antiquity was that in which the brothers, Amphion and Zethus, discuss and defend their disparate ways of life: Zethus advocates the practical activity of the man of affairs and Amphion the private and leisured life of the artist and intellectual.[27]

---

[24] On the *Symposium*, see Bacon 1959, Anton 1974, Clay 1975, Sider 1980a, Patterson 1982: especially 84–90, Nussbaum 1986: 122–35 and passim. Kuhn 1941 and 1942 discusses general links between Plato's dialogues and Greek tragedy and attempts to demonstrate that Plato scripted the *Republic* as a "true tragedy." Halliwell 1984a: 50–8 argues that the *Phaedo* comes the closest of Plato's dialogues to "philosophical tragedy." Arieti 1991 offers "dramatic" interpretations of a number of dialogues. For a detailed list of scholars who have suggested that the *Symposium* and other Platonic dialogues are comic or tragic (or both), see Mader 1977: 71–7. Mader himself argues that no single dialogue is "comic" or "tragic"; rather, they are simultaneously "anti-tragic" and "meta-comic" (which is to say, neither tragic nor comic). See also Nussbaum's excellent "interlude" on "Plato's anti-tragic theater" (1986: 122–35).

[25] Arieti 1991: ch. 5 uses the Euripidean subtext as a starting-point for interpreting the *Gorgias* "as drama." See also my "Plato's *Gorgias* and Euripides' *Antiope*: a study in generic transformation" (Nightingale 1992), which has been substantially revised for this chapter.

[26] 484e, 485e–486a, 486b, 486c. For an examination of the (minor) deviations of these citations from their Euripidean originals, see Dodds 1959: *ad loc.*

[27] Dodds 1959: 276. Reconstructions of the *Antiope* (dated *circa* 408) are found in Schaal 1914, and, more recently, Kambitsis 1972. See also Wecklein 1923, Pickard-Cambridge 1933: 105–13, and Snell 1964: ch. 4, who follows Schaal's reconstruction very closely.

Their debate thus centered on the comparative merits of the life of politics and the life of intellectual cultivation.[28] Plato's *Gorgias* stages a similar debate. In this dialogue, Socrates attempts to persuade a recalcitrant Callicles – as well as Gorgias and Polus, the interlocutors whose arguments Callicles takes over – that the life of the philosopher, rather than that of the powerful orator and politician, is the best and happiest for humankind.

Note, however, that there are important differences between the two debates. In particular, while Euripides draws a simple contrast between the non-intellectual man of affairs and the intellectual who has opted out of civic life, Plato's characters are more complex. On the one hand, Callicles (unlike his prototype Zethus) is no enemy to intellectual pursuits: as he says at 485a, he considers it "a fine thing to partake of philosophy to the extent that it serves one's education." In fact, he explicitly reproves those who do not practice philosophy in their youth:

For when I see a youth practicing philosophy I approve, and it seems to me to be fitting, and I believe that this person possesses the liberal culture proper to a free man, but the person who does not practice philosophy I consider illiberal – a man who will never think himself worthy of any fine or noble action. (485c–d)

As these passages suggest, Callicles considers "philosophy" the appropriate education for the future politician. What Callicles argues, then, is that a person should practice philosophy in youth and turn to politics when he becomes an adult. Socrates, on his part, also diverges from his tragic predecessor. Whereas Amphion had totally removed himself from civic affairs, Socrates is a quite different animal. As he says to Callicles at 500c, the questions that subtend their entire argument are:

[first,] what sort of life one ought to live, whether it be the kind of life to which you invite me, engaging in manly pursuits such as speaking in the assembly and practicing rhetoric and *doing politics in the way in which you are doing politics*, or whether it be a life spent in the practice of philosophy; and [second,] in what way the one differs from the other. (my italics)

In this passage, Socrates does not oppose philosophy to politics. Rather, he suggests that the difference between the two pursuits is precisely what needs to be determined; since Callicles is "doing politics" in a specific way, it is quite possible that the philosopher may be playing the politician in a very different manner. When Socrates says at the end of the argument that he is one of the very few men in Athens who engages in "the true

[28] Euripides may have derived the notion of the life of intellectual cultivation and contemplation from the Pythagoreans (see, e.g., Joly 1956: 21–40, Guthrie 1962: 204–12, and Carter 1986: ch. 6, esp. pp. 133–7). Dodds 1959 finds numerous Pythagorean elements in the *Gorgias* (see pp. 20, 26–7, 297–8, 300, 303, 337–40, 373–6, 383).

political art" (521d), we are reminded that the "philosophy" which he is advocating includes practical and political activities.[29]

One of the things that is at stake in this debate, then, is the true nature of this thing called "philosophy." Note that when Callicles discusses "philosophy" in his famous diatribe, he refers to it as an activity that is practiced by a number of people. He clearly does not think it necessary to define philosophy, nor does he attempt to distinguish different kinds of intellectual inquiry. Although he takes the adult philosophizers to task for continuing their studies, there is no suggestion that they are doing anything different from the youths who practice philosophy: the point is that the adults are engaging in the same practice for a much longer time. Clearly, Callicles is using the term "philosophy" in the broad sense of intellectual cultivation or "higher" learning that was discussed in chapter 1; it is an activity that is not inherently antithetical to political life in the Athenian democracy provided that it is treated as a means rather than an end in itself.[30]

Socrates, however, has a quite different conception of philosophy. After suggesting that he is in love with philosophy on the one hand and Alcibiades on the other (481d), Socrates says to Callicles at 482a–b:

[Philosophy] speaks the things, my friend, which you now hear me saying, and she is far less unstable than my other beloved; for the son of Clinias says one thing at one time and another at another, but philosophy is always consistent. And she speaks the things which you just now found so shocking, and you yourself were present when these things were said. So you must either refute philosophy by proving that to do injustice and, having done injustice, to evade the penalty is not the greatest of all evils; or, if you leave this unproved ... then Callicles will not agree with you, Callicles, and he will be in discord for all of his life.

In this passage, Socrates indicates that philosophy involves self-consistent argumentation concerning justice and (we infer) related issues of ethics and politics. But his claims for philosophy are substantive as well as formal. For, as Socrates insists, it is philosophy that claims that to suffer wrong is better than to do wrong; philosophy is thus wedded to a specific world-view – a world-view that the people whom Callicles identifies as practitioners of philosophy would almost certainly reject. By identifying

[29] See also 521a and *Apology* 31c, where Socrates says: "ἰδίᾳ ... πολυπραγμονῶ." As Reeve 1989: 159 suggests, in this paradoxical line Socrates indicates that he is "neither private nor political, but somehow both at once."

[30] Callicles' notion of philosophy (which is clearly rejected by Plato) chimes with the general view as Socrates describes it at *Republic* 497e–498a: "At present ... those who take up [philosophy] approach the most difficult part of it when they are youths just out of boyhood, in the interval before they take up household management or moneymaking, and then they give it up; and these are considered the most philosophical of men (οἱ φιλοσοφώτατοι ποιούμενοι)."

himself as the mouthpiece of philosophy, in fact, Socrates indicates that his own arguments and activities represent true philosophy. If he is one of the very few Athenians who is practicing the true art of politics, we can infer, he is also one of the very few who is engaged in philosophy. Plato, then, does not oppose the contemplative to the practical life in the *Gorgias*. Rather, he attempts to distinguish two kinds of intellectual cultivation: one which serves the aspiring politician in a democracy or a tyranny, and one which serves the true art of politics.

It should be emphasized that the *Gorgias* is the first dialogue in which Plato sets out to narrow the definition of "philosophy" by appropriating the term for his own intellectual activities and commitments.[31] The dichotomy that Plato draws in this dialogue between φιλοσοφία and ῥητορική, of course, is a fundamental part of this project. Interestingly, Schiappa claims that the word ῥητορική is found for the first time in extant Greek literature in the *Gorgias*; he suggests that Plato may have coined this term in an effort to "limit the sophistic art of *logos* to affairs in the law courts and the assembly ..."[32] As Schiappa argues:

There is a tendency to treat rhetoric as a given in Plato's *Gorgias*. That is, it is usually assumed that there was a discrete set of activities or a body of teachings that were consensually regarded as *rhētorikē* and toward which Plato directed his critical abilities. A more likely situation was that Plato thought the Sophists' art of *logos* was in danger of being ubiquitous and hence in need of definitional constraint.[33]

If Schiappa is right about *rhētorikē*, then the first explicit and systematic definition of the art of rhetoric would go hand in hand with the first attempt to define philosophy. In attempting to define his own territory, as it seems, Plato had to define and delimit his rivals' terrain.

A similar, if less explicit, polarization is found in Plato's attack on the tragedians in the *Gorgias*. For by incorporating Euripides' *Antiope* as a subtext for his own drama, Plato is able to set his own new hero in opposition to the tragic hero. This new hero, of course, is the philosopher. And just as Socrates is juxtaposed with the "hero" of the *Antiope*, so also is true philosophy contrasted with the genre of tragedy as a whole. As Chance has rightly suggested, interpreters of Plato need to attend to "the

---

[31] I follow the standard dating of the dialogues outlined by Guthrie 1975: 50.

[32] Schiappa 1991: 40–9, esp. 46 (and appendix B). Schiappa (pp. 209–10) points out that the evidence for dating Alcidamas' *On the Sophists* at 391–90 BCE is tenuous at best; he argues that the speech is a response to Isocrates' *Panegyricus*, and thus must be dated after Plato's *Gorgias*. See also Cole 1991: 173 n. 4, who also argues for a later dating for *On the Sophists* (he places it in the 360s).

[33] Schiappa 1991: 47. Cole 1991: ch. 1 and passim also argues that the concept of "rhetoric" is an invention of the fourth-century philosophers (cf. Halliwell 1994).

thoroughness with which he analyzes how *not* to think, speak, and act."[34] In the remainder of this chapter, I will investigate the ways in which Plato's intertextual encounter with the genre of tragedy contributes to his ongoing effort to distinguish true or "philosophic" discourse from genres of speech and thought that make a false claim to wisdom.

III

In composing the *Gorgias*, Plato deliberately appropriated fundamental thematic and structural elements from Euripides' *Antiope*. Not only does the brothers' debate and its conclusion inform the *agōn* between Socrates and Callicles, but the *deus ex machina* that brings the *Antiope* to a close provides a structural model for the eschatological myth at the end of the *Gorgias*. Plato thus invites his readers to juxtapose his dialogue to its tragic model, and he reinforces this message by persistently probing at the nature of the tragic and the comic. At the heart of Plato's critique of tragic wisdom, finally, is a detailed and complex portrait of its newly-invented adversary: philosophy.

Euripides' *Antiope* is dated *circa* 408–407 BCE.[35] The plot hinges on the rescue of Antiope, the daughter of Nycteus (the late king of Thebes), from her murderous uncle and aunt, Lycus and Dirce, by her long-lost sons, Amphion and Zethus. In order to save the woman that will turn out to be their mother, however, the brothers must put aside their differences. Amphion and Zethus rehearse these differences in the famous *agōn*. In spite of powerful arguments, Amphion is finally worsted in this debate and yields to his brother. They then proceed to engineer their mother's rescue, though they are prevented at the last minute from killing their uncle by Hermes, who makes an appearance at the end of the play. Hermes restores order by restraining the angry brothers and establishing them as the rightful rulers of Cadmeia. He also pronounces that the music from the lyre of Amphion will cause the stones and trees to move unaided and form the walls of Thebes. The *deus ex machina* thus not only provides a resolution to the plot but also resolves the question raised in the *agōn* between the two brothers: though Amphion lost the argument with his brother, he is nonetheless vindicated by Hermes at the end of the play, for it is his music that will build the walls of Thebes.

A brief examination of the brothers' famous debate will enable us to

---

[34] Chance 1992: 20. In this detailed study of the *Euthydemus*, Chance argues that Plato sets up eristic as "the antipode to his own philosophical method" (p. 19). See Nehamas 1990 for an excellent analysis of Plato's attempt to differentiate philosophy from "eristic" and "sophistry."

[35] For the dating of the *Antiope*, see Kambitsis 1972: xxxi–xxxiv.

assess the *Gorgias'* debt to the *Antiope*.[36] In fr. 22K (186N),[37] Zethus says to his brother:

πῶς γὰρ σοφὸν τοῦτ' ἔστιν, ἥτις εὐφυῆ
λαβοῦσα τέχνη φῶτ' ἔθηκε χείρονα;

For how can this be wise, this art which gets hold of a man with a good nature and makes him worse?

What is the nature of the musical "art" that Zethus finds so repugnant? The opening line – "for how can this be σοφόν?" – must be a response to a claim of Amphion's that the musical life is connected with wisdom. As Cicero testifies in the *de Inventione* 1.50.94, "Amphion apud Euripidem ... vituperata musica *sapientiam* laudat."[38] This claim is borne out by Zethus' remark in fr. 10.5–6K (188.5–6N) that Amphion should embrace hard work, "leaving to others these subtle sophisms which will make [him] dwell in an empty house" (ἄλλοις τὰ κομψὰ ταῦτ' ἀφεὶς σοφίσματα, | ἐξ ὧν κενοῖσιν ἐγκατοικήσεις δόμοις). The phrase "subtle sophisms" clearly suggests that Amphion's musical pursuits include intellectual inquiry. Finally, fr. 6K (1023N; cf. 5K [192N]) gives good evidence of Amphion's intellectualist bias: he sings a cosmogonic hymn that hails aether and earth as the origin of all things.[39]

Why, then, does Zethus inveigh against the cultivation of the intellect? We have seen in fr. 10K (188N) that he considers his brother's pursuits antithetical to material success. And the notion that such pursuits actually corrupt the individual emerges in fr. 22K (186N). Both of these themes recur in fr. 8K (187N):

---

[36] Discussions of the brothers' debate are found in Joly 1956: 64–8, Goossens 1962: 648–52, and Carter 1986: 163–73.

[37] I use Kambitsis' edition of the *Antiope* (1972; designated by "K"). As an aid to the reader, I have placed Nauck's numeration of the fragments (designated by "N") after that of Kambitsis.

[38] Cf. *Rhet. ad Herennium* 2.27.43, where Zethus and Amphion (in Pacuvius' *Antiope*, which was modelled on Euripides' play) are accused of abandoning the true subject of their debate, which is music, for a discussion of wisdom and virtue: "uti apud Pacuvium Zethus cum Amphione, quorum controversia de musica inducta disputatione in sapientiae rationem et virtutis utilitatem consumitur." Cf. Cicero, *de Orat.* 2.37.155–6, where Pacuvius' Zethus is said to have "declared war" on "philosophy" (similarly, Cicero, *de Rep.* 1.18.30; Aulus Gellius, *Noct. Att.* 13.8.4–5). Dio Chrysostomos, too, in his discourse "On trust," says that Zethus "admonished his brother, since he did not think it right for him to practice philosophy" (ἐνουθέτει τὸν ἀδελφόν, οὐκ ἀξιῶν φιλοσοφεῖν αὐτόν, 73.10). Note that the word "philosophy" is not found in Euripides' *Antiope*.

[39] On Amphion's cosmogonic hymn, see Wecklein 1923: 56, Snell 1964: 73, Kambitsis 1972: xii–xiii, 30–2. That Amphion was especially concerned with (what we now call) natural philosophy is evinced by a passage from Probus which includes Euripides in a group of thinkers who posit two cosmic principles: "consentit in numero Euripides, sed speciem discriminat. terram enim et aetherem inducit principia rerum esse in Antiopa" (*in Verg. Ecl.* 6.31). Cf. Philostratus, *Imagines* 1.10.

ἀνὴρ γὰρ ὅστις εὖ βίον κεκτημένος
τὰ μὲν κατ' οἴκους ἀμελίᾳ παρεὶς ἐᾷ,
μολπαῖσι δ' ἡσθεὶς τοῦτ' ἀεὶ θηρεύεται,
ἀργὸς μὲν οἴκοις καὶ πόλει γενήσεται,
φίλοισι δ' οὐδείς· ἡ φύσις γὰρ οἴχεται,
ὅταν γλυκείας ἡδονῆς ἥσσων τις ἦ.

For the man who, though he possesses a good livelihood, ignores and neglects the things in his house and, taking pleasure
in songs, always pursues this, will be a lazy idler in his house
and in the city, and to his friends will be a nobody. For nature
is gone when a man is worsted by sweet pleasure.

Here, Zethus claims that the intellectual life is bad for the individual, his
household and friends, and even his city: it is selfish, lazy, and ignomin-
ious. The emphasis on *phusis* in frr. 22K (186N) and 8K (187N), moreover, reveals that Zethus believes in the virtues and status conferred on
individuals by nature rather than those developed through self-culti-
vation.[40] Intellectual and musical pursuits may result in cleverness (τὰ
κομψὰ ... σοφίσματα, 10.5K) but not, according to Zethus, in wisdom
(σοφόν, 22.1K).

Amphion responds to his brother on all of these counts.[41] In fr. 15K
(193N), first of all, he denigrates the active life of *polupragmosunē*:

ὅστις δὲ πράσσει πολλὰ μὴ πράσσειν παρόν,
μῶρος, παρὸν ζῆν ἡδέως ἀπράγμονα.

Anyone who engages in many activities that he need not engage in is foolish, when he can live free from business in a
pleasant fashion.

The *apragmōn* person lives more pleasantly, claims Amphion, yet he also
is useful to his city and friends:

ὁ δ' ἥσυχος φίλοισί τ' ἀσφαλὴς φίλος
πόλει τ' ἄριστος· μὴ τὰ κινδυνεύματα
αἰνεῖτ'· ἐγὼ γὰρ οὔτε ναυτίλον φιλῶ
τολμῶντα λίαν οὔτε προστάτην χθονός.

The quiet man is both a safe friend to his dear ones and the
best man for the city. Do not praise dangers. I am no friend of
the overbold sailor or the ruler of the land. (fr. 17K [194N])

---

[40] As Carter 1986:171 observes, "The character of Zethos has strong aristocratic colouring."
Zethus' aristocratic temperament finds a parallel in the character of Callicles.

[41] According to Kambitsis (1972: xxiv–xxx), Zethus initiates the debate by criticizing music.
When Amphion responds by linking the musical life to the life of the mind, Zethus
counterattacks by inveighing against the intellectual life, and is again answered by Amphion. Similarly, Schaal 1914: 9–21, Wecklein 1923: 58–62, Snell 1964: 83–92.

Here, Amphion suggests that the busy practical man is ambitious and unreliable and therefore potentially harmful to his friends and city. He strikes another blow for the cultivation of the intellect in fr. 19K (200N):

γνώμαις γὰρ ἀνδρὸς εὖ μὲν οἰκοῦνται πόλεις,
εὖ δ᾽ οἶκος, εἴς τ᾽ αὖ πόλεμον ἰσχύει μέγα·
σοφὸν γὰρ ἕν βούλευμα τὰς πολλὰς χέρας
νικᾷ, σὺν ὄχλῳ δ᾽ ἀμαθία πλεῖστον κακόν.

For by a man's intelligence cities are managed well and the household is managed well, and moreover in war it has great strength. For one wise piece of counsel conquers many hands, but ignorance in the mass of the people is the greatest evil.

Judgment and intelligence are what benefit the city and the household, not unthinking action.

Finally, having argued that his mode of life will confer the greatest benefits on both friends and country, Amphion vouches for the supreme happiness it brings the individual:

εἰ δ᾽ εὐτυχῶν τις καὶ βίον κεκτημένος
μηδὲν δόμοισι τῶν καλῶν θηράσεται,
ἐγὼ μὲν αὐτὸν οὔποτ᾽ ὄλβιον καλῶ,
φύλακα δὲ μᾶλλον χρημάτων εὐδαίμονα.

If someone who is fortunate and possesses a livelihood will pursue no fine things in his house, I will never call him blessed, but rather a fortunate guard of money. (fr. 16K [198N])

Although it is hard to pin down exactly what Amphion means by the "fine things" (τῶν καλῶν, line 2) whose pursuit leads to blessedness, it is probable that he is referring to the cultivation of the intellect.[42] In any event, it is clear from the rest of the fragment that Amphion does not consider the possession of wealth and good fortune the determinants of a "blessed" life (ὄλβιον, line 3). So far from being supremely happy, the rich man who does not pursue "fine things" is merely a good guard of money. Amphion, in sum, accepts the criteria that Zethus has set up for the best kind of life – namely, whether it is beneficial to one's family, friends, and city as well as good for the individual. But he denies that political activity and the status and success that go with it satisfy these criteria. It is in fact the leisured life of intellectual culture which is both beneficial to others and supremely good in itself.[43]

[42] As Snell 1964: 87–8 and Kambitsis 1972: 53–4 suggest.
[43] Whereas Snell 1964: 89 says that Amphion "*yields* to the argument of utility for house and state, brought forward by Zethos" (my italics), Carter is probably right in seeing this move as a "progression" rather than a concession: "Amphion has made an important

IV

How does the *agōn* between Socrates and Callicles in the *Gorgias* imitate and transform its tragic model? Callicles, as I have mentioned, explicitly casts himself in the role of Zethus at 485e. In addition, he repeatedly alludes to the *Antiope* in his argument, quoting directly from Zethus' polemics at least four times in his explosive *rhēsis* (484e, 485e–486a, 486b, 486c). Callicles, of course, champions the life of power, distinction, wealth, and pleasure that issues from the mastery of rhetoric. Although Callicles differs from Zethus in important ways,[44] many of his arguments do in fact chime with those of his tragic predecessor. Adapting a passage from the *Antiope* (fr. 9K [185N]) at 485e–486a, for example, Callicles exclaims:

Socrates, I am quite friendly towards you. And I suppose I feel now what Zethus (whom I mentioned before) felt towards Amphion in Euripides. For I am moved to say to you the same things that he said to his brother: "you neglect, Socrates, what you ought to care for, and, though you possess a noble nature (φύσις) and spirit, you call attention to yourself with your childish antics. Neither could you advance a proper argument in the councils of justice, nor utter anything probable and persuasive, nor offer any brilliant counsel on another person's behalf."[45]

According to Callicles, too much philosophy perverts a good nature and renders a man unable to help himself or others in the world of affairs. Callicles thus follows Zethus in celebrating the political life, though he diverges from his predecessor by insisting that this kind of life is necessarily grounded in rhetorical prowess.

At 486b–c, Callicles invokes Zethus once again:

And, indeed, Socrates, "how can this be wise, this art which gets hold of a man with a good nature and makes him worse" [= fr. 22K (186N)], rendering him unable to help himself or to save either himself or others from the greatest dangers, and allowing him to be robbed of his entire substance by his enemies and to live completely without honor (ἄτιμος) in his own city? (486b–c)

progression in his debating position. He is no longer arguing from a point of view of pure *apragmosunē*, of political passivity, but maintaining that he can, in certain circumstances, be more useful to the city than his brother" (1986: 169).

[44] In addition to the differences mentioned above, note also that while Zethus denounces pleasure (which is attested by frr. 7K [395 + 184N] and 8K [187N]), Callicles wants *both* power/prestige *and* limitless pleasure. Clearly, Zethus is more old-fashioned than Callicles. But his traditionalism intersects with Callicles' anti-traditional stance at a crucial juncture: each bases his arguments on the erroneous belief that power, prestige, and money make for the good life.

[45] The Greek text translated here is Dodds' (1959). Cf. J. Burnet 1903: *ad loc.* The lines in quotation marks are an adaptation of *Antiope* fr. 9K (185N). Dodds discusses this adaptation on pp. 276–7.

Like Zethus, Callicles harps on the intellectual's ruined nature, his poverty, his lack of honor or distinction, and his inability to help himself or others. As he says to Socrates in another allusion to the *Antiope* at 486c–d,

practice what will make you seem wise, "leaving to others those subtleties" – whether one should call them nonsense or rubbish – "which will make you dwell in an empty house"; do not emulate those men who investigate these trifling matters but those who have a livelihood (βίος) and a reputation (δόξα) and many other good things.[46]

Zethus, as we have seen, wanted to acquire the wealth, power, and distinction of the man of affairs. Callicles, however, carries this pursuit to a dangerous extreme: for he aims, ultimately, at absolute power. He therefore does not suggest, as Zethus did, that the life he advocates is good for the city, for he would be hard pressed to prove that a self-seeking tyrant is good for a state.

At 506b, when the argument has reached a point where Callicles refuses to go on, Socrates asserts that he would have liked to continue the dialogue with Callicles until he had "paid him back with the speech of Amphion in reply to that of Zethus." Socrates is forced to conclude the argument by continuing the elenctic questions and answers alone (except for occasional half-hearted rejoinders by Callicles) and, finally, by launching into the long closing speech that contains the myth depicting the fate of the soul after death. It is in these passages that Socrates provides Amphion's "answer" to Zethus.[47] Let me briefly rehearse this response. At 502e, Socrates poses the question whether politicians have as their goal that "the citizens become as perfect as possible through their speeches." Callicles responds that some act in the interests of the citizens and others do not. Though Callicles had not tried to argue that the life of the powerful rhetorician is necessarily good for the city, Socrates insists that rhetoric has an invariably bad effect on the city; even the statesmen that Callicles admires have made the city worse instead of better (518e–519d). In fact, Socrates goes so far as to suggest that he is one of the very few who

---

[46] The parts of this passage put in quotation marks are identical to fr. 10.5–6K (188.5–6N) except for the exclusion of the word σοφίσματα after ἀφείς. This exclusion does not alter the sense of the line.

[47] Note that Socrates' responses contain a number of allusions to the *Antiope*, such as at 526c where he avers that "the soul of a philosopher who has minded his own business and hasn't meddled in many affairs (οὐ πολυπραγμονήσαντος)" will journey to the Islands of the Blessed after death. This statement recalls Amphion's defense of the *apragmōn* man in fragment 15K (193N). Again, at 521e1–2, Socrates admits that he will not be able to speak effectively in a lawcourt since he has refused to dabble in the "subtleties" (τὰ κόμψα) that Callicles has recommended (cf. *Apology* 17a–18a). Here, Socrates turns the tables on his opponent: whereas Callicles had echoed Zethus (fr. 10K [188N]) by dubbing philosophical musings "subtleties," Socrates transfers this epithet to the rhetorical "art" espoused by Callicles.

have practiced true statesmanship in Athens, "since those things which I say on each occasion I say not aiming at gratification, but rather at what is best ..." (521d).

It is the philosopher, according to Socrates, who confers the greatest benefit on his city, and this same person turns out to be the ideal friend and relative. At 507e–508a, Socrates shows that the intemperate and unjust man adulated by Callicles is wholly incapable of friendship, and he adds at 508b (cf. 509b) that the philosopher alone can offer vital aid to his friends by exposing the sickness in their souls. Finally, the philosophical life renders the individual happy and blessed. For, as Socrates repeatedly indicates, happiness derives solely from virtue and is therefore immune to the malice of other people. And in the eschatological myth he positively trumpets forth the claim that, so far from corrupting a person's nature, philosophy will land him in the Islands of the Blessed (526c).

V

It should be clear by now that the *Antiope* plays a surprisingly prominent role in the *Gorgias*. Certainly the references to Euripides' play go beyond "poetic coloring."[48] Nor is Plato simply trying to "remind the reader that the debate between the practical and the contemplative life was already engaged in the fifth century."[49] In order to comprehend Plato's interaction with Euripides' tragedy, I suggest, we need to look beyond verbal and even thematic echoes. For Plato's allusions to the *Antiope* must surely conjure up its dramatic action and structure.

Consider the plot and denouement of Euripides' tragedy. In the *Antiope*, Zethus' arguments – which are echoed by Antiope herself, as we discover from fr. 32K (206N)[50] – overpower those of Amphion. As Horace describes the events to his friend Lollius in *Epistles* 1.18.39–45:

> nec tua laudabis studia aut aliena reprendes,
> nec cum venari volet ille, poemata panges.
> gratia sic fratrum geminorum Amphionis atque
> Zethi dissiluit, donec suspecta severo
> conticuit lyra. fraternis cessisse putatur
> moribus Amphion: tu cede potentis amici
> lenibus imperiis...

---

[48] Dodds 1959: 275.
[49] Dodds 1959: 275.
[50] The fact that Antiope shares Zethus' point of view underlines the unpopularity of Amphion's beliefs (which provides another parallel between Amphion and the much-despised Socrates).

>You will neither praise your own pursuits nor find fault with
>those of others, nor when that man wishes to go hunting will
>you be composing poems. In this way the friendship between
>the twin brothers Amphion and Zethus was broken up, until
>the lyre on which the stern brother looked askance was si-
>lenced. Amphion is thought to have yielded to the *mores* of his
>brother: you, too, must yield to your powerful friend's gentle
>orders ...

This passage suggests that Amphion admits defeat and agrees to turn his
back on the musical life.[51] If Amphion is persuaded to adopt his brother's
mores after losing the debate, then we would expect him to plunge into a
life of action. The plot bears this out, for it is Amphion who threatens
to kill his uncle Lycus at the end of the play. Hence the opening lines
of Hermes' speech: "stop, king Amphion, this murderous assault" (fr.
48.67–8K). In this speech, which is almost completely preserved, Hermes
commands Amphion to take up the lyre and celebrate the gods with
songs, so that the rocks and trees will be charmed by the music and come
unaided to form the walls of Thebes. "Zeus gives this honor (τιμή) to you
and I give it with him, since I am the one who gave you this gift" (96–7).
It was no less than Hermes, we discover, who had given Amphion the lyre
in the first place, and he reminds the youth here that music is not only his
god-given calling but will in fact be of the greatest aid to the city. Hermes,
then, belatedly adjudicates the brothers' debate about the best kind of life
and reverses the verdict that the brothers had reached for themselves.[52]
Amphion is to abandon the life of action he has recently adopted and re-
sume his divinely inspired calling. The *deus ex machina*, in sum, unveils a
divine perspective on the events of the drama that runs counter to that
achieved by the human characters.

How does the drama in the *Gorgias* reenact this narrative structure?
One important dramatic parallel is that Socrates, like Amphion, is unable

[51] Unfortunately, nothing in the fragments indicates why and in what way Amphion capitulates to Zethus. Conjectures are offered by Wecklein (1923: 61–2), Snell (1964: 90–2),
and Kambitsis (1972: xxiii–xxiv, xxix n. 3). All of these scholars believe that Amphion did
not give up his principles but rather agreed to accommodate himself to a more active life.
Horace's claim (*Epistles* 1.18.43) that Amphion "is thought (putatur) to have yielded ..."
to his brother may indicate that Amphion's concession was patently ambivalent.

[52] Hermes directs seven and a half lines to Amphion and one and a half to Zethus. Some
scholars have suggested that this numerical disparity evinces Euripides' valorization of
Amphion and his lifestyle (Goossens 1962: 651–2, Hausmann 1958: 52). Kambitsis 1972:
122 endorses this interpretation, though he believes that several lines may have dropped
out of the text after line 89 – lines which would have been directed towards Zethus (the
same conjecture was made by Roberts 1935: 165–6). Either way, Hermes' revelation that
Amphion's music will build the walls of Thebes clearly offers a retrospective judgment of
the debate staged earlier; as Snell 1964: 92 suggests, this revelation "shows the superiority
of a life dedicated to the muses."

to convince his opponents by his arguments. All three of Socrates' interlocutors, of course, are ensnared by his logic and shown to be contra-
dicting themselves. To be sure, these contradictions lend credence to Socrates' own arguments, which none of the interlocutors is able to refute and
which Socrates himself considers to have won the day (see, e.g., 508e–
509a). But in spite of the fact that Socrates succeeds in confounding his
interlocutors with his logical argumentation and keen psychological acu-
men,[53] the dramatic interplay in the dialogue reveals that none of his
companions is in fact persuaded by what he says. Certainly Socrates'
claims seem to have no effect on the conceited and complacent Gorgias.
Polus actually laughs in Socrates' face at 473e and, though he seems the
most tractable of Socrates' opponents, he nonetheless remains an un-
believer. He says at the end of their argument that, although they may be
consistent with the stated premises, Socrates' claims still strike him as
"strange" or "absurd" (ἄτοπα, 480e).

Callicles' allergy to Socrates is especially virulent. As soon as he begins
to sense the weakness of his own arguments, Callicles sneers, "I don't
know what your sophistries mean" (497a). Shortly after that, he starts to
agree with everything Socrates says "in order that the argument may be
finished and to gratify Gorgias" (501c). Callicles is totally out of sym-
pathy with Socrates' positions, as his scornful and abusive demeanor
reveals. He says outright on a number of occasions that he is "un-
persuaded" by Socrates (493d, 494a, 513c). And at one point he simply
refuses to go on: "If you will obey me," he says, "you will bid goodbye to
this argument, or else converse with someone else" (505d).[54] As Socrates
himself admits just before relating the closing myth, "this man will not
allow himself to be benefited or to experience the very thing we are now
discussing – being disciplined" (505c). Here, Socrates reminds us that, so
far from being converted, Callicles has made little if any progress.[55]

At 472b–c, Socrates contrasted his style of inquiry, which invites only
one other person into a dialectical search for the truth, to that used in the

---

[53] Scholars who have analyzed the logical argumentation in the *Gorgias* include: Vlastos
1967, Santas 1979: ch. 8, Irwin 1979: passim, Klosko 1984. Cf. Kahn 1983 and McKim
1988, who assert that the elenchus has a crucial psychological aspect that has been ignored by scholars who have interpreted it as a method of logical analysis. McKim (who
critiques Kahn as well as Vlastos) persuasively argues that Socrates' method is "psychological, not logical – not to argue them into believing [the Socratic "Axiom" that virtue is always beneficial and vice harmful] but to maneuver them into acknowledging that,
deep down, they have believed it all along" (p. 37).

[54] On Callicles' response to Socrates' arguments, see Dodds 1959: 352, 358, Irwin 1979: 233,
Kauffman 1979: esp. 118, and Lewis 1986: esp. 195–6.

[55] The Stranger in the *Sophist*, describing the Socratic teaching technique, emphasizes that it
removes the conceit of knowledge and brings people to be "angry at themselves and
gentle to others" (230a–e). This is precisely what Socrates fails to achieve with Callicles.

lawcourts, where a person can call in a number of witnesses to testify to what he is saying. According to Socrates, he aims to produce but one witness for his views – his interlocutor. As he puts it at 472b, "If I cannot bring forward you yourself as a single witness who agrees with what I'm saying (μάρτυρα ... ὁμολογοῦντα περὶ ὧν λέγω), I consider that I have accomplished nothing worth speaking of in the matter under debate." But isn't this precisely what Socrates fails to achieve in the *Gorgias*?[56] Though Socrates succeeds in refuting his opponents at the logical level, their responses to these arguments reveal that none of them is in the least persuaded that the philosopher is happier than the orator. And this lack of persuasiveness becomes more prominent as the dialogue reaches its close: Callicles grows progressively more alienated and sarcastic and Socrates is finally left to complete the investigation by himself. Socrates' move from duet to solo hammers home the unsuccessful result of his discussions.[57] Since his method by definition must involve another individual, his conclusion of the argument *by questioning and answering himself* at 506c–509c is a poignant signal of his failure to win his companions over.[58]

Even more pointed is Socrates' surprising departure from the dialectical

[56] Vlastos 1983a: 48 says that "*to compel Polus to 'witness' for* not-p *Socrates would have to give Polus a logically compelling proof that* p *is false*" (his italics). But giving a "logically compelling proof" will not necessarily make an interlocutor "a witness who agrees with" (μάρτυρα ... ὁμολογοῦντα) one's views (472b7). At 474a5–7, Socrates claims that he knows how to "furnish one person as a witness" to his views *and* how to "secure the vote of" (ἐπιψηφίζειν) that one person. None of the interlocutors in this dialogue "agrees" with Socrates in the sense of giving him their vote. Kahn 1983: 115–18 suggests that Socrates "defeats" all three interlocutors insofar as he "forces them to confront the incoherence of their own position, and thus to make a first step towards that recognition of their ignorance which is the beginning of wisdom" (p. 116). While Socrates does expose his opponents' inconsistencies, his inability to make them "witness" to his views provides a dramatic dimension to the dialogue that should not be ignored.

[57] It is not fortuitous, I think, that Socrates glosses his move from dialogue to monologue by conjuring up a scene from a comedy by Epicharmus (Plato calls Epicharmus "the greatest master of comedy" at *Theaetetus* 152e4–5). When Callicles asks him to carry on the argument alone, Socrates says he will do this "in order that the saying of Epicharmus applies to me: 'Let me single-handedly manage what two men spoke about before'" (505e; the line quoted is an Attic equivalent of Epicharmus DK B16). Olympiodorus claims that Epicharmus wrote a comedy in which two people speaking in dialogue later gave way to one who spoke for both of them (34.13 Westerink [1970: 177]). By assimilating himself to a comic character at this crucial juncture, Socrates reminds us that there is something funny (feeble?) about this move away from his cherished dialectical method.

[58] Socrates concludes this conversation with himself at 509a, after proclaiming that his own views are "held firm and bound together by arguments of steel and adamant" (508e–509a). At this point, Socrates returns to the theme of rhetoric, inviting Callicles to re-enter the discussion. Callicles obliges, but he says repeatedly that he is only answering the questions in order to "complete the argument" and to "gratify" Socrates (501c7, 510a1–2, 513e1, 514a4, 516b4). Given the link that Socrates so noisily forges in this dialogue between "gratification" and "flattery" (e.g. 521a–b), Callicles' desire to "gratify" Socrates (and Gorgias, 501c8) betrays his unregenerate nature.

method in his mythic harangue at the end of the dialogue. Recall that, on several occasions earlier in the drama, Callicles accuses Socrates of descending to the tactics of a "mob-orator" (δημηγόρος, 494d1, 482c5; cf. e4). Shortly before launching into his myth, Socrates concedes this point (519d5–7): "truly you have compelled me to play the orator (δημηγορεῖν), Callicles, by being unwilling to answer." When Callicles retorts, "and you would not be able to speak, unless someone were answering you," Socrates responds, "it seems I can; now, at any rate, I am stretching out many of my speeches . . ." (519d–e). In light of his repudiation of speechifying at the very opening of the text (448d, 449b–c) – of "rhetoric" over and against "dialogue" (448d9–10) – Socrates' exhibition of *makrologia* at the end of the dialogue is of great dramatic importance.[59] Callicles' refusal to participate in the conversation forces Socrates to retreat into rhetoric.

Socrates' inability to make Callicles "witness" to the merits of philosophy is closely tied to – one might even say prefigures – his failure to convince the jury at his own trial. Like his arguments in the *Gorgias*, the speech Socrates gives at his trial takes the form of a defense of the philosophical life: he fails to persuade on both occasions. Socrates' trial is clearly prophesied a number of times in the *Gorgias*, and this encourages the reader to juxtapose Socrates' argument with Callicles to the defense he makes at his trial.[60] Take, for example, Callicles' outburst at 486a–b:

Doesn't it seem to you disgraceful to be in the condition I think you are in – you and the others who advance ever further into philosophy? For, as it stands, if anyone should arrest you or any other such person and lead you away to prison, saying that you are acting unjustly when you are not, you know that you would not be able to handle yourself, but you would reel and gape and have nothing to say, and when you came before the court, even if your accuser was very common and wicked you would be put to death if he should choose to punish you with death.

Later in the piece, Socrates admits that he could easily be prosecuted and put to death in a city like Athens (521c–d), and adds that his trial would be "like that of a doctor prosecuted by a cook before a jury of children" (521e). These ominous allusions to Socrates' trial remind the reader of his ultimate inability to defend the philosophical life before his all-too-human fellow Athenians. Polus seems almost to sum it up at 473e

---

[59] Kahn says that, in the closing myth, Plato "uses his privileged *persona* to speak directly to the audience, as in an Aristophanic *parabasis*" (1983: 104). But it is the dramatic character Socrates, not Plato, who is in fact speaking. Socrates' retreat into a persuasive mode after failing to convert his companions by way of logical argumentation is what makes this dialogue especially dramatic.

[60] As Dodds 1959: 368 and Irwin 1979: 181, 240 observe.

when he says, "don't you think that you are already refuted when you say things which no human being would accept?"

Like Amphion, then, Socrates is depicted in the *Gorgias* as unable to persuade his opponents to embrace the philosophical life. And like Amphion, Plato's drama indicates, he will be vindicated by the gods. Before examining this vindication, let me muse on a fascinating way in which it is prepared for in the dialogue. At the beginning of his debate with Callicles, Socrates says that he would be delighted to find a device for testing souls analogous to the stones that are used to test gold.[61] If he were to find a really good specimen of this miraculous device, he could establish that his own soul had been well nurtured and in need of no further testing (486d). He then exclaims that he has found just such a "godsend" in the person of Callicles because he is the ideal elenctic partner (486e). The word for "godsend" is, importantly, ἕρμαιον. It is more literally translated as a "gift from Hermes." This word is emphasized in the dialogue by its recurrence at 489c1, where Callicles angrily hurls it back at Socrates. Why all this fuss about a gift from Hermes? We recall that in the *Antiope* the lyre was given to Amphion by Hermes – this is why the god comes in person to vindicate the musical life at the end of the play. But in what sense could Callicles be seen as the god's gift to Socrates as the lyre was to Amphion?

Socrates explains that his excitement over Callicles issues from his desire for an elenctic partner who not only possesses wisdom and good will but is ready to speak his mind. Both Gorgias and Polus had proved less than ideal interlocutors because, as Callicles and (later) Socrates note (482d–e, 487a–b), they had suppressed their actual opinions at crucial points in the argument. Since Socrates' method is designed to test his own and his partner's soul as well as the arguments they construct,[62] it can only bear fruit when both participants are well disposed to one another and frank about their beliefs.

Socrates, of course, is being ironic when he calls Callicles wise, friendly, and frank.[63] Nor is he surprised when Callicles proves an unruly elenctic partner who cannot be brought to "agree" with Socrates' views. Nonetheless, there may be a sense in which Callicles plays the role of the godsent instrument to Socrates: it is through the *inconsistency* of Callicles' argument that the compelling *consistency* of Socrates' argument is re-

[61] Note that this conceit is found in several Euripidean tragedies: *Medea* 516–19 and *Hippolytus* 925–31 (cf. Theognis 119–24).

[62] Kahn 1983: 75–80 and passim rightly stresses this feature of the Socratic elenchus. The elenchus is analyzed by R. Robinson 1941: especially chs. 2 and 3 and, more recently, by Vlastos 1983a and 1983b. For critiques of Vlastos' position, see Kraut 1983, Brickhouse and Smith 1984, and Polansky 1985. Kahn 1983 and McKim 1988 discuss the psychological as well as the logical elements of the elenchus.

[63] McKim 1988: 40 notes that Callicles lacks frankness as well as wisdom and friendliness.

vealed. The lack of harmony that is evinced by Callicles' inconsistent
arguments – the fact that "Callicles will not agree with Callicles" (482b)
and that he "never says the same things about the same subjects" (491b) –
points up by contrast Socrates' self-consistent arguments and, correlatively, his well-tuned soul.[64] Perhaps Callicles is right when he peevishly
suggests at 489c1 that Socrates "considers it a godsend (ἕρμαιον) if someone makes a slip in expression." For it is Callicles' slips – which invariably expose the inconsistencies of his argument – that lead Socrates to
conclude at 508e–509a that his own views "are held fast and bound by
arguments of adamant and steel," and will remain so as long as nobody
can refute them.[65]

It is an interpretative leap, no doubt, to say that Callicles is a kind of
heaven-sent gift to Socrates. But even if we refuse this leap, the reiteration
of the word ἕρμαιον in the *Gorgias* cannot but recall the *deus* in the *Antiope*, and it functions as a harbinger of the divine vindication of Socrates
that occurs in the closing myth. As we have seen, although his argument
with Callicles makes him more sure of his own position, Socrates is unable to persuade his companions to agree with him. Given that Socrates'
unpersuasiveness in this dialogue looks forward to his fatal unpersuasiveness at his trial, vindication becomes necessary. To achieve this vindication, Plato borrows and transforms Euripides' *deus ex machina* – a dramatic
device that the tragedians, as Plato suggests in the *Cratylus*, have used in
an ignorant and expedient fashion. Perhaps we should call in divine aid,
Socrates says in that dialogue, "like the tragic poets, who, when they are
at a loss, take refuge by raising up the gods on the machine" (425d).[66]

[64] This is bolstered by 482b–c: if Callicles cannot refute his claims, says Socrates, then
"Callicles will not agree with you, Callicles, but will be out of tune (διαφωνήσει) for his
whole life. And I at any rate think it better, my good man, that my lyre be discordant and
out of tune (ἀνάρμοστόν τε καὶ διαφωνεῖν), and any chorus I might train, and that the
majority of mankind should disagree with me and oppose me rather than that I, being one
man, should be out of tune (ἀσύμφωνον) and inconsistent with myself." Here, the soul is
pictured as a lyre-like instrument whose proper tuning and playing is the most important
activity in a person's life. Since Callicles' soul is out of tune, he is in dire need of philosophical therapy. As Dodds 1959: 260 points out, musical metaphors "run through
Plato's ethical discussions from first to last." Nonetheless, they are especially prominent
in this dialogue (see, e.g., 457e2, 480b4, 482b6, 482b8, 482c2, 486c5, 503e8).
[65] While scholars have noted the uncharacteristic confidence that Socrates exudes here
(Dodds 1959: 16, Vlastos 1983b), most have failed to observe that Socrates does not in
fact defeat his interlocutors on his own terms: he does not make any of them "a single
witness in agreement with" his views (472b; cf. 474a).
[66] We need to distinguish Socrates' retreat into mythic discourse from Plato's use of the
dramatic device of the *deus*. Though he is fully confident of his own views, Socrates is "at
a loss" with respect to his unyielding interlocutors; he therefore moves into the mythic
mode. Plato, however, is in no way "at a loss"; he appropriates the tragic device of the
deus to serve a new and anti-tragic purpose. Cf. *Cleitophon* 407a8, where Socrates is said
to address his exhortations ὥσπερ ἐπὶ μηχανῆς τραγικῆς θεός.

Something very like a *deus ex machina*, I suggest, manifests itself at the close of the *Gorgias*. This occurs when Socrates changes key towards the end of the dialogue, modulating into the discourse of *muthos* (523a).[67] The myth runs as follows.[68] In the reign of Cronus, the souls of men who had reached the day of their death were judged by other living men. As a result, the wrong people were sent both to Hades and to the Islands of the Blessed, for evildoers could deceive the human judges with their handsome bodies, good families, and great wealth, and they could supply plenty of witnesses who would testify that they had lived righteous lives when their day of judgment arrived. Dazzled by these external trappings and by the testimony of the witnesses, the judges pronounced unsound verdicts. When Zeus took the reins of power, he rectified this situation. Humans were made to stand trial after death, disembodied and devoid of all trappings; and gods, rather than humans, sat in judgment. These divine judges, of course, would send virtuous and philosophical people to the Islands of the Blessed and visit the rest of mankind with appropriate punishments.

Socrates' myth goes beyond the mere narration of the rewards for virtue and punishments for vice in the afterlife. For it places special emphasis on the disparity between human and divine judgment of souls: whereas humans reach false conclusions by judging one another according to criteria that are external and deceptive, the divinities judge on the basis of virtue alone and thus can always reach a true verdict about a person's soul.[69] The divine judges, as the myth shows, will actually reverse the verdicts that the humans had pronounced when they had given judgment in the age of Cronus. Just as Hermes champions Amphion in the *Antiope*, the divine judges in Plato's myth will vindicate the philo-

[67] Although Socrates asserts that the story is "true" and not a "myth" (523a), it is nonetheless a rhetorical (rather than a dialectical) discourse. Note that Plato has prepared the reader for the myth by positing at the beginning of the dialogue a good kind of persuasion. As Socrates says to Gorgias at 454e, "do you want us to posit two kinds of persuasion, the one creating belief without knowledge and the other creating knowledge?" Rhetoric, of course, will be placed in the first of these two classes. It is possible that Plato believed that his myth was an example of the second or good kind of persuasion and thus to be distinguished from what he calls "rhetoric."

[68] For a recent discussion of this myth, see Annas 1982a: 122–5 (Annas provides a useful bibliography on the subject of Plato's myths/views on myth in her first footnote). Interestingly, Olympiodorus in his commentary on the *Gorgias* calls the closing myth a νέκυια, and he puts the myths at the end of the *Phaedo* and the *Republic* under the same rubric (46.8–9 Westerink [1970: 240–1]). It is probable that Olympiodorus recognized a νέκυια in Er's journey to the afterworld in the *Republic* and then applied this term to the other eschatological myths. The myth in the *Gorgias*, however, evokes not a νέκυια but a *deus ex machina* from the genre of tragedy.

[69] Annas 1982a: 122 notes "the extraordinary prominence given in this myth to the judges, and to the details of their judging ..."

sopher. In a trial before these judges, claims Socrates, it is Callicles who will be unable to defend himself: he will "reel and gape" and receive the stiffest of sentences. Though Socrates was unable to persuade his interlocutors (and, eventually, the citizens of Athens) of the superior merits of the philosophical life, the false judgments accorded to him by these human beings will be reversed by the gods in the final judgment.

The myth, then, provides a god's-eye view of the issues dealt with in the dialogue. Though Plato does not go so far as to give voice to a divinity who will reverse a false verdict and pronounce a true one, his mythical portrayal of the replacement of fallacious human judges by divine ones that will vindicate the seemingly defeated philosopher plays the same dramatic role as the *deus ex machina* in the *Antiope*.[70] If this is on target, then it is reasonable to conclude that Plato conceived this, the first of his eschatological myths, as a conscious imitation of the closure of a Greek tragedy. What attracted Plato to the *Antiope*, in short, was not only the debate about the merits and demerits of the intellectual life but the vindication of that life by a god. The divine perspective articulated in this and other Greek tragedies by the gods themselves is thus achieved in the Platonic dialogue through the vehicle of myth. The myth allows Plato to do what he could never do through logical argumentation – to introduce a radically different and, indeed, "divine" perspective on human affairs.[71]

VI

As I have argued, Plato consciously adapted a tragic model when he wrote the *Gorgias*. What would motivate the author of the piercing diatribe in the *Republic* against poetry in general and tragedy in particular to attempt such an adaptation? A brief foray into Plato's musings on the tragic and the comic will help to answer this question.[72] In the *Republic*,

---

[70] Euripides' treatment of the gods, of course, is very often ironical, especially in the *deus ex machina* scenes (*contra* Spira 1960, who sees the *deus* as a "healing" device which brings a "restoration of order"). Whether or not Hermes provided a triumphant or even satisfactory resolution to the *Antiope*, Plato was free to use the device non-ironically in his own drama. His conception of the gods as perfectly good beings allows him to invest the gods with the ethical authority they lack in Euripidean tragedy.

[71] I am not suggesting that Plato meant the myth *literally*. Rather, it functions *literarily*: it situates Socrates in a different narrative by shifting to a "divine" perspective in a dramatic closing gesture.

[72] For a detailed analysis of Plato's meditation on the nature of the comic and the tragic, see Patterson 1982: esp. 78–84 (see also Halliwell 1984a: 50–8, who comes to similar conclusions about Plato's views on tragedy). Patterson suggests that Plato portrays Socrates as a truly tragic (i.e. serious) character *who appears comic* to the average person. As Patterson puts it, "one can forge a direct link between the truly tragic (in the sense just described) and the *apparently* laughable: to the many, the philosopher will inevitably appear ridiculous or laughable and definitely not worth taking seriously" (p. 80).

Socrates repeatedly insists that tragedy is by no means the serious (σπουδαῖος) thing that people think it is. At 608a, for example, he says of tragedy, "we must not take seriously (οὐ σπουδαστέον) such poetry, as though it is something that lays hold of the truth and is a serious thing (σπουδαίᾳ)."[73] Socrates claims at 602b that tragedy is a "mimesis" that is παιδιάν τινα καὶ οὐ σπουδήν, and even goes so far as to call it φαύλη ("base," "inferior") at 603b.[74] The same denigration of tragedy emerges in Plato's *Laws*. In that text, after distinguishing comedy and tragedy as genres concerned with (respectively) γελοῖα (816d9, e5; cf. γέλωτα, e10) and σπουδαῖα (817a2), the Athenian proceeds to contrast the "so-called serious" creations of the tragedians (τῶν δὲ σπουδαίων, ὥς φασι, τῶν περὶ τραγῳδίαν ἡμῖν ποιητῶν, 817a2–3) with the "most beautiful and finest tragedy" that he and his interlocutors are themselves producing in their construction of a good code of laws (ἡμεῖς ἐσμεν τραγῳδίας αὐτοὶ ποιηταὶ κατὰ δύναμιν ὅτι καλλίστης ἅμα καὶ ἀρίστης, 817b2–3). Here, Plato not only denies that tragedy is truly "serious," but confers upon his own creations the title of serious tragedy.

Though Plato gives many reasons throughout his corpus for doubting the seriousness of tragedy, let me focus on an argument from the *Philebus* about the comic and the tragic. A given person, Socrates says in his discussion of the mixed pleasures of the soul, can be self-ignorant (have a conceit of knowledge) about his external goods, his bodily goods, or the goods of his soul (48d–e). This last kind of self-ignorance – that about the goods of the soul – is the most common, and it usually takes the form of an overestimation of one's own virtue and wisdom (49a). Socrates goes on to link this self-ignorance explicitly to comedy and implicitly to tragedy at 49a–c. In this passage, after suggesting that "all who foolishly hold this false opinion about themselves" should be divided into "those who are influential and powerful and those who are the opposite," Socrates says:

Divide them in this way, then, and all those who are weak and unable to retaliate when laughed at, if you say that they are "ridiculous" (γελοίους), you will be speaking the truth. But as for those who are powerful and able to retaliate, you

---

[73] Note that Aristotle also defines tragedy as concerned with σπουδαῖα (e.g. *Poetics* 1448a1–2, 1448a26–7, 1449b9–10; cf. 1449b1) and comedy as concerned with φαῦλα or γελοῖα (1448a2, 1448b36–8, 1449a32–7). For a discussion of these terms, see Lucas 1972: 63, 87.

[74] Here, Plato is talking about "mimetic art" in general, but he singles out tragedy for special mention: "those who write tragic poetry, whether in iambics or epic verse, are all imitators (μιμητικούς) in the highest degree" (602b). That Plato places epic under the rubric of tragedy reminds us that, for the ancients, epic poetry, like tragic drama, is a "serious" art form dealing with "serious" matters. Thus Aristotle says in the *Poetics* that Sophocles resembles Homer because "both of them imitate serious people" (1448a26–7), and that epic poetry resembles tragedy insofar as it is an imitation of σπουδαῖοι (1449b9–10).

will give the most correct account if you call them "fearsome" and "hateful." For the ignorance of the powerful is hateful and shameful – since the ignorance itself and its images [in poetry] are harmful to anyone near. But the ignorance of the weak belongs in the ranks of the ridiculous ... (49b–c)

A self-ignorant person who is powerless and unable to retaliate when wronged, in other words, is a comic character, while self-ignorance in a powerful person renders him/her dangerous and fearsome and therefore, we infer, the kind of character found in tragedy.[75] Here, Plato subtly conflates tragedy with comedy by indicating that both feature individuals characterized by self-ignorance.

The *Gorgias*, of course, was written before these discussions of tragedy and comedy. But note how it anticipates these discussions.[76] At 502b–d, Socrates places "the lofty and marvellous poetry of tragedy" – a highly ironic turn of phrase[77] – under the rubric of rhetoric: tragedy is a "species of rhetoric" which "we do not much admire, for we describe this as a kind of flattery" (d5–8). Just as rhetoric "treats people like children, attempting only to gratify them" (e7–8), tragedy aims at "pleasure" and "gratification" (c1) and is of no benefit to the city. This deflation of tragedy chimes with the rejection of the "seriousness" of tragic drama found in later dialogues.

These repudiations of tragic "seriousness" bring Plato's transformation of a tragic model in the *Gorgias* into sharper focus. For they invite us to explore the ways in which this "imitation" reflects upon the nature of what Plato calls "philosophy." Note, first of all, that the opposition created between tragedy and philosophy is bolstered by Plato's explicit and repeated emphasis on the question of what is "serious" (σπουδαῖον) and what is "ridiculous" (καταγέλαστον). For example, after petulantly inquiring at 481b whether Socrates "is serious (σπουδάζει) or joking (παίζει)," Callicles goes to great lengths to portray Socrates as downright "ridiculous." He says at 484d–e that philosophers show themselves to be καταγέλαστοι (e1) when they enter into practical affairs both public and private, and he claims at 485a–b that it is not only καταγέλαστον (a7) for a man to pursue philosophy in his adulthood and old age but in fact signals an immature childishness that is worthy of a beating. Callicles' portrait of Socrates is in fact strikingly comic.[78] At 485d–e, for instance, he

---

[75] Socrates mentions tragedy explicitly at 50b, where he says that "in threnodies and tragedies and comedies, not only in dramas but in the tragedy and comedy of life as a whole, pains are blended together with pleasures ..." As this statement indicates, Socrates' arguments apply to real individuals as well as to dramatic characters.

[76] Plato's *Ion* provides further evidence that his distaste for poetry's claims to "seriousness" developed early in his career.

[77] Dodds 1959: 324 points out that "σεμνός is nearly always ironical in Plato."

[78] Clay 1975: 243 notes that γελοῖος is one of "*the* Socratic epithets."

pictures the philosopher as slinking into a remote corner to whisper to three or four boys. And Callicles embellishes his comic portrayal when he says that Socrates would "reel and gape" if he were ever to be brought into court (486b), and that the defenseless philosopher can even be "boxed on the ears" with impunity (486c).[79] Callicles thus portrays Socrates as a comic character very much in keeping with the comic persona delineated in the *Philebus* – the ignorant fool who is powerless to retaliate when harmed. In the eyes of the non-philosophical person, we infer, a philosopher like Socrates appears both foolish and comic. This is in fact dramatized when Polus laughs in Socrates' face at the suggestion that the tyrant is the most unhappy of men (473e).

But Socrates will turn the tables on those who ridicule him. "Do not take what I say as if I were joking (παίζοντος)," he says at 500b–c, "for you see that our discussion concerns what kind of a life one ought to live – and on what subject should a man who has even a little intelligence be more serious (μᾶλλον σπουδάσειέ τις)?" The subject that philosophy addresses is the most "serious" of issues and, as Socrates suggests at 509a, anyone who attempts to argue against the philosopher will always appear καταγέλαστος. Since injustice is the greatest of evils, Socrates says at 509b, and the unjust man actually harms himself by his wicked deeds, it is in fact this man rather than the philosopher who is defenseless and therefore "ridiculous" (καταγέλαστος). It is, finally, Callicles and men of his kind who will "reel and gape" when they come up for trial in the afterlife (527a). Callicles' picture of the powerful orator and the helpless and ridiculous philosopher is thus reversed by Socrates. It is the philosopher who is serious and the orators and unphilosophical people ridiculous.

Plato's drama, then, overturns its tragic model in crucial ways. Note in particular that the tragic character Zethus – whom Plato would have considered ignorant but nonetheless fearsome by virtue of his ability to punish his enemies – gives way to the "ridiculous" Callicles. Callicles' helplessness in the final tribunal renders him more comic than tragic. In addition, while Amphion not only failed to persuade Zethus but even acceded to his brother's dangerous ignorance, Socrates has fully satisfied himself, if not his listeners, that his arguments are sound. Unlike Amphion, Socrates does not move one inch towards the life that his opponent champions. It is for this reason, of course, that he will eventually be put to death. Socrates, then, is not the self-ignorant persona that Plato finds in the tragic genre. While Amphion foolishly capitulates to his brother

---

[79] Dodds 1959: 278 suggests that ἐπὶ κόρρης τύπτοντα means "punched in the jaw." I choose to translate the phrase literally (though it's equally funny either way).

and plunges into a life of action that leads him to attempt an impious murder, Socrates holds fast to his convictions in spite of his inability to persuade others to accept the truth of his claims.

Should we conclude that Plato's adaptation of the *Antiope* is a deliberate attempt to transform a "so-called serious" tragedy into a truly serious one? This solution is, I think, too simple. For Plato is not, after all, writing tragedy. Not only does he opt for prose rather than poetry, but he brings on stage a hero who is neither *spoudaios* nor *geloios* (or, perhaps, a strange blend of both). While he urges the reader to resist Callicles' portrayal of Socrates as a foolish comic character, Plato also refuses to elevate Socrates to tragic heights. Note, in particular, that Plato's Socrates uses ordinary, even common language[80] – language that is, in fact, a real irritant to his aristocratic companions. As Alcibiades says in the *Symposium*, "[Socrates] speaks of pack-asses and blacksmiths and cobblers and tanners, and he always seems to say the same things in the same language, so that anyone who was inexperienced or thoughtless would laugh at his arguments" (221e–222a). In the *Gorgias*, in fact, Socrates seems almost to revel in his lack of refinement. In one noteworthy passage, Socrates speaks of compulsive itchers (494c), birds that defecate at the same time as they eat (494b),[81] and the dread *kinaidos* who not only offers his body for another man's penetration, but actually enjoys this unmanly sexual role (494e). Callicles cringes at these coarse references (494e), just as earlier he berated Socrates for continually talking about foods and drinks and doctors and cobblers and fullers and cooks (490c, 491a) – for, in short, his incessant recourse to "things vulgar and common" (φορτικά καὶ δημηγορικά, 482e). The question is thus raised as to what is truly vulgar and what noble, what is ridiculous and what serious. The categories have become unsettled: philosophy demands that we rethink these terms.

In the *Gorgias*, as I have argued, the tragic subtext is made to serve Plato's purposes in a number of ways. For Plato criticizes his model even as he imitates its themes and structure. The "seriousness" of the tragic hero is ridiculed in order that a new kind of hero can enter the stage. The intertextuality in this dialogue is thus a clear case of parody.[82] It should

---

[80] This is surely one of the reasons why Aristotle (*Poetics* 1447b10–11) mentions the *Sōkratikoi logoi* in the same breath as the mimes of Sophron (who represented working-class men and women speaking in a low Doric dialect).

[81] As the scholiast glosses the χαραδριός: ἅμα τῷ ἐσθίειν ἐκκρίνει (see Dodds 1959: 306).

[82] Interpreters may differ about the degree of polyphony present in this work. It could be argued that, in spite of Socrates' insistence that death is not a tragedy, and in spite of Plato's attempts to parody the tragic genre, Socrates still emerges as a tragic figure (in the traditional sense). For those who decide that tragedy is not completely stifled in the *Gorgias*, a further question arises: does Plato deliberately grant tragedy an independent (if muted) voice, or is he simply unable to devalue the genre of tragedy to the extent that he would like?

be emphasized, moreover, that Plato targets the genre of tragedy as a whole even as he "imitates" a single text. For by parodying the *Antiope*, Plato picks a quarrel with all the tragedians. This contest, in fact, is fought on quite specific grounds. As Halliwell claims, it is the "combination of high status and merit with the display of an exceptional vulnerability to suffering – a combination which affirms the imbalance between virtue, ἀρετή, and happiness – that makes the tragic hero the antithesis of Plato's good man."[83] It is, finally, to define and dramatize this good man – or, to be more precise, this new kind of sage called the "philosopher" – that Plato clashes with his tragic predecessors. Socrates, the *Gorgias* urges, is heroic but not tragic, in spite of his undeserved fate.

Plato's interaction with the tragedians, in sum, was more complex and extensive than is generally believed. For, by entering into the parodic mode, Plato was able to criticize tragedy on a number of specific grounds and to set up "philosophy" as a serious rival to tragic drama.[84] But we should not forget that this famous quarrel with "serious" poetry was, in Plato's own day, a mere whisper.

[83] Halliwell 1984a: 54. For a similar (and much fuller) argument, see Nussbaum 1986: 378–94 and passim.

[84] It should be emphasized that Plato's handling of poetic discourse is hardly homogeneous: different genres of poetry will receive different treatment precisely because they differ as discursive forms and as socio-political practices. "Philosophy" will illuminate and be illuminated by different genres in different ways. Each instance where Plato incorporates poetry (or rhetoric) into his dialogues, then, deserves a separate investigation.

3 Eulogy, irony, parody

There is nothing either precise or calibrated about praise and censure.

Cervantes, Prologue to *Novelas ejemplares*

I would rather err on the side of praising the undeserving than castigating where blame is due. Unmerited praise passes for ingenuousness on the part of the giver, but if you paint in his true colours someone whose conduct calls for nothing but censure, this is attributed to your own sick judgement and not to his deserts.

Erasmus, Letter to Martin Dorp

By setting philosophy in opposition to poetry, Plato was able to distinguish his version of wisdom and the wise man from those of the poetic tradition. But an equally menacing opponent presented itself in the form of rhetoric – a mode of discourse whose difference from "philosophy" was far more difficult to mark. Plato, of course, went to great lengths to differentiate philosophical from rhetorical discourse. But he did not simply attack the "art of rhetoric" as a whole: as a cultural critic, he was acutely aware of the ways in which different genres of rhetoric reflected and reinforced Athenian ideology. While Plato was clearly concerned with rhetoric in all its aspects, there was one genre that he found especially pernicious: the rhetoric of praise. This kind of rhetoric was a beast with many heads. It found its way into many different genres of discourse and was offered up to disparate audiences in a number of different performative contexts. It was thus much more difficult to target than the deliberative rhetoric of the assembly and the forensic rhetoric of the lawcourts, which had a distinct form, purpose, and context of performance. It is no surprise, then, that Plato attacks the discourse of eulogy from different angles in different dialogues. Again and again, Plato sets the encomium in diametrical opposition to the discourse of the philosopher: philosophy is defined by the "otherness" of eulogy. At the same time, however, Plato exploits the rhetoric of praise and invective in his efforts to champion his own "philosopher" over all other claimants to wisdom. Since praise is the discourse of value and commendation, a protreptic writer like

Plato could hardly steer clear of it.[1] Yet Plato's own use of praise collides with his repeated claim that this kind of discourse is fundamentally anti-philosophical.

In order to understand Plato's critique of encomiastic rhetoric, we must first analyze the multiple manifestations of the discourse of praise in the social and political context of late fifth and fourth-century Athens. Praise, of course, reaches back to the very beginnings of the poetic tradition as we know it. But, by late fifth-century Athens, prose had become the primary vehicle for eulogy. Aristotle, in fact, identifies praise and blame as the discourse that constituted the entire epideictic genre of rhetoric (*Rhetoric* 1358b12–13). It is worth rehearsing the criteria that Aristotle uses to distinguish the three branches of rhetoric, since his classification has had such great impact upon the way in which we moderns conceptualize ancient rhetoric. Aristotle begins by suggesting that the different branches of rhetoric are directed to different kinds of listeners: whereas deliberative and forensic rhetoric are addressed to "judges" who are to vote on a certain course of action, epideictic rhetoric is delivered to "spectators" who are concerned with "the skill of the speaker" (1358b2–8; cf. 1391b7). He then turns to subject matter: deliberative rhetoric is characterized by exhortation and advice, forensic rhetoric by accusation and defense, and epideictic rhetoric by praise and blame (1358b8–13). Finally, deliberative rhetoric deals with the future and its "telos" is "the expedient and the inexpedient," forensic rhetoric deals with the past and its telos is "the just and the unjust," and epideictic rhetoric deals with the present (though it may also include the past and the future) and its telos is "the honorable and the shameful" (1358b13–29). While this classification has many virtues, it offers little insight into the diversity of the epideictic genre and the specificity of its many branches. I believe that Aristotle's formal analysis needs to be supplemented with an investigation of encomiastic rhetoric in its socio-political context. In particular, we need to pay more attention to the different kinds of encomiastic speeches and to the different contexts for their delivery.[2]

Let me briefly survey the prose encomium down through the first half

---

[1] For discussions of praise discourse in the poetic tradition, see Fraustadt 1909: 8–41, Schroeder 1914, Bundy [1962]/1986: passim, Nagy 1979: ch. 12 and passim, Gentili [1985]/1988: ch. 7, R. Martin 1989: 75–7, 89–145 and passim. Note that Aristotle suggests in his *Poetics* that all poetic genres evolve from the discourse of praise and blame (1448b).

[2] As Russell and Wilson 1981: xx observe, Aristotle wrongly identified "the oratory of 'praise and blame' with everything that is not actual forensic or deliberative speech." In fact, there were many rhetorical speeches that did not involve praise and blame which would rightly be classified as epideictic. Let me emphasize that I am concerned only with those branches of the epideictic genre that do involve praise and blame; I will therefore not offer an analysis of epideictic rhetoric *in toto*.

of the fourth century.[3] The encomium with the most ancient pedigree was the funeral oration or *epitaphios*. The funeral oration was delivered by an Athenian politician to the people of Athens at the end of a year of war; the speech was devoted to praising the men who died on the field of battle and, even more importantly, the democratic city that they died for.[4] Though Pericles' oration in Thucydides 2.35–46 is the first extant example of this type of speech, the *epitaphios* probably originated in the second quarter of the fifth century (*circa* 470–460 BCE).[5] This kind of eulogy had a very specific function and character. As Loraux observes, the *epitaphios* was "born of lyric poetry and in competition with it"; the funeral oration "uses poetic themes but reinterprets them from a resolutely political perspective."[6] It is precisely the civic character and political context of the funeral oration, she notes, that is concealed by Aristotle's classification of the *epitaphios* as epideictic rhetoric:

> the civic character of the funeral oration prevents us from applying to it Aristotle's definitions of the epideictic genre. In these definitions the polis is singularly absent: "neither citizen nor judge," the listener is a mere spectator, "drawn there solely by the pleasure of seeing an artist in speech at grips with the difficulties of his profession" ... It is not enough, then, to see the funeral oration as an epideictic speech. An institution of the city cannot be confused with the invention of a rhetor, and the epideictic genre therefore seems more like a neighboring genre than like a larger whole.[7]

While Loraux is right to insist on the political orientation of the *epitaphios*, she may be too quick in accepting Aristotle's account of the epideictic genre as adequate for other kinds of prose eulogies. Is the polis really "absent" in the case of these other eulogies? I will return to this question shortly. At present, I want to highlight a crucial disjunction within the genre of the *epitaphios*. Whereas the funeral oration originated and renewed itself as a public speech composed for a specific occasion, it is clear that a number of specimens of this genre were not composed for

---

[3] Since my study focusses on Plato's response to the encomiastic genre, my survey covers speeches composed before or during Plato's lifetime. For detailed discussions of the extant prose encomia of the late fifth and early fourth century, see Fraustadt 1909: 42–90 and Buchheit 1960: chs. 1–2.

[4] Demosthenes says that the funeral oration is a uniquely Athenian institution (*Against Leptines* 141). For detailed analyses of the genre of the *epitaphios*, see Ziolkowski 1981, Loraux [1981]/1986, and Thomas 1989: ch. 4.

[5] For the dating of the beginnings of the funeral oration, see Loraux [1981]/1986: 56–60. Hyperides' *Epitaphios*, which is dated at 323-322 BCE, reveals that the funeral oration was still being delivered in the late fourth century.

[6] Loraux [1981]/1986: 231.

[7] Loraux [1981]/1986: 225; cf. p. 78: "Since they end with an exhortation and have so much in common with a political speech, the epitaphioi cannot be placed in the purely ornamental category of *logoi epideiktikoi* ..."

delivery at the public burial: the funeral oration of Gorgias and probably
that of Lysias would have been read to small audiences at the intellectual
gatherings that met at so many venues – both public and private – in
classical Athens; and Plato's parodic funeral oration in the *Menexenus*
was clearly not designed to be delivered before the Athenian *dēmos*.[8]
Loraux suggests that priority must be given to the political orator over
the logographer, since the logographic *epitaphioi* were mere imitations of
the institutional *epitaphioi*.[9] But it seems reasonable to suppose that, once
the logographers had turned the *epitaphios* into a literary genre, the influence went both ways – that the "occasional" orators came to emulate
the logographic speeches even as the logographers were imitating the
"true" *epitaphioi*. The result would be a fruitful interaction between the
"occasional" speech delivered before the Athenian *dēmos* at the public
burial and the "non-occasional" compositions of private intellectuals.[10]
To be sure, the occasional speeches had a much greater impact insofar as
they reached the entire Athenian public, but it would be a mistake to
banish the non-occasional speeches to the realm of art-for-art's-sake. For
these speeches served to recycle the political discourse of the institutional
orations in a number of different performative contexts.[11] The institutionalized eulogy of the Athenian democracy was thus frequently renewed and broadly circulated, since the occasional speech that was
delivered annually could be heard reverberating at a number of venues
in Athens that lacked the political or institutional markings of the "true"
epitaphios.[12]

A second branch of the prose encomium has been dubbed the "festival"

---

[8] Gorgias' *epitaphios* is generally agreed to be a rhetorical exercise – an "imitation" of the
genre (Kennedy 1963: 156, J. Martin 1974: 194, 196, Loraux [1981]/1986: 226). Some
believe that the *epitaphios* attributed to Lysias was also a rhetorical exercise (Jebb 1962.I:
206–10; cf. Loraux [1981]/1986: 91). The parodic nature of Plato's *Menexenus* is demonstrated by Vlastos [1964]/1981: 188–201, M. Henderson 1975, and Loraux [1981]/1986:
264–74, 311–27 and passim; cf. Kennedy 1963: 158–64 and Kahn 1963.

[9] Loraux [1981]/1986: 11.

[10] I have chosen to designate the speech that is delivered before a specific audience at a
specific civic occasion an "occasional speech," and the speech that is delivered before any
group of listeners at informal gatherings a "non-occasional speech." The distinction here
is not that between oral and written discourse, since "occasional" speeches such as the
funeral oration were very likely composed before delivery with the aid of writing and the
"non-occasional" speeches were designed to be read aloud at informal gatherings (silent
reading being the exception rather than the rule in this period).

[11] One should note that the discourse of the funeral oration makes its way not only into
historical, philosophical, and sophistic writings, but also into comedy and tragedy (see
Loraux [1981]/1986: 11 and passim). While some of these texts criticized the genre and
others reinforced it, all testify to the currency of this kind of discourse.

[12] Note that at Plato's *Menexenus* 239c the speaker explicitly suggests that his praise and
commemoration will supply material for future poets who will celebrate the same exploits.
Here, the *epitaphios* looks forward to its reverberation in other genres of discourse.

speech, which comprised orations delivered at panhellenic festivals as
well as at the festivals of a single city like Athens. In the former case,
of course, the speech was addressed to an audience of citizens from all
the Greek city-states. Examples of this kind of speech are Gorgias'
Olympicus, Pythicus, and *Encomium of the Eleans,* and Lysias' *Olympicus.*[13] In Plato's *Hippias Minor,* Hippias speaks of "entering the contests"
(ἀγωνίζεσθαι) at Olympia and being unbeaten (364a), but there are no
remains of any of his speeches. In fact, the only complete speech of this
kind that is extant is Isocrates' *Panegyricus,* which was certainly not delivered by its author at the occasion of a panhellenic festival. It is possible
that someone else performed in his stead; if not, then his speech has the
same "non-occasional" status that we found in the logographic funeral
orations.

What is the character of this kind of eulogy? So far as one can tell from
the extant evidence and testimonia, the panhellenic festival speech was a
"mixed" speech rather than a pure encomium, since it combined the discourse of praise and blame with the rhetoric of advice found in deliberative oratory. Isocrates' *Panegyricus,* for example, which explicitly sets
out to rival the panhellenic festival speeches delivered by the sophists (3–
4), combines an exhortation to the Greeks to unite and turn their energies
against Persia with a eulogy of Athens as the natural leader of the Greeks.
There is invective, too, against the discordant and hostile behavior of
various Greek cities, and especially Sparta. It is worth recalling here the
report that Antisthenes composed a speech for the Isthmian festival whose
purpose was "to censure and praise the Athenians, Thebans, and Lacedaemonians"; as the story goes, the speech was not delivered, since Antisthenes backed down when he saw flocks of people arriving from those
cities.[14] Even if this story is pure fiction, the description of this festival
speech as a combination of eulogy and censure is instructive. The evidence suggests, then, that at least some such speeches were written to stir
up both the friendly and the hostile feelings that the Greeks felt towards
one another. While Aristotle is right to say that the audience of epideictic
speeches did not consist of "judges" who were to vote on a practical or
political issue, his suggestion that they were simply "spectators" who were
evaluating the "skill of the speaker" misses the mark in the case of the
festival speech. For the discourse of praise and blame, aimed as it was at
one or another city-state, could hardly have been received as mere enter-
tainment. It is quite likely, in fact, that the panhellenic festivals were more
than a little politically charged; given that peaceful periods were the ex-

[13] On Gorgias' *Olympicus* and *Pythicus,* see Philostratus, *Lives of the Sophists* 1.9, 493–4.
An encomium of the Eleans is attributed to Gorgias by Aristotle (*Rhet.* 1416a1–3).
[14] Diogenes Laertius 6.2, quoting from Hermippus.

ception rather than the rule in classical Greece, the resentment and hatred fueled by the many wars among the Greeks must surely have been felt at such festivals.[15]

In the case of a speech written for the festival of a single city, of course, the audience would consist primarily of that city's denizens and would thus have a different political orientation from that at the panhellenic festivals. An example of this kind of speech is Isocrates' *Panathenaicus*, where the majority of the speech is devoted to the praise of Athens and censure of the Spartans. Here, the panhellenic "advice" is conveyed almost exclusively by way of praise for Athens' contributions to Greece (both military and cultural) and her victories over the barbarians who were the common enemy of all Greeks. The eulogy for Athens is thus much more extensive than it was in the *Panegyricus*, and the arguments for panhellenism more muted. These differences between the *Panegyricus* and the *Panathenaicus* suggest that the rhetoricians of the classical period tailored their discourse to the different audiences at the different kinds of festivals. This is corroborated by Philostratus, who offers the following account of the difference between Gorgias' *Epitaphios* and his *Olympicus*:

The epitaphios, which [Gorgias] delivered to the Athenians ... is composed with extraordinary cleverness. For although he was inciting the Athenians against the Medes and the Persians and was arguing with the same [panhellenic] intention as he did in the Olympian Oration, he mentioned nothing about concord with the rest of the Greeks, since the speech was addressed to the Athenians, who had a passionate desire for hegemony (which they could not acquire without choosing an aggressive course of action). But he focussed on praises for the Athenian victories over the Medes, indicating to them that victories over the barbarians demand hymns of praise, while those over the Greeks call for threnodies. (*Lives of the Sophists* 1.9, 493–4)

According to this account, the audience and context determined both the content and the orientation of Gorgias' texts. There is solid evidence, then, that politics played a role in the composition of festival speeches. So far from being "absent," the polis exerts a manifest influence over the genre of the festival speech.

Another branch of the prose encomium consisted of eulogies for contemporary individuals. Extant examples are Isocrates' *Evagoras* and Xenophon's *Agesilaus*. If we are to believe Isocrates, who claims that he was the first to compose a prose eulogy for a contemporary individual,

[15] Cf. Isocrates' idealizing account of the panhellenic festivals at *Panegyricus* 43–5. We need not accept this description of the harmony and amicability of these festivals; even if there was a good deal of fellow-feeling, it is hard to believe that the Greeks could fully transcend their differences even for a short time.

this kind of encomium got started at a relatively late date.[16] As he says in the *Evagoras* (8), a speech written sometime after 374 BCE,

I know that what I intend to do is difficult – to eulogize in prose the virtue of a man. The greatest proof is this: those who concern themselves with philosophy venture to speak on many other subjects of every kind, but none of them has ever attempted to write about such things.

Eulogies of good men have been the province of poetry, he goes on to say, but a prose writer should not be afraid to rival the poets in this endeavor (8–11). Whether or not Isocrates was in fact the first to compose a eulogy of this kind, we have good evidence that this brand of eulogy rose swiftly to popularity: Aristotle is cited as saying that, after Xenophon's son Gryllus died on the battlefield (in 362 BCE), "innumerable (μυρίοι) authors, who wrote at least in part to gratify his father, composed epitaphs and encomia for Gryllus";[17] and Aulus Gellius (10.18) reports that when Mausolus, the ruler of Caria, died in 353 BCE, Theopompus, Theodectes, and Naucrates competed with eulogies written in his honor.[18] Given that all these speeches were written upon the death of a "worthy" individual, it seems reasonable to suggest that this branch of the encomiastic genre was in part fostered by the *epitaphios*: the praise that the *epitaphios* conferred upon the dead Athenian warriors as a group (and, indeed, on Athens as a whole) is now bestowed upon a single individual. This kind of encomium, of course, has an aristocratic flavor that is at odds with the democratic ethos of the *epitaphios*. As Russell and Wilson suggest, "It is clear, however, that, even in the free *poleis* of the fourth century, the taste for personal encomium was growing. This taste was naturally much strengthened by the increasing monarchical tendencies of political life."[19] Not surprisingly, we find explicit references in Isocrates'

---

[16] Many scholars have accepted Isocrates' claim (e.g. Burgess 1902: 115, Fraustadt 1909: 57–60, Marrou [1956]/1964: 121, Buchheit 1960: 64–75, Russell and Wilson 1981: xv, Poulakos 1987: 318; for further bibliography on this topic, see Owen 1983: 20 n. 36). Cf. J. Martin 1974: 188, who identifies the eulogy of Alcibiades in Isocrates' *De Bigis* (written in the early 390s) as the first extant encomium on a contemporary person (cf. Owen 1983: 20–1). Consider also the following candidates: (1) Stesimbrotus of Thasos' Περὶ Θεμιστοκλέους καὶ Θουκιδίδου καὶ Περικλέους, which praises Cimon at the same time as it criticizes Themistocles and Pericles (*FGrH* 107F1–11); (2) Polycrates' eulogy of Thrasybulus, which is mentioned by Aristotle at *Rhetoric* 1401a34–6 and the scholiast on that passage (see Radermacher 1951: 132); (3) Xenophon's eulogy of Cyrus at *Anabasis* 1.9. Note also Plutarch (*Cons. ad Apoll.* 118e–f), who attributes a long paragraph in praise of Pericles to Protagoras. In order to resolve this scholarly dispute, agreement as to what constitutes an encomium would have to be reached.

[17] Diogenes Laertius 2.55.

[18] Note also the Isocratean eulogies that postdated the *Evagoras*: 3.29–47 (on Nicocles), 9.3–5 (on Archidamas), and 15.101–139 (on Timotheus).

[19] Russell and Wilson 1981: xvi. Note that both of the extant speeches from this branch of the encomium emphasize the panhellenism of the kings whom they praise. In the *Eva-*

Evagoras to the archaic eulogies of tyrants and other "worthy" men written by poets such as Pindar.[20] Like these poetic models, this kind of encomium is directly concerned with contemporary political life.

We move, now, to a branch of the encomium that I call "pure non-occasional encomia." This category comprises eulogies that do not imitate or interact with an "occasional" speech; written by sophists and other intellectuals, these encomia circulated primarily by readings at (relatively) small gatherings. The "pure non-occasional encomia" can be divided into two groups: the serious and the "paradoxical." Examples of the former are eulogies for mythological heroes (such as Prodicus' encomium of Heracles) and for gods (such as the speeches in praise of Eros in Plato's *Symposium*). One might also put in this category the encomium written for a beloved boy and delivered in sympotic contexts, such as pseudo-Demosthenes' *Erotic Essay*.[21]

The "paradoxical" encomium, on the other hand, was a eulogy for a person or thing that was generally held to be unpraiseworthy if not despicable.[22] This kind of encomium seems to have originated in the late fifth century and was especially popular in the fourth. Extant examples of the paradoxical encomium are Gorgias' *Encomium of Helen*, Isocrates' *Busiris* and *Helen*, and the praise of the non-lover attributed to Lysias in Plato's *Phaedrus*. Ancient sources testify that many other such eulogies were composed during this period. Athenaeus, for example, reports several encomia for courtesans: the sophist Alcidamas, a pupil of Gorgias, wrote in praise of Nais, and the orator Cephalus eulogized Lagis.[23] Alcidamas is also said to have written an encomium on death,[24] and the Athenian rhetorician Polycrates composed encomia on infamous mythological figures such as Busiris and Clytemnestra, as well as on mundanities such as pots, pebbles, and mice.[25] The sophist Lycophron, Aristotle tells

---

goras, Isocrates represents the Cyprian monarch as "the champion of Greek areté and Greek character on the most easterly outpost of Hellenism against the Asiatic power of Persia" (Jaeger 1944: 86). And Xenophon dwells on the "philhellenism" of the Spartan king Agesilaus and his manifold battles against the Persians on behalf of Greece (see, e.g., *Agesilaus* 7.4–7).

[20] Race 1987 details Isocrates' use of Pindaric *topoi*.

[21] Note also the erotic eulogies described in Plato's *Lysis* (204d). These prose encomia were clearly derivative from the poetic eulogies known as *paidika* (on this genre of poetry, see Gentili [1985]/1988: 113 and Kurke 1990: 86–8).

[22] For discussions of this kind of eulogy, see Burgess 1902: 157–66, and Pease 1926.

[23] Athenaeus 13 592c.

[24] Cicero, *Tusc.* 1.48.116.

[25] Busiris: Isocrates, *Busiris* 4, and Quintilian, *Inst.* 2.17.4; Clytemnestra: Quintilian, *Inst.* 2.17.4; pots and pebbles: Alexander, son of Numenius, Περὶ ῥητορ. ἀφορμῶν, in Spengel 1853.III: 3 (see also Russell and Wilson 1981: xxiv–xxv); mice: Aristotle, *Rhet.* 1401a13–15, 1401b15–16.

us, composed a eulogy for the lyre,[26] and Zoilus, an orator who studied under Polycrates, wrote an encomium on Polyphemus.[27] Finally, Isocrates mentions encomia composed for bumblebees and salt,[28] and Aristotle refers to eulogies of dogs, words, Hermes, and Paris.[29]

Minus the erotic eulogy and the parodic compositions of Plato (which will be discussed below), "pure non-occasional encomia" are generally identified as "display-pieces" composed by sophists or teachers of rhetoric. As Kennedy has indicated, however, these compositions were not merely "rhetorical displays of ornamentation." To be sure, they were in part designed as show-pieces to attract pupils and followers; but they also functioned as models or "lessons in method" within the context of the "higher education" that was on offer at Athens.[30] As remote as they may seem from political discourse, then, the non-occasional encomia played a vital role in teaching students of rhetoric to manipulate the discourse of praise and blame in public fora. When Cicero says that Gorgias "wrote encomia and invectives because he considered it the peculiar function of the orator to magnify a thing by praising it and to diminish it again by censuring it" (*Brutus* 12.47), we are alerted to the direct connection between the sophistic show-pieces and the political rhetoric of their pupils. Thus Protagoras is said by Eudoxus to have "taught his pupils to praise and blame the same thing" (DK 80 A21). And note that Prodicus distinguished between "esteem" (εὐδοκιμεῖν) and "praise" (ἐπαινεῖσθαι) on the ground that the former is heartfelt and the latter a eulogy in words which belies a speaker's true beliefs.[31] These reports suggest that the discourse of praise and censure was a central part of the teaching of the early sophists; we can infer that the later teachers of rhetoric composed "non-occasional" eulogies for the same purpose.

Clearly, both serious and paradoxical encomia could be put to use in an educational context. But why the penchant for paradox? To answer this question we need to move beyond the pedagogical function of the paradoxical encomium and to focus instead on its peculiar use of praise. This kind of encomium is a sort of parody of serious or orthodox uses of

[26] DK 83.6 (= Aristotle, *Soph. El.* 15.174b)

[27] Scholium on Ps.-Plato, *Hipparchus* 229d (see Radermacher 1951: 200). Zoilus' encomium for the people of Tenedos, which Strabo quotes from (6.271), may also have been "paradoxical."

[28] *Helen* 12; cf. Plato, *Symp.* 177b, where Eryximachus alludes to the encomium on salt.

[29] Dogs, Hermes, words: *Rhet.* 1401a13–25; Paris: *Rhet.* 1401b20–3, cf. 1398a22. Some scholars attribute the encomium of Paris to Polycrates (see Fraustadt 1909: 59); cf. Blass 1962.II: 371, who suggests that this eulogy may have been written by Theodectes (to whom the Suda ascribes an encomium of Paris).

[30] Kennedy 1963: 167–73; so also Cole 1991: ch. 5.

[31] If the evidence of Plato's *Protagoras* (337b) is sound.

praise. Or, to be more precise, the paradoxical encomium is parasitic upon the serious encomium: its mockery and paradoxes operate precisely by virtue of their deviance from serious praise. The paradoxical encomium must therefore be interpreted in relation to serious or official genres of praise rather than viewed as an isolated and inconsequential literary phenomenon. As Rosalie Colie says in her fine study of the "epidemic" of paradoxical discourse in the Renaissance,

> one element common to all these kinds of paradox is their exploitation of the fact of relative, or competing, value systems. The paradox is always somehow involved in dialectic: challenging some orthodoxy, the paradox is an oblique criticism of absolute judgment or absolute convention.[32]

The paradoxical encomia, in short, implicitly assert the relativity of all values. For to suggest that any object, no matter how base, can be exalted by an artful manipulation of rhetoric is to suggest that there is no absolute standard for the proper conferral of praise. The parody involved in the paradoxical encomium, then, does not undermine the discourse of praise *per se*; rather, it exposes the contingency of the value systems that regulate the orthodox use of praise. In fact, the discourse of praise is exalted even as the traditional objects of praise are called into question. To successfully call a bad or paltry thing good is to exhibit the role that rhetoric plays in creating and dismantling "orthodox" beliefs and values. The paradoxical encomium thus had a special relevance for would-be politicians studying to learn the art of rhetoric: silly as these encomia may seem, they are peculiarly well-suited to the study and practice of political oratory.

As this survey has shown, prose encomia came in a number of different varieties in the classical period, each of which had a different orientation to the social and political life of the city. This genre of rhetoric had a very wide circulation, reaching the uneducated public as well as the cultured elite. As I have suggested, in spite of their different audiences, the occasional and the non-occasional eulogies interacted in important ways. On the one hand, the occasional encomium provides a model for the writers of non-occasional encomia to imitate or parody. But, at the same time, the non-occasional encomia could serve to instruct students in how to compose a speech of praise for delivery at a public and/or political "occasion."

It must be emphasized that it is the very simplicity of the discourse of praise that allows it such a broad range of habitation. For underlying all of the genres of eulogy is a basic binary scheme: what is praised is good (without, or with very few qualifications), and what is contrary to this is

[32] Colie 1966: 10.

bad. The simplicity of this scheme, in fact, is what makes the genre so formulaic. Certainly the writers of the fourth century had little difficulty in systematizing the genre.[33] Isocrates seems to have been the first to lay down the rules in his *Busiris*. First and foremost, he says, "it is necessary for those who wish to eulogize a person to represent him as possessing a greater number of good qualities than he actually possesses . . ." (4). Both Aristotle and the author of the *Rhetorica ad Alexandrum* echo this principle in their discussions of laudatory writing, labelling it (innocuously) "amplification" (αὔξησις).[34] Isocrates' eulogy of Busiris also illustrates the "good qualities" that should be attributed to a subject of praise: famous and/or noble ancestors (10), outstanding achievements (11–23 and passim), and the possession of virtues such as courage, wisdom, piety, temperance, and justice (11–29).[35] In addition, Isocrates explicates the most essential techniques of the genre. In sections 30–5, he stresses the importance of using "probable" and "credible" material; since the facts are a matter of dispute, he says, the successful eulogist proceeds by "reasoning from what is probable" (ἐκ τῶν εἰκότων σκοπούμενος, 35). And in sections 7–8, Isocrates gives Polycrates a lesson in the all-important trope of σύγκρισις or "comparison," which elevates and exalts the subject by juxtaposing it to a comparandum that is inferior if not base.[36] To be sure, not every prose eulogy includes every one of these *topoi*, but basic to all of them is the amplification of the laudandum to the status of extraordinary goodness and/or nobility; any material that serves this purpose is included, any that doesn't is occluded.

The genre of the prose encomium, in sum, permeated many areas of Athenian life in the late fifth and fourth centuries. Delivered at funerals, festivals, symposia, in the schools, in private residences, and at other in-

[33] As Russell and Wilson 1981: xiv observe, the encomium was rapidly systematized by the school of sophistic rhetoric. The rules for composing encomia were explicated as early as Isocrates' *Busiris*. Aristotle's *Rhetoric* (1366a23–1368a37) and the *Rhetorica ad Alexandrum* (1425b36–1426b22) offer even more detailed and technical outlines of the "system."

[34] E.g., Aristotle, *Rhet.* 1368a22–3, 26–9; *Rhetorica ad Alexandrum* 1425b36–40. That exaggeration and distortion is the norm in encomiastic discourse can be readily glimpsed if one compares Xenophon's rather critical handling of Agesilaus in the *Hellenica* to his eulogistic *Agesilaus*, or Euripides' contradictory treatment of Capaneus in the *Supplices*: the "hubristic" Capaneus conjured at lines 496–9 is praised less than four hundred lines later in the funeral oration of Adrastus as a model of temperance, loyalty, and good faith (857–871). Collard 1972: 44 notes that Adrastus' funeral oration is designed not to document the particularities of the dead men but rather to "illustrate a wide range of social and civic virtues acquirable by any man if he schools himself to them."

[35] Isocrates places special emphasis on wisdom and piety in the *Busiris*, but courage, justice, and temperance are given due stress by Aristotle and the author of the *Rhetorica ad Alexandrum*, and are generally found in extant encomiastic speeches.

[36] Aristotle (*Rhet.* 1368a19–26) and the author of the *Rhetorica ad Alexandrum* (1441a27–32) also endorse the technique of "comparison" (σύγκρισις), and give illustrations of how it should be used.

tellectual gatherings, the encomium involved at core a conferral of value – a statement of who or what is good (and bad). In addition to catering to the aesthetic sensibilities of the Athenians, it played an important role in the schooling of future civic leaders and politicians, and was regularly harnessed in the construction and reinforcement of Athenian ideology.

In analyzing the scope and impact of the prose eulogy, finally, we must not ignore its interaction with the discourse of praise that is not packaged in a formal speech or composition. When a speaker in an assembly, a lawcourt, or any other public context uses the language of praise – a phenomenon which is abundantly attested in Herodotus, Thucydides, Aristophanes, and the orators – he is not delivering a formal encomium; yet his informal use of praise has a great deal in common with the formal speeches of praise that we have been examining. To cite but one example, the speech of the Athenians at Plataea in Herodotus 9.27 – which is an informal enunciation of (self-) praise in a political context – finds direct parallels in the formal, "epideictic" genre of the funeral oration.[37] Although Aristotle and Theophrastus segregated the discourse of eulogy and invective from the practical and political rhetoric of the lawcourts and assemblies,[38] it is clear that praise and blame pervaded these and other public fora in classical Athens.[39]

Plato shows a keen eye for the "informal" enunciation of praise in the practical and political spheres. Consider, for example, the following vignette from the *Phaedrus*. At 260b–c, Socrates describes a scene in which person A knows that person B thinks that a horse is the tame animal that has the longest ears. Person A, who also doesn't know what a horse is, seeks to persuade person B to buy a donkey by "composing a speech of praise for the ass, though calling it a horse, saying that it is the most valuable animal to possess both at home and at war, useful as a mount in battle, capable of carrying supplies, and beneficial for many other purposes." Both Socrates and Phaedrus agree that this scenario is γελοῖον (260c), which conjures up the paradoxical branch of the encomium. But this is no epideictic show-piece, since the mock encomium is placed in the context of a business transaction in which one person tries to get the other

---

[37] As Loraux [1981]/1986: 65 points out.

[38] As Quintilian observes (*Inst.* 3.7.1–3).

[39] The practical/political use of praise is ubiquitous in Aristophanes, Thucydides, and the Attic orators. Note that Aristotle seems to have recognized his error in segregating praise discourse from practical and political rhetoric, for he says at *Rhetoric* 1367b37–1368a9 that "the discourse of praise and advice-giving have a common aspect; for those things which you advise by way of deliberative rhetoric become encomia by way of a change in discourse ... So that, when you wish to praise something, consider what you would advise, and when you wish to offer advice, consider what you would praise."

to buy an ass.[40] Person A, in short, uses praise to sell the donkey, capitalizing on his knowledge of what person B thinks a horse is. Having described this private negotiation, Socrates proceeds to outline its analogue in the public sphere. This occurs, Socrates says, when an ignorant orator addressing an equally ignorant populace proceeds "not by praising a miserable donkey as being really a horse but by praising something bad as being really good." "Having studied the opinions of the multitude," this kind of orator "persuades them to do what is evil instead of what is good" (260c). While the latter situation is "terrible" rather than "ridiculous," both involve the persuasion of an ignorant audience by means of false praise, and in both cases the person who enunciates the praise stands to gain something thereby. Here, Plato suggests that encomiastic discourse plays a vital role in the world of *praxis* and, indeed, of exchange: the expedient use of praise can pay dividends in the form of money, honor, or power. It should go without saying that Plato considered this to be the rule rather than the exception in Athenian political transactions.

Plato approaches the practical and political impact of praise from a very different angle in the *Republic*. At 492a–b, Socrates suggests that the language of praise and censure is the most effective tool for "educating and molding" people, be they young or old, male or female.[41] This occurs, he explains,

when the multitude, sitting together at the assemblies or in the lawcourts or in theatres or camps or any other public gathering, with a great uproar censure some of the things that are said or done and praise others, both in an excessive way, by shouting and clapping – and, wherever they are, the rocks and the region send back an echo, doubling the volume of the praise and the censure. In such a situation, what state of heart, as the saying goes, will a young person possess? What sort of private education will hold out against this – who will not be overwhelmed and swept away, carried by the current of such praise and censure wherever it may lead, and thus be brought to say that those same things are good and evil which the crowd has pronounced so, and even to do what they do and be such as they are? (492b–c)

Here, Plato focusses on the expression of praise and censure by the public as a whole, and the effect that this torrent of praise and blame has on the individual. The stakes here are very great, since it is no less than the basic values of the citizens and the city that are being promulgated in these public gatherings. It is precisely this extraordinary power of public praise,

---

[40] Note that Plato legislates against using praise (ἔπαινος) in the sphere of business at *Laws* 917b–c.

[41] Cf. *Protagoras* 326a, where Protagoras reports that "many ... praises and encomia of the great men of old" are taught to children in primary schools "so that the child will emulate and imitate them and long to become a man such as those."

in fact, that Plato chooses to harness in the *Laws*, where the discourse of praise and blame is subject to strict control and is used to regulate those areas of the citizens' lives that cannot be controlled by law.[42]

In these and other passages, Plato deals with the "informal" use of praise as it is manifested in public and in private life. As we will see, his critiques of the "formal" eulogies that belong to the epideictic genre echo and expand his attacks on "informal" praise. This parallelism indicates that Plato sees a fundamental continuity between the formal or "epideictic" encomia and the praise that is so often used in practical and political affairs – that his targeting of one or another branch of the prose encomium is grounded in a philosophic critique of praise discourse in general.

II

Plato's critique of the encomiastic genre, then, was not simply a literary polemic. But what exactly is at stake in his repeated attacks on the discourse of praise? Plato targets the encomiastic genre in three separate dialogues: the *Lysis*, the *Menexenus*, and the *Symposium*. In each of these dialogues, Plato not only criticizes a given use of praise, but he invites the reader to juxtapose the language of eulogy with the discourse of the philosopher. Plato's opposition to eulogy, in short, is part and parcel of his attempt to both define and legitimize philosophy.

Many studies have been devoted to Plato's handling of the funeral oration in the *Menexenus*.[43] Loraux, for example, has persuasively argued that Plato set out to parody and criticize the *epitaphios* and its celebration of Athenian ideology.[44] Rather than go over the ground that Loraux and others have covered so thoroughly, I will confine myself to a few observations about this text. It is at the opening of the dialogue that Plato explicates the nature of the *epitaphios* and the impact that this kind of eulogy had on the Athenian people. As Socrates says at 234c–235b,

Indeed, Menexenus, to die in battle appears to be a fine thing in many ways. For the dead man gets a noble and magnificent funeral even though he happens to be poor, and even if he is base he receives a eulogy which is spoken by men who are wise and who do not utter random praises but have prepared their speeches a long time before. These men deliver eulogies so beautifully that, by ascribing to each in-

---

[42] See, e.g., 730b–c , 801e–802a, 822d–823a (esp. e8–a1), 829c–e. Note also Callicles' assertion of the power of public praise and censure at *Gorg.* 483b–c.

[43] Kennedy 1963: 158–64 nn. 50–6, gives a useful survey of the scholarship on the subject. More recently, see Vlastos [1964]/1981: 188–201, M. Henderson 1975, and Loraux [1981]/ 1986: 264–74, 311–27 and passim; cf. Kahn 1963. For discussions of the genre of the funeral oration, see Ziolkowski 1981, Loraux [1981]/1986, and Thomas 1989: ch. 4.

[44] Loraux [1981]/1986: 264–74, 311–27 and passim.

dividual both what he has and what he does not have, and achieving such beautiful variety in their language, they bewitch our souls. And when they eulogize the city in every possible way and praise those who have died in battle and all of the ancestors who lived before us and we ourselves who are still living, I myself am greatly ennobled by their praise, Menexenus, and on each occasion I am transfixed as I listen and am charmed, so that I instantly come to believe that I have become greater and nobler and more beautiful.

In this short passage, Socrates slyly registers a number of criticisms of the *epitaphios*. In particular, he indicates that orators who are considered to be wise mix the false in with the true, that the eulogy/eulogist is unable to distinguish between the good men and the base, and that the speech so puffs up the Athenians that they imagine themselves to be better than they really are. What mode of discourse could be more alien to that of Socrates – the man who devoted himself to truth, who spent his entire life investigating human virtue and vice, who took every opportunity to deflate the Athenians and to expose their false conceit of knowledge? As Loraux suggests, "delivered to all equally, this oration, as a political speech, knows no distinctions, and thus sets itself in opposition to Socratic speech, which is concerned wholly and entirely with difference and singularity."[45] The self-praise of the Athenians, then, is diametrically opposed to Socrates' disavowal of knowledge and his unfinished search for virtue.

The *Lysis* addresses itself to a branch of the encomiastic genre very different from that of the *epitaphios*, namely, the eulogy for a beloved boy delivered at symposia and other small gatherings. But while the *Lysis* deals with a non-occasional and personalized genre of eulogy which is quite different from the public and official discourse of the *epitaphios*, it nonetheless makes explicit what was implicit in the *Menexenus*: the fundamental antinomy between encomiastic rhetoric and Socratic discourse. Whether it is bestowed upon one individual or the city as a whole, the discourse of praise is antithetical to the project of the philosopher.

At the opening of the *Lysis*, two young men – Ctesippus and Hippothales – accost Socrates and invite him to visit a wrestling school where some good-looking boys are attending a festival of Hermes.[46] Socrates soon learns that Hippothales is in love with a boy named Lysis. Indeed, as Ctesippus informs Socrates, Hippothales has "deluged" his companions with "poems and prose speeches" (τὰ ποιήματα ... καὶ συγγράμματα) for the young Lysis (204d). Socrates asks Hippothales to "display" (ἐπίδειξαι) these compositions and to demonstrate that he knows "what is proper for

[45] Loraux [1981]/1986: 315.
[46] On the opening of the *Lysis*, see A. Taylor 1949: 65–6, Friedländer [1957]/1964: 92–3, Hoerber 1959: 15-21; for a more extended treatment, see Bolotin 1979: 69–82, who shows how Socrates systematically exposes the selfishness of Hippothales' love.

a lover to say of his beloved either to his face or to others" (204e–205a). But he qualifies this request in an important way: he does not want to hear the actual verses but rather to learn their "content" (διάνοια). He wishes to discover from Hippothales, as he puts it, "in what way you deal with your beloved" (205b). Socrates, in short, is concerned with the ethical and pedagogical rather than the aesthetic quality of the compositions.

The scornful Ctesippus gives Socrates the information he seeks. Hippothales' compositions have nothing personal (ἴδιον) to say about Lysis: all he talks about are Lysis' ancestors, their wealth, the horses they owned, and their victories in the panhellenic contests (205b–c). Indeed, Hippothales even proclaims that Lysis' forefather, who was descended from Zeus, played host to his "kinsman" Heracles (205c–d). This is the stuff that eulogies are made of, and Socrates recognizes their encomiastic character immediately: "my ridiculous Hippothales, are you composing and singing an encomium (ἐγκώμιον) for yourself before you have achieved a victory?" (205d). When Hippothales denies that he has written these encomia "for himself," Socrates maintains that his eulogies for Lysis are in fact designed for self-glorification, since the compositions will commemorate Hippothales' own victory should he triumph over the boy. But the trouble does not end here. For Socrates adds that Hippothales' encomia are filling Lysis with self-conceit (206a). The compositions are actually damaging the boy and, by making him more proud, cheating the slighted lover of his prize (206b). Though the encomia may appear to exalt both the author and his beloved, they actually serve to harm them both.

Hippothales begs Socrates for guidance, and Socrates agrees to demonstrate in an actual conversation with the boy "what one must say to him instead of those things" that Hippothales has composed (206c). Socrates' method of handling the young is thus directly juxtaposed with the lover's encomiastic approach.[47] Socrates proceeds to engage Lysis in a conversation about friendship. He refutes Lysis' ideas on this subject and then hammers home the point of the lesson:

Is it possible, Lysis, for a person to have a high notion of himself in matters of which he does not yet have any notion? ... For you cannot be highminded if you are still mindless. (210d)

Lysis, chastened by Socrates' elenctic technique, readily confesses his ignorance. And at this crucial juncture, Socrates turns to address the un-

---

[47] Tecuşan 1990: 243 suggests that Socrates' conversation with the youths in the *Lysis* is "an example of good courtesy, set in contrast to Hippothales' sympotic fashion of wooing." As I see it, the contrast centers on discourse (and its effects), not on manners.

named person to whom he is relating the entire dialogue (i.e. the reader).
"When I heard him answer this," Socrates says,

> I looked at Hippothales and almost made a mistake. For it occurred to me to say:
> "This is the way, Hippothales, to converse with your beloved, humbling and di-
> minishing him rather than puffing him up and pampering him, as you did." (210e)

The moral is thus made explicit: Socrates' elenctic method is diametrically
opposed to the language of the encomium. It does not aim at gratification
or glory, nor does it promulgate falsehoods that instil in the auditor
a proud and stubborn ignorance. On the contrary, it encourages self-
knowledge in the boy by robbing him of his false conceits.

Plato's critique of the erotic encomium, however, is not simply a matter
of the style, the content, and the effects of this kind of discourse. For
consider the social context of this kind of speech. The encomia described
in the *Lysis* are composed by an older male for the boy he loves. As
Dover has shown, the erotic relationship between an older and a younger
male in the aristocratic circles of ancient Athens included a prominent
pedagogical aspect.[48] This is made explicit in Pausanias' speech in Plato's
Symposium (184b-e): the lover gives the boy practical, ethical, and intellectual guidance in exchange for the "gratification" that he seeks from
his beloved.[49] What Plato indicates in the *Lysis* is that a non-philosophical lover cannot in fact play the role of a true educator. For desire drives
this kind of lover to pursue his own interests instead of the boy's. Hippothales resorts to encomia, Plato suggests, precisely because he hopes that
flattering his beloved will induce him to pay back the favor. Of course,
Hippothales is not consciously proposing this exchange; indeed he seems
quite ignorant of what is at stake. The reader, however, is clearly meant
to recognize the folly of Hippothales' erotic discourse: for his flattering
encomia emerge as a sort of payment offered for the things he craves.
Hippothales' "intellectual" offerings and the sexual favors that he wants
in return are both reduced to the level of commodities: so far from offering an education in virtue, Hippothales' "pedagogy" would corrupt both
him and his beloved by turning their relationship into a commercial
transaction.

In the *Lysis*, of course, it is only in the opening scene that Plato cri-

---

[48] Dover 1980: 4–5. Note that in extant erotic eulogies, the lover both praises and counsels
the boy; as Ps.-Demosthenes puts it in the *Erotic Essay* (2), his speech will "on the one
hand, praise the lad and, on the other, counsel him concerning his education and choice of
life." The first two speeches in the *Phaedrus*, though deviating from the standard erotic
eulogy (the first being paradoxical and the second tending towards blame rather than
praise), both give a good deal of advice to the boy.

[49] As Dover 1964 demonstrates, Aeschines' portrayal of the homoerotic practices of upper-
class Athenians in *Against Timarchus* is in fundamental accord with that of Pausanias.

tiques the lover's encomia. But this scene has important ramifications for the rest of the dialogue. For, by setting up encomiastic discourse as a foil for Socratic discourse, Plato asks us to analyze not only what Socrates says, but how and to whom he says it and what sort of effect it produces on its audience. The dialogue, then, does not simply illustrate the Socratic method by showing the philosopher in discussion. For the method is also demarcated by way of its opposition to another brand of "discourse offered to the young." By creating this opposition, Plato stakes out the territory of philosophic language; he both defines and defends this new mode of discourse.

III

It is in the *Symposium* that we find Plato's most sustained and complex treatment of encomiastic discourse. For, in this dialogue, Plato not only illustrates and comments on the vices that inhere in the encomiastic genre, but he juxtaposes Socrates' ironic "praises" of his interlocutors with traditional encomiastic discourse, thus inviting the reader to explore the relation between Socratic irony and the rhetoric of eulogy. In addition, the *Symposium* exhibits two untraditional "encomia" – Socrates' eulogy for Eros and Alcibiades' for Socrates – that illustrate and investigate the ontological underpinnings of the rhetoric of praise. The *Symposium*, then, attacks the encomium in a variety of ways: by parody and explicit criticism, by ironic gesture and generic transgression. But perhaps the most distinctive feature of this critique is that Plato allows Socrates to appropriate the discourse of eulogy, thus blurring the sharp contrast between philosophical and encomiastic discourse that was drawn in the *Menexenus* and *Lysis*.

I begin this investigation of praise discourse in the *Symposium* by highlighting some of the overt criticisms that Plato levels against the encomium. Note, first of all, that the dialogue invites the reader to locate the speeches on Eros within a specific branch of the encomiastic genre. For Plato explicitly mentions the playful encomia of "sophists" such as Prodicus (who eulogized Heracles) and "wise men"[50] such as the one who wrote on salt (177b).[51] Here, Plato conjures up that branch of the enco-

---

[50] As Bury 1932: 19 and Dover 1980: 88 note, the "wise man" in question is generally agreed to be Polycrates, an Athenian teacher of rhetoric.

[51] Also mentioned are poetical hymns for the gods and paeans (177a), which occupy a branch of literature quite different from that of the encomiastic pieces of the sophists and teachers of rhetoric. See Harvey 1955 for a discussion of ancient conceptions of the "encomium" and the "hymn." Plato himself says that the "hymn" is characterized by "prayers directed to the gods" (*Laws* 700b); the speeches in the *Symposium*, however, offer praise rather than prayers (cf. Socrates' second speech in the *Phaedrus*, which contains

miastic genre constituted by "pure non-occasional eulogies": the eulogies
written by sophists and teachers of rhetoric as display-pieces and tools of
pedagogy. By targeting this branch of the genre, Plato attacks the expedient manipulation of the rhetoric of praise that was being taught to
aspiring politicians in democratic Athens.

How do the speeches in the *Symposium* reflect the genre and what is
Plato's response to their generic features? One of the most prominent
features of the encomia of the fifth and fourth centuries is the agonistic
stance adopted by their authors.[52] In the *Symposium*, the contest of words
is initiated when Phaedrus insists on the novelty and importance of his
theme; the very act of recalling the writers who have failed to eulogize
Eros signals the competitive nature of the enterprise.[53] The speakers who
come after Phaedrus – Pausanias, Eryximachus, Aristophanes, and Agathon – follow suit. Each begins his speech by addressing himself to the
speech(es) which preceded his; each attempts to offer a more adequate
and beautiful encomium. Not surprisingly, the challenge increases with
the number of contestants: as Eryximachus indicates at 193e, were Agathon and Socrates not so clever, they might be "at a loss for words" after
"the many and various things that have been said." The result is a series
of attempts to achieve originality within determinate generic boundaries –
to manipulate stock techniques ("amplification" and "comparison") and
material (the ancestry, accomplishments, and virtues of the subject), and
yet produce something superior to the other offerings.

Socrates foregrounds this agonistic feature of the genre by jabbing at
the verbal "competition." As he says to Eryximachus at 194a, for example, "you have competed beautifully (καλῶς ... ἠγώνισαι), Eryximachus;
but if you were in my present position – or rather in the one I shall be in
when Agathon has also spoken – you too would be in great fear ..."
When Socrates ironically confesses his fear of performing badly (194a;
198a–199b) and so becoming a "laughingstock" (199b), his pretense ex-

---

a number of hymnic features). On the generic features of the hymn, see Bundy 1972, Janko
1981, and Race 1982. Why does Plato mention hymns in the *Symposium*? Probably because the subject matter of his eulogies is a god. Given that Plato explicitly identifies the
prose eulogies of the sophists and teachers of rhetoric (and that his own eulogists all speak
in prose), these must be seen as his primary target.

[52] Examples of the agonistic stance adopted by encomiasts: Isocrates, *Busiris* 4–6, *Helen* 14–
15, *Evagoras* 8–11, 36; Plato, *Menexenus* 239b–c. Loraux [1981]/1986: 241 and passim
discusses the agonistic aspect of the funeral oration. Cf. Griffith 1990, who argues that
Greek poetry from its very beginnings had a prominent agonistic component.

[53] Cf. Phaedrus' instigation of a competition between Lysias and Socrates in the *Phaedrus*
(235d, 257c). For a fascinating investigation of Phaedrus' challenge to Socrates in its literary and its cultural context, focussing in particular on Phaedrus' claim that he will set
up statues of himself and Socrates in Delphi and/or Olympia (235d–236b), see Morgan
1994.

poses the real anxieties felt by his fellow encomiasts. The encomiastic genre, Socrates suggests, is a contest with winners and losers – a contest where the language of commendation is a vehicle for the author's pursuit of glory.

Extant prose encomia from the fifth and fourth centuries exhibit another regular feature: a polished and often poetic style that calls attention to the author's literary prowess. The author celebrates himself as much as his subject matter by his ostentatious use of stylistic devices (most especially that of amplification, which gives the speech a "totalizing" look). Socrates makes fun of this self-conscious style in his hyperbolic response to Agathon's καλόν ... καὶ παντοδαπὸν λόγον (198b2): so "stunned" (ἐξεπλάγη, 198b5) was he by the beauty of the words and phrases that he seriously considered running away out of shame (198b–c). He is "at a loss" (198a7), and lays claim to a gripping panic: "I feared that Agathon would end by sending the head of Gorgias – clever at speaking in speeches – against my speech and thus turn me to stone by striking me dumb" (198c). Agathon's speech, in short, was a stylistic *tour de force* designed to take the listeners' breath away – to preempt all discourse by striking people dumb.

A genre's emphasis on style necessarily affects its content. As we have seen, Isocrates admitted quite frankly in his *Busiris* (4) that "it is necessary for those who wish to eulogize a person to represent him as possessing a greater number of good qualities than he actually possesses ..." This aspect of the genre, which is abundantly represented in the *Symposium*,[54] left it especially vulnerable to Plato's attack. As Socrates says at 198d–e,

> For I in my stupidity thought that one should speak the truth about whatever is eulogized ... And I was quite proud, thinking that I would speak well, since I knew the truth about praising any given thing. But now, as it seems, to praise something well is not this [i.e. telling the truth] but rather ascribing to the subject the greatest and most beautiful qualities, whether these things are true or not. If they are false, it does not matter. For it was proposed, as it seems, that each of us would seem to eulogize Eros, not that we would actually eulogize him.

Socrates had initially embraced the encomiastic enterprise because he hoped that each of the speakers had some knowledge about Eros – Eryximachus, Phaedrus, Pausanias, and Agathon because they were involved

---

[54] For example, the speakers contradict one another with little concern for accuracy: if Phaedrus can suggest that Eros is the oldest of the deities because he is the most beneficent (178b–c), Agathon can counter that Eros, the most beautiful god, must necessarily be the youngest (195a). And numerous inconsistencies can be found even within individual speeches. After dilating on Eros' "delicacy" (195c–d), "softness" (195e, 196a), and fondness for flowers and scents (196b), for instance, Agathon insists on his "temperance" and "manly courage" (196c–d). Agathon's mania for amplification well illustrates the tendency towards untruth that inheres in this rhetorical device.

in love affairs, and Aristophanes because Aphrodite was so central to his profession as comic poet (177e). Socrates is thus disappointed when the encomia evince a rhetorical technique – a τρόπον τοῦ ἐπαίνου (199a4) – that will have no truck with truth.

A lie, of course, must have some substance. Encomiastic discourse by definition offers value judgments and prescriptions. This aspect of the encomium was, in Plato's eyes, especially pernicious, for the manipulation of praise (and blame) had the power to indoctrinate the people most in need of instruction – "the ignorant" (199a). Plato underlines the ideological stakes for which the encomiasts are playing in a number of passages. Take, for example, the way in which Pausanias' notion of "good" Eros is unmasked later in the dialogue. Pausanias, of course, had proclaimed that the good and "heavenly" kind of love affair is achieved when the older lover confers virtue and knowledge on the boy and receives sexual gratification in return (181c–185d). Later on, when Socrates refuses Alcibiades' offer of sexual favors in exchange for virtue and knowledge (218c–219d) – an exchange that Socrates dubs "bronze in exchange for gold" – he retrospectively rejects Pausanias' recommendation that virtue be exchanged for gratification. For Socrates' handling of Alcibiades indicates that knowledge and virtue should not be reduced to a commodity for exchange – indeed, that true virtue and knowledge *cannot* be handed over in any kind of exchange.[55]

The encomiasts create false ideologies, Plato indicates, because they have no notion of the truth. This is vividly dramatized when, in a short elenctic dialogue, Socrates refutes Agathon's contention that Eros is replete with virtue. For Agathon is forced to concede that he did not know what he was talking about: κινδυνεύω, ὦ Σώκρατες, οὐδὲν εἰδέναι ὧν τότε εἶπον (201b11–12). Here, Plato has Agathon speak for all the encomiasts.

IV

Thus far Plato's criticisms of the encomiastic genre echo his critique of rhetoric in general. But what about the most fundamental aspect of the genre: its use of praise? In order to fully comprehend the problem of praise, we must advert to the praise discourse in the *Symposium* which transgresses the boundaries of the encomiastic genre: Socrates' singular uses of praise – both in his conversation and his encomium – and Alci-

---

[55] Cf. 175d, where Socrates denies that wisdom can be transferred from one person to another "like water, which flows from the fuller into the emptier cup when you connect them with a piece of yarn." As I suggested in chapter 1, where the seduction scene is discussed in detail, Socrates does not believe that wisdom can be exchanged or handed over like material possessions.

biades' eulogy of Socrates. These untraditional expressions of praise are crucial for an understanding of Plato's response to encomiastic rhetoric.

Let me investigate first the commendation that crops up in Socrates' conversation: the overweening praise of others that goes under the heading of irony. Recent investigations of Socratic irony have centered on the philosopher's disavowal of knowledge.[56] But as least as central to Socrates' ironic technique was the extravagant praise that he so often bestowed upon his acquaintances.[57] This aspect of Socratic irony was regularly discussed by Renaissance thinkers: one of them even thought that Socrates' habit of heaping praise upon undeserving people was the origin of the mock encomium![58] Plato's Socrates tends to pour on the praise when he encounters pretentious people such as Euthyphro, Ion, and Hippias.[59] But he also makes an especially obtrusive use of this technique with his companions in the *Symposium*.

At 175e, for example, Socrates claims that his own knowledge is something "paltry and disputable as a dream" (φαύλη τις ἂν εἴη, ἢ καὶ ἀμφισβητήσιμος ὥσπερ ὄναρ οὖσα), whereas Agathon's, which "shone so brightly" when his tragedy was performed in front of "more than thirty thousand Greeks," is "brilliant and possessed of a great future" (λαμπρά τε καὶ πολλὴν ἐπίδοσιν ἔχουσα). Again, at 194a–c, Socrates remarks upon the "courage" (ἀνδρεία) and "highmindedness" (μεγαλοφροσύνη) exhibited by Agathon at the competition. Even more blatant is Socrates' hyperbolic response to Agathon's flowery encomium – an effusive enunciation containing what is probably the longest informal speech of praise delivered by Socrates in Plato's corpus (198a–c). Agathon spoke so "marvelously" (θαυμαστῶς), Socrates says in that passage, that no-one would be able to compete against him. The "beauty of the words and phrases" positively "stunned" (ἐξεπλάγη) Socrates, who feared that he would be struck dumb and turned to stone. He even considered running away out of shame, he confesses, since he knew that he could never produce anything close to this masterpiece. Socrates also uses ironic praise, of course, in his dealings with Alcibiades. When Alcibiades offers his

---

[56] See, e.g., Burge 1969, Guthrie 1971: 126–9, Vlastos [1987]/1991: ch. 1, Gooch 1987. For more wide-ranging discussions of Socratic irony, see Ribbeck 1876, Friedländer [1954]/1958: ch. 7, Booth 1974: esp. 269–76, Gourinat 1986, and Griswold 1987: esp. 76–82.

[57] According to Theophrastus (*Characters* 1.2), one of the characteristic actions of the ironic individual is "to praise to their faces people he has attacked behind their backs." Though Theophrastus' portrait of the ironist is not especially reminiscent of Socrates, his identification of insincere praise as ironic is instructive.

[58] D. Knox 1989: passim shows the pervasiveness of the notion of irony as "blame by praise or praise by blame" in medieval and, especially, Renaissance thinkers. The gentleman who derived the mock encomium from Socratic irony was Caspar Dornau (1577–1632; see Knox 1989: 105).

[59] See, e.g., *Euthyphro* 5a, *Ion* 530b–c , *Hippias Minor* 364a–b.

(allegedly) beautiful body to the philosopher, for example, Socrates warns: "you must see in me an incredible beauty – greatly superior to even your own good looks ... But be more careful, blessed man, for I may be a mere cipher who has deceived you" (218e–219a). Here, Socrates praises Alcibiades' looks even as he calls his own gifts into question.

Socrates' effusions in the *Symposium* are all too familiar to readers of Plato. But consider: in this dialogue, Socrates' ironic praises are uttered *in the context of a meditation on praise discourse*. This context demands that the reader take stock of Socrates' ironic flights rather than dismiss them as mere local color. How should we interpret Socrates' hyperbolic praise? What is the relation between this kind of praise and encomiastic discourse? And, finally, how do we distinguish the dissimulation inherent in Socrates' ironic praise from the lies of encomiastic rhetoric?

It should come as no surprise that the beneficiaries of Socrates' praises often accuse him of arrogant mockery – of using praise for the purposes of blame. When Agathon hears the comparison of his own brilliant knowledge to Socrates' paltry state of mind, for instance, he calls Socrates a ὑβριστής (175e7). Alcibiades, too, accuses Socrates of "hubris" (215b7, 219c3–5, 222a8), begging his listeners to act as judges of the "arrogance" (ὑπερηφανία, 219c6) of the philosopher. Alcibiades claims that Socrates' "ironizing" is at the root of his hubristic behavior:

For you observe that Socrates is erotically inclined towards beautiful people and is always hanging around them in a state of dazzled admiration; and, in addition, he is ignorant of everything and knows nothing ... Believe me, it doesn't matter to him at all if someone is handsome, but he looks down on this more than anyone would imagine, and the same is the case if someone is rich or has some other privilege deemed a blessing by the crowd. He considers all these possessions worthless and all of us mere nothings, I tell you, and he spends his entire life ironizing and playing games with people (εἰρωνευόμενος δὲ καὶ παίζων πάντα τὸν βίον πρὸς τοὺς ἀνθρώπους διατελεῖ). (216d–e)

Here, Alcibiades links Socrates' disavowal of knowledge with his admiration for others: both are insincere and therefore "ironic."[60] According

---

[60] Cf. Vlastos 1991: 33–42, who argues that, in calling Socrates an "ironist," Alcibiades is not accusing him of *willful or intentional* deception (the common sense of the Greek word εἰρωνεία) but rather of irony in the modern sense of the word. To be sure, *Plato wants his readers to perceive* that Socrates did not intend to deceive Alcibiades, but this does not mean that *Alcibiades is aware that Socrates was not intending to deceive.* As Vlastos himself admits (41), Alcibiades was very definitely deceived by Socrates. Alcibiades says explicitly at 222b that Socrates has "deceived" many people by pretending to be their lover (οὓς οὗτος ἐξαπατῶν ὡς ἐραστής). Since the words εἰρωνευόμενος (216e) and εἰρωνικῶς (218d) are put in Alcibiades' mouth, they must be interpreted according to his perception of Socrates. It is the shortcomings of Alcibiades' interpretation of Socrates that invite the reader to seek a different explanation of Socrates' indirection. Where Alcibiades sees intentional deception, Plato and the reader see something different from both sincerity and mendacity.

to Alcibiades, Socrates is toying with his companions: he pretends to admire and love them but actually considers them worthless. He not only looks down on the beauty and other external endowments of his associates, but he actually scorns the people themselves.[61] His admiration and praise, as it seems, are a disguise for contempt.

This contempt, as I have mentioned, is labeled "hubris." We should recall that the Athenians considered hubris an offense not against a private individual but rather against the community as a whole.[62] If Alcibiades' interpretation of Socrates' behavior is correct, his "ironizing" would be a threat to the Athenian *dēmos* – indeed to democracy itself. As Dover explains,

to establish that an act of violence was hubris rather than assault it was necessary to persuade the jury that it proceeded from a certain attitude and disposition on the part of the accused: that is to say, from a wish on his part to establish a dominant position over his victim in the eyes of the community, or from a confidence that by reason of wealth, strength or influence he could afford to laugh at equality of rights under the law and treat other people as if they were chattels at his disposal.[63]

Socrates' irony, then, at least if Agathon and Alcibiades have assessed it correctly, is a willful assertion of superiority over his fellow citizens – a subtle but unmistakable declaration of pre-eminence that defies the egalitarianism of the democracy.[64]

Is this interpretation of Socrates' irony correct? In particular, when

[61] It is crucial to grasp the difference between Diotima's claim that the lover who ascends the ladder must "become a lover of all beautiful bodies and slacken his violent love for one boy, looking down on it [i.e the violent love] and considering it a small thing" (ἑνὸς δὲ τὸ σφόδρα τοῦτο χαλάσαι καταφρονήσοντα καὶ σμικρὸν ἡγησάμενον, 210b), and Alcibiades' assertion that Socrates "considers all these possessions [i.e. beauty, wealth, etc.] worthless and *all of us mere nothings*" (ἡγεῖται δὲ πάντα ταῦτα τὰ κτήματα οὐδενὸς ἄξια καὶ ἡμᾶς οὐδὲν εἶναι, 216e). Diotima's lover scorns *his own obsessive love*; he does not feel contempt for his beloved but rather for physical beauty and the obsession that it generates. Alcibiades, by contrast, claims that Socrates scorns *the men he pretends to love*.

[62] Dover [1978]/1989: 35.

[63] Dover [1978]/1989: 35. Fisher 1990 argues along the same lines: "the essence of *hubris* is the deliberate attack on the *timē* (honour) of another. That is, it is constituted by intentional, often gratuitous action, frequently but by no means always violent, and specifically designed to inflict shame and public humiliation" (p. 126). Cf. Gagarin 1977, whose emphasis on Socrates' ascent above his mortal station through philosophy obscures the fact that what Agathon and Alcibiades are accusing Socrates of is the *arrogant assertion* of his own superiority and their inferiority – of a deliberate attempt to establish a dominant position over men who should by rights be treated as equals.

[64] Agathon and Alcibiades are probably not using the word "hubris" in its technical legal sense; as Dover [1978]/1989: 34–5 observes, accusations of "hubris" were commonly used for emotional effect in a variety of rhetorical situations. Nonetheless, the accusations of "hubris" remind the reader that Socrates was in fact judged and condemned as a threat to the Athenian *dēmos* and its egalitarian ethos.

Socrates commends or admires a person, is he simply playing a game of scornful mockery?[65] That there is some form of censure in Socrates' extravagant praise cannot be doubted. But does this censure derive, as Alcibiades suggests, from an attitude of superiority and, indeed, hostility towards his fellow human beings? Is Socrates' irony merely a clever way of getting one-up on his associates? If so, then it would be properly classified as a form of invective – the genre of rhetoric diametrically opposed to that of the encomium. As Aristotle explains in the *Rhetoric*, irony is a species of ὀλιγωρία or contempt.[66] Contemptuous actions, he says, must be distinguished from those performed for the sake of retaliation or for some other benefit.[67] For the contemptuous action is done solely for the sake of pleasure – a pleasure that derives from the thought that, as Aristotle puts it, "by treating others badly a person shows his own superiority."[68] As a species of contempt, then, irony must be linked to the discourse of invective. This is made explicit in the *Rhetorica ad Alexandrum*, which recommends irony as an ingredient for speeches of invective.[69]

Should we identify Socrates' ironic praise with the rhetoric of invective? Plato provides the answer to this question at the very opening of the dialogue. There we find Apollodorus, the devotee of Socrates who narrates the dialogue, engaging in true invective. He begins by accusing his companion Glaucon of being "more wretched than anyone" (173a). Though Glaucon asks Apollodorus not to "mock" him (μὴ σκῶπτ', 173a), the would-be Socrates only turns up the volume:

when I listen to other kinds of discourse, and especially that of you rich businessmen, I am annoyed and I pity you, my companions, because you think that you are doing something when in fact you are doing nothing. And perhaps you think that I am a failure, and I think that you think the truth. I, however, don't just *think* that you are a failure, but *know* it for sure. (173c–d)

[65] It is necessary to handle the question whether Socrates' disavowal of knowledge is insincere (and therefore "ironic" in the original sense of the word) separately from the question whether his effusive praises are insincere. Socrates' use of praise, which is the focus of this investigation, cannot be completely sincere. But this does not necessarily mean that Socrates' disclaimer of knowledge is also insincere. A full analysis of Socratic irony, of course, would have to take both of these aspects into account.
[66] Contempt is analyzed at *Rhet.* 1378b–1379b (irony is mentioned explicitly at 1379b30–1; note that Aristotle identifies hubris as one of the three genera of ὀλιγωρία). In the ethical treatises, of course, Aristotle speaks rather differently of irony, identifying it as the opposite of boastfulness: although both irony and boasting involve dissembling, the ironic individual is more commendable in that he avoids pompousness (see, e.g., *NE* 1108a, 1127b, *EE* 1233b–1234a). Since my investigation centers on ironic *praise of others* (rather than ironic *self-deprecation*), the discussions of irony in the ethical treatises are not as pertinent as the one in the *Rhetoric*.
[67] *Rhet.* 1378b23–6, 1379a33–4.
[68] *Rhet.* 1378b27–8.
[69] *Rhetorica ad Alexandrum* 1441b24–7.

I believe that Plato wanted the reader to contrast Apollodorus' abusive rhetoric not only with the speeches of praise that follow but with the language used by Apollodorus' hero and mentor, Socrates. Note, for example, the pointer that Plato puts into the mouth of Glaucon:

> You are always the same, Apollodorus. For you are always inveighing against (κακηγορεῖς) yourself and others, and you seem to actually consider all men wretched except for Socrates, beginning with yourself ... You are always raging (ἀγριαίνεις) at yourself and everyone except for Socrates. (173d)

By reproaching himself, Apollodorus succeeds in imitating Socrates' self-deprecating style; but when he reviles his companions, he fails to emulate the philosopher's ironic handling of others. Apollodorus, in short, opts for invective instead of irony. But his invective is as inflammatory as the encomiasts' rhetoric of praise. By debasing the human race and exalting Socrates, Apollodorus enters into the competitive mode that characterized the encomiasts. When Apollodorus goes on to challenge Glaucon to call him "mad" and "crazy," Glaucon rightly reminds him that this is not the time for a "competition" (οὐκ ἄξιον περὶ τούτων ... νῦν ἐρίζειν, 173e4).

If we juxtapose the language of Apollodorus with that of Socrates, we discover that Socrates' ironic treatment of the people he encounters is fundamentally different from Apollodorus' abusive approach. While Socrates' effusions can hardly be taken for true praise, neither can they be identified with invective. For the discourse of invective, like that of the encomium, is essentially combative: the speaker seeks to glorify his own views (and therefore himself) by abusing someone else's.[70] But Socrates' ironic praise moves in another direction altogether. This "praise" does of course call other people's claims to knowledge and virtue into question. It is in fact meant to unsettle individuals who have a high opinion of their own capacities. But Socrates does not resort to invective – to saying that they are stupid while he is wise. Rather, he attempts to defuse this zero-sum competition by insisting that he has not achieved knowledge either.[71]

---

[70] Apollodorus tries to conceal this by acting as though Socrates, rather than he, is superior to other people. But Apollodorus clearly thinks that his association with and imitation of Socrates lifts him above other people. Cf. Socrates' response to Anytus' claim in the *Meno* that Socrates is "too ready to abuse people" (94e): "[Anytus] thinks that I am slandering (κακηγορεῖν) these men, and he also believes that he too is one of them. But if he ever discovers what slander really is, he will cease to be angry; as it stands, he is ignorant of this" (95a). Though Socrates does criticize men such as Pericles and Thucydides in this dialogue, he denies that he is slandering them. First, he is speaking the truth rather than maligning them and, second, his critique is not designed to elevate him at the expense of others.

[71] This occurs in the dialogues (most of them early) where Socrates is actually using the "Socratic method." In the *Symposium*, of course, Socrates claims that he knows "nothing except τὰ ἐρωτικά" (177d). As I will suggest below, Socrates indicates here that he only

His ironic praise thus challenges others to prove that they are wise. If they take up this challenge, Socrates can use his elenctic method to show them that, like him, they lack wisdom and should inquire again into the matters which they had believed they understood.[72] Socrates' ironic praise is, of course, a kind of rhetoric, but it is a rhetoric that clamors for a cooperative dialectical quest. So far from comprising hubristic self-assertion, Socratic irony is designed to combat this arrogant quality in others.

V

If Alcibiades misses the mark when he labels Socrates' irony "hubris," what are we to make of the rest of his eulogy of Socrates? This eulogy stands out from the others in its positioning within the dialogue, its subject matter, and its style.[73] Indeed, Alcibiades' fevered attempt to get at the truth about Socrates might seem to suggest that he is delivering precisely the kind of eulogy that Socrates himself had hoped to receive from his fellow encomiasts – an encomium that speaks the truth. Does Alcibiades' eulogy, by aiming at the truth, serve as a corrective to the false speeches of the other encomiasts? And is Plato therefore placing his own encomium of Socrates in the mouth of Alcibiades?

Certainly Plato would not be the only Socratic writer to engage in eulogy. Xenophon, for example, says at the end of his *Apology*, "for myself, observing the wisdom and nobility of the man, I am compelled to mention him, and when I mention him I am compelled to praise him" (34.1–4).[74] Isocrates refers to a group of writers who "make it their custom to praise" Socrates (*Busiris* 6), and Athenaeus even suggests that the discourse of *all*

---

knows "the things to do with desire" – i.e. the erotic path towards wisdom. This does not include the body of knowledge that the desire for wisdom is aiming at.

[72] Needless to say, Socrates' elenchus does not always succeed. Traits such as vanity, competitiveness, and complacency often render the interlocutor unable to submit himself to the cooperative enterprise of philosophical conversation: he may take offense (e.g., Callicles and Thrasymachus), or he may simply ignore the force of Socrates' refutation and continue to parade his "knowledge" (e.g., Euthyphro, Ion, Hippias).

[73] Particularly unusual is the mixture of praise and censure in this eulogy. Though it was not uncommon for an encomiast to use an invective against some unworthy subject as ballast for his commendation of his principal subject, to praise and blame the same individual in a single speech is quite another matter. Alcibiades' encomium does of course cleave to some of the standard features of the genre. Though it makes no mention of Socrates' ancestry, it attributes to Socrates the virtues of temperance (219b–d, 219e–220d), justice (219e), courage (220d–221c), and wisdom (221e–222a and passim). In addition, Alcibiades exploits the device of "comparison" to suggest that Socrates is *unlike* any human being who ever existed (221c–d). On the genre of the speech, see Belfiore 1984a: 142–3. For examinations of Alcibiades' speech in its political and social context, see Gagarin 1977 and Schein 1974.

[74] Note also the encomium Xenophon pronounces on Socrates at the end of the *Memorabilia* (4.8.11).

the Socratic writers amounted to eulogy and invective: "for to these men," he concludes after detailing a number of "invectives" pronounced by Socratic writers, "no advisor is good, no general wise, no sophist of any worth, no poet of any use, and no populace capable of reasoning; only Socrates [deserves these epithets]."[75]

In the *Symposium*, I will suggest, Plato resisted the temptation to eulogize Socrates. Indeed, so far from planting his own praise of Socrates in the mouth of Alcibiades, Plato may even have designed this encomium as a reminder that others had missed the mark in their eulogies of Socrates. In creating Alcibiades' encomium, Plato chose to portray an infamous and ignoble man struggling – and failing – to praise a philosopher. The pleonectic Alcibiades is the last person to understand the ironic Socrates, and his lack of understanding cannot but compromise his praise. Alcibiades misinterprets Socrates, and this misinterpretation warns the reader not to construe the encomium as proper praise of Socrates. Alcibiades' eulogy is thus designed to be a caveat against an ignorant conferral of praise.

Alcibiades, of course, insists that he will only tell the truth (214e). He even invites Socrates to contradict him if he says anything false (214e–215a). This encourages the reader to accept his eyewitness reports of the specific things that Socrates said and did. But when Alcibiades puts forth his own subjective views about Socrates – when he begins to *interpret* Socrates – we must prick up our ears.[76] Take, for example, Alcibiades' claim that when "even a poor speaker" rehearses Socrates' *logoi* before any kind of listener – "be it man, woman, or child" – the audience is invariably spellbound (215d). This is in fact explicitly contradicted at the beginning of the dialogue.[77] For recall that Glaucon, who comes to Apollodorus for an account of the symposium, had already heard another version which was totally unsatisfying: the speaker, Glaucon says, "was unable to say anything clear" (172b). This disparity reminds us that Alcibiades' interpretation of Socrates' *logoi* is subjective and idiosyncratic.[78]

How much credence should we attach to Alcibiades' reading of Socrates? Nussbaum has suggested that Alcibiades' interpretation of Socrates

[75] *Deipnosophistae* 5 220e. See also 11 504e–509e, where Athenaeus takes Plato to task for the numerous "invectives" that he wove into his dialogues. Athenaeus is, of course, hostile to Socrates and his circle; his statements must be taken with a grain of salt.

[76] I do not mean to imply that the fictive Alcibiades is necessarily reporting actual facts about the historical Socrates. Rather, *within the fiction of Plato's dialogue*, some of what Alcibiades says is factual and some subjective interpretation.

[77] As Halperin 1992: 115 points out.

[78] Note that Socrates calls Alcibiades' eulogy into question twice: first, at 214e, where he asks whether Alcibiades is going to "mock" him by way of praise; and, second, at 222c–d, where he says that Alcibiades' eulogy was designed to make trouble between Agathon and Socrates. These remarks warn us against taking everything Alcibiades says at face value.

is based on a special kind of knowledge – one that contrasts with the philosophical knowledge endorsed by Diotima.[79] As Nussbaum puts it, Alcibiades "suggests that the lover's knowledge of the particular other, gained through an intimacy both bodily and intellectual, is itself a unique and uniquely valuable *kind* of practical understanding ..."[80] To be sure, Alcibiades does appear to have been in love with Socrates (and perhaps he still is).[81] He also claims that he has come to understand Socrates through this love affair. But can he really play the role of Nussbaum's "knowing" lover? Consider her description of the "know-how" of this individual:

> The lover can be said to understand the beloved when, and only when, he knows how to treat him or her: how to speak, look, and move at various times and in various circumstances; how to give pleasure and how to receive it; how to deal with the loved one's complex network of intellectual, emotional, and bodily needs. This understanding requires acquaintance and yields the ability to tell truths ...[82]

I have no quarrel with Nussbaum's conception of the "lover's knowledge" in itself. But I must disagree with her suggestion that Alcibiades possesses this knowledge. While Alcibiades is profoundly stirred by Socrates, he chooses to run away from him rather than take the risky course of understanding, and truly loving, this strange man.[83]

Plato's Alcibiades is a wonderfully compelling and seductive figure. But he is also a man of limited imagination, as his encomium abundantly reveals. For, in spite of his very real charm, Alcibiades betrays his love of power and honor at almost every turn. Imprisoned in a competitive world that operates according to the logic of the zero-sum game, he is compelled to interpret human interaction in terms of an ongoing struggle for power. He claims, for example, that he was "enslaved" to Socrates (219e3–5, cf. 215e6–7), and says three times that he was constrained to do "whatever Socrates bid him" (216b3–4, 217a1–2, 218a6–7). Spurning this bondage,

---

[79] Nussbaum 1986: ch. 6.

[80] Nussbaum 1986: 190.

[81] For the role reversal of lover and beloved in Socratic dialogues, see Halperin 1986: esp. 68–72.

[82] Nussbaum 1986: 191.

[83] Nussbaum 1986: 191–2 seems to anticipate this criticism when she says that "with the failure of physical intimacy a certain *part* of practical understanding is lost to Alcibiades. There is a part of Socrates that remains dark to him, a dimension of intuitive responsiveness to this particular person, an aptness of speech, movement, and gesture, that he can never develop, a kind of 'dialectic' that is missing." Nevertheless, she claims, "Alcibiades can tell the truth about Socrates' unique strangeness even though his aims were frustrated" (p. 191). But is the lack of "physical intimacy" really the only thing that limits Alcibiades' understanding of Socrates? As I will argue, Alcibiades' vision of Socrates is far dimmer than Nussbaum supposes; Alcibiades has other loves besides Socrates that are competing for his soul.

Alcibiades turns the tables by playing the "run-away slave" (δραπετεύω, 216b5). But Alcibiades is not simply running away from Socrates; he is running towards something more enticing. As Alcibiades himself admits, he was "conquered by the honor conferred by the crowd" (ἡττημένῳ τῆς τιμῆς τῆς ὑπὸ τῶν πολλῶν, 216b). As much as he harps on his enslavement to Socrates, he cannot conceal that all the while he loved something else more.

What fuels this story of slavery and rebellion is Alcibiades' desire to get hold of Socrates – to come into possession of his knowledge. Alcibiades had realized, he says, that Socrates was ἄτρωτος – "unwoundable" – by money (219e), so he decided to bribe him with sex. He believed that, as he puts it, "by gratifying Socrates' desire I could hear everything that the man knew" (217a). At first he plays it coy, but soon resolves to "attack the man by direct assault" (μοι ἐπιθετέον εἶναι τῷ ἀνδρὶ κατὰ τὸ καρτερόν, 217c). He tells Socrates that he wants to become "the best man possible" (ὅτι βέλτιστον), and he is ready to barter not only his body but the property belonging to himself and his friends (218c–d). "Having sent forth my darts," he says, "I thought that [Socrates] was wounded" (τετρῶσ-θαι, 219b). Alcibiades "plots" (217c8, d3), "attacks" (217c5), "shoots" (219b3–4), "wounds" (219b4). This is the language of *erōs* – an *erōs* that seeks to dominate and overpower.[84] Alcibiades, of course, fails to overpower Socrates, and his account of this failure is telling: Socrates, he says, "was so much the victor – he looked down on me, he mocked at my good looks, and he committed hubris ..." (οὗτος τοσοῦτον περιεγένετό τε καὶ κατεφρόνησεν καὶ κατεγέλασεν τῆς ἐμῆς ὥρας καὶ ὕβρισεν, 219c).

Alcibiades sees the world in terms of winners and losers, victors and victims. Socrates' refusal to be manipulated is therefore interpreted by Alcibiades as an arrogant attempt to dominate. Ironically, Socrates is in fact refraining from taking advantage of Alcibiades by rejecting his offer of sex. Contrary to Alcibiades' claims, Socrates refuses both to overpower and to be overpowered. He thus attempts to cancel Alcibiades' game of cat and mouse. Note how Socrates diagnoses the problem: when Alcibiades has offered his favors to Socrates, the philosopher observes that Alcibiades' proposal is wildly unfair.[85] Alcibiades, he says, is scheming to get more than his share (πλεονεκτεῖν, 218e5). Even in the act

---

[84] Socrates himself refers to Alcibiades' violent and jealous behavior at 213c–d (though his claims are no doubt exaggerated). For an interesting analysis of Alcibiades' "jealousy," see Fantham 1986: 47–50. In addition to his (psychological) feelings of jealousy, Fantham notes Alcibiades' "tendency towards assault" (50).

[85] Why didn't Socrates tell Alcibiades this in the first place? And why didn't he express it in plain and unequivocal terms? Gagarin 1977 sees this (among other things) as a failure on Socrates' part. Cf. Vlastos 1991: 42, who suggests that Socrates adopted this approach because "he wanted Alcibiades to find out the truth for himself by himself."

of erotic seduction, this is a man who wants to enrich himself at the expense of others.

Alcibiades' attempt to seduce Socrates, I suggest, cannot be disentangled from his passion for honor and power. Alcibiades thinks he sees some treasure underneath Socrates' philosophical conversations – something different from and better than the *logoi* that Socrates engages in. He thinks that Socrates' philosophical life has borne fruits that he can hand over – fruits that he is willfully concealing from his companions. Alcibiades wants to possess Socrates' knowledge; but he does not want to live the philosophical life. Though Alcibiades claims to have a share in "the madness and frenzy of philosophy" (218b), he does not comprehend that philosophical activity is an end in itself. He says that he stopped up his ears to the siren-voice of Socrates because he was afraid that he would "grow old sitting next to Socrates" (216a). Here, Alcibiades seems unable even to imagine what a life dedicated to philosophy would be like, let alone why it would be choiceworthy in itself. We can only infer that he wanted knowledge for private and political ends rather than for ethical improvement.

Since Alcibiades' character distorts his perceptions, we must be especially wary when he claims to reveal the "inner" Socrates. Given our own desire to get at the core of Socrates, it is worth pausing over Alcibiades' excavation. Socrates, he says, is like one of those "silenuses" found in statuary shops, which have the figure of an ugly satyr on the outside but contain images of the gods on the inside (215a–b). These satyrs have pipes or flutes in their hands, and this links them with Marsyas, the satyr whose musical abilities rivalled those of Apollo. Socrates resembles these satyrs in his physical appearance, but also because his own brand of "music" has the same power to bewitch as Marsyas' had (215b–c). Alcibiades returns to this comparison at the end of his speech, where he adds that Socrates' *logoi* themselves resemble the silenus statues (221d–222a). For these *logoi* have a ridiculous exterior that conceals their beautiful core. Socrates, Alcibiades says, appears to be speaking about pack-asses, smiths, cobblers, and tanners, and thus he seems laughable to the untutored mind. But these unprepossessing *logoi* must be opened up. For a glimpse of their interior reveals that they are replete with virtue and, indeed, are "the most divine" of all discourses (222a).

It is tempting to accept Alcibiades' revelation of Socrates' beautiful inner core. But consider what is at stake. First of all, Alcibiades' claims fly in the face of Socrates' characteristic denial that he possesses wisdom and virtue. Thus, if Alcibiades is right, then Socrates is lying. Alcibiades in fact makes this perfectly clear in his speech. Socrates seems to be attracted to beautiful people, Alcibiades says, and he claims to "be ignorant of everything and know nothing" (216d2–4). But this is only Socrates' "outward appearance" (τὸ σχῆμα αὐτοῦ). This is the cloak that he "puts around himself on the outside" (ἔξωθεν περιβέβληται, d5). In fact, Alcibiades asserts,

> it doesn't matter at all to him if someone is handsome, but he looks down on this more than anyone would imagine, and the same is the case if someone is rich or has some other privilege deemed a blessing by the crowd. He considers all these possessions worthless and all of us mere nothings ... (216d–e)

According to Alcibiades, Socrates possesses a "divine and golden and perfectly beautiful and marvelous" interior that elevates him over other people (216e–217a). From this lofty position, Socrates looks down on humankind with an attitude of arrogant superiority – a superiority that he asserts by way of concealment and dissimulation. As Alcibiades says to Eryximachus at 214c–d, "do you believe what Socrates said just now? Or are you aware that everything is the opposite of what he says?"[86]

Alcibiades, then, indicates that Socrates is in full possession of wisdom and the other virtues, but that he is hiding – and, indeed, hoarding – these valuable goods. In this regard, Alcibiades' portrait of Socrates bears comparison with that of another encomiast of Socrates, namely, Xenophon. A brief foray into Xenophon's account of Socrates will bring Alcibiades' claims into better focus. From the opening sections of the *Memorabilia*, Xenophon insists that Socrates did nothing in secret; so far from hiding anything from his associates and fellow citizens, he was completely φανερός – "conspicuous" or "visible" – in all his activities. A few quotations will illustrate this point: Socrates was "conspicuous (φανερός) in sacrificing both at home and at the public altars of the city, and he was not hidden (ἀφανής) in his use of divination" (1.1.2); "he was always visible (ἐν τῷ φανερῷ), for in the morning he went to the public walking-places and the gymnasia, and when the agora was full he was visible (φανερός) there, and he spent the rest of the day wherever it was likely that the most people would gather" (1.1.10); "he was conspicuous (φανερός) beyond all men in serving the gods, and rather than corrupting the young, as his accuser charged against him, he was conspicuous (φανερός) in his attempts to stop those who had wicked desires from indulging them ..." (1.2.64); "and concerning justice he did not hide (ἀπεκρύπτετο) his beliefs, but he even demonstrated (ἀπεδείκνυτο) them by his deeds ..." (4.4.1); "that Socrates revealed (ἀπεφαίνετο) his beliefs

---

[86] Here, Alcibiades appears to be referring back to Socrates' claim that Alcibiades gets violent when Socrates so much as looks at anyone else. But Alcibiades' statement in this passage represents his general view of Socrates' discourse.

plainly to those who associated with him, I think has been made clear from what has been said" (4.7.1).

In chapter 1, I discussed Isocrates' transference of the notion of "visible property" to the symbolic realm of "philosophic" knowledge; as I suggested, Isocrates conceptualizes his knowledge as a possession that can be given or spent just like material capital. In the passages quoted above, we find the same vocabulary of "visible" knowledge and virtue as we did in Isocrates, though it is difficult to tell whether Xenophon is consciously alluding to the economic notion of "visible property." Whether or not this was a deliberate strategy, Xenophon's claim that Socrates' wisdom and virtue are "visible" and not "hidden" operates according to the same logic as the arguments made about "visible" and "invisible" property in the economic sphere. As we saw in chapter 1, the distinction between visible and invisible property is called into play when there is a question whether a citizen has used his wealth for the benefit of the city or has hoarded it for private expenditure. Within the context of the Athenian polis, where public benefaction was the price that wealthy people paid for participating in political life, a citizen who "hid" his wealth was not behaving in proper democratic fashion. In the *Memorabilia*, of course, Xenophon is partly concerned to dispel the idea that Socrates was hiding any *wicked* activities or ideas from the public view. But he also suggests that Socrates was not hiding or hoarding any *good* things from the city – useful possessions such as wisdom and virtue. Whereas a hostile Charicles is quoted at 1.2.36 as reprimanding Socrates because he always "asks questions to which he knows the answer," Xenophon insists that Socrates is not hiding what he knows but is using it for the benefit of the city. In fact, Xenophon portrays Socrates' activities as a kind of liturgy or expenditure:

> But Socrates made the city glorious in the eyes of other men far more than Lichas, who is famous for his benefactions to the city of the Lacedaemonians. For Lichas used to entertain the foreigners who were in Sparta during the Festival of the Dancing Boys, but Socrates passed his entire life spending what belonged to him (τὰ ἑαυτοῦ δαπανῶν) and lavishing the greatest benefits on those who wanted them. For he sent his associates away after making them better than they were. (1.2.61)

Here, in a move very similar to the one that Isocrates makes in the *Antidosis*, Xenophon metaphorizes Socrates' knowledge as wealth that has been expended for the benefit of the city.

In contrast to Xenophon, Alcibiades claims that Socrates is hiding his knowledge. Insisting that none of Socrates' associates really know him, Alcibiades says that he will "reveal" (δηλώσω, 216d1) the true Socrates, whose golden interior he claims to have "seen" (216e7). Indeed, Alcibiades even suggests at 217e that he will not allow the extraordinary deeds of Socrates to remain "invisible" (ἀφανίσαι). Alcibiades, of course, attempts to make Socrates visible by describing and praising his character and actions.[87] But by insisting that Socrates has kept himself hidden – that he has refused to share his wealth with his fellow citizens – Alcibiades subtly suggests that Socrates is acting undemocratically. As Humphreys observes,

Visible property – especially real property – was related to openly acknowledged social position and commitments. Its owner's wealth and status could be easily assessed, he could not evade tax obligations, his kin knew what they could expect from him. With "invisible" property in cash and loans a man could conceal his wealth and evade social obligations: it was difficult to "place" him socially.[88]

If, as Alcibiades suggests, Socrates was concealing and hoarding his knowledge, then he was open to the charge of evading his social and political obligations.[89] We are left with the picture of a man who possessed all of the virtues and yet did not use them for the benefit of the city. Note that Alcibiades never portrays Socrates as a public benefactor. On the contrary, his possession of wisdom and virtue has only served to make Socrates scorn his fellow democrats. In the context of Athenian political practices, then, Alcibiades' revelation of Socrates' extraordinary virtue and wisdom emerges as censure rather than praise.

The logic of Alcibiades' reasoning may be summarized as follows: (a) Socrates must be either ignorant or wise; (b) he cannot be ignorant, therefore he is wise; (c) since he denies that he is wise, he is therefore concealing his knowledge; and (d) this act of concealment reveals that he is toying with people whose inferiority he scorns. It is possible to attack each of these claims, but an assault on (a) will nip the problem in the bud. Why must Socrates be either ignorant or wise? Isn't there some third path? Alcibiades' frame of mind, I suggest, is the same as the one exhibited by Agathon earlier in the dialogue. Recall how Socrates said in his speech that he used to be like Agathon – he used to think that Eros was

---

[87] Note Kurke's discussion of the interaction of the discourse of praise and "visible property" found in Pindar and other poets of the sixth and fifth centuries (1991: ch. 9).

[88] Humphreys 1983: 10.

[89] As E. Cohen 1992: 8 (see also Gabrielsen 1986: 111–12) remarks about the concealment of material property, "In the *aphanēs* market, investments and ownership were cloaked in secrecy, as protection from creditors, tax collectors, and other potential adversaries. Yet the existence of the secret sphere was much bruited, rumors of nonexistent wealth were rampant, and allegations of tax avoidance or creditor evasion were frequent." In other words, a person was often thought to possess much more wealth than he in fact did – a situation which would make him vulnerable to various legal challenges. The case of Socrates might be seen as analogous: people thought that he was concealing "wealth" that he did not in fact possess.

either a god or a mortal, either beautiful or ugly, either wise or ignorant (201e–202e). Diotima dismantled this binary scheme by introducing Socrates to a tertium quid: midway between beauty and ugliness, mortality and immortality, ignorance and knowledge, Eros both loves and lacks wisdom. Perpetually on the move, Eros is the quintessential *philosophos*.

In Alcibiades' speech, Socrates is *sophos*, and therefore godlike and lacking in desire, rather than the *philosophos* who restlessly pursues true wisdom. But, as the dialogue as a whole indicates, Plato does not endorse Alcibiades' view. Indeed, he refuses to perfect and reify Socrates – to turn him into an immobile statue such as Alcibiades finds on Socrates' inside. Alcibiades' encomium of Socrates, then, cannot be the final word. Its systematic misreading of Socrates invites us to challenge Alcibiades' world of masters and slaves, of haves and have-nots, and to explore the region of the in-between. Alcibiades attempts to memorialize Socrates – to catch, kill, and stuff his protean subject. But Socrates will not sit still to be praised.

Alcibiades' encomium of Socrates, in sum, beautifully evinces the folly of praise. For, in addition to the fact that the speaker is ignorant, the subject of praise – the human soul, whose essence is lack and desire, mobility and alteration – is beyond the grasp of the simplistic rhetoric of eulogy. To be sure, Alcibiades' account of Socrates' actions does elicit the reader's admiration, but his inability to get at the core of Socrates reminds us that we, too, may have misunderstood this complex figure. By provoking this *aporia*, Alcibiades' speech calls for inquiry rather than idolatry.

It is no accident, finally, that Plato put this speech into the mouth of a famous (and, indeed, infamous) politician. The foolish use of the language of praise, he reminds us, poses a very real danger for the city as a whole.

VI

In light of Plato's manifold criticisms of eulogy, Socrates' encomium of Eros raises a number of important questions. First of all, is the speech properly called a "eulogy"? And, even if it is not a true encomium, why does Socrates embrace the rhetorical mode? How are we to interpret this foray into enemy territory?

We have seen how Socrates makes fun of the competitiveness of his fellow encomiasts in the *Symposium*. We are not surprised, then, when he prefaces his own speech with a noisy refusal to contribute his offering in an agonistic manner. As he says at 199b, he is willing to speak "in his own fashion" (κατ' ἐμαυτόν), but not "in competition with your speeches" (οὐ πρὸς τοὺς ὑμετέρους λόγους). Again, when he has succeeded in eliciting a confession of ignorance from Agathon, he will not play the victor: to Agathon's admission that he is unable to argue against Socrates (σοὶ οὐκ ἂν δυναίμην ἀντιλέγειν), Socrates counters that it is the truth that Agathon is unable to contradict, since Socrates himself can easily be challenged (οὐ μὲν οὖν τῇ ἀληθείᾳ ... δύνασαι ἀντιλέγειν, ἐπεὶ Σωκράτει γε οὐδὲν χαλεπόν, 201c). The real competition, Socrates suggests, is the search for wisdom; he and Agathon are not competitors but teammates who must meet the challenge together.

How does Socrates' encomium bear this out? Whereas the previous encomiasts began their speeches with criticisms of the other encomia, Socrates commences by putting himself on the same footing as Agathon. He used to believe the very things that Agathon has just enunciated, he says, and was only disabused of these ideas by a stern teacher.[90] Indeed, so far from using his speech to glorify his own cleverness and skill, Socrates casts himself in the role of the less-than-brilliant student of a mere woman![91] This unlikely teacher must repeatedly condescend to her "astonished" (208b) pupil: she insists that "even a child" is smarter than Socrates (204b), she chafes at his ignorance (207c), she doubts his ability to grasp the highest mysteries (210a). Socrates for his part treats her as a formidable and all-knowing mentor (206b, 207c), and is quite willing to admit his own ignorance and need of instruction (206b, 207c). The form of Socrates' eulogy, then, functions to deflate the speaker and defuse the competition that inheres in encomiastic discourse.[92]

The substance of Socrates' eulogy, too, explodes the conventions of the encomiastic genre. Eros is not a god, we are told, and is in fact poor, tough, dirty, barefoot, and homeless; though not ignorant or evil, he lacks wisdom and virtue. Conceived in a one-night stand[93] by two not very distinguished divinities (Poros and the beggar Penia), Eros gets his poverty and ugliness from his mother, and his ability to scheme after the

---

[90] Cornford 1971: 122 explains Socrates' assumption of the status of ignorant student as "a masterstroke of delicate courtesy" whereby Socrates "avoids making his host look foolish." But Plato's Socrates can hardly be accused of courtesy: we must look elsewhere for the explanation of this act of self-deflation.

[91] For a fascinating analysis of Diotima's presence in the dialogue, see Halperin 1990: ch. 6.

[92] The Socrates who attends the drinking party is clearly not the person that he claims he used to be. The disparity between the Socrates whom Diotima accuses of being stupidly infatuated with young boys (211d) and the Socrates who resists Alcibiades' enticements suggests that Socrates has made some headway in his erotic pursuits. But this does not mean that Socrates has made it to the top of the ladder: Diotima actually doubts that Socrates can achieve these heights (210a), and Socrates' claim that he knows "nothing but ta erōtika" suggests that he understands the journey but not the journey's end.

[93] Or is it a rape? Whatever it is, it's not very savory and highly unerotic! God knows how Poros managed it while collapsed in a drunken sleep.

things he lacks – beauty, virtue, wisdom, etc. – from his father. Eros, then, is deprived of both the ancestry and the personal qualities that encomiasts invariably strive to document. To be sure, he does have one saving grace: he loves beauty and wisdom and can drive the human soul towards the highest goods. But, since he never achieves knowledge and virtue, he isn't praiseworthy is any ordinary sense.

The ugly and barefoot Eros cannot but conjure up Socrates. And the parallel seems apt, since Socrates is so often portrayed by Plato as an intermediary between human souls and the virtue and wisdom he prods them to seek – as a gadfly, a sting-ray, a midwife.[94] But if Socrates is like Eros, then he too must be lacking in virtue and wisdom; he too must be situated somewhere between ignorance and knowledge, vice and virtue. Socrates' repeated insistence in the early dialogues that he does not have real knowledge about the things he seeks encourages us to accept the parallel between Socrates and Eros.[95] In the *Symposium*, of course, Socrates claims that he knows "nothing except τὰ ἐρωτικά" (177d). As Lowenstam has suggested, "when Socrates claims knowledge of *ta erō-tika*, he is not asserting that he possesses a certain type of substantive knowledge but that the only thing he knows is how much he lacks and desires knowledge."[96] Socrates, in other words, understands that humans are, by nature, needy beings who long for a knowledge that they can never fully attain. He knows that he lacks true knowledge and that he must dedicate his life to its pursuit.

To the extent that he praises Eros, then, Socrates celebrates the philosopher and therefore himself. If Socrates does in fact deliver a speech of praise, then he would be praising himself for knowing that he did not possess true knowledge – for knowing "nothing except *ta erōtika*." Certainly Socrates suggests in Plato's *Apology* that his consciousness of his own ignorance makes him "wiser to some small extent" than other people (21d). Here in the *Symposium* Socrates is on the verge of extolling his own *lack* of wisdom.

[94] Burnyeat 1977 suggests that the Socrates of the *Symposium* has a very different style of pedagogy from that of the "midwife" (which is found in the early dialogues and is articulated in the *Theaetetus*); as he argues, the *Symposium* "presents a middle period Socrates, argumentative still but with positive doctrine of his own or learned from Diotima" (p. 9). I would argue that Socrates transmits Diotima's "doctrines" (rather than "positive doctrines of his own") in his speech, and that his ironic behavior at the drinking party is very much in keeping with the Socrates of Plato's early period.
[95] The fact that Socrates supersedes Eros as the subject of eulogy further invites us to link the two.
[96] Lowenstam 1985: 88. Roochnik 1987 comes to a similar conclusion. As he says on p. 128, "To understand *ta erōtika* is thus to understand the primacy of the question, that mode of discourse emanating from the knowledge of ignorance" (so also Reeve 1992: 93).

But can the celebration of a being who lacks wisdom and virtue be dubbed encomiastic?[97] Socrates is careful to mention that his speech may not in fact be a eulogy at all (212c). As we have seen, Socrates transgresses the boundaries of the encomiastic genre in fundamental ways. In addition to these generic transgressions, Diotima's teaching explicitly states that human beings are always in flux, and that they do not possess any qualities in a stable or lasting way (207c–208b). Even knowledge is something that needs to be replenished by "practice" (μελέτη, 208a). Humans want to possess the good forever (ἔστιν ... ὁ ἔρως τοῦ τὸ ἀγαθὸν αὐτῷ εἶναι ἀεί, 206a), she says, but they are unable to achieve this in a straightforward way. Owing to their temporality, they cannot possess knowledge and the other virtues once and for all; the best one can hope for is to conceive and give birth to these things, and to spend one's life rearing and nourishing these children (212a). Virtue and knowledge, in short, are the fragile fruits of an ongoing creative process, not objects that can be won like a trophy.

Socrates' "eulogy," then, insists upon motion – the movement towards "birth-giving in the presence of the Beautiful." This speech critiques encomiastic discourse by refusing to finalize, to reify, to memorialize its subject. To be sure, a stable and unchanging Form shimmers at the summit of the climb. But the vision of the Form of Beauty does not in fact provide an ending to the questing soul's journey.[98] Rather, it plays the midwife to the pregnant philosopher – it brings children into the light that need nurture and sustenance (212a). Human desire cannot be fulfilled once and for all; human beings cannot escape motion. Socrates' speech, then, calls into question the very possibility of the "good man" whose perfect virtue is the paradigmatic subject of the encomiastic genre. It is a brilliant parody that explodes the encomiastic genre from within. Note, however, that Socrates' speech is not a "mock" or "paradoxical" encomium; for it does not celebrate a trivial or disreputable subject – it does not, in short, call a worthless thing "good." Rather, Socrates insists on the existence of absolute goodness and on the impossibility of the perfect instantiation of this goodness in the human world. This is an ontology which challenges the binary logic of the rhetoric of praise and blame. Since human life is, by definition, unstable and unfinalizable, it simply cannot be apprehended by the rhetoric of eulogy.

[97] For an excellent analysis of the ways in which Plato calls into question the "truth" of Socrates' speech, see Belfiore 1984a. Belfiore rightly queries whether this speech is "an encomium, the truth, or something else" (p. 149). See Patterson 1991: 211–14 for a discussion of what it means to "praise correctly" in the context of a philosophic love-affair (such as the one Diotima adumbrates).
[98] As D. Frede 1993: 414 observes.

VII

Plato's critique of the many manifestations of encomiastic discourse
evinces two aims. First, to show how the rhetoric of praise that pervades
classical Athens can damage individuals and, indeed, the city as a whole.
And second, to demonstrate the antithesis between praise discourse and
the language of the philosopher. As we have seen, Plato sets the rhetoric
of praise in opposition both to ironic discourse, which systematically undermines the binary logic of good vs. bad, and to the methods of elenchus
and dialectic, which destroy the conceit of knowledge and set the soul
in perpetual motion towards knowledge and virtue. As each of Plato's
critiques suggests, the language of praise is false when it attaches the
predicates "good" or "wise" to objects that are neither good nor wise.
But the *Symposium* goes further, since it introduces an ontological
scheme in which human beings and affairs can never be truly good. If
one accepts this ontology – where only the Forms are perfect and good
– one can never attach the predicates "good," "wise," etc., to objects in
the human world without qualification. In this case, the language of
eulogy will always be false, since it insists on the perfect virtues of its
laudandum.

Plato's own rhetoric, however, flies in the face of this trenchant critique.
Ironically, it is in the middle dialogues – which usher in the metaphysical
scheme that is adumbrated in the *Symposium* – that Plato makes a regular
practice of using encomiastic rhetoric for his own purposes. Take, for example, the end of the *Phaedo*, where a short eulogy is pronounced for the
dead Socrates: "such was the end, Echecrates, of our companion, a man
who was, as we may say, of all those of his time whom we have known,
the best and the wisest and the most just" (118a15–17). To be sure, it is
Phaedo and not Plato who speaks these lines, but the entire trajectory of
the dialogue bolsters this claim. Loraux, in fact, suggests that the *Phaedo*
is a kind of funeral oration for Socrates; as she argues, Socrates is assimilated to the perfected philosopher and set up as an "epic hero or new-
style hoplite."[99] Here, the ironic and idiosyncratic Socrates of the *Symposium* and other dialogues is eclipsed: the philosopher is portrayed as
sophos. In the *Republic*, moreover, the lengthy description of the philosopher in books 5–7 attributes all of the virtues to this individual, and even
suggests that he will attain the vision of the Form of the Good. Finally, in
the *Theaetetus*, the philosopher is said to be "similar to god" insofar as he
is as just and holy as it is possible for a man to be (176b–c). Although
Plato stops short of attributing divine goodness to his philosophers, they

[99] Loraux 1989: 30 and passim.

have reached the pinnacle of human goodness and can therefore be called wise and virtuous.[100]

As we saw in chapter 1, Plato often defines his philosopher by juxtaposing him to "false" and "base" claimants to wisdom. Note that this gesture is identical to the rhetorical strategy that is at the heart of encomiastic discourse: the trope of *sunkrisis*, whereby the laudandum is exalted by a "comparison" with something (allegedly) inferior or base. This binary logic pervades the middle dialogues of Plato. To cite but a few examples: the comparisons in the *Gorgias* and *Theaetetus* of the rhetorician and the philosopher; the opposition between the "lovers of wisdom" and the "lovers of sights and sounds" in *Republic* book 5, between the philosophers and the "banausic" pretenders to philosophy in book 6, and between the philosopher and the tyrant in book 9; and the antithesis set up in the *Phaedrus* between the "serious" and the "trivial" farmer, which is used to distinguish the philosopher from all other laborers in the fields of language. Either one is a philosopher or one is not: in these passages, there seems to be nothing in between.[101]

Perhaps Plato's assertion in many middle dialogues that the philosopher can – and, indeed, must – achieve true knowledge and virtue justifies his praise of this unique individual. But Plato's penetrating critiques of encomiastic rhetoric nonetheless cast a shadow over his appropriation of this kind of discourse for his own purposes. Is this collusion with "antiphilosophical" discourse defensible? In the next chapter, I will discuss a dialogue in which Plato takes a very different approach to defining philosophy – an approach which allows him to grant "alien" genres a positive role in the philosophic enterprise.

[100] Note that Plato also pronounces eulogies on non-human subjects. For example, at *Rep.* 358d and 589b–c, Plato designates the arguments in favor of both injustice and justice as "encomia" (Socrates makes it clear at 589b–c that the encomiast of injustice is a liar and the encomiast of justice a truthteller); note also *Phaedrus* 266a–b, where Socrates says that his first speech "abused" (ἐλοιδόρησεν) bad love and his second "praised" (ἐπήνεσεν) good love. I will discuss the *Phaedrus'* use of praise and blame in chapter 4.

[101] As I have already indicated (ch. 1 n. 18), Plato sometimes defines philosophy as the *pursuit* of the Forms – a search that can never be concluded – and at other times as the *knowledge achieved as a result of this pursuit.* Likewise, the philosopher can be the erotic quester or the consummate knower. Although one might argue that the latter is favored in the later dialogues, a text like the *Phaedrus* warns against adopting a simple developmental scheme. One should remember that Plato's "definitions" of philosophy are highly rhetorical, and vary depending on context.

4   Alien and authentic discourse

Heard melodies are sweet, but those unheard
Are sweeter.

Keats, "Ode on a Grecian Urn"

language is a virus from outer space.

William S. Burroughs

We believe that we live in the "age of information," that there has been
an information "explosion," an information "revolution." While in a
certain narrow sense this is the case, in many important ways just the
opposite is true. We also live at a moment of deep ignorance, when vital
knowledge that humans have always possessed about who we are and
where we live seems beyond our reach. An Unenlightenment. An age of
missing information.

Bill McKibben, The Age of Missing Information

As we have seen in the previous chapters, Plato attempts in a number of
dialogues to distinguish philosophy from traditional genres of discourse.
Philosophical language, he suggests, is not only new and different: it is
superior to all other kinds of discourse. The *Phaedrus*, however, takes a
different tack. For it abandons the notion that traditional genres of poetry
and rhetoric are inherently "unphilosophical." This means that it is at
least possible for one or another genre to make a positive contribution to
the project of philosophy.[1] The *Phaedrus* targets a number of generic
subtexts, but handles each in a different way: while some genres are subjected to parody, others are granted full semantic autonomy. In the latter
cases, Plato disrupts the boundaries that he had previously drawn between "philosophy" and "non-philosophic" discursive practices.[2] In fact,
the *Phaedrus* repeatedly signals its rapprochement with "unphilosophi-

---

[1] Note that even if every existing specimen of a genre is in some way misguided from the
point of view of the philosopher, the basic structure and orientation of the genre *per se*
need not be rejected out of hand.

[2] The crossing of boundaries is dramatized in the dialogue when Socrates ventures "outside
of the wall" of the city (ἔξω τείχους, 227a3). We are promptly informed that Socrates is a
stranger in this region since he never journeys beyond the city's boundaries. As Phaedrus

cal" language. How, then, does this dialogue mark the boundaries of philosophy? In the *Phaedrus*, I will argue, Plato defines the language of the philosopher by reference to the concept of authenticity. In this rich and subtle meditation on the problems of authorship and authority, the philosopher is identified as the person who makes his *logoi* his own by testing the multifarious "alien" *logoi* which confront him both from without and from within. As he recollects and relearns the Forms, the philosopher develops "authentic" *logoi* by measuring them against the truths he has discovered by dialectical investigation.

At the opening of the *Phaedrus*, Socrates criticizes some unnamed "wise men" who attempt to reduce myths to historical events. According to Socrates, those who take this approach to mythic discourse must account for monsters such as centaurs, the Chimaera, the Gorgon, Pegasus, and hordes of other "impossible" creatures (229c–e). It is not fortuitous that Socrates mentions mythological creatures whose bodily forms are composed of a mixture of the parts of different animals. For, after privileging the pursuit of self-knowledge over the inquiry into mythological monsters, Socrates pointedly resuscitates just such a monster in the very next line: "I investigate not these things but myself, [to find out] whether I happen to be an animal more complex and more angry than the Typhon" (230a). Like the other monsters mentioned in this passage, the Typhon is a marvel of miscegenation. But the Typhon has an added feature that must be taken into account. For, as Hesiod's detailed description of this creature in the *Theogony* reveals (819–35), what distinguished the Typhon was not simply his hundred snake heads with their dark tongues but the fact that each tongue could utter sounds of every kind: on the one hand, they could speak in such a way that "the gods could understand"; on the other hand, they could imitate the "voices" of animals such as bulls, lions, puppies, and hissing snakes.[3]

The Typhon's plurivocality, I will suggest, reverberates in several important ways in this dialogue. Note, first of all, that the monster's voices *conspire* in both the root and the regular senses of the word: because they derive from a single being, they literally breathe together; but they also can be said to conspire with and against one another, depending on their divine or bestial orientation. The *Phaedrus* will illustrate, first of all, the conspiracy of the voices within a single human soul. As we discover in the

puts it at 230d, "you do not go out of the city into the land across the border (ἐκ τοῦ ἄστεος οὔτ' εἰς τὴν ὑπερορίαν ἀποδημεῖς), and in fact you never seem to go outside the wall (ἔξω τείχους)."

[3] Griswold 1986: 40 suggests that the Typhon's multilingualism symbolizes the nature of "rhetoric" which, as he observes, "will have so broad a meaning in the *Phaedrus* as to include all the discourses with which we communicate with ourselves and others."

palinode, each of the three parts of the soul has a voice; the charioteer and his horses quarrel and negotiate, exhort and vituperate. This quarrel within the soul, moreover, finds a parallel in the discursive strategy of the dialogue. For a conspiracy of voices is also taking place at the level of the text. Like the miscegenated monsters that Socrates evokes, the *Phaedrus* has a composite nature. Much ink has been spilled on the "two halves" of the text and the question of the dialogue's unity.[4] But, even within each half of the text, a plurality of voices can be heard. It is the typhonic aspect of both the soul and the text that I will take as my focus in this chapter.

Let me begin by explicating the nature and operations of "alien discourse." This phenomenon pervades the *Phaedrus*, but nowhere is it illustrated more clearly than in the famous conversation between the Egyptian deities, Theuth and Thamus. For, in his pronouncement upon the harmfulness of writing, Thamus says that "[writing] will produce forgetfulness in the souls of its learners because they will neglect to exercise their memory; indeed, on account of the faith they place in writing they will recall things by way of *alien marks external to them* (ἔξωθεν ὑπ' ἀλλοτρίων τύπων) and not from within, themselves by themselves (ἔνδοθεν αὐτοὺς ὑφ' αὑτῶν)" (275a). In this passage, written discourse is identified as an "alien" which imposes itself on an individual from without; having established itself in a person's psyche, it precludes internal and autonomous thought and speech.[5] Although this passage focusses exclusively on written discourse, Socrates says explicitly at 277e–278a that spoken discourse which is delivered "for the sake of persuasion without investigation or teaching" has the same liabilities as the written word. As this latter passage indicates, Thamus' discussion of the written word actually illustrates a problem that is not confined to writing, namely, the narcotic effects of "alien" discourse. Thus when Socrates claims at 235c–d that he is not the author of his (first) speech, but has "been filled through the ears with *alien streams* (ἐξ ἀλλοτρίων ... ναμάτων διὰ τῆς ἀκοῆς), like a pitcher," it is clear that the *logoi* which Socrates has *heard* function in the same way as *written* discourse – as aliens that have (allegedly) occupied Socrates' psyche.

The *Phaedrus* depicts a private conversation held on the banks of a river outside of the walls of Athens. Yet a startling number of voices find their way onto the scene or, more accurately, into the mouths of

---

[4] For some recent discussions of the dialogue's unity, see Rowe 1986a, 1989 and Heath 1989a, 1989b.

[5] Cf. *Protagoras* 347e–348a: "Thus gatherings of this kind, if they include men such as many of us claim to be, have no need of alien voices (ἀλλοτρίας φωνῆς) or of the poets, whom it is impossible to question concerning the things that they say ... But [men such as we are] eschew such gatherings, associating instead directly with each other and using their own *logoi* to test and be tested by one another."

the two interlocutors. Let me begin with the most obtrusive category of "alien discourse" in the *Phaedrus*: that reported as "hearsay." The verb ἀκούειν and its cognates occurs 55 times in this dialogue. We are repeatedly invited to overhear things that both Socrates and Phaedrus have heard, although the two make different uses of hearsay. Hearsay, in fact, is thematized in the opening scene of the dialogue, when Phaedrus promises to tell Socrates about the *logoi* of Lysias if he has leisure "to hear" (ἀκούειν, 227b8). Socrates replies that "to hear" (τὸ ... ἀκοῦσαι) about these things is more important to him than any business (b9–11). Good, says Phaedrus, since ἡ ἀκοή is especially suitable for the ears of Socrates (c3). Socrates then expresses his passion "to hear" (ἀκοῦσαι) the *logoi*, no matter whether he has to follow Phaedrus as far as Megara (d2–4). We are not yet through with this verbal repetition. For, when Phaedrus suggests that his memory may not be adequate to the task of rehearsing Lysias' speech, Socrates insists that he knows that Phaedrus, "hearing (ἀκούων) the speech of Lysias, heard (ἤκουσεν) it not once but many times" (228a6–8). In fact, Socrates conjectures, Phaedrus was in the process of learning the speech by heart directly from the book when he met another person who is "sick for the hearing of speeches" (τῷ νοσοῦντι περὶ λόγων ἀκοήν, b6–7). Socrates even suggests that Phaedrus would force his speech upon him (βίᾳ ἐρεῖν) "whether or not anyone is willing to hear" (ἑκὼν ἀκούοι, c3).

How does the theme of hearing and hearsay play out in the dialogue? It will come as no surprise, I think, that Phaedrus has a penchant for repeating what other people say. In addition to his rehearsal of the speech of Lysias, Phaedrus quotes, for example, the doctor Acumenus, who has recommended walks on the roads (227a); the politicians who rail at the practice of logography (257c); the rhetoricians who deny that orators must have knowledge of the truth (259e–260a); people who have defined rhetoric as an art confined to public gatherings (261b); the authors of books on rhetoric (266d); and Hippocrates' theories on the physiology of the human body (270c). Rather than examine these passages in detail, I will rehearse but one. At 259e–260a, Phaedrus reports to Socrates what he has heard (ἀκήκοα) about the practitioners of oratory. Later in the passage, after suggesting that the art of rhetoric operates in both the public and the private sphere, Socrates turns to Phaedrus and asks: "or what have you heard about this?" (ἢ πῶς σὺ ταῦτ' ἀκήκοας; 261b2). Phaedrus claims that he has heard that rhetoric is exercised in lawcourts and public assemblies, "but beyond this I haven't heard anything" (ἐπὶ πλέον δὲ οὐκ ἀκήκοα, 261b5). Have you only "heard" (ἀκήκοας), responds Socrates, of the rhetorical manuals of Nestor and Odysseus ... and are you "without the hearing" (ἀνήκοος) of those of Palamedes? (b6–8).

Clearly, the text highlights Phaedrus' reliance on the opinions and statements of other people.

Socrates' use of hearsay is quite different from that of Phaedrus. Before, during, and after his first speech Socrates insists that he has been invaded by a disparate group of tongue-snatchers. Denying his own authorship of the speech, he attributes it to wise men and women of old (235b), to Sappho, Anacreon, and some unnamed prose writers (235c), to the Muses (237a), and to the local nymphs (238d; 241e); it is at this point, in fact, that Socrates says that he has been "filled through the ears with alien streams, like a pitcher" (235c–d). But note the way that Socrates glosses this claim. When Socrates disagrees with Phaedrus' assessment of Lysias' speech at the opening of this passage, Phaedrus replies: "where have you heard (ἀκήκοας) anything better than this?" (235c1). "It is clear that I heard it (ἀκήκοα) from somebody," Socrates responds, "since I know that I didn't invent it myself … but, on account of my stupidity, I have forgotten just this thing – how and from whom I heard it" (ἤκουσα, c2–d3). As Griswold has observed, Socrates is engaging in a sort of ironic mimicry in this passage, "pretend[ing] that he is very much like Phaedrus into whom Lysias' speech has been poured."[6] But the pointed use of the vocabulary of hearsay shows that Socrates is also bringing the theme of alien discourse to the fore.

In addition to the spoken word, as I have suggested, writing is a conveyor of hearsay. Plato in fact encourages us to link writing and hearsay at several points in the dialogue. At 268c2–3, Phaedrus makes fun of the person who thinks he is a physician by virtue of his ability to induce certain effects in a body through the use of drugs: this person thinks he is a doctor when he has only picked up some techniques "hearing them from a book or somewhere" (ἐκ βιβλίου ποθὲν ἀκούσας). Again, at 271c, referring to the authors of books on rhetoric, Socrates says to Phaedrus: "those writers, whom you have heard …" (οἱ νῦν γράφοντες, ὧν σὺ ἀκήκοας). But the most emphatic conflation of things read with things heard is in the Egyptian story itself. For Thamus pointedly suggests that people who rely on the written word will be πολυήκοοι rather than πολυγνώμονες – "hearers of many things" as opposed to "learners of many things" (275a7–b1).[7]

Why, we must ask, is alien discourse such a problem, and what does

[6] Griswold 1986: 53; cf. pp. 28–9. Cf. Berger 1990: 97.
[7] Schenkeveld 1992 investigates the use of ἀκούειν and its cognates to signify "to read" in Greek literature. He shows that word is used in this sense as early as the fifth century. The connection that Plato draws between hearing and reading, then, is not unusual. But the connection takes on added meaning in light of the dialogue's exploration of the unthinking internalization of *logoi* by hearing and by reading.

Plato think that we should do about it? Alien discourse is presented to an individual on another person's authority; it is an external voice that seeks to be made internal. This is a simple enough concept, but it is important to distinguish two quite different players in the transaction of alien discourse. On the one hand, there is the person who *transmits* the alien discourse by setting him/herself up as some kind of authority; obviously, anyone can be quoted as an authority, but only some few people achieve the status of public "authorities," and it is this group who play the leading role in the transmission of alien discourse. The second player, on the other hand, is the individual who *receives* the *logoi* , whether by hearing or by reading; this person is invited to accede to the authority of the first player.

II

How does Plato deal with the first player? Let us go back to the alien voices that Socrates names as authorities for his first encomium. By ascribing his speech to not one but a number of disparate authors, Socrates problematizes the very notion of individual authorship. Is there a single author of any public speech or composition? Even a piece written by a single, identifiable author may itself derive from "alien streams." When, we must ask, can an author call his *logoi* his own?[8] Socrates adverts explicitly to this issue at 235e, where he responds to Phaedrus' request that Socrates deliver a speech in which he "avoids the things" (τούτων ἀπεχόμενος) that Lysias said (235d7–8). Socrates answers that he certainly cannot come up with "other things that go beyond all of these" (i.e. the things Lysias said); "even the poorest writer," he adds, "could not have this happen." What Socrates is saying here, albeit with an ironic twist, is that even the best writer in a given genre is not the sole author of his *logos*. But he indicates this in a backhanded way, by stating that no writer who set out to compose an encomium for a non-lover could ever be so incompetent as to avoid the kinds of things that Lysias says – that any writer, no matter how ignorant and unskilled, would necessarily make use of the commonplaces of the genre.

It is important to note how Socrates glosses this claim. For he goes on to say at 235e–236a:

Take, for example, the subject of this speech – who do you think, in claiming that it is right to show favor to the non-lover rather than the lover, avoiding praise of the

---

[8] Note that the problem of the authenticity of Lysias' speech may have been anticipated by Plato. As Ferrari 1987: 210 has pointed out, Plato must have realized that "the longer the embedded text [of the Lysias speech] lay preserved within the book written around it, the more likely it was that subsequent readers would find themselves unable to determine its authenticity."

good sense of the one and censure of the foolishness of the other (which are necessary commonplaces), will then have anything else to say? No, these things, I
believe, must be allowed and granted to the speaker. And in the case of arguments
such as these, one ought to praise not the discovery (τὴν εὕρεσιν) but the arrangement, whereas in the case of those that are not necessary commonplaces and difficult to discover (χαλεπῶν εὑρεῖν), one ought to praise the discovery as well as the
arrangement.

In this passage, Socrates indicates that Lysias, whose encomium on the
non-lover would have been considered a novel and inventive idea, was
simply rehearsing the standard *topoi* of the encomiastic genre: the bestowal of praise and blame fueled by binary oppositions such as sensible/
senseless, beneficial/harmful, mad/sane. This is not to say that Socrates is
accusing Lysias of quoting someone else word for word. The point is that
he is writing within a specific genre which provides him with the kinds of
things that he must say and constrains him from deviating into other
modes of discourse. Socrates suggests, in short, that Lysias' speech is derivative insofar as it reuses the genre's stock of "necessary commonplaces."[9] Whether Lysias has "discovered" anything is not discussed; but
Socrates will suggest later in the dialogue that only the *logos* which a
person possesses "as something that has been discovered (εὑρεθείς)" can
properly be called his own (278a5–b1).[10] Hackforth notes that what
Socrates refers to in this passage is the true *logos* that has been "discovered" by the method of dialectic.[11] In Plato's sense of the term, then,
"discovery" is something that can never be found in a non-philosophical
discourse.

As Burger points out, Socrates' privileging of "discovery" over
"arrangement" in the passage quoted above marks a deliberate correc-
tion of the claims that Isocrates makes at *Helen* 11–13.[12] There, Isocrates
contrasts "*logoi* that are of general import and trustworthy" (κοινοὶ καὶ
πιστοί, 11) – which handle themes which are "serious" and "well-known"
– with "trivial" ones on obscure themes. In the case of the former, "it is
rare to discover things that nobody has ever said before" (σπάνιον εὑρεῖν ἃ

---

[9] Note the pointed use of the verb ἀκήκοας at the opening of Lysias' speech (which is repeated verbatim twice after its original delivery; 262e1–2, 263e6–7): "You know about my
affairs, and in what way I think that we will be benefited if these things come to be, you
have heard" (ἀκήκοας, 230e6–7). This opening seems more like an ending than a beginning, as Socrates himself points out later in the dialogue (264a–e). Perhaps the speaker's
suggestion that the boy (= audience) has already heard the arguments is meant to remind
the reader that the *logos* has in fact been heard before in the sense that it rehearses generic
commonplaces.
[10] I will discuss this passage in more detail below. Note that Plato uses the word εὑρίσκω and
its cognates to refer to the activity of the philosopher at 252e7, 266a5, a7, and 274c2.
[11] Hackforth 1952: 162 n. 1.
[12] Burger 1980: 118.

μηδεὶς πρότερον εἴρηκε), whereas in the latter writings "whatever a person chances to say is completely original" (ἅπαν ἴδιόν ἐστιν) (13). Note also that in the *Panegyricus*, Isocrates acknowledges that the sophists have already spoken on his theme (3–4) and claims that writers should not "avoid the things which others have spoken about before" (8–9). Since the "deeds of the past are left behind as an inheritance common to all," the wise writer is the one who "uses them at the opportune time, possesses thoughts that are fitting on each subject, and arranges them well (εὖ δια-θέσθαι) with his words" (9). Isocrates, then, champions the reuse of time-honored material over the hunt for novelty, which inevitably leads the author off the beaten track and into areas that are irrelevant if not stupid.[13]

It is important to observe that Isocrates' notion of "discovery" is completely different from Plato's. For, as the quotes above reveal, Isocrates equates "discovery" with the use of novel or obscure material. Plato, by contrast, indicates that "discovery" is based on recollection of the Forms; this actually precludes invention and novelty since it involves finding something that has been there all along.[14] For Isocrates, then, "discovery" is akin to invention or originality; by avoiding all commonplaces and inherited truths, one "comes up with" something totally new. In Plato's view, this kind of discovery (which is exemplified by Lysias' speech) is nothing other than a clever manipulation of generic commonplaces. For this reason, it is not very different from rearranging traditional material, which is precisely what Isocrates wants to privilege over "discovery." Indeed Plato competely dismantles the opposition that Isocrates draws between "arranging" inherited truths and "discovering" novel ideas: in Plato's eyes, the different authorial approaches exemplified by "Lysias" and Isocrates are equally inauthentic since neither is based on true knowledge; both "author" discourse that is alien to their souls.

It is worth examining several more passages from Isocrates, since the claims that he makes for his writings illuminate Plato's project in important ways. Both *ad Demonicum* and *ad Nicoclem* were written between 375 and 372, which places them immediately before the composition of the *Phaedrus*.[15] Both are deliberate attempts to imitate in prose the poet-

[13] See also *Helen* 10–11. But note that Isocrates himself claims in the *Helen* that he will "leave out all the things that have been said [about Helen] by others" (15): he thus seems to suggest in this speech that he can be both topical and inventive, both traditional and innovative.

[14] Plato's repeated use of the word εὑρίσκω in an ironic sense to describe the "discoveries" of various orators and rhetoricians underscores his rejection of the traditional notion of "discovery" (see, e.g., 267a4, 267b3, 273b3).

[15] The *ad Demonicum* is dated at 374–2 (Jebb 1962.II: 85), and *ad Nicoclem* at just after 374, when Evagoras, the father of Nicocles, died. The dating of the *Phaedrus*, of course, has

ical genre called *hypothēkai*.[16] As Kurke observes in her recent investigation of this genre, *hypothēkai* were characterized by "a collection of
injunctions and traditional wisdom, loosely strung together with gnomic
material."[17] As Isocrates puts it in *ad Nicoclem* 41,

> In discourses of this sort we should not seek for novelties, since it is impossible to
> say anything paradoxical or unbelievable or outside of accepted beliefs, but we
> should consider that man the most accomplished who is able to collect the greatest
> number of those things which are scattered among the ideas of others (ἐν ταῖς τῶν
> ἄλλων διανοίαις) and to speak most beautifully about them.

As this passage shows, Isocrates is not merely assuming the authoritative
voice of traditional advice poetry; he is culling his actual material from
"the ideas of others." As was customary in Greek education from the very
beginning, Isocrates hands over traditional moral precepts to the young
in the hope that they will internalize them. As he puts it at section 38:
"practice speaking about noble pursuits so that you will become accustomed to think things that are similar to the things spoken (ἵνα συνεθισ-
θῇς ὅμοια τοῖς εἰρημένοις φρονεῖν)."

Consider, finally, the programmatic statements that Isocrates enunciates at *ad Demonicum* 12:

> It is not possible for a person who is not filled up with many fine *akousmata* (τὸν
> μὴ πολλῶν καὶ καλῶν ἀκουσμάτων πεπληρωμένον) to be disposed in [the proper]
> frame of mind; for bodily things are by nature developed by suitable exercises,
> while the soul is developed by serious discourses (σπουδαίοις λόγοις). Therefore I
> will attempt to lay down (ὑποθέσθαι) concisely by what pursuits you will most
> successfully advance towards virtue and be held in high repute in the eyes of all
> other men.

"*Akousmata*" – the precepts that are "heard" throughout a culture – can
"fill" the soul with "serious" ideas.[18] Indeed, as we learn in section 19,
"*akousmata* are better than much wealth; for wealth quickly fades away,
whereas *akousmata* last for all time." Finally, as Isocrates suggests towards the end of the speech,

> I have chosen ... to leave behind precepts for the years to come; for it will be easy
> for you to perceive the usefulness of these things, but it will be difficult to find a

---

been the subject of much debate. For a summary of this controversy, see de Vries 1969: 7–
11; de Vries (tentatively) assigns it to the 360s.

[16] Isocrates explicitly describes his work as ὑποθήκας ὡς χρὴ ζῆν at *ad Nicoclem* 3. In the *ad Demonicum* 5, he refers to his speech as a παραίνεσις which, as Kurke 1990: 91 observes, is used as a synonym for *hypothēkai*.

[17] Kurke 1990: 90.

[18] Cf. *Helen* 11, where Isocrates claims that τὸ σπουδάζειν (which he is doing in his speech) is much more difficult than τὸ παίζειν (exemplified by discourses that handle unusual and paradoxical subject matter).

person who advises you with goodwill. In order that you do not seek to learn from another things which I have excluded, and that you may draw from this as from a treasure-house, I thought that it was necessary to leave out none of the counsels which I have to give. (44)

Isocrates thus claims that his speech offers counsels that are complete and self-sufficing; it is, in fact, an eternal repository of true and useful *akousmata.*[19]

I am not so much interested in exploring the polemic between Plato and Isocrates on these topics.[20] More important for my purposes is that Isocrates explicates (and endorses) a phenomenon that had been in operation for centuries in Greek culture: the transmission of ethical and political ideologies by way of the repetition of time-honored precepts and stories. Plato's target, I would argue, is not simply Isocrates; rather, it is the very notion of the inherited "truths" of which Isocrates is simply another transmitter. Authors of traditional *logoi*, Plato urges, should not be considered authorities if they are merely recycling the ideas and generic commonplaces handed down to them by others; unless they have "discovered" what they have to say, these authors are not speaking authentically.

III

We come now to the second of the two players mentioned above: the individual who receives the alien discourse. It should be clear by now that Plato wants individuals to speak for themselves rather than rehearse the language of others. But what exactly is the self, and under what conditions can it be said to author its own discourse?[21] Plato does not give a full answer to these questions in the *Phaedrus*. But he does provide some clear pointers. Consider, for example, Socrates' second speech in the dialogue, where we are ushered inside the human soul to witness a struggle between the rational part (figured as a charioteer) and the appetitive part (figured as a black horse). What is especially startling about this struggle is that it involves a good deal of discussion and argument. Note, in particular, the eloquence of the black horse: first, he gets the other parts of

[19] For a discussion of *akousmata* or aphorisms in early Greek literature, see Barnes 1983.

[20] A recent analysis of the ongoing polemic between Plato and Isocrates is found in Eucken 1983 (see also de Romilly 1975: esp. ch. 3). For the treatment of Isocrates in the *Phaedrus*, see Howland 1937, de Vries 1953 and 1971, Coulter 1967, Burger 1980: 115–26. Little has been done with the *ad Nicoclem* and the *ad Demonicum*, however; I believe that their relationship with the *Phaedrus* deserves careful consideration.

[21] For a provocative analysis of Plato's notion of the "self," see C. Taylor 1989: 115–27; Long 1992a and 1992b discusses concepts of the self developed and articulated in the ancient philosophical tradition, especially in Presocratic and Stoic thinking.

the soul to "agree to do his bidding" (ὁμολογήσαντε ποιήσειν τὸ κελευό-
μενον, 254b3); when they break this agreement, he "censures" (ἐλοιδόρησεν) and "reviles" (κακίζων) them for "abandoning their post out of
cowardice and unmanliness" (c7–8); having "agreed to their request that
they put the matter off" (συνεχώρησεν δεομένων εἰς αὖθις ὑπερβαλέσθαι,
d2), he later "reminds them when they pretend to have forgotten"
(ἀμνημονεῖν προσποιουμένω ἀναμιμνήσκων, d3–4); he then compels the
other parts to approach the boy "with the same proposals" (ἐπὶ τοὺς αὐτοὺς λόγους, d5–6) and, when the lover is lying down with his beloved, he
"has something to say to the charioteer, and claims that he deserves a
little enjoyment in exchange for so much suffering" (ἔχει ὅτι λέγῃ πρὸς τὸν
ἡνίοχον, καὶ ἀξιοῖ ἀντὶ πολλῶν πόνων σμικρὰ ἀπολαῦσαι, 255e5–256a1).
In spite of his appetitive and irrational nature, the black horse can negotiate, argue, vituperate, and persuade. Indeed he is even said to have an
"evil-speaking tongue" (κακηγόρον γλῶτταν, 254e3–4).[22]

The appetitive part of the human soul, then, does not simply comprise
brute and irrational desires; for it also houses what we might call the discourse of these desires.[23] Given that each part of the soul has a different
set of desires and motivations, it stands to reason that each will ally itself
with a different sort of *logos*. Different kinds of *logoi*, the *Phaedrus* indicates, represent different parts of the soul. When the charioteer resists
and eventually subdues the black horse, then, he must overcome not only
his physical appetites but the seductive arguments which champion that
kind of pleasure. In this struggle within the soul, competing modes of
discourse as well as competing desires come into collision. Socrates' second speech, of course, offers only a brief description of the collision between the *logoi* in the soul. To gain a clearer sense of this intra-psychic
verbal competition, we must look elsewhere in the dialogue.

In his book on the *Phaedrus*, Ferrari argues persuasively that the
speeches in favor of the non-lover made by Lysias and Socrates should be
directly linked with the voices of the black horse and the white horse
(respectively) in Socrates' second speech. As Ferrari puts it,

Lysias' non-lover speaks with the voice of the lustful black horse, for whom there
can be no ethical conflict but at most a prudential deferral of the immediate sat-
isfaction of pleasure for the sake of its future maximisation; Socrates' man adds to

---

[22] For a detailed study of the eloquence of the black horse (and, correlatively, of the brute
violence of the charioteer), see Ferrari 1985.
[23] As Ferrari 1985 and 1987: esp. 185–203 observes. It could be argued that the *Republic*
also assigns different kinds of "*logoi*" to the different parts of the soul (especially in books
8–10). On the psychology set forth in the *Republic*, see Annas 1981: ch. 5, Moline 1981:
ch. 3, J. Cooper 1984, Patterson 1987. As these scholars have observed, Plato locates desire in all three parts of the soul; cf. Nussbaum 1986: ch. 5, who allocates all desire to the
appetitive part of the soul.

this drama the voice of the white horse, who seeks honour with the same un-reflective determination that his black yoke-mate applies to the pursuit of pleas-ure, and so can do nothing but bluntly resist the other's aims when they come into conflict with its own; and although both characters claim to speak with the voice of reason, what we have yet to hear is reason's true voice . . .[24]

If this is on target, then the *logos* of the black horse is aligned with the speech of Lysias by virtue of its valorization of physical pleasure. These "prudential" discourses cannot question the value of this or any other end but can only represent and rationalize the unexamined goals of the ap-petitive part of the soul. The *logos* of the white horse would resemble the ashamed lover of Socrates' first speech; both have honor as their unexamined end. Only the charioteer has the capacity to investigate and choose between the various goals and ends. It is of course in the third speech – Socrates' palinode – that we find a depiction of the charioteer's choice between ends and, if not a full investigation of the nature of each end, at least a vivid picture of the stakes in this contest.

The three speeches in the *Phaedrus*, then, are examples of the kinds of *logoi* that represent the different parts of the human soul. It should be emphasized, however, that the soul may contain many other kinds of *logoi* than the three set forth in the *Phaedrus*. In particular, the appetitive part of the soul, as the *Republic* makes clear, is a monster with many heads. As Socrates says in book 9, "the third part [of the soul], because it has many forms (διὰ πολυειδίαν), we are not able to designate by one distinctive name . . ." (580d–e). He goes on to say at 588c that the human soul, insofar as its nature is composite, resembles monsters such as Chi-maera, Scylla, and Cerberus; more specifically, it can be likened to a monster made up of a man, a lion, and a beast that is "variegated and many-headed, having the heads of tame and wild animals all around, and having the capacity to change and grow all these things out of itself" (588c). This passage, which finds a clear parallel in the opening scene of the *Phaedrus*, reminds us that the human soul can be more or less typhonic. In particular, that part of the soul portrayed by the black horse can contain a great number of "voices" which differ not only in style but in the ends that they champion. But all of these would share in the same cognitive limitations revealed by the speech of Lysias' non-lover; none would be able to analyze or evaluate the various ends or goals that are presenting themselves to the soul.

If this is on target, then alien discourse cannot simply be defined as something external to a soul. For we have now seen that alien discourse

---

[24] Ferrari 1987: 102. Griswold 1986: 67, 116, seems to be moving in the same direction.

can lodge itself within a soul precisely because the soul has desires and motivations that are represented by different kinds of *logoi*. There are certain *logoi* that the black and white horses *want* to hear, as it were, and it is by way of the soul's conspiracy with these alien voices that external language becomes internal language.[25] Since human beings are continually making the language of others their own, the very boundaries of the self are called into question. What I take Plato to be indicating is that a human soul's authentic voice does not comprise the manifold voices that reside within it – it is not coextensive, in short, with all the soul's internal voices. The authentic voice is something that needs to be identified and developed by way of philosophical inquiry. Since this kind of inquiry involves testing the truth of different *logoi*, the practice of philosophy demands that a person examine and evaluate not only external discourse but also the voices within. This person will discover that some of his internal voices are in fact alien in the sense that they do not represent the wisdom-loving part of the soul.

We are now able to see why the *Phaedrus* keeps recurring to the problem of alien discourse – whether it be conveyed by the spoken or the written word, whether it comes from without or within the soul. Note that Socrates actually spells this out for Phaedrus in the passage where he narrates the Egyptian story. "I can relate an ἀκοήν from the ancients," he says at 274c, "although only they know the truth; but if we could discover (εὕροιμεν) the truth, would we still be concerned with human opinions (ἀνθρωπίνων δοξασμάτων)?" Here, Socrates indicates that his own story is merely hearsay, and he explicitly contrasts what he is about to do – relate something that he has heard – with the activity of discovering the truth. In spite of this pointer, however, Phaedrus' only response to the story is that Socrates has made it up (275b). Since Phaedrus has failed to get the message, Socrates tries again. In the olden days, he says, people were perfectly happy to listen to the words of an oak or rock, so long as they spoke the truth; "but to you, perhaps, it matters who the speaker is and where he comes from; for you do not consider this thing alone – whether what is said is true or not" (275b–c). In this passage, Socrates

---

[25] Plato does not analyze the precise mechanics of the act of internalizing discourse in the *Phaedrus*. In particular, where are the false opinions within the soul lodged (i.e. do they reside in the lower parts, or can the rational part itself be the seat of error)? Plato appears to address this question in *Republic* 10, where he divides the soul into a "superior" and an "inferior" element (603a). The latter element is described as "opining (δοξάζον) contrary to measure" (603a1; cf. 603d, where Socrates mentions souls that contain "opposing opinions [δόξας] about the same things"). As Belfiore observes (1983: 52–3), the "inferior" element should not be identified with the irrational parts of the soul. The inferior element is swayed by these parts, but its essence is false cognition.

gives explicit instructions for handling hearsay: do not search for an authority on whom to rely; develop your own authority by investigating the validity of the things you hear.

Given this and other suggestions in the *Phaedrus* that philosophical investigation is necessary for the development of an authentic voice, why does Plato include alien discourse in his own texts? Why not stick to portrayals of philosophers developing their authentic voices by way of dialectical investigation? Why not at least steer clear of those voices that address themselves to the lower parts of the human psyche – voices which could well become internal aliens that impede the development of the true and authentic voice?

In a famous passage in the *Republic*, Socrates deplores ποικίλη μίμησις ("complicated mimesis") with its dangerous representation of τὸ ἀγανακτητικόν τε καὶ ποικίλον ἦθος ("the irritated and complicated character", 604e–605a); this kind of mimesis fosters the lower parts of the soul, he adds, for when people vicariously participate in ἀλλότρια πάθη, they unwittingly convert "what is alien into what is their own" (ἀπὸ τῶν ἀλλοτρίων εἰς τὰ οἰκεῖα, 606b). In the *Phaedrus*, by contrast, Socrates issues an endorsement of "complex" – *poikilos* – discourse. For, at 277c, Socrates describes the person who possesses the art of rhetoric as someone who will "offer to the complex soul (ποικίλη ψυχῇ) *logoi* that are complex and that include all modes (ποικίλους ... καὶ παναρμονίους), and to the simple soul *logoi* that are simple." Given that human souls can be more or less typhonic – that they house any number of voices that can be in discord or in concord – they must necessarily be doctored by different kinds of *logoi*.

It will come as no surprise that Phaedrus is a person who possesses an especially complex soul. Socrates describes him at 257b as "going in two directions" (ἐπαμφοτερίζῃ) because he is wavering between Lysias and Socrates.[26] If Lysias would only turn towards philosophy, Socrates adds, then Phaedrus would no longer be pulled in two directions. As this passage indicates, the struggle in Phaedrus' soul is not between reason and

---

[26] Interestingly, the word ἐπαμφοτερίζειν is a technical term in Aristotle for animals and plants whose anatomical features place them in two different categories of being. Sea anemones, for example, "waver" between plants and animals (*PA* 681a36–b2); apes, monkeys and baboons "waver" between human beings and quadrupeds (*HA* 502a16–18); the ostrich "wavers" between a bird and a quadruped (*PA* 697b14–18), the seal between a land animal and a water animal (*HA* 566b27–31), and the bat between a creature of the air and a creature of the land (*PA* 697b1–3). As Aristotle describes such creatures in the *Parts of Animals* (697b3–4), "they belong to both classes or to neither." Although none of the plants and animals that Aristotle mentions is, technically, a monster, their dual natures lend them a freakish aspect. Aristotle's unclassifiable creatures provide a neat analogue for Phaedrus' complex and "wavering" psyche (and for the many other monsters conjured in the *Phaedrus*). On Aristotle's use of ἐπαμφοτερίζειν, see Peck 1979: lxxiii–lxxv.

appetite but rather between different *logoi* that represent different desires
and aims – *logoi* such as those of Lysias and Socrates. Phaedrus is complex, then, not only because he possesses a tripartite soul, but because so
many competing *logoi* have lodged themselves within his psyche. As Socrates puts it coyly at 242a–b, Phaedrus is "divine about discourses" (θεῖος
... περὶ τοὺς λόγους), for he has "produced more *logoi* than anyone else in
his generation, either by delivering them himself or by compelling others
to speak." Recall the "delight" (γάνυσθαι) that Phaedrus takes in Lysias'
speech (234d); his willingness to use force on Socrates to get him to deliver
the first speech (236c–d); his assertion that Socrates' announcement that
he will make a second speech is the "most pleasant" utterance imaginable
(243b); his suggestion that he will get Lysias to make another speech "in
competition" with Socrates' (257c); and, finally, his extraordinary response to Socrates' question whether he would like to carry the inquiry
further: "what else should one live for ... other than pleasures such as
these?" (258e). As these passages reveal, Phaedrus' philology is undis-
criminating and oriented towards pleasure; it is precisely this addiction to
logoi that has fostered the typhon in his soul.[27]

Clearly, the character of Phaedrus serves to dramatize the typhonic soul
and its need for "complex discourse." It should be emphasized, however,
that all souls are complex to the extent that they are tripartite: even a
"simple" person like Socrates must come to grips with discourse which is
geared towards the lower parts of his soul.[28] Part of philosophy, then,
must involve a critical engagement with *logoi* that do not represent the
wisdom-loving part of the soul. To be sure, philosophic souls will not
need the kind of doctoring that Phaedran types require. But they will have
to explore different kinds of *logoi* in an effort to understand how each
kind operates upon (or within) the human soul. The philosopher, then,

---

[27] On Phaedrus' weakness for *logoi*, see Griswold 1986: 28–9 and Ferrari 1987: 6–9, 27–9.
Morgan 1994 offers a detailed analysis of Phaedrus' challenge to Socrates to make a
speech in response to that of Lysias at 235d–236b.

[28] The distinction between "simple" and "complex" souls made at 277c must be interpreted
in conjunction with 270d, 271a, and 230a. Socrates says at 270d that they need to investigate whether the soul is by nature "simple or multiform" (ἁπλοῦν ἢ πολυειδές), and at
271a that the true rhetorician must grasp the exact nature of the soul and explain
"whether it is one and uniform or whether, like the shape of the body, it is multiform"
(πότερον ἓν καὶ ὅμοιον πέφυκεν ἢ κατὰ σώματος μορφὴν πολυειδές). In the first passage,
"multiform" is opposed to "simple," whereas in the second, "multiform" is opposed to
"one and uniform." Does Plato equate "simple" with "one and uniform"? The palinode
indicates that no human soul is "simple" in this sense. Thus, when Socrates says that a
"simple" soul needs a "simple *logos*" (277c), he must mean that some human souls are
relatively simple rather than "one and uniform" (which would preclude tripartition). Note
also Socrates' claim at 230a that he investigates himself in order to discover whether he is
"a creature more complicated and furious than the typhon, or something gentler and
more simple" (my italics).

must make every kind of *logos* his/her business. It is for this reason that the ποικίλος λόγος constituted by the *Phaedrus* is useful both for Phaedran types and for people pursuing philosophy. For even as it prompts the former to begin to harmonize their souls, it aids the latter in investigating the liabilities and potentialities of traditional kinds of discourse.[29]

IV

I turn now from the alien voices that inhabit the soul to those that inhabit the text. What sort of voice would be alien in the context of a Platonic dialogue? It might seem, at first glance, that any discourse that is not dialectical is alien to philosophic discourse. This would mean that the distinguishing feature of philosophic discourse is a formal one: if the method of dialectic is present, so also is philosophy; if it is absent, then something alien to philosophy is occurring. But this is surely not the case. One can converse in a dialectical mode and not be pursuing the truth. And, correlatively, one can be pursuing the truth and not be engaging in dialectic. A different and, I think, more fruitful approach to this problem is to follow Bakhtin and identify *genres of discourse* alien to that of the text in which they are embedded. In other words, genres that have a separate existence outside of the genre of the Socratic dialogue are alien to Plato's text simply by virtue of generic differentiation. Note that we are no longer talking about alien voices spoken or heard by individuals but rather the alien discourse of a genre.

Before examining the generic "aliens" in the *Phaedrus*, let us briefly recall Bakhtin's notion of parodic discourse: parody occurs when the alien genre "is a completely passive tool in the hands of the author wielding it. He takes, so to speak, someone else's meek and defenseless discourse and installs his own interpretation in it, forcing it to serve his own new purposes."[30] Intertextuality is non-parodic, on the other hand, when the author grants the alien genre full semantic autonomy. In this chapter, I would like to employ an alternative terminology that Bakhtin used for distinguishing parodic and non-parodic intertextual modes: that of "active" and "passive double-voiced discourse." "Active double-voiced discourse" is a synonym for parody: it is in "active" double-voicing that

---

[29] The "complexity" of the dialogue, in short, cannot be explained by reference to the over-complex souls of Phaedrus and the unphilosophical readers. For this kind of interpretation encourages a very reductive reading of the dialogue: the complexity of the text is seen as a mere medicine for lesser souls; philosophical souls, it implies, will not be benefited by such a discourse. I cannot agree with this line of argument. For Plato's incorporation of alien discourse into the *Phaedrus* – which is, after all, what makes the text "complex" – offers a number of vital lessons to the student of philosophy.

[30] Bakhtin 1984: 197.

the author imposes his will upon an alien genre – the author is the active party, the alien text is the passive victim. Correlatively, "passive double-voiced discourse" is a synonym for non-parodic discourse: in this case, the author assumes a more passive stance, thus allowing the alien genre to play an active and relatively autonomous role in his text.[31] Although this alternative terminology may grate on the ear, I believe that it is especially well suited to a dialogue like the *Phaedrus*, whose powerful intertextual encounters are embedded in a narrative describing the sexual life of philosophers, with its peculiar blend of active and passive elements.

How, then, does Plato handle alien genres in the *Phaedrus*? Is he conspiring with or against these intruders? My first analysis will deal with a relatively simple example of one such conspiracy in the *Phaedrus*: Socrates' story of Theuth and Thamus. This story, I will argue, beautifully illustrates the intertextuality that is characteristic of this dialogue, and can serve as a starting-point for a fuller exploration of the many other alien voices in the *Phaedrus*.

In searching for a subtext for the tale of Theuth and Thamus, scholars have almost invariably turned to the figure of Prometheus, who was credited in some mythic traditions with the invention of writing. Hackforth, for example, claims that "the inventor of writing in Greek legend was Prometheus; but he was unsuitable for Plato's purpose, since it would have been difficult to make anyone play against him the part that Thamus plays against Theuth."[32] But there was another tradition which attributed the invention of writing to Palamedes, whose story provides a far more suitable subtext for our passage. It should be emphasized that Palamedes was a very conspicuous figure in fifth-century Athens. The tragic playwrights Aeschylus, Sophocles, and Euripides each wrote a *Palamedes*. Euripides' play, in fact, is explicitly imitated in Aristophanes' *Thesmophoriazusae* (769–84, cf. 848), which parodies the scene in which Oeax, Palamedes' brother, attempts to send his father the news of Palamedes' death by writing it on the oars of a ship and launching them into the sea.[33] Clearly Aristophanes expected his audience to recall the details of

---

[31] Readers familiar with Bakhtin will note that I have altered his terminology in one simple way. For I have reversed Bakhtin's use of the words "active" and "passive," which is why in my scheme "active" double-voiced discourse is a synonym for parody and "passive" double-voiced discourse denotes non-parodic hybridization. It is important to emphasize that, although Bakhtin's epithets are reversed, the Bakhtinian conception of the two kinds of double-voiced discourse remains the same. I have chosen to reverse the epithets in order to draw a parallel between active/passive intertextual encounters and active/passive sexual encounters.

[32] Hackforth 1952: 157 n. 2. See also de Vries 1969: 248, Burger 1980: 93, and Rowe 1986b: 208–9; cf. Derrida [1972]/1981: 84–94, who explores the relation between Theuth and the Greek god Hermes.

[33] For a reconstruction of the *Palamedes* of Euripides, see Scodel 1980: ch. 2.

Euripides' play. One should note, too, that Gorgias composed a speech of defence for this hapless hero (DK B11a); the rhetorical potential of Palamedes' predicament is obvious. Finally, Palamedes' fame as a literary figure is clearly attested by a passage from Plato's second letter: the encounter between a sage and a man of power is a popular *topos* in poetry and other discourses, the letter runs; witness that of Periander and Thales, Pericles and Anaxagoras, Cyrus and Croesus, Creon and Tiresias, Agamemnon and Nestor, and Odysseus and Palamedes (311a–b).

Plato gives us several reasons for looking to Palamedes rather than Prometheus for the subtext of the Egyptian tale. First, he describes Theuth as the inventor of number (ἀριθμόν) and its attendant arts, draughts and dice (πεττείας τε καὶ κυβείας) and, finally, writing (γράμματα) (274c–d). This is a singular collection of inventions, yet it is precisely this unlikely combination that Palamedes claims for himself in Gorgias' speech: γράμματα, ἀριθμός, and πεσσοί.[34] Both draughts (*pessoi*) and dice (*kuboi*), moreover, make an appearance in a fragment from Sophocles' *Palamedes*:

> οὐ ...
> ... χρόνου τε διατριβὰς σοφωτάτας
> ἐφηῦρε φλοίσβου μετὰ κόπον καθημένοις,
> πεσσοὺς κύβους τε, τερπνὸν ἀργίας ἄκος;

> didn't he invent the wisest ways for passing time for the men
> when they were sitting idle after the toil of war – draughts and
> dice, a sweet remedy for idleness? (fr. 479 Radt)

Finally, consider the arresting image in Euripides' tragedy (fr. 578N), where Palamedes designates γράμματα as λήθης φάρμακα – "a drug that cures forgetfulness." Theuth's claim in Plato's tale that γράμματα are a μνήμης τε γὰρ καὶ σοφίας φάρμακον (274e) – a "drug for memory and wisdom" – clearly imitates this tragic passage. Even with the scant remains of the tragedies, the echoes of the dramas of Palamedes in Plato's story are difficult to deny.[35]

---

[34] DK B11a.30. See also Plato's *Republic* 522d, where Palamedes is credited with the invention of ἀριθμός. Note, too, that Palamedes is explicitly mentioned at *Phaedrus* 261b–d, where Socrates identifies "Palamedes of Elea" as the inventor of eristic. Most scholars agree that this is a reference to Zeno.

[35] Ferrari 1987: 280–1 n. 21 has documented these parallels. He does not, however, offer any analysis of the allusions to the Palamedes story in Plato's text. Euripides describes writing as a φάρμακον (*Palamedes* fr. 578N) and Sophocles as an ἄκος (*Palamedes* fr. 479 Radt) and (probably) as an ἄκεστρον (*Palamedes* fr. 480 Radt; though we lack the context for the word in this fragment, it seems likely that it was used in reference to writing. Note that Hesychius glosses ἄκεστρον with "φάρμακον"). These fragments suggest that the notion of writing as a drug or cure was already a *topos* in the tragedians.

Why would Plato invoke the tragic story of Palamedes in this scene?[36] Recall, first of all, the plot of the story. As Scodel has suggested in her reconstruction of Euripides' *Palamedes*, "There appears to have been a tragic (and later a rhetorical) Palamedes, whose story was, of course, not treated in exactly the same way by any two authors, but whose character and fate seems to have been more fixed within tragedy than in the case of many mythological personages."[37] The basic ingredients of this tale are as follows. Odysseus was jealous of Palamedes' wisdom and contrived to frame him as a traitor to the Greeks. Therefore, having buried some gold in Palamedes' tent, Odysseus forged a letter which appeared to be written by Palamedes to the Trojan king Priam; the letter mentions the gold which Priam has given to Palamedes in exchange for his betrayal of the Greeks. The letter is eventually "discovered," and its contents are corroborated by the presence of the gold in Palamedes' tent. Palamedes is put on trial and condemned to death.[38]

If Plato is deliberately alluding to the story of Palamedes, then the Egyptian tale is the site of a fascinating instance of generic appropriation. For, as I will argue, Socrates' story both conjures and corrects its tragic predecessor. Consider, first, the tale of Theuth and Thamus. In this dry little story, we witness a miniature dramatic dialogue. The dramatic context is supplied at the beginning, when we are told that Theuth has brought his inventions to Thamus in order to convince him that they should be disseminated throughout Egypt (274d). The dialogue now begins. Theuth proudly suggests that writing will be a drug for memory and wisdom, and Thamus disagrees. Theuth, he insists, has gotten it all wrong: "you, who are the father of writing," he says, "because of your affection [for your child], have claimed for it a power which is the opposite of that which it possesses" (275a). Thamus proceeds to summarize his own views about the damaging effects that writing would produce, em-

---

[36] Cf. the reference to Palamedes in the *Apology* (41a–b), where Socrates describes the pleasure he would experience if, after his death, he could converse with characters such as Ajax and Palamedes and "any other of the ancient heroes who met his death through an unfair trial"; if death should bring him this boon, he adds, he might "compare his own experience to theirs" (ἀντιπαραβάλλοντι τὰ ἐμαυτοῦ πάθη πρὸς τὰ ἐκείνων). Although the *Phaedrus* does not juxtapose Palamedes' fate with that of Socrates, Plato's critical reading of the Palamedes story in this dialogue may shed light on the passage from the *Apology*. For, if we "compare" (or "contrast," which is another meaning of ἀντιπαραβάλλοντι) Socrates' fate with that of Palamedes, as the *Apology* asks us to do, we will discover a crucial difference between these structurally similar stories: Palamedes (and Ajax) died miserably, whereas Socrates' death is serene and *truly* heroic. Note that Xenophon (*Apol.* 26; cf. *Mem.* 4.2.33) and Libanius (*de Socratis Silentio* 28) also compare Socrates' fate to that of Palamedes.
[37] Scodel 1980: 43.
[38] The most detailed ancient accounts of this plot are Hyginus 105, Servius on *Aen.* 2.81, and the scholium on Euripides' *Orestes* 432.

phasizing that it would in fact obstruct learning and recollection. And that is the end of the story.

The tragic subtext enriches this tale in a number of ways. First, and most obvious, the fact that Palamedes was destroyed by the agency of his own invention – the forged letter – supplements Socrates' tale of an overfond father with a terrifying story of parricide and betrayal. For the father of writing will be killed by his own child. Theuth, of course, plays the role of Palamedes *prior* to his bestowal of writing upon the Greeks; Theuth's proud insistence on the power of his newly discovered drug is now loaded with irony. Socrates' subsequent suggestion, moreover, that writing is an illegitimate son who needs his father to defend him since he cannot defend himself (275e–276a) echoes and inverts the logic of the tragic drama: Palamedes attempts to deny that he has fathered the letter, but the child speaks differently about its paternity. Finally, when we hear Socrates asserting that the wise man will not sow the seeds of his discourse in a written text (276c), since a written text cannot speak if questioned and can easily get into the hands of people who do not understand (275d–e), we are reminded of how the Greeks condemned Palamedes on the basis of the forged letter. The tragic subtext, in short, affirms and dramatizes Plato's message.

Plato was clearly drawn to the Palamedes story because of its depiction of the destructive power of the written word. But, while the plot of the story serves Plato's purposes perfectly, its tragic trajectory collides with the aims and claims of philosophy. It is for this reason that Plato incorporates into his tale a critique of the tragic interpretation of the story. For, in the tragic version of the tale, a wise man is worsted by one who is merely clever. As Xenophon puts it, "haven't you heard of the sufferings of Palamedes? All of the poets say that he was destroyed by Odysseus, who envied his wisdom" (*Mem.* 4.2.33). Scodel observes that Palamedes enjoyed the reputation of being "the perfect σοφός."[39] A clash between him and the wily Odysseus, then, amounts to a contest for wisdom.

It is worth noting the persistent references to the theme of wisdom in several of the fifth-century handlings of the Palamedes story. In the scant fragments of Euripides' *Palamedes*, for example, this theme obtrudes itself no less than four times:

> fr. 581N: "thousands of us may be generals, but some one or two men in a long span of time may be wise (σοφός)."
>
> fr. 583N: "I will never praise the wisdom (τὸ σοφόν) of the man who speaks well, when the deeds which he speaks about are shameful."

[39] Scodel 1980: 43.

fr. 580.3–5N: "all men – both those who are friends of the Muses and those who dwell apart [from them] – toil on behalf of money, and he who has the most is the wisest (σοφώτατος)."

fr. 588N: "you killed, you killed, O Danaans, the all-wise (πάν-σοφον) nightingale of the muses, who harmed no-one."

These passages suggest that this tragedy brings two different kinds of wisdom into conflict – Odysseus' calculating cleverness and Palamedes' beneficial inventiveness and cultured intelligence. In Gorgias' speech, too, the theme of wisdom comes to the fore. Palamedes says in sections 25–6, for example, that Odysseus has accused him of both wisdom and madness, since he has called him clever but also accused him of treachery. Since no-one in his right mind would become a traitor, Palamedes would have to be both wise and insane. After inquiring from Odysseus whether he thinks that "wise men are sensible or senseless," Palamedes goes on to conclude: "if I am wise, then I committed no wrong, but if I committed a wrong, I am not wise."[40]

What Plato objected to in the Palamedes story, I submit, was its emphatic suggestion that an "all-wise" man could meet a tragic end. It is for this reason that Plato offers a corrective in his little Egyptian dialogue. Theuth, like Palamedes, claims that writing is a powerful and beneficial drug. When Thamus explains to him that he is behaving like a doting father and is completely mistaken about his invention, he is clearly indicating that Theuth is *not* wise. It is for this reason that he addresses him as ὦ τεχνικώτατε Θεύθ (274e) – "O most skilled Theuth" – and informs him that it is one thing to invent something and another thing to judge whether it will benefit or harm its user (274e). Here, Plato segregates the technical skill and inventiveness displayed by Theuth from the wisdom that enables a person to make judgments about the ethical and political ramifications of a given *technē*. Theuth emerges as a clever inventor whose pride in his creations has obstructed his judgment. When he blithely informs Thamus that he thinks that his inventions should be given to the Egyptians (274d5–6), we are reminded that his bad judgment could have serious consequences for himself and others.

Clearly, the Egyptian dialogue asks us to reinterpret the tragic subtext. For, if Theuth is not wise, then neither is Palamedes. In addition, Palamedes can no longer be seen as the benefactor he was taken to be, since his inventions are judged by Thamus to bring more harm than aid to human beings.[41] These retrospective assessments of the subtext, then,

---

[40] On the methods of argumentation used by Gorgias in the *Palamedes*, see Long 1984.

[41] Plato may also have objected to Palamedes' invention of dice and draughts as the "most wise way of passing time" (Sophocles, *Palamedes* fr. 479 Radt). Cf. the meditation on good and bad ways of passing time at *Phaedrus* 276d.

invite us to reevaluate the story of Palamedes. In particular, we are asked
to see Palamedes' death as due to his ignorance about the nature of his invention; if he had understood the true power of writing, Plato suggests, he
could have avoided his fate. Instead of the story of a wise and good man
who comes to a tragic end, we are presented with an alternative tale in
which a proud and self-deceived man is hoist with his own petard. But
this, of course, is not a tragedy. This scene, then, offers an excellent example of parody or "active double-voiced discourse." For Plato foists his
own interpretation on the tragic tale and, in so doing, rejects what he
takes to be the most distinctive "semantic intention" of the genre of
tragedy: the claim that a good man can be reduced to wretchedness.[42] By
appropriating the tragedy of Palamedes, Plato transforms the alien voice
into his own.

Plato's parody of the tragic story of Palamedes provides a standard
against which we can adjudge his handling of other alien voices in the
text. As we will see, this is a dialogue in which Plato does not always opt
for "active" double-voicing. And this should come as no surprise. For, in
a dialogue that challenges the traditional ideology of active and passive
roles in the erotic sphere – the philosophic lover being passive in his
surrender to the invasion of love and active in his pursuit of truth – it is
fitting that the author would refuse to play a consistently dominant role
in his interaction with alien genres of discourse.[43]

Plato's pointed refusal of parody emerges in several fascinating instances of intertextuality in the *Phaedrus*. Consider, first, his use of the
genre of the encomium, which is the most prominent type of alien discourse in the dialogue.[44] The case of the encomiastic speech of "Lysias"
is, I believe, fairly straightforward. For Plato simply incorporates a complete text from an alien genre into his dialogue, but subverts it by placing
it in a new context.[45] By making Lysias' speech the first in a series of

[42] For a fuller investigation of Plato's "imitation" of the genre of tragedy, see chapter 2. See
also Kuhn 1941 and 1942, Bacon 1959, Clay 1975, Sider 1980a, Patterson 1982: esp. 84–
90, and Halliwell 1984a: 50–8.

[43] For discussions of the male homoerotic love affair as it was articulated and enacted in
Greek (and especially Athenian) culture, see Dover [1978]/1989, and Halperin 1986 and
1990. As Halperin 1986: 68–72 points out, Plato overturns and reconceives the traditional
role of the "active" lover and the "passive" beloved in the *Phaedrus* and other dialogues.

[44] Not coincidentally, the discourse of praise and blame is a major component of most of
Isocrates' speeches. Although Plato's treatment of praise discourse in the *Phaedrus* is not
simply directed against Isocrates, Plato must have been aware of Isocrates' proclivity for
this mode of discourse. One should recall that the very great majority of Lysias' speeches
were forensic, and thus make only passing use of the discourse of praise and blame. I
would suggest that Isocrates is subjected to much greater criticism than Lysias in this
dialogue.

[45] It does not matter whether Plato has composed this speech or not; it is alien to the Platonic dialogue simply by virtue of belonging to the encomiastic genre.

three speeches, each of which supersedes its predecessor(s), Plato puts it
in its place: the *logos* of Lysias appears simplistic, strained, and downright
silly when compared with the other two speeches. In addition, if we accept
that the three speeches are designed to reflect and represent the three parts
of the soul, then Lysias is shown to be the spokesman for but one part of
the soul, and that the most obnoxious. In short, the Lysias speech proceeds according to the rules of the encomiastic genre, but its semantic intention is altered by its new surroundings.

In Socrates' first speech, on the other hand, Plato begins to disrupt the
discourse of eulogy and censure from within. For Socrates' insistence
at the opening that they cannot proceed without agreeing on a definition
of "the essence of each thing" (237c) calls into question the subjective and
arbitrary conferral of praise and blame that was an essential feature of
the genre. In addition, when Socrates refuses to finish, claiming that his
speech of censure (καὶ ταῦτα ψέγων) has stolen into the lofty realms of
epic discourse (241e), Plato alerts us to the boundaries – and, indeed, the
boundedness – of the genre. This disruption invites us to reflect upon the
limitations of the rhetoric of censure and eulogy as a vehicle for representing truth. Unlike the Lysias speech, Socrates' speech is deliberately
left unfinalized. This indicates that Socrates *cannot* finish his speech by
remaining within the confines of the encomiastic genre. For Socrates can't
even complete the censorious part of the speech without slipping into a
mode of rhetoric loftier than that used for the discourse of blame.

What, then, are the limitations of the discourse of praise and blame?
Socrates' first speech gives us a clue: he insists that the eulogy cannot
proceed without a definition of the subject (237c–d), but then proceeds to
offer a definition of *erōs* that is completely contradicted in his second
speech. Clearly, it is not enough simply to offer a definition; the definition
itself must be grounded in truth.[46] Note that Socrates says when looking
back at his speeches that they achieved "clarity" and "consistency" because they "defined what *erōs* is, whether rightly or wrongly" (εἴτ᾽ εὖ εἴτε
κακῶς, 265d). The possibility that his first definition may have been in-
correct is explicitly raised here. Any definition can be asserted, but only a
correct definition will stand up to scrutiny. The trouble with the genre of
the encomium is that it cannot demonstrate the truth of a definition and
still remain an encomium.

At the heart of the encomiastic genre is an assertion of a given set of
values by way of the binary logic of good versus bad. As long as one stays
in this binary mode, it will be impossible to ground one's claims by way of
argumentation. Note that Socrates positively parades the binary logic of

---

[46] As Griswold 1986: 177 observes.

his own speeches in his retrospective analysis. At 265a, for example, he claims that "the two speeches were opposites, for the one asserted that it is necessary to gratify the lover and the other the non-lover." Even more pointed is the passage at 265e–266b:

just as in the case of a single body, things come in sets which have the same name – things that are designated by "left" and "right" – so also the two speeches conceived of madness as a single principle within us. The one speech cut off the portion on the left and did not cease from cutting until it discovered (ἐφευρών) within us that which we call "left-handed love" (as it were), which it justly censured; and the other speech led us towards the portion of madness on the right and discovered (ἐφευρών) a love that has the same name as the first but is divine, and it held this up to view and praised it as being the cause of the greatest good for man.

This technical description of Socrates' two speeches immediately strikes the reader as inadequate.[47] Crucially, it leaves out the very principle by which one "discovers" the goodness or badness of a given object. It is not enough merely to divide things in half, for this division depends on a prior knowledge or "discovery" of what is truly valuable for human beings.

The analogy of the human body used in this passage follows hard upon Socrates' famous claim that "every logos should be constructed like a living being, having a body of its own, so that it is not without a head (ἀκέφαλον) or without a foot, but has a middle and extremities..." (264c). Here, we are reminded of the need for more than just the body parts that come in twos. For, in addition to the feet and the limbs, we are explicitly told that the logos needs a head. It must go beyond the binary logic of the encomiastic genre. It must also have a head or reasoning principle which enables it to serve the truth.[48]

Thus far, we have focussed on that part of Plato's handling of the encomium which is critical and parodic. This might suggest that Plato incorporated the encomiastic genre into this dialogue in order to discredit or subvert it, just as he did with the tragic story of Palamedes. To the extent that he does discredit the encomiastic genre, Plato can be seen to be engaging in "active" double-voicing; certainly the first two encomia are

---

[47] Both Griswold 1986: 173–201 and Ferrari 1987: 59–67 note the inadequacy of Socrates' retrospective comments. Though their interpretations differ, each suggests that the technical description and analysis of the speeches ignores the fundamental question of how one discovers what is truly good and valuable.

[48] This passage is usually taken to mean that Plato is issuing an endorsement of a logos that is an organic unity. For a recent exchange on this subject, see Rowe 1986a and 1989 and Heath 1989a and 1989b. Those who want to defend this position (such as Rowe and Heath) are faced with the problem of the apparent disunity of the Phaedrus itself. I have chosen to explore the notion of a logos that has a head – a notion that is dramatized when Socrates covers his head during the delivery of his first speech – rather than to pursue the concept of unity. For the notion of the "headless" logos, see also Gorgias 505d.

not granted full semantic autonomy. But, unlike tragedy, the genre of the encomium admits of a "good" use, and for this reason it need not always be the passive partner in its interaction with Platonic discourse.

Let me turn now to Socrates' second speech. It is important to note that Socrates retrospectively glosses his first speech as an invective and his second as an encomium. For he says at 266a–b that the first speech "censured" the bad kind of lover, with his "left-handed" madness, and the second "praised" the good kind of lover, who is the blessed recipient of "right-handed" madness (cf. 265c). Even the second speech, he suggests, used the same binary oppositions between mad and sane, harmful and beneficial, noble and shameful, as the earlier speeches did. This gloss, however, is only partially true, since the "palinode" moves well beyond the confines of the encomiastic genre. In fact, it ranges from the analytic discourse of the short "proof" of the immortality of the soul to the poetry of *erōtika pathēmata*, from the physicalist language of the medical writers (heating, cooling, infecting, teething) to the apocalyptic utterances of the mystery religions. Finally, it does indeed contain an encomium of the good lover as well as a hymn to the god of Love. To call this speech a "myth" is misleading, for this might seem to denote a simple rather than a composite creature.[49] It is the multiplicity of genres of discourse that characterizes this *poikilos logos*.

We have seen that Socrates was on the verge of transgressing the boundaries of the encomiastic genre in his first speech. In the second speech, it is the non-encomiastic genres of discourse that provide the grounding for the right use of praise. Since praise and blame are assertions of value, they depend upon an understanding of what is truly valuable. This kind of rhetoric, then, must be tethered to a system of value that has been tested and "discovered" by way of philosophical investigation. In Socrates' second speech, Plato offers a vivid depiction of the locus of human value. By locating human souls in a cosmic scheme both by way of the analytic "proof" of the immortality of the soul and by the mythic narrative about the soul's preincarnate peregrinations, Plato lays the foundation for the proper conferral of praise and blame.

In the second speech of Socrates, then, encomiastic discourse is allowed to do just what it is meant to do – to praise a given object (in this case, the philosophic lover) and devalue its opposite (the non-lover). The genre of the encomium thus plays an active role in the generation of meaning. To be sure, the genre is given free rein to the extent that it bolsters the claims of philosophy. But it is not, in this speech, stripped of either its "semantic

---

[49] Socrates makes this explicit at 265b, where he says that he has "blended together" (κεράσαντες) his *logos*.

intentions" or its traditional generic features. For the discourse of eulogy is not parodied or criticized. It conspires *with* the philosophic material.

Plato, then, does not always opt for "active double-voiced discourse" in the *Phaedrus*, and nowhere is this more evident than in his handling of the genre of lyric love poetry. Socrates, of course, mentions Sappho and Anacreon as sources of his first speech (235c), but this genre of poetry has even more impact on his second speech.[50] Certainly the genre makes its most obvious incursion into the *Phaedrus* in this latter speech, when the language of Sappho's famous *phainetai moi* – with its vivid evocation of the fire running beneath the skin, the cold sweat, and the trembling that grips the lover – is used to depict the *pathos* of the philosophical lover when he begins to sprout wings.[51] But this particular allusion is just the beginning, since the entire narrative of the lover's encounter with his beloved in the second speech is replete with the discourse of lyric love poetry.

It is hard to imagine a genre more antithetical to the project of philosophy than that of the lyric love poem. Consider Anne Carson's description of this genre:

Consistently throughout the Greek lyric corpus, as well as in the poetry of tragedy and comedy, eros is an experience that assaults the lover from without and proceeds to take control of his body, his mind and the quality of his life. Eros comes out of nowhere, on wings, to invest the lover, to deprive his body of vital organs and material substance, to enfeeble his mind and distort its thinking, to replace normal conditions of health and sanity with disease and madness. The poets represent eros as an invasion, an illness, an insanity, a wild animal, a natural disaster. His action is to melt, break down, bite into, burn, devour, wear away, whirl around, sting, pierce, wound, poison, suffocate, drag off or grind the lover to a powder.[52]

In the poets, then, the discourse of *erōs* centers on invasion, madness, the

---

[50] See Fortenbaugh 1966 for a discussion of several allusions to Sappho and Anacreon in Socrates' speeches. Carson 1986 offers a rich analysis of the genre of Greek love poetry and Plato's meditation on it in the *Phaedrus*.

[51] Indeed, as Carson 1986: 155–7 observes, the wings themselves, which are so elaborately described in Socrates' speech, find a parallel in the erotic poetry of both Sappho and Anacreon (fr. 31.6 *PLF*; fr. 378 *PMG*, respectively). Note, too, that Plato's depiction of the tripartite soul echoes Anacreon's address to a boy whom he calls the "charioteer of my heart" (τῆς ἐμῆς | ψυχῆς ἡνιοχεύεις, fr. 360 *PMG*); Sappho's declaration in fr. 51 *PLF* – "I do not know what I should do; my thoughts go in two directions" (οὐκ οἶδ' ὄττι θέω· δίχα μοι τὰ νοήμματα) – may also anticipate Plato's psychology. See Carson 1986: 7–9 and passim for the *topos* of the divided self in lyric love poetry. Carson does not explore the connection between this *topos* and the divided soul that is dramatized in Socrates' second speech. Anacreon's mention of the charioteer invites us to posit a direct influence.

[52] Carson 1986: 148.

destruction of the very boundaries of the self. At first glance, this genre
hardly seems to lend itself to philosophic pursuits. How does Plato handle
this unlikely bedfellow?[53]

It could be argued that Plato incorporates the genre of lyric love poetry
into his dialogue merely in order to discredit or correct it. Carson, for
example, argues that "there is an enormous difference" between the erotic
attitudes of Plato and those exhibited in the poetic tradition.[54] This difference, she suggests, is best grasped by focussing on the way in which
Plato "reimagines" the lyric conception of the wings: "Wings are no
foreign machinery of invasion in Plato's conception. They have natural
roots in the soul, a residue of its immortal beginnings."[55] Plato's divergence from the poetic tradition on this and other points is hardly surprising. But, as I will argue, Plato yields to the discourse of lyric love poetry
in fundamental ways.

In Socrates' second speech, the madness of *erōs* is identified as a kind of
enthusiasmos (ἐνθουσιάσεων, 249e1; ἐνθουσιῶντες, 253a3). This term, of
course, indicates the inhabitation or seizure of a human soul by a god.
The references in the dialogue to the myths of Boreas and Oreithuia
(229b–d) and Zeus and Ganymede (255c) serve as dramatic reminders of
the god-snatches-human theme, and the terminology of seizure is explicitly used to describe Eros' invasion of the human soul at 252c: ὁ
ληφθείς (c3); ὅταν ὑπ' Ἔρωτος ἁλῶσι (c5–6).[56] We need not interpret
these passages literally, of course. Griswold, for example, suggests that
"divine erotic madness is not so much sent from gods external to the
individual as sparked from a source within him, as is suggested by its association with anamnesis."[57] While I would hardly insist that Plato's
philosophical lover is literally seized by the god Eros, I must challenge the
suggestion that the lover is not subject to "foreign machinery of invasion"
(Carson) or to forces that are "external to the individual" (Griswold). For
a good deal of the second speech depicts the lover as being invaded from

---

[53] It goes without saying that *erōs* plays a critical role in the psychology of Plato's middle
period. But it is one thing to identify love as a *principle and motive force* of the human
psyche, and quite another to adopt the *discourse* of love constructed by the genre of lyric
love poetry. My investigation centers on the latter.

[54] Carson 1986: 155.

[55] Carson 1986: 157.

[56] Compare Socrates' (ironic) claim that he has been "inspired" and "snatched" by the
nymphs (241e and 238d respectively). He also says at 234d that, as he listened to
Phaedrus' speech, he came to "share in the Bacchic frenzy." These passages thematize
the notion of inspiration, thus anticipating the "good" kind of inspiration depicted in
Socrates' second speech.

[57] Griswold 1986: 75.

without; at least part of the role that he plays is passive in the sense that he is acted upon by external forces that are beyond his control.[58]

From the very beginning, the lover is "driven out of his mind" (ἐκπλήττονται, 250a), and perhaps the best word for his condition thereafter is *permeable*. For his soul is repeatedly penetrated by a variety of liquid influxes. At 251b1–2, for example, he is described as "receiving the stream of beauty in through the eyes" (δεξάμενος γὰρ τοῦ κάλλους τὴν ἀπορροὴν διὰ τῶν ὀμμάτων); at 251b5, "nourishment flows in upon him" (ἐπιρρυείσης δὲ τῆς τροφῆς); when he gazes upon the beauty of the boy at 251c, his soul "receives particles from there that come at him in a stream" (ἐκεῖθεν μέρη ἐπιόντα καὶ ῥέοντ' . . . δεχομένη); at 251e, he is "irrigated by the streams of desire" (ἐποχετευσαμένη ἵμερον); and at 253a, the philosophic lovers are said to "draw the liquid of inspiration from Zeus like the bacchantes" and to "pour this out over the soul of the beloved" (κἂν ἐκ Διὸς ἀρύτωσιν ὥσπερ αἱ βάκχαι, ἐπὶ τὴν τοῦ ἐρωμένου ψυχὴν ἐπαντλοῦντες).[59] Another powerful influx, finally, is described at 255c: when the lover spends time with the beloved, "then the fountain of that stream (ἡ τοῦ ῥεύματος ἐκείνου πηγή) which Zeus called 'desire' when he was in love with Ganymede moves in great volume upon the lover; part of it flows into him, but part of it overflows outside of him because he is filled up (ἡ μὲν εἰς αὐτὸν ἔδυ, ἡ δ' ἀπομεστουμένου ἔξω ἀπορρεῖ)"; this overflow then reverses direction and flows into the beloved, who thus undergoes the same kind of *pathos* as the lover. As these passages indicate, the soul is the receptacle of various liquid streams that "flow into" and "fill" it. It thus plays a role analogous to that of the passive partner in sexual intercourse.

But this is only part of a very complicated story about the μεταβολή (251a) that the soul undergoes as a result of the experience of *erōs*. This μεταβολή begins when the soul is gripped by love and invaded by streams of beauty and desire. Like the lover of lyric poetry, Plato's philosopher is subject to a massive assault both in body and in soul. Driven out of his mind, he shudders and sweats, he is tickled and pricked. Note, too, that the lover of lyric poetry is both passive (as the helpless victim of an invasion by love) and active (as the pursuer of a beloved object). A similar combination of passivity and activity is found in Plato's scenario, where the lover is passive to the extent that he is invaded by beauty, yet is active in his pursuit of both the boy and of the Forms. To be sure, the similarity

[58] I am not suggesting that the lover is passive in the sense that he does nothing. On the contrary: he is supremely active at the same time as he is passive (= acted upon; subject to powerful and irresistible external forces).

[59] The last passage cited is difficult to construe. Hackforth 1952: 100 n. 2 seems right in suggesting that "the point is that in both sorts of divine madness [i.e. that of the bacchant and that of the lover] the immediate subject of possession 'infects' another or others."

of the two schemes serves to highlight a critical difference: the lyric lover wants to possess the beloved (both physically and psychically), whereas the philosophical lover aims to enlist the beloved in a mutual search for an object of desire that each has loved and lost. But this corrective does not discredit the genre of the love lyric as a whole; even if the object of desire is altered in Plato's scheme, many aspects of the lyric conception of love are left intact.

Consider one more notion that Plato borrows from the genre of lyric love poetry: the alteration of the boundaries of the psyche brought on by the assault of love. Like his lyric predecessors, Plato's lover experiences major psychic fluctuations. For things are crossing the soul's borders going in both directions. On the one hand, streams are flowing into the soul; on the other hand, the wings are pushing their way out. The growth of the wings, in fact, alters the entire configuration of the soul. And it should be emphasized that, even when they are fully grown, they have to be continually nourished by philosophy. There are no fixed or final boundaries of the soul, since a given set of boundaries is always subject to change.[60]

I am not suggesting that Plato defers to the genre of love poetry at every point; far from it. Nonetheless, the extent to which he respects and preserves the "voice" of this genre is quite remarkable. Indeed, it is precisely by leaving the genre of love poetry – with its discourse of madness, invasion, and the destruction of the boundaries of the psyche – more or less intact that Plato is able to create one of the most extraordinary paradoxes in his entire corpus: the notion that reason and madness, at a certain level, converge.[61] Fittingly, this paradox itself finds its source in the genre of lyric love poetry; as Anacreon says in fr. 428 *PMG*: "I'm in love and I'm not in love; I'm crazy and I'm not crazy" (ἐρέω τε δηὖτε κοὐκ ἐρέω | καὶ μαίνομαι κοὐ μαίνομαι).[62] In sum, the double-voiced discourse that occurs at the heart of Socrates' second speech is, like Plato's philosophical lover, both passive and active.

In a fascinating essay on the treatment of the Simonides poem in Plato's *Protagoras*, Anne Carson concludes: "You can always tell the poetry from the prose in a Platonic dialogue. The poetry is what keeps unmixing itself from everything else."[63] There can be no doubt that Socrates' "interpretation" of Simonides' poem in the *Protagoras* is one of

---

[60] Cf. the description of the ongoing metabolism that characterizes both the body and the soul of human beings in the *Symposium* (207c–208b).

[61] Griswold 1986: 112 discusses this convergence.

[62] See Carson (1986: 3–9 and passim) for a discussion of the element of paradox that characterizes the genre of lyric love poetry.

[63] Carson 1992: 128.

the most blatant examples of active double-voicing in Plato's writings: the poem can "mix" with philosophic discourse only after Socrates forces his own ideas upon this unwilling text. The *Phaedrus*, however, is a quite different animal. For, in this dialogue, poetry and other traditional genres of discourse do not always "unmix" themselves from philosophic discourse. Indeed, as Socrates says of his second speech, he has "mixed together (κεράσαντες, 265b8) a not unpersuasive *logos* and playfully sung a mythical hymn ... to Eros" (265b–c).

V

In the *Phaedrus*, Plato enters into a "dialogue" with a variety of traditional genres of discourse – a dialogue that invites the reader to engage with the different genres critically, examining the roles that they play in the culture at large as well as the ways in which they impact upon the soul. This dialogue with "alien" genres is, I would like to suggest, analogous to ordinary philosophical dialogue. After all, when engaging in a philosophical dialogue, one must either test one's own ideas by submitting them to the criticism of others or else test another person's ideas by introducing one's own criticisms and ideas. In either case, one is necessarily dealing with *other people's logoi*. To be sure, there is an important difference between these two kinds of dialogue: in the former case, one is testing alien *genres* of discourse, whereas in the latter case, it is the *ideas and arguments* of others that are tested by arguments in the same mode. But this does not mean that the former activity is not a part of philosophy. For, as the *Phaedrus* indicates, the activity of philosophy is a perpetual engagement with the discourse of others, whether that discourse be presented in an analytic or a non-analytic mode.

As we have seen, the *Phaedrus* illustrates the need for the philosopher to test and examine all modes of discourse. In particular, the dialogue urges, genres that carry with them the authority of tradition need to be carefully analyzed, since they are the ones that human beings have been bombarded with since childhood. Plato was fully aware of a notion that has been discussed by a number of modern and postmodern theorists, namely, the social construction of the self. In fact, no Greek thinker understood more than Plato about the ways in which society – and especially the discourse that it uses – determines the ideas and desires that make up the human psyche. Unlike so many twentieth-century thinkers, however, Plato believed that the human psyche is not completely constituted by way of social interaction. Since the soul has a history that predates its sojourn on earth, it is possible for an individual to rediscover a pre-social self. But this requires Herculean labor, since it demands no

less than a lifetime of critical inquiry, part of which is devoted to analyzing the manifold *logoi* circulating within the society in an effort to discover how they interact with the human soul and whether or not they are
consonant with the pursuit of truth.

What, then, does the *Phaedrus* tell us about "authentic" discourse? It
seems intuitively correct to say that authentic discourse is philosophic
discourse. But herein lies the problem: what exactly is "philosophic discourse," in Plato's view? Should we identify it with what Plato calls dialectic? This would be unhelpful, in part because it is such a slippery term
in Plato; as Robinson has rightly observed, "The fact is that the word
'dialectic' had a strong tendency in Plato to mean 'the ideal method,
whatever that may be.' In so far as it was thus merely an honorific title,
Plato applied it at every stage of his life to whatever seemed to him at the
moment the most hopeful procedure" (his italics).[64] But even if one could
identify the formal criteria of dialectic, it would be possible for a person
to be meeting these criteria and still not be philosophizing in Plato's sense
of the word.[65] This leads to the conclusion that philosophic discourse
cannot be identified by formal or stylistic criteria alone. But, if this is the
case, then how can it be identified?

Plato's approach to this problem in the *Phaedrus* is somewhat oblique.
Nowhere does he say "the nature of philosophic discourse is x." Nor do
we find him explicitly contrasting the philosopher's mode of discourse
with that of, say, the poets (as in the *Ion*), the orators (as in the *Gorgias*),
or the encomiasts (as in the *Lysis* and *Symposium*). To be sure, the character Socrates serves to dramatize the philosopher at work. But this only
makes matters more difficult, since Socrates uses so many different modes
of discourse in this dialogue.

It is in the "second half" of the dialogue that the nature of philosophic
discourse is addressed. The discussion begins with a peculiar act of classification: the creation of a supergenre called "logography." The word
"logography," of course, was traditionally used to describe the activity of
writing a speech for another person to use in a lawcourt. But Socrates
argues that this term should be used to designate any act of writing, regardless of the genre. At the close of this scene, in fact, Socrates explicitly
groups together "anyone who has written or will write anything, whether
it be a political or a private composition, either in meter, as a poet, or
without meter, as an ordinary person" (258d). By placing every kind of
writing under a single rubric, Socrates ignores all formal and generic dis-

[64] R. Robinson 1941: 74.
[65] Cf. Nehamas 1990, who indicates that dialectic can never be reduced to a mere formal
method, since it cannot be dissociated from the metaphysics of Plato, particularly the
theory of Forms.

tinctions between written compositions. Here, Plato invites us to meditate on all these genres *qua* written discourse. This move is important, for it is the first step in an argument designed to separate philosophy from other discursive practices.

To be sure, Socrates does not explicitly announce that his aim is to fence off philosophy. In fact, in the passage just discussed, Socrates says that the subject of their conversation is "the method of writing well or badly" (258d). But note how this long discussion concludes. At the end of the dialogue, Socrates tells Phaedrus to go and make the following announcement to Lysias and the composers of speeches, to Homer and the poets, and to Solon and the lawgivers:

> if he has written these things [i.e. speeches, poems, or laws] with knowledge of the truth, and is capable of defending them by submitting to cross-examination, and is able to show in his speech that his writings are of little worth, such a person should not be labelled by reference to these writings but rather to the things about which he is serious. (278c–d)

If an individual fulfills these criteria, Socrates continues, he should be called a "philosopher" (278d4); if he does not, he should be called "a poet or a composer of speeches or a writer of laws" (278e1–2).[66] This passage reveals that one of Socrates' goals in this half of the dialogue is to distinguish the philosopher from all other laborers in the fields of language.

According to what criteria, we must ask, does Socrates draw this boundary line? It should be emphasized that the distinction that Socrates has drawn between spoken and written *logoi* is not sustained throughout the discussion. Even as early as 259e, Socrates suggests that what they are examining is how one "writes *and speaks* well or badly" (ὅπη καλῶς ἔχει λέγειν τε καὶ γράφειν καὶ ὅπη μή). The division between spoken and written discourse, we begin to see, requires amendment. This point is made explicit at 277e, where Socrates champions the person

> who believes that there is necessarily a great deal of playfulness in writings on any subject, and that no discourse has ever been written, either in meter or in prose, that is worth any great seriousness, and that no discourse has ever *been spoken* (λεχθῆναι), such as those speeches delivered in the fashion of rhapsodes for the sake of persuasion without investigation and teaching (ἄνευ ἀνακρίσεως καὶ διδαχῆς), [that is worth any great seriousness].

[66] Note that this point is made in a simple (and not a contrary-to-fact) conditional: if a person has composed speeches or poems or lawcodes, but knows the truth about his subject and can demonstrate the inferiority of his writings by way of discussion, then it is right that he be called a philosopher. This means that the philosopher *may in fact have written poems or speeches or lawcodes*; what distinguishes him is his knowledge of the issues and his awareness that writing is inadequate as a medium for conveying truth.

Here, Socrates indicates that some spoken discourse has the same liabilities as written texts, namely, that which is delivered for the sake of persuasion rather than for investigation and teaching.[67]

Clearly, philosophic discourse is a special *kind* of spoken discourse. But
how exactly is it identified? One way of approaching this question is to
take the passage quoted above as providing the key: philosophic discourse
is that which is spoken for the sake of "investigation and teaching" rather
than "persuasion." Both Heath and Rowe, in their recent debate over the
question whether the palinode should be classified as philosophical, exemplify this approach. Hence Rowe argues that the criteria for identifying
a discourse as philosophical are (*a*) the presence of the author of the *logos*
and his capacity to defend it, and (*b*) "the right *intention* on the author's
part: he must compose his *logos* with the *intention* of teaching (rather than
merely persuading); that is, of initiating or continuing the two-way process of communication on which teaching depends (or which teaching is)"
(his italics).[68] Heath echoes this statement in his postscript, when he says
that "Rowe accepts that the presence or absence of questioning is not, as
such, decisive ... and that there is no *formal* impediment to the palinode
being teaching ... We must look, therefore, at the attitudes and intentions
of Socrates himself and his interlocutor" (his italics).[69]

I agree with both scholars that philosophic discourse cannot be identified by formal criteria alone. But, as I see it, there is a consideration that
is prior to the questions whether (*a*) the author is present and able to defend his *logos*, and (*b*) he composes his *logos* with the intention of teaching and initiating further investigation. For what must first be determined
is *the author's relation to his own logos*. Take the case of Socrates: is the
palinode with its many *logoi* alien or authentic vis-à-vis his own psyche?
Has he transformed (or is he in the process of transforming) these alien
logoi into his own? Certainly Socrates shows full awareness of the nature
and, indeed, the ubiquitousness of alien discourse. Recall his claim at the
beginning of the dialogue that he makes it a priority to examine himself to
discover whether he is complex, like the Typhon, or a simpler sort of
creature (229e–230a). Clearly, part of Socrates' task is to make sure that
his soul does not resemble that monstrous beast with a hundred snakey
heads which speak in different tongues – to rid himself, in short, of the
alien voices within. Given that Socrates repeatedly recurs to the problem
of alien discourse, we may infer that the *logoi* which make up his palinode

---

[67] As Burger 1980: 101–4, Griswold 1986: 209, and Ferrari 1987: 208–12 observe, the distinction that Plato draws between spoken and written discourse is qualified in this and
other passages.

[68] Rowe 1989: 183.

[69] Heath 1989b: 190.

have been previously subjected to analysis. Even if Socrates cannot ground these *logoi* in complete knowledge of the essence of good and evil, we know that he has spent a lifetime investigating precisely these issues. In addition, Socrates is the first to undermine his own authority, which is a further sign of the extent of his self-scrutiny. Ultimately, of course, we cannot ascertain what goes on in the soul of Socrates or anyone else: it is the alien discourse in our own souls that must be our first concern. By offering in the *Phaedrus* a dramatization of and a meditation on the nature and varieties of alien discourse, Plato demands from the reader a vigilance concerning all *logoi*, external or internal, analytic or non-analytic.

When all is said and done, Plato does not offer a definition or even a description of *philosophic discourse* in the *Phaedrus*. Rather, he chooses to identify and describe *the philosopher*. It is worth examining how Plato makes the shift from a discussion of *logoi* to a discussion of the *authors of logoi*. In the Egyptian tale, Plato focusses on the written word and the effect it has on the reader: its "external marks" substitute for recollection, which comes from within (274e–275b). Note that this takes place "because of the faith [readers] put in writing" (διὰ πίστιν γραφῆς, 275a3). As Socrates suggests at 275c–d, the real problem occurs when the people who have "left behind" the writings and those who have "received" them believe that they contain "something clear and certain." There is nothing inherently evil in the written word, as it seems; it is the attitude of the authors and readers that creates the problem. But doesn't the very nature of the written word encourage this wrongful attitude? Socrates says in the next section that a written text is like a painting in the sense that it always says the same thing and cannot answer if questioned; in addition, it is available to all viewers and is unable to protect itself if someone attacks it (275d–e). This analogy reminds us of the limitations inherent in the medium of writing. But it does not indicate that the medium is *intrinsically* harmful; indeed, why should a written text be any more harmful than a painting, which shares in these limitations? The medium is only harmful if it is used for the wrong purposes. This use is itself determined by human agency: that of the author, on the one hand, and of the reader, on the other.

Given this emphasis on human claims and conceptions about writing, it is no surprise that the dialogue concludes with a discussion of the author's attitude towards his own writings. At 276b, the author is compared to a farmer faced with two alternatives. On the one hand, he can plant his seeds "in the gardens of Adonis" (276b). In the gardens used in the Adonia festival, the plants are destroyed before they develop seeds. As the paroemiographer Zenobius explains, the gardens "are sown in clay vessels and grow only to the point of becoming green; they are carried away along with the dying god and are thrown into springs."[70] The alternative to planting this "festive" garden is to practice the "art of husbandry": to sow the seeds "in the place that is fitting" and to tend them until they reach maturity. Obviously, a "wise farmer" (ὁ νοῦν ἔχων γεωργός) will only indulge in the former activity "in play and for amusement" (παιδιᾶς τε καὶ ἑορτῆς χάριν); when he is "serious" (σπουδῇ, 276b3; ἐσπούδακεν, b6), he will look to his husbandry (276b).

The wise farmer, of course, is analogous to the philosopher. For only the philosopher can rear up *logoi* in his own soul "which are not fruitless but contain a seed" (οὐχὶ ἄκαρποι ἀλλὰ ἔχοντες σπέρμα, 277a1); this seed, in turn, can be planted in other souls, where "other *logoi* growing in other minds are able to make [the seed] immortal forever" (277a).[71] It is important to note that the philosopher's *logoi* enter into another person's soul *as seeds*; the philosopher does not hand over knowledge that is ready-made (or, to continue the analogy, fully grown), since knowledge can only be achieved if the student rears up the seeds himself. As Socrates says at 278a–b, the philosopher is the person who thinks that

only in the *logoi* that are taught and spoken for the sake of learning and really written in the soul concerning the just and the beautiful and the good can clarity and perfection and serious worth be found. Such *logoi* should be identified as the speaker's legitimate offspring – first, the *logos* that is in him, if it is in him as something that has been discovered (ἐὰν εὑρεθεὶς ἐνῇ),[72] and then those *logoi* that are the offspring and brothers of this *logos*, if any have grown in a worthy manner in the souls of others.

[70] Zenobius 1.49 (Leutsch and Schneidewin 1965: 19). For some recent discussions of the Adonia festival, see Detienne [1972]/1977: 64–6, 78–80, and Winkler 1990: 189–93. Winkler points out that Plato's discussion of the gardens of Adonis in the *Phaedrus* ignores the fact that these gardens are part of a women's rite (p. 192). Of course the ancient Athenian reader could readily picture the women climbing onto the rooftops with their miniature gardens and (as they are said to do in Aristophanes' *Lysistrata* 393–6) drunkenly shouting, "woe for Adonis!" and "beat your breasts for Adonis!" Readers familiar with the festival are thus encouraged to identify the "bad farmer" with the female celebrants.

[71] The passage at 276e–277a does not mention that part of the process where the philosopher rears up the crop in his own soul, since it starts at the point where he is sowing the seeds of his *logoi* in other souls. I have included this earlier stage in the process on the basis of 278a, which makes it clear that the philosopher must first "discover" *logoi* about justice, beauty, etc. for himself; only then can he offer his seeds to others.

[72] Note Hackforth's gloss on this line (1952: 162 n. 1): "In the clause ἐὰν εὑρεθεὶς ἐνῇ the emphasis falls on the participle. A man's legitimate spiritual children are primarily those truths which he himself has discovered by a process of dialectic, and secondarily those which, while logically consequent upon the former, are actually reached, again dialectically, by others."

It is in this description of the philosopher that the notion of authentic discourse comes to the surface. For we are now apprised of a *logos* that is inside the soul "as something that has been discovered." We have already seen that there can be any number of *logoi* in a person's soul which have not been "discovered": these are, of course, internal "aliens." Authentic discourse, by contrast, is "discovered" in Plato's special sense of this word. It is not invented or created by the soul but rather found in the process of recollecting the Forms. Authentic discourse, then, is grounded in philosophical investigation that both begins and ends with the vision of the Forms; it is "discovered" by way of a dialectical pursuit of true reality.

If authentic discourse is that which resides in the philosopher as something that has been discovered, then why shouldn't it be presented in written form? One answer to this question is that the philosopher knows that his writings, even if they could convey his own "authentic" *logoi*, are by definition "alien" to others. In addition, the philosopher understands that alien discourse will damage souls which accept its authority and internalize it unthinkingly. It is for this reason that he refuses to recognize the authority of any untested *logos*; it is only by investigation and analysis that a person makes his *logoi* his own. Clearly, a person who believes that the external imposition of authority is antithetical to the project of philosophy will refuse to claim that his own writings are true and authoritative. A person whose discourse is authentic, in short, will necessarily refrain from imposing his authority on others.

A second answer, however, might be added to the first: authentic discourse shouldn't be presented in written form because it *can't* be presented in this medium. Although the notion of a "discovery" might suggest a product that can be neatly packaged and given away, the dialogue explicitly states that writing cannot contain anything "clear" or "steadfast" (σαφὲς καὶ βέβαιον, 275c6). This is a paradoxical claim, since common sense would indicate that it is in writing, rather than speech, that these qualities are to be found. But, as Plato reveals, a written text cannot respond to questioning; its discourse is fixed and unchanging. In opposition to the fixity of the written text, Plato sets up a "living" *logos*, which is of course the spoken dialogue. This achieves steadfastness and clarity not by virtue of packaging the truth in some finite (and final) set of formulations, but by its ability to keep the pursuit of truth in motion. If, in the category of spoken discourse, it is the ongoing philosophical conversation that enables one to achieve authenticity, then it is clear that the written text is simply the wrong container for authentic discourse. To be sure, a written text may serve to initiate or lay the groundwork for a philosophical dialogue, but it must find a way to usher the reader outside its narrow bounds – to announce itself as an unauthoritative and, indeed, "alien" discourse.

In a recent article on the dialogue form, Michael Frede insists that we take seriously the point that is made explicit in so many Platonic texts, namely, that "it is exceedingly difficult, if possible at all, to get oneself into a position in which one can speak with authority, with some kind of justified confidence, out of expertise and knowledge, about a certain subject matter."[73] Perhaps the greatest difficulty, he argues, centers on the fact that "beliefs about these subject matters, like virtue, reality, justice, evil, do not form relatively small, isolated clusters; they form sheer endless chains which ... determine, or help to determine, our whole life and the life of the society we live in."[74] Even in the middle and late dialogues, Frede concludes, Plato is not putting forth his own ideas in a dogmatic or authoritative way. While Plato clearly had positions on the matters he investigates, he adopted the dialogue form precisely because he did not consider his own views as final. The *Phaedrus* offers abundant support for Frede's argument. As Socrates sums it up at 278d: the gods alone can be designated as *sophoi*; humans are, at best, *philosophoi*.[75]

As I have suggested, authentic discourse must be identified with "the *logos* that is in [a person], if it is in him as something that has been discovered" (278a). This formulation does not insist that the truth has been discovered in its entirety; it only specifies that there are *logoi* inside the philosopher which have been discovered by way of an inquiry guided by the Forms. But, if a person has not achieved perfect knowledge, then some of his *logoi* will not yet be authentic; in addition, the person will continually be confronted with new *logoi*, which must themselves be naturalized or deported.

A useful analogue for this ongoing process is found in Bakhtin's notion of the human psyche and its confrontation with alien discourse:

When someone else's ideological discourse is internally persuasive for us and acknowledged by us, entirely different possibilities open up. Such discourse is of decisive significance in the evolution of an individual consciousness: consciousness awakens to independent ideological life precisely in a world of alien discourses

[73] M. Frede 1992: 214.
[74] M. Frede 1992: 215.
[75] Note also Socrates' response to Phaedrus' suggestion that the project of mastering the art of speech may be beyond human abilities: "but it is a fine thing even to strive after things that are good, and to suffer whatever may come to pass" (274a–b). Here, Socrates hints that the path may have no end. At 262d, Socrates claims that he himself does not possess "the art of speaking." I take these passages to indicate that complete wisdom is an ideal which can never be achieved by humans. The portrait of the true rhetorician at 271a–272b, then, offers a goal at which to aim rather than an attainable epistemic state.

surrounding it, and from which it cannot initially separate itself; the process of distinguishing between one's own and another's discourse is activated rather late in development. When thought begins to work in an independent, experimenting and discriminating way, what first occurs is a separation between internally persuasive discourse and authoritarian enforced discourse, along with a rejection of those congeries of discourses that do not matter to us, that do not touch us.[76]

Bakhtin sets what he calls "internally persuasive discourse" over and against discourse that is "externally authoritative." In the normal course of psychic development, the former will develop out of the latter: "One's own discourse and one's own voice, although born of another or dynamically stimulated by another, will sooner or later begin to liberate themselves from the authority of the other's discourse."[77] But the alien origins of internally persuasive discourse are never fully overcome; for even internally persuasive discourse is "half-ours and half-someone else's."[78]

Like Bakhtin, Plato was concerned about the development of one's own authority by way of a critical appraisal of the "authority of the other's discourse." But for Plato, the task of developing an authentic voice is far more difficult than merely ensuring that discourse is "internally persuasive"; certainly the task of ridding oneself of alien discourse is not something that happens in the normal course of psychic development. Most of the discourse that is "internally persuasive" in Bakhtin's scheme, in fact, would be identified as alien in Plato's. For, as we have seen in the *Phaedrus*, part of the human soul is naturally disposed to welcome internal persuasion which is false and harmful. It is for this reason that Plato would insist that authentic discourse can only be achieved by way of philosophical inquiry; it must be grounded in the ongoing investigation of the Forms, which alone guarantee the kind of authenticity he is after.

Bakhtin, of course, does not suggest that alien discourse must be tested by reference to a standard whose essence is absolute truth.[79] This is what accounts for the gulf between these two thinkers' conceptions of authentic discourse. Nevertheless, the model that Bakhtin proposes illuminates Plato's enterprise. Particularly relevant, I think, is Bakhtin's insistence that the project of testing and overcoming alien discourse is unending –

[76] Bakhtin 1981: 345. On the psychological theories of Bakhtin and his circle, see Emerson 1986, and Morson and Emerson 1990: ch. 5.
[77] Bakhtin 1981: 348.
[78] Bakhtin 1981: 345.
[79] Although, as Hirschkop 1990 has observed, Bakhtin contradicts himself at times by slipping into the Kantian notion of value. As Hirschkop puts it (p. 20), "Values with an impeccably Kantian pedigree are thus juxtaposed with those of mundane sociological origin."

that the human psyche is engaged in a lifelong dialogue with *someone else's discourse* (be it individual or generic). As we have seen, Plato believed that even the most advanced philosophic souls can never come to an end of dialogue. On the one hand, truth itself cannot be fixed in a finite set of propositions; and, on the other hand, there will always be new "voices" that keep the conversation going. Plato's philosopher, then, must endlessly revise the text of his soul. When the text is completed, in the ideal world, the author will finally be born.

5   Philosophy and comedy

> The people who throng the streets shout at each other, their voices rising from the mass of heads and floating upwards towards the church spires and the great copper bells that clang at the end of the day. Their words, rising up, form a thick cloud over the city, which every so often must be thoroughly cleansed of too much language. Men and women in balloons fly up from the main square and, armed with mops and scrubbing brushes, do battle with the canopy of words trapped under the sun.
>
> The words resist erasure. The oldest and most stubborn form a thick crust of chattering rage.
>
> Jeanette Winterson, *Sexing the Cherry*

Scatology and eschatology: at first glance, Attic comedy seems completely removed from the discourse of philosophy. But while Plato shows a serious aversion to laughter (see, e.g., *Rep.* 388e), he is arguably more indebted to comedy than to any other literary genre.[1] It is in comedy, of course, where Socrates gets his start as a literary character. As Diskin Clay has suggested, "Socrates *kōmōidopoioumenos* is ... significant for the history of the *Sōkratikoi logoi* as they are to be placed in the context of ancient literary genres."[2] But how exactly does comedy impact upon the Platonic dialogue? In Plato's *Apology*, Socrates mentions the comic playwrights as being among his "first accusers" (18a–e). We might expect, then, that Plato would be consistently hostile to the genre of comedy, since it made his own hero into a ridiculous buffoon. Certainly Plato does

---

[1] See L. Cooper 1922: ch. 10 and Mader 1977 for Plato's notion of the comic and the relation between the Platonic dialogue and Old Comedy (especially Aristophanes). Mader takes the discussion of comedy in the *Philebus* (47b–50b) as representing *the* Platonic theory of laughter – a theory that can be applied to most if not all of Plato's excursions into the ridiculous (cf. de Vries 1985 for a brief but cogent rebuttal of this approach). For a survey of previous scholarship on comedy in Plato and/or Plato's discussions of comedy, see Mader 1977: esp. 72–7 (and note his appendix documenting the words for laughter, the ridiculous, abusive mockery, and comedy, pp. 130–2). Brock 1990 offers an insightful analysis of Plato's imitations of comedy, focussing primarily on the reuse of comic *topoi* and techniques in the dialogues (e.g., colloquial language, word-play, the coinage of words, vulgarity, imagery, stylistic parody, satire on individuals, and comic character-types).

[2] Clay 1994: 41.

172

not hesitate to criticize comedy, as we see in *Republic* 10, where Socrates lashes out against low or "ridiculous" poetry, of which comedy is the primary vehicle in classical Athens (606c).[3] Here and elsewhere, Plato makes it quite clear that he considers comedy a force to be reckoned with in the Athenian democracy. Strangely, however, he treats Aristophanes far better than Agathon in the *Symposium*: it is the comic poet who, despite his humorous style, enunciates the more compelling discourse on *erōs*. Plato, in fact, was reported by the anecdotal tradition to have kept a copy of Aristophanes under his pillow. Although this is no doubt a fiction, it reminds us that Plato's relationship with comedy is more complex than it may at first appear.

As I will argue, Plato's relationship with comedy is complex precisely because the genre of comedy is complex. Indeed, it is even more complex than this investigation will indicate, since Old Comedy gave way to the ever-elusive genre of Middle Comedy during Plato's lifetime. Given the scant remains of Middle Comedy, it is difficult to make many general statements about the genre, let alone identify dramas that provided subtexts for Plato's dialogues.[4] I will therefore confine myself to Old Comedy, which, as we will see, offers solid material for intertextual analyses. It should be emphasized, however, that Old Comedy did not simply disappear at the advent of Middle Comedy: genres don't change overnight, and the appearance of new generic forms is entirely compatible with the ongoing use of old forms as well as with the reproduction of older texts. We know that the "great" tragedies of the fifth century were regularly performed in fourth-century Athens.[5] In the case of comedy, however, "it has been generally assumed that Old comedy was too Athenian and too ephemeral to be reperformed after its first occasion, even at Athens,

---

[3] Note, however, that Plato's primary concern in this passage is "serious" poetry; comedy only enters the picture as an afterthought (at 606c).

[4] For the genre of Middle Comedy, see Dover 1968b: esp. 144–9, Webster 1970: chs. 1–3, Arnott 1972. Emphasizing the "continuity" between Old and Middle comedy, these scholars suggest that the "development" of the genre of comedy from the late fifth to the late fourth century BCE was by no means as linear and progressive as the simple categories of "Old," "Middle," and "New" Comedy would lead us to suppose. Note that the "serious" aspect of Old Comedy is still in evidence in Middle Comedy: the extant material contains many references to political and social issues and personages (Webster 1970: 23–50, Dover 1968b: 146–7, Arnott 1972: esp. 69–70, 79–80, Carrière 1979: 278–85 and passim). Aristotle says at *NE* 1128a22–4 that the jokes of the "old" and the "new" comedies differ insofar as the former used "direct abuse" (αἰσχρολογία) whereas the latter use "innuendo" (ὑπόνοια). This indicates that comedy was still conveying some sort of "abuse" in Aristotle's day (though precisely what Aristotle meant by the "old" and the "new" comedy is under debate; see, e.g., Janko 1984: 204–6 and passim).

[5] On the reproductions of fifth-century tragedies in fourth-century Athens, see Webster 1954 and Easterling 1993.

let alone elsewhere."[6] But, as Taplin has shown in *Comic Angels*, vase-paintings from Southern Italy and Sicily offer good evidence that Old Comedy was reproduced in Megale Hellas in the fourth century. If people this remote from fifth-century Athens could enjoy Old Comedy, there is a strong likelihood that this kind of drama was also reproduced in fourth-century Athens. We may take issue, then, with Henderson's claim that Plato's and Aristotle's objections to obscenity and *Rügekomödie* were anachronistic, since these aspects of comedy had "already expired of old age and social uselessness."[7] If Old Comedy was reproduced in fourth-century Athens, and if Middle comedy did not completely abandon the political advice and abuse that characterized Old Comedy, then the philosophers' arguments are more pertinent.

What, then, is so complex about the genre of Old Comedy? This kind of comedy, of course, is a purveyor of "the ridiculous." But it is not simply funny. For it regularly deals with vital social and political issues and even claims to offer sage advice and criticism to the Athenian *dēmos*. As the chorus announce in the *Frogs*, they will say "many things that are ridiculous and many that are serious" (πολλὰ μὲν γέλοια ... πολλὰ δὲ σπου-δαῖα, 389–90). Comedy, as the extant plays and fragments attest, is (among other things) a dispenser of blame and praise – a social critic that claims to speak the unvarnished truth. As Henderson suggests,

the comic poets, despite their jokes, argue vehemently and purposefully about the most important and divisive issues of the day. The positions they advocate or denounce represent those of actual groups, and their techniques of persuasion and abuse are practically identical with those used in political and forensic disputes.[8]

To the extent that it addresses itself to social and political issues, Old Comedy can be said to have a "serious" side.[9] If we are to understand the impact that comedy had on the genre of the Platonic dialogue, I believe, we need to consider both the ridiculous and the serious aspects of the genre of comedy.

I will begin with the first of these two strands: comedy's traffic in the ridiculous. Unlike the "serious" aspect of comedy, its humorous or "ridiculous" side has never been questioned. Plato himself has a good deal to say about comic ridiculousness. In the *Republic*, of course, Socrates banishes the comic poets along with their "serious" counterparts. As he says at 606c (cf. 388e):

---

[6] Taplin 1993: 3.
[7] J. Henderson 1991: 29.
[8] J. Henderson 1990: 273.
[9] I will discuss the vexed question of the "seriousness" of comedy in fuller detail below.

Does not this same principle apply to the ridiculous? For if you would be ashamed to play the buffoon yourself, but you greatly enjoy this in a comic representation or when you hear it in private, and you do not detest it as being base, you are doing the exact same thing as we described in the case of the pitiable. For that part of you which you restrained when it longed to play the buffoon (since you feared the reputation of clownishness) you give rein to in the latter situations and, making that part vigorous, you unwittingly become a comedian since you have been carried away so often in private.

When he comes to the "second-best city" in the *Laws*, however, Plato takes a different approach to the production of comedy; though he still believes that comedy can corrupt its viewers, he seems to have decided that the genre could be put to good use if handled properly. As the Athenian Stranger remarks at 816d–e,

It is necessary to observe and to understand shameful bodies and ideas and the part played by those engaged in comic enactments of the ridiculous, be it in speech, in song, in dance, or in the comic imitations of all of these things. For it is not possible to learn the serious without the ridiculous, or any contrary without its opposite, if one is to be a wise man. It is, however, impossible for a person to put both of these things into action if he is to have even a little share in virtue; rather, it is precisely for this reason that it is necessary to learn these things, namely, so that we never do or say anything ridiculous out of ignorance when we need not.

In order to learn the truth about both the "serious" and the "ridiculous," then, the latter must be confronted rather than avoided.[10] The Athenian goes on to stipulate, however, that comedies can only be acted by slaves or foreigners and never by the citizens of Magnesia (which is the name he gives his new city). No freeborn person, in fact, is even allowed to "learn" a comedy (816e). What they need to "learn," we infer, is the nature of the ridiculous; this is quite different from learning or mastering the text of a comedy. The Athenian adds, moreover, that comic productions must "always" contain "some novel (καινόν) element" (816e). As England glosses this last suggestion, "if we must have unedifying spectacles on the stage, they should be *varied* – so as to do less harm than we should get from familiarity with *one* such spectacle."[11] Interestingly, the Athenian states in this same passage that tragedy will not be allowed in Magnesia at

---

[10] Note that Socrates says in the *Republic* that it is necessary to have knowledge of "mad and base men and women, though one must do and imitate nothing of this kind" (396a). Clearly, Plato did not think when he wrote the *Republic* that watching comedies could help people to learn the nature of base and ridiculous characters.

[11] England 1921.II: 258 at 797d9 (his reading here follows that of Ritter on 816e). The notion that comedy, which depicts "base" subjects, should be varied recalls the Athenian's repeated suggestion that "good" genres should be kept pure since their adulteration leads the viewers to lawlessness and the conceit of knowledge (656d–657b, 669c–670a, 700a–701a).

all (817a–d): the genre of comedy, we infer, has the capacity to illustrate what is truly ridiculous (though only those comedies will be allowed in Magnesia which echo the sentiments of the lawgiver[12]) whereas "the so-called serious poets" of tragedy (817a) can never hit the mark in representing what is truly serious.

Unlike the *Laws*, the *Republic* deals with comedy in its present state; the idea that some select group of approved comedies might be used to present a spectacle of what is truly ridiculous is simply not addressed. But the *Republic* is in accord with the *Laws* on the need for understanding the true nature of the ridiculous. In fact, in a lengthy passage in book 5, Socrates explicitly criticizes comic poets for dispensing ridicule in a fashion that is ignorant and contrary to truth. The passage runs as follows:

"Perhaps then," I said, "many of the things which we are saying, being contrary to our customs, would seem ridiculous (γελοῖα), if our words are translated into deeds." "Quite true," he said. "What, then," I said, "is the most ridiculous thing (γελοιότατον) you note in them? Isn't it the idea of women exercising naked in the gymnasia with the men, and not only the young women, but also the older ones, just like the old men in the gymnasia who, though wrinkled and unpleasant to look at, nonetheless indulge in exercise?" "Yes, by Zeus," he said, "it would seem ridiculous (γελοῖον), at least under present conditions." "Then," I said, "since we have set out to speak, we must not fear the jokes made by educated wits (τὰ τῶν χαριέντων σκώμματα) – all those kinds of things that they would say about such a revolution, and about gymnastics and culture and not the least about the [women's] bearing of arms and riding of horses ... But since we have begun to speak, we must advance towards the rough part of our legislation, after begging these people not to practice their regular profession but rather to be serious (μὴ τὰ αὑτῶν πράττειν ἀλλὰ σπουδάζειν). And we will remind them that not so long ago it seemed shameful and ridiculous (γελοῖα) to the Greeks (as it still does to many barbarian peoples) for men to be seen naked, and when first the Cretans and then the Lacedaemonians instituted the practice of gymnastics, it prompted the clever men of those times to make a comedy (κωμῳδεῖν) of all of these things ... But when, I suppose, it became apparent to people who had experience of these matters that to uncover such things is better than to veil them, then what appeared ridiculous (γελοῖον) faded away before that which reason revealed to be best." (452a–d)

This passage occurs near the opening of book 5, just after Socrates agrees to discuss the difficult question of the role of the women in the guardian class. In this passage, Socrates portrays the comic poets (both past and present) as responding to new ideas that are "contrary to custom" with mockery and ridicule. In so doing, they reflect the opinion of the majority, which is bound to see any truly radical idea as ridiculous. Socrates clearly disagrees with the comedians' conception of what is

---

[12] On the censorship of literature in the *Laws*, see Nightingale 1993b.

ridiculous, and he therefore begs them to stop being comic poets for a moment and to take these issues seriously. He then corrects their mistaken assessment of the ridiculous, suggesting that "experience" will prove that radical proposals such as these are not in fact ridiculous.

Socrates' criticism of the comedians' portrayal of the ridiculous brings us to our first example of the inclusion of a comic subtext in a Platonic dialogue. For, in the rest of book 5, Socrates will defend a number of ideas that find direct parallels in Aristophanes' *Ecclesiazusae*: the capacity and fitness of females to rule; the common possession of material goods (cf. *Eccl.* 590–4, 597–610, 667–75), women (cf. *Eccl.* 613–34), and children (cf. *Eccl.* 635–50); and the establishment of common meals (cf. *Eccl.* 715–16).[13] It should be emphasized, however, that the relationship between these two texts is by no means straightforward. While the *Republic* is chronologically later, most scholars have been loath to accept that Aristophanes was the source of the ideas found in Plato.[14] Rather, it is generally agreed that both authors are reworking material from a philosophic source from the late fifth / early fourth century.[15] Note that Plato indicates in the passage quoted above that the comedians are *responding* to the novel ideas of others rather than cooking up these ideas themselves. By portraying the comic poets as reactionary rather than innovative, Plato indicates that they got their material from the innovative ideas of other people.[16]

If this is on target, then we can say (with Ussher) that Plato did not "copy" his communistic ideas from Aristophanes. But does it follow from this that Plato did not "refer to" Aristophanes' handling of this material?[17] It is hard to believe that, when Plato came to rework and publish this material, he could simply ignore its handling by Aristophanes. To be

---

[13] See Adam 1902.I: 350–1 for a list of specific parallels between *Republic* 5 and the *Ecclesiazusae* "in idea, or in language, or in both idea and language."

[14] For a summary of the scholarship on the question of the relation between *Republic* 5 and the *Ecclesiazusae*, see Adam 1902: appendix 1 to bk. V, and Ussher 1973: xv–xx.

[15] We can only speculate about who this source is: the most prominent contenders are the Socratic circle (especially Antisthenes or Plato himself) and Protagoras.

[16] As Adam suggests (1902.I: 282 at 452b12): "If – with the majority of modern critics – we hold that the *Ecclesiazusae* is earlier than Book V, and if we consider the play as at least in some measure directed against theories on communism and the position of women with which the Socratic school sympathized, it is easy to interpret Plato here as *addressing a rebuke to the comic stage in the form of a further challenge*" (my italics). One need not insist that Aristophanes wrote his play as a parody of or a polemic against some group of philosophical thinkers (a parody which the public at large was hardly likely to appreciate). For my purposes, it is sufficient that Aristophanes borrowed (rather than invented) the communistic material because he saw its rich comic potential. But even if Aristophanes had the best intentions, he still managed to provoke a response from Plato, who clearly took the ideas much more seriously than Aristophanes did.

[17] As Ussher 1973: xx claims.

sure, Plato does not refer to Aristophanes by name. But his criticism of the ignorant mockery of the comic poets, together with his repeated emphasis on ridicule and the ridiculous in book 5,[18] offers strong evidence that Plato was, at least in part, responding to Aristophanes' comedy. Plato did, then, "include" the *Ecclesiazusae* in book 5, but this inclusion is complicated by the fact that it is Aristophanes' *mockery* of the ideas, rather than the *ideas themselves*, which Plato sets out to challenge. Plato in fact disentangles the communistic ideas from their comic rendering by making Socrates suggest that this material is "serious" and not "ridiculous." The point is hammered home at the end of our passage, where Socrates states the moral (so to speak) of his story:

And this is what was made clear: he is foolish who considers anything ridiculous except evil, and who tries to raise a laugh by looking to any other pattern of ridiculousness than ignorance and evil or sets up any other standard of the beautiful than the good. (452d–e)

Ignorance and evil, in short, are the proper material for ridicule; the subject matter for serious discourse is goodness and virtue. Where the comic poets go wrong, Plato indicates, is by making fun of ideas and people that are in fact good. In the case of the *Ecclesiazusae*, of course, we moderns may find a rather sympathetic rendering of the communistic ideas. But whatever we may think, Plato seems to have found in the play a straightforward mockery of new ideas.[19]

Plato's critique of the comedians in this passage can also be extended to the hostile portrait of Socrates drawn by Aristophanes and other poets of Old Comedy. For in these comedies, a good man is subjected to ridicule by playwrights who are ignorant of their subject. This is bolstered by the fact that, in the explicit definitions of the philosopher found in Plato, Socrates insists that the philosopher will seem "ridiculous" to the unphilosophic viewer. We have already seen how, in the *Gorgias,* Callicles portrays Socrates and his practice of philosophy as ridiculous. The same *topos* appears in the *Republic* at the end of the narration of the allegory of the cave (516e–517a). There Socrates observes that, since the philosopher who journeys back into the darkness of the cave is temporarily blinded

---

[18] Leaving aside the references to "comedy" and "the ridiculous" in the passage at 452a–d (which is quoted in the text above), the following references are found in book 5: γελᾶν (451b2, 457b1, b3), γέλως (451a1, 473c7), ἐκγελᾶν (473c8), γελοῖος (454c6, c7, 456d11, 457b2, 463e1), καταγέλαστος (455c8, 467a9). This repetition both thematizes and problematizes the ridiculous.

[19] One should recall that the interpretations of poems found elsewhere in Plato reveal a less than sensitive reader: the rather simplistic suggestion in *Rep.* 5 that comic poets attack novel ideas (rather than explore them in a humorous and lighthearted manner) is in fact entirely in keeping with the discussions of poets elsewhere in the corpus.

because of the brilliant illumination he has just experienced, his condition
will inevitably be misunderstood by those imprisoned in the cave. As he
puts it at 517a: "would he not produce laughter (γέλωτ᾽ ἂν παράσχοι),
and would it not be said of him that, having journeyed upwards he had
returned back with ruined eyes, and that it is not a good idea even to
attempt to go up?" The correct response is spelled out at 518a–b: "an intelligent man," says Socrates, would realize that a person's vision can be
disturbed either by a movement from darkness to light or by a movement
from light to darkness. Therefore, if he should come across someone
whose vision is disturbed, "he would not laugh (γελῷ) unthinkingly" but
would first determine which of the two kinds of disturbance the person is
suffering from, and if it should be the latter, he would call the person
happy rather than ridiculous.

This *topos* plays an especially prominent role in the definition of the
philosopher in the *Theaetetus*. The passage begins with Socrates' obser-
vation that "those who have occupied themselves with philosophy for
a long time, when they go into the lawcourts, appear to be ridiculous
speakers" (γελοῖοι ... ῥήτορες, 172c). Recalling the anecdote that a
Thracian servant "mocked" Thales because he fell into a pit as he was
contemplating the heavens, Socrates claims that "this same joke applies to
all who spend their life practicing philosophy" (174a–b). For the philosopher "provokes laughter (γέλωτα) not only in Thracian girls but in the
multitude as a whole" (174c). His awkwardness "makes people think he
is a fool" and, because of his inexperience in human affairs, "he seems
ridiculous" (γελοῖος, 174c–d). The philosopher, in turn, finds the multitude
ridiculous.[20] Indeed, it is partly because he laughs at them that he is held
up to ridicule (174c8–d1; 175b). But, as in the *Gorgias*, Plato turns the
tables on those who mock the philosopher. For, as Socrates says at 175b–
d, when the average person is forced into the philosophic arena and made
to answer the questions that concern philosophers, it is he who will "provoke laughter" (γέλωτα ... παρέχει, d4–5) as he "stammers" in response.

Clearly, Plato wants to set the record straight regarding "the ridiculous." While he does "include" a comic subtext in the *Republic*, he adds
instructions for handling this material.[21] For he not only invites the

---

[20] Socrates offers a detailed account of the laughter of the philosopher at 174d–175b.

[21] Cf. Saxonhouse 1978, who argues that Plato is purposely creating a ridiculous and ugly
city in the *Republic* (his overall purpose being "to set private justice within the soul in
opposition to the justice which the political unit can never achieve" [p. 889]). According
to this argument, Plato reuses Aristophanes' comic material *without transforming it*: he
wants Callipolis to appear as comic as the city portrayed in the *Ecclesiazusae*. Saxonhouse
fails to consider the passage in book 5 which criticizes comedy (452a–e), as well as the
persistent references in the *Republic* to the opposition between what *seems ridiculous* and
what is *truly ridiculous*.

reader to meditate on the true nature of the ridiculous, but he makes it quite clear that the people who are in the business of ridicule often get it all wrong. As Socrates puts it at 457b, the person who makes a mockery of what is in fact good " 'plucks the unripe fruit of the ridiculous' and knows neither what he laughs at nor what he is doing." The comic poets (as well as those who encourage and imitate their brand of ridicule) are thus both criticized and corrected. We may smile at the notion of correcting a comic poet: to what extent are the comedians aiming for truth or even accuracy? As we will see in the next section, Old Comedy did in fact claim to offer valuable criticism and advice to the *dēmos*; as social critics operating from an authorized position within the democracy, the comedians often elicited a "serious" response.

II

Thus far, I have been discussing Plato's response to the "ridiculous" or humorous side of comedy. As many passages attest, Plato is critical of the comedians' ignorant portrayal of the ridiculous. At the same time, however, Plato shows clear signs of putting comic humor to good use: Euthyphro, Ion, Hippias, and Alcibiades, to name only a few, have a great deal in common with comic characters. Many scholars, of course, have identified "comic" elements in Plato's dialogues (especially the *Symposium*).[22] To cite one rather extreme example, Saxonhouse argues that the entire political edifice erected in the *Republic* was designed to be seen as ridiculous.[23] As she argues, "If it is funny in Aristophanes, why isn't it funny in Plato?"[24] As this quotation reveals, Saxonhouse is addressing the question of whether a dialogue or a portion of a dialogue can be said to be *ludicrous or funny*. Whether or not they would agree with Saxonhouse's "comic" reading of the *Republic*, many scholars who have discussed the relation between Plato and comedy evince the same basic methodological assumption: that Plato's debt to comedy is measured by his inclusion of material that is ludicrous, humorous, or funny.

As I see it, this methodology relies on the general and transhistorical notion that comedy is funny. But what is at stake here is Plato's relationship to a specific and quite idiosyncratic genre: that of Old Comedy. As we have seen, Old Comedy is indeed ridiculous and funny and Plato does address this aspect of the genre in his dialogues. But, unlike many

---

[22] Greene 1920, Bacon 1959, Bloom 1968: 380–2 and passim, Clay 1975, Saxonhouse 1978, Woodruff 1982a: esp. 100–3, Brock 1990, Arieti 1991: ch. 7 and passim.
[23] Saxonhouse 1978. Saxonhouse follows Bloom (1968: 380–2 and passim) in many respects.
[24] Saxonhouse 1978: 891.

other comic genres, Old Comedy contains a good deal of material that has serious social and political import. As Dover suggests,

The fact that the privilege of Comic ridicule was suspended by law from 440/39 to 437/6 shows that it was not always regarded as a light-hearted family game; nor can we read Aristophanes without becoming aware of passages which strike home in a way that fun does not.[25]

According to Henderson, the comic poets conceived of themselves

as public voices who could, indeed were expected to, comment on, and seek to influence public thinking about matters of major importance – the same matters that were being or might be presented to the voting *dēmos* in other settings and in different ways, by competitors in a tragic competition, for example, or by speakers in an assembly, or by litigants in a law court.[26]

What was the nature of this "public voice" of comedy? This "voice" emerges perhaps most clearly in the parabases, where the chorus speaks for or on behalf of "the poet" and offers criticism and advice on vital political issues. But the comic poet can also convey criticism and commentary by way of the characters and plot of his drama. The following quotations from Aristophanes will serve to exemplify the "public voice" of comedy:

DICAEOPOLIS: Bear me no grudge, spectators, if, being a beggar, I speak before the Athenian people about the city in a comic play. For comedy also knows what is just. And I shall utter things that are terrible but just (τὸ γὰρ δίκαιον οἶδε καὶ τρυγῳδία. | Ἐγὼ δὲ λέξω δεινὰ μέν, δίκαια δέ). For Cleon cannot slander me now, saying that I speak ill of the city (τὴν πόλιν κακῶς λέγω) when strangers are present. For we are alone: it is the Lenaea and there are no foreigners here. (*Acharnians* 496–505)[27]

CHORUS: Our poet says that he deserves great rewards from you, since he kept you from being deceived by foreign and novel speeches, from taking pleasure in flattery, and from swallowing everything open-mouthed ... [And even the king of Persia] asked about our poet – which of the two cities he regularly abuses (εἴποι κακὰ πολλά). For he said that these people were superior by far and would easily conquer in the war, since they have this man as an adviser. (*Acharnians* 633–5; 647–51)

---

[25] Dover 1968b: 129. If the "decree of Syrocosius" (a law banning comic invective against individuals "by name" which was supposedly introduced in 415/414 BCE) is genuine, it adds further weight to the notion that comedy impacted upon Athenian social and political affairs. *Contra* Halliwell 1984c, who argues that the decree is a scholiast's invention, see Sommerstein 1986 (and, similarly, Atkinson 1992) who contends that the decree did exist, but that it did not impose a ban on naming *all* individuals; rather, it confined itself to those condemned for impiety in the mutilation of the Herms and the profanation of the Mysteries.

[26] J. Henderson 1990: 271–2.

[27] See Taplin 1983 for a discussion of comedy's identification of itself as "τρυγῳδία."

CHORUS: Demos, you have power, since all men fear you like a tyrant. But you are easily led astray, and you enjoy being fawned upon and deceived, and are always gaping at the orator who is speaking. You have intelligence, but it has gone abroad. (*Knights* 1111–20)

CHORUS: It is just for the holy chorus to offer good advice to the city and to instruct it ... [a long speech follows, including blame, praise and advice] ... But even now, you foolish people, change your ways and make use of good men once again ... (*Frogs* 686–7; 734–5)

PRAXAGORA: You, the Athenian *dēmos*, are responsible for these things, since you took your wages from the public purse but were looking for what each of you might gain in private. (*Ecclesiazusae* 205–7)

As these passages indicate, comedy features (among other things) a voice which claims the authority to criticize and correct the Athenians; unlike other public speakers, who flatter and deceive the *dēmos*, comedy will "speak" and "teach" what is "just" and "true."

As many scholars have emphasized, we should not interpret this "public voice" of comedy as necessarily representing the poet's own views.[28] For we cannot simply pull these passages out of context and confer upon them the privilege of conveying the (extra-fictional) "voice of the poet." As Bowie suggests, "'Aristophanes the man', the social commentator ironically viewing the events of the play from without, is not to be found ... his 'personal' statement in the parabasis is no more than the play in miniature; he is as much a literary construct as his hero."[29] According to this argument, the fictional dramas of the comedians do not give us direct access to the minds of the poets who wrote them. But, even if the "personal statements" of the "poet" are taken to be a literary construct, we may still believe that the "voice" which utters these statements has something serious to convey. To be sure, an interpreter's assertion that a statement is serious or comic will always be subjective; no doubt the individual members of the Athenian *dēmos* would have reacted differently to the same material. In addition, as Goldhill claims, the comic and the serious in this kind of drama have a tendency to "mutually infect each other's status."[30] But the fact remains that comedy incorporated the genre of invective as one of its many voices, and the genre is still recognizable in spite of its comic surroundings. As Rosen has shown in *Old Comedy and the Iambographic Tradition*,

the Athenian comic poets were aware of both the distinguishing poetic features of the Ionian iambos and the appropriateness of these features to their own genre.

[28] See, e.g., Carrière 1979: passim, Bowie 1982, Goldhill 1991: ch. 3.
[29] Bowie 1982: 40.
[30] Goldhill 1991: 222.

This awareness, moreover, reflected their realization that the satirical and antagonistic elements of their plays derived from an impulse fundamentally similar to that of the iambic ψόγος.[31]

While the exact degree of seriousness in a given comic passage will always be disputable, the presence of invective as a regular and quite distinct feature in this genre is not in doubt.[32]

The connection between comedy and invective, of course, is attested by a number of ancient writers, including the comedians themselves.[33] Aristotle says in the *Poetics* that comedy evolved out of the iambic lampoon (1448b–1449a). He also calls the comedians κακολόγοι in the *Rhetoric* (1384b10) and identifies comedy as a species of αἰσχρολογία in the *Politics* (1336b4, b20–3). In the latter passage, in fact, Aristotle indicates that all αἰσχρολογία will be banished from the good state, except in the case of religious events at which the "law allows mockery." "Iambic lampoons and comedy," which are part of the festivals of Dionysus, are thus permitted, but Aristotle stipulates that the young shall be forbidden to attend these performances. Finally, in the *Nicomachean Ethics*, stating his preference for the "new" comedies which use "innuendo" rather than "direct abuse," Aristotle goes on to say: "comic joking (σκῶμμα) is a form of verbal abuse (λοιδόρημα), and the lawgivers forbid certain kinds of verbal abuse; perhaps they ought to prohibit some forms of joking also" (1128a22–31). Clearly, Aristotle takes comic mockery seriously, otherwise he would not venture the suggestion that their jokes be subjected to law.

Comedy's conferral of abuse and invective is also attested by the "Old Oligarch," who explicitly complains about the politicization of the comedians' abusive discourse:

[The Athenians] do not allow comedians to speak abusively of the *dēmos*, so that the people do not hear themselves spoken ill of. But they allow this in the case of private individuals, if anyone wishes to abuse someone, knowing full well that the

---

[31] R. Rosen 1988: 37. See also Koster 1980: 72–6, and J. Henderson 1991: 17–19.

[32] The question whether Old Comedy contained any "serious" import has been debated by a number of scholars. Those who believe that comic satire was "serious" in the sense that it contained ascertainable elements of political import and/or conviction are, e.g., Ste. Croix 1972: 231–44, 355–71, Carrière 1979: esp. 41–50, R. Rosen 1988 (with important qualifications), J. Henderson 1990 and 1993, Edwards 1991 and 1993; disbelievers are Gomme 1938, Bowie 1982 and 1993, Halliwell 1984b and 1993, Reckford 1987: esp. 443–51, 475–82, and Heath 1987. It is important to note that, even if one does not take the *positive advice* that comedy offers as "serious," this does not entail that the *criticisms* offered are not (at least to some degree) serious. As J. Henderson 1991: 12 suggests, the genre of comedy was designed for promulgating "negative criticism and scurrilous exposures" rather than "positive enlightenment" on social and political questions.

[33] For a discussion of comedy's reflection on its own discourse of invective, see Edwards 1991.

person who is attacked in comedy will not, for the most part, belong to the populace or the masses, but will be wealthy or nobly born or powerful. There are some poor commoners – though they are few – who are attacked in comedy, but only if they are meddlesome and are seeking to place themselves above the *dēmos*, so that the people are not angry that such individuals are abused. (2.18)

The statements of the Old Oligarch, of course, can hardly be taken as neutral reportage. But they do remind us that the censure of the comedians was uttered in a specific socio-political context and that at least some people took this censure very seriously indeed.[34]

It should be emphasized that the comedians were not the only Athenians who deployed invective in public fora. For the orators and politicians offered many of the same criticisms of the *dēmos* as the comedians did: its inferiority to the great Athenians of yore, its empowerment of bad leaders, its love of flattery, its gullibility, and its susceptibility to mendacious demagogues.[35] These similarities are striking, but one should also note the differences between the abusive discourse of comedy and oratory. Consider Ober's remark about the orator's critical statements: "Although each criticism had its particular context and was intended to put the speaker in the best light and his opponent in the worst, the thread running through the various topoi of blame is clear enough: the orator 'attacks' the people for not living up to their own ideals."[36] If one looks at this "thread" rather than at the context of these utterances, it is easy to see the parallel with comedy. But if one focuses on the contexts in which oratory and comedy are performed, the differences are immediately apparent. In particular, the orator had to acquire and maintain power by persuading the people to back him on specific issues; his abuse was invariably put in the service of this goal. The case of comedy is more complex. To be sure, the comedians were competing for prizes and needed to please the *dēmos* if they were to win the day. But, unlike the orators, they did not need to persuade the people to pursue an immediate course of action; rather, their criticism was part of their attempt to invite the *dēmos* to take a good hard look at itself – to reflect upon the ways in which the democratic government and its citizens can go awry. Given these aims and the festival context, the comedians could afford to censure the Athenians with much greater freedom and on a wider range of issues than oratory. Comedy, in

[34] For discussions of the Old Oligarch's remarks on comedy, see Carrière 1979: 44–5 and passim, and J. Henderson 1990.
[35] Dover 1974: 23–33 analyzes the *topoi* and other elements shared by comedy and oratory. For a succinct discussion of the orators' use of the discourse of blame, see Ober 1989: 318–24. On Demosthenes' criticisms of demagogues and the *dēmos*, see Montgomery 1983: esp. 20–8; Montgomery also notes the similarities and differences between Demosthenes' censure and that of Aristophanes (27–8).
[36] Ober 1989: 320.

short, had a good deal to offer Plato that no other social critic in Athens was able to provide.

III

Plato addresses comic criticism quite explicitly in the *Laws*. In his discussion of the regulations concerning "abuse" (κακηγορία) in book 11, the Athenian begins by asserting that there will be but one law on this topic: "no one shall abuse anyone" (934b). But he modifies this position when he turns to the question of the abuse uttered in comedies:

[in our legislation for Magnesia], should we divide the practice in two, according to whether the ridicule is conferred in jest or in earnest (τῷ παίζειν καὶ μή), and should we allow a person to ridicule someone without animosity (ἄνευ θυμοῦ), but forbid it when he is in earnest and passionate (συντεταμένῳ δὲ καὶ μετὰ θυμοῦ)? (935d–e)

The Athenian offers the following answer to this question. On the one hand, the comedians and other poets of invective "will never be allowed to ridicule any of the citizens, either in words or in mimicry, whether it be with or without animosity" (935e). They may, however, subject non-citizens to ridicule, with the following caveat: "those who have been given permission to write about others, as we specified previously, will be allowed to confer ridicule in play and without animosity; but they are not allowed to do this in a serious way or with animosity" (936a).[37] Who, then, is permitted to write these comedies? This is explicated in book 8, where the Athenian discusses compositions involving praise and blame:

Not everyone may write these kinds of compositions. First, the person must be more than fifty years old, and those who are skilled in poetry and music but have done no fine or illustrious deed will not be allowed. But all those who are good and esteemed in the city, being the craftsmen of fine deeds – let their poems be sung, even if they possess no skill in poetry. (829c–d)[38]

Only the "good" may write comedies, presumably because they alone will use ridicule correctly. And even their comedies must be submitted to the Minister of Education, who must first judge whether the ridicule is "playful" or fueled by "animosity" (936a–b).

As these passages indicate, Plato saw the "serious" side of comedy. But while he clearly gave a good deal of thought to the place of comic criti-

---

[37] I follow England's text here, which deletes περί του (1921.II: 198).

[38] In this passage, the Athenian is talking about compositions containing praise or blame of the citizens (which is quite different from the ridicule and abuse that the comedies will level against non-citizens). But it is clear that the Athenian is looking back to this passage when he discusses *kakēgoria* in book 11.

cism in a good city, his dialogues indicate that he felt differently about its role in a bad city such as democratic Athens. To be sure, Plato must have believed that his understanding of the serious and the ridiculous gave him the right to indulge in criticism; certainly he did not refrain from attacking his fellow citizens or the city as a whole. It should be emphasized that Plato uses some form of invective in every dialogue. Our concern here, however, is with those dialogues where Plato's criticism is based on a comic subtext. For what is at stake here is his reuse of comic material and the significance of this intergeneric aspect of Plato's texts.

Let me begin with a comedy which offered an irresistible subtext for a Platonic dialogue: Eupolis' *Flatterers* (*Kolakes*), which won first prize at the Dionysia in 421 BCE. As scholars have long observed, the setting and the subject of this comedy find a direct parallel in Plato's *Protagoras*.[39] For Eupolis' comedy represented the flock of flatterers found at the house of the wealthy Callias – a flock which included Protagoras, who probably had a speaking role (frr. 157, 158 *PCG*).[40] The *Protagoras*, of course, is also set at Callias' house, and its "chorus" is a flock of sophists and their followers. Although it is easy to see the comic aspects of the *Protagoras*, the paucity of extant fragments from the *Flatterers* makes it impossible to analyze Plato's dialogue from an intertextual perspective. Perhaps the only detail we can nail down is Plato's reenactment of the chorus of flatterers that was featured in Eupolis' comedy. As Socrates describes the sophists' "dance" in the house of Callias:

And I myself, when I saw this chorus (τοῦτον τὸν χορόν), was especially delighted at how well they took care never to hinder Protagoras by getting in front of him; and when he and his followers turned and reversed their course, the listeners divided their ranks on one side and the other in a fine and orderly way, and moving round in a circle, they took up their stations behind him each time with beautiful precision. (315b)

Here, Plato clearly alludes to the chorus of flatterers in Eupolis' comedy and, indeed, to Protagoras' former incarnation as a comic character. Note that, in Plato's rendition, Protagoras is figured both as the object of fawning adulation and as the leader (and therefore a member) of this chorus. It is likely that Plato was using the comic subtext to portray his own "chorus" of sophists as a group of flatterers. Certainly flattery is an important theme in the *Protagoras*: as Carson has shown, Plato takes both Protagoras and Simonides to task for being salesmen or purveyors of praise.[41]

---

[39] See, e.g., Wilamowitz 1920.I: 140, Norwood 1932: 190, Arieti 1991: ch. 7.

[40] Chaerephon was also dubbed a "flatterer" of Callias in this play, but there is no evidence in the extant fragments that he appeared as a speaking character (180 *PCG*).

[41] Carson 1992: 122 and passim. Note also *Theaetetus* 161e, where Socrates says that Protagoras was "playing to the crowd" (δημούμενον) when he enunciated his "man is the

Although any conclusions we reach about Plato's reworking of the *Flatterers* must necessarily be speculative, it seems reasonable to suggest that Plato found the comedy congenial to his own project. Rather than correcting the comedy, then, he seems to have harnessed its censure of the sophists. The double-voicing involved here is thus not parodic, since the abusive "voice" of comedy is granted full semantic autonomy within the Platonic dialogue.

A similar use of comic invective is found in the *Gorgias*. We have seen in chapter 2 that Callicles and Socrates portray each other as "ridiculous." But the dialogue's relation with comedy goes beyond these two characters. When Socrates offers a detailed account of rhetoric as a species of "flattery" at 462d–463c, for example, he says that this definition may "make a comedy" (διακωμῳδεῖν, 462e7) of the profession of the sophist and orator. Clearly, this does not mean that his portrayal of rhetoric will be funny or raise a laugh; in fact, there is very little humor in the *Gorgias*. Rather, the reader is invited to look for comic abuse and invective, and this is easy to find.

A number of abusive tropes in the *Gorgias* find direct parallels in Old Comedy, and particularly in Aristophanes' *Knights*.[42] Note, for example, Socrates' statement at 481d–e that Callicles is the lover (*erastēs*) of the Athenian *dēmos* and is unable to contradict or oppose anything his "beloved" says; if the Athenian *dēmos* disagrees with something he proposes, Socrates adds, Callicles "changes positions and says whatever the *dēmos* wants to hear." This recalls the vivid portrayal of Demos (the Athenian *dēmos* personified) and his lovers, the Paphlagonian and the Sausage-seller, in the *Knights*. The Paphlagonian, who represents the Athenian politician Cleon, is portrayed as both the servant and the lover of Demos: he "crouches before his master, wheedling, fawning, flattering, and deceiving him" (47–8); he feeds and gorges Demos (e.g. 51–7; 715) and claims to be his *erastēs* (732). The plot of course centers on the Sausage-seller's competition with the Paphlagonian for Demos' favor. The Sausage-seller pronounces himself a "rival lover" (*anterastēs*, 733), and proceeds to outdo the Paphlagonian by flattering Demos and promising to feast him in even greater style and abundance (not for nothing is he a dealer in sausages).

The *Gorgias* reworks a number of these themes. Aristophanes' vocabulary of love and passionate desire – which is well brought out in the Paphlagonian's declaration at line 732 that he "cares for" (φιλῶ) Demos and is his "lover" (ἐραστής) – finds a parallel in the language of φιλία,

---

measure" doctrine. Plato's contention that the sophists as a group are salesmen who give the people what they want to hear is discussed in chapter one.

[42] As Brock 1990: 48–9 observes.

ἔρως, and χάρις (with its overtones of sexual gratification) in the *Gorgias*. To be sure, the use of erotic language in the political sphere is not unique to Aristophanes: Pericles' statement in the funeral oration that the Athenians must become *erastai* of their polis (Thucydides 2.43.1) is one of many examples.[43] But it is only in the writers of Old Comedy that we find the *dēmos* personified and portrayed as the literal object of sexual desire.[44] As Rothwell observes,

A figurative "love of country" may not have seemed unduly strained or improper when Pericles used it, but Aristophanes took it in a literal sense, and, in an Aristophanic *reductio ad absurdum*, portrayed Cleon as a homosexual *erastēs* who was attempting to seduce Demos who, in turn, was portrayed as an *erōmenos*.[45]

In the *Gorgias*, after declaring Callicles a "lover" of the *dēmos*, Socrates points out that his companion will have to "become as similar as possible to the Athenian *dēmos*, if [he] is going to be loved (προσφιλής) by them and powerful in the city" (513a). Again, at 513b–c, Socrates says,

you must be not just an imitator but similar in your very nature to them if you are going to forge a genuine friendship (φιλίαν) with the Athenian *dēmos* ... So, then, whoever can make you as like as possible to the people will make you a politician and a rhetorician in the way in which you long (ἐπιθυμεῖς) to be one. For each man rejoices when he hears words that match his character, and is vexed by an alien character.

Later, when Callicles refuses to abandon his own inconsistent positions, Socrates sums up the problem as follows: "it is *erōs* for the *dēmos*, dwelling in your soul, which is opposing my position" (513c). For all his bluster, Callicles exhibits a penchant for pleasing other people, as his oft repeated expression of his desire to "gratify" his companions attests (χαρίζεσθαι, 501c8, 513e1, 514a4, 516b4).

Flattery, of course, plays a pivotal role in the attempts to seduce Demos in the *Knights*. In fact, the whole of Aristophanes' comedy is devoted to satirizing, on the one hand, the ways in which Athenian politicians fawn on the *dēmos* to serve their own private interests and, on the other hand, the *dēmos'* tendency to empower those politicians who dem-

---

[43] For a discussion of the rhetoric of *erōs* in the political discourse in Athens, see Connor [1971]/1992: 96–8, Arrowsmith 1973, and Rothwell 1990: 37–43. For the discourse of *erōs* in Thucydides, see Cornford 1907: ch. 12.

[44] The *dēmos* is portrayed as the object of sexual desire in Eupolis 346 *PCG*. It is personified in Eupolis 227 *PCG*, 346 *PCG*, and Plato Comicus 201 *PCG*. Note that the description of Demos (= the *dēmos*) as "hard of hearing" (ὑπόκωφον) at Aristophanes' *Knights* 43 – an image which is also found in Eupolis' *Cities* (227 *PCG*) – finds a parallel in Plato's comparison of the *dēmos* to a shipmaster who is "hard of hearing and slightly blind" (ὑπόκωφον δὲ καὶ ὁρῶντα ὡσαύτως βραχύ τι, *Republic* 488a–b).

[45] Rothwell 1990: 40.

onstrate or at least declare their willingness to serve it. Which is the master and which the slave? At one moment Demos claims that he is not deceived by the fawning politicians but is in fact controlling them by means of the "ballot box" (1141–50); at another, the Sausage-seller explains to Demos that he has been completely fooled by the politicians' false protestations of love (1340–5). The overall picture is one of mutual bondage, since neither party is really in control. A very similar picture of democratic "rule" emerges in the *Gorgias*. As we have seen, the entire dialogue revolves around Socrates' definition of rhetoric as a "knack" for producing "gratification and pleasure" (ἐμπειρία ... χάριτός τινος καὶ ἡδονῆς ἀπεργασίας, 462c) – as, in short, a species of "flattery" (κολακεία, 463b1, etc.). This discourse of flattery, Socrates suggests, operates in an especially pernicious way in a democracy. For the rhetorician must necessarily gratify the *dēmos* if he wants power in this kind of regime; so far from being powerful and free to do as he wishes, he is effectively enslaved to the mob. Nor is the *dēmos* really empowered, since it is swayed by the specious flattery and gratification offered by the rhetoricians. Since each party is ignorant of the good, each enslaves itself to the gratification offered by the other.

In the *Knights*, as we have seen, the "service" that the politician offers to the *dēmos* is assimilated to the act of feasting. The exchange between the Paphlagonian and the Sausage-seller at 714–18 offers an excellent example of the metaphors of food and feasting that pervade the comedy:

ss: How strongly you believe that Demos belongs to you.
p: Yes, for I know just the tidbits to feed him (ψωμίζεται).
ss: And, like nurses, you feed (σιτίζεις) him badly. For, when you have chewed (μασώμενος) it, you place a little in his mouth, but you yourself swallow (κατέσπακας) three times as much as he.

The *Gorgias*, too, with its emphasis on the rhetorician's procurement of pleasure, makes a prominent use of metaphors of feasting. Take, for example, Socrates' response at 518b–c to Callicles' suggestion that men such as Themistocles, Cimon, Miltiades, and Pericles were "upright and good citizens in the city":[46]

it is as if, when I asked you to name the good ministers of the body – either past or present – in the field of gymnastics, you should say to me in all seriousness, "Thearion the baker and Mithaecus the author of the Sicilian cookbook and Sarambus the inn-keeper – these men are marvellous ministers of the body, the first providing bread, the second gourmet food, and the third wine." Perhaps, then, you would be angry if I said to you, "Sir, you understand nothing about gym-

[46] This phrase is Socrates': he recapitulates at 518a–b the claim that Callicles made at 503c.

nastics; you speak of servants and men who cater to the appetites, but who have no proper understanding of these things – men who, if they happen to win praise when they have stuffed and fattened (ἐμπλήσαντες καὶ παχύναντες) the people's bodies, will eventually rob them of even the flesh that they had to begin with." (518b–c)

Here, the Athenian statesmen who have "stuffed the city with harbors and dockyards and walls and tribute and other nonsense of this kind" (519a) are assimilated to cooks and tavern-keepers who fatten the people on unhealthy food. This analogy, of course, picks up on the direct parallel that Socrates draws between rhetoric and gourmet cookery at 462d–465e (cf. 500e–501c). And the same image recurs in Socrates' famous claim that, if he were to be dragged into court, he would resemble a doctor being accused by a cook in front of a jury of children (464d, 521e–522a).

By portraying them as lovers, as flatterers, as cooks, Plato does indeed "make a comedy" of the rhetorician and the politician in the *Gorgias*. For he uses a number of recognizable comic *topoi* to bolster his own critique of Athens. Clearly, Plato is not correcting or parodying comedy but rather harnessing its "voice of criticism." In the case of the *Gorgias*, the appropriation of comedy does not include much humor. But when Plato borrows from comedy in other dialogues – such as the *Protagoras* and the *Symposium*[47] – we find a good deal of humor mixed in with the satire.

IV

As I have attempted to show, comedy presented Plato with a number of different possibilities, as even the (relatively) few remains from this genre attest.[48] Though he objected to the comedians' ignorant use of ridicule, Plato was quick to appropriate comedy's "voice of criticism" for his own dramas. Note also that both genres claim authority on the basis of the "fact" that they "dare" to utter the truth. Or, to be more precise, both genres feature a "voice" which claims to speak the truth. Compare, for example, the following passages from Aristophanes' *Acharnians* and Plato's *Gorgias*:

CHORUS: But you must never surrender [this poet]; for he portrays what is just in his comedies (ὡς κωμῳδήσει τὰ δίκαια). He says that he will teach you many fine things, so that you will be happy, not fawning or bribing or deceiving or cheating you or currying your favor, but teaching the things that are best (ἀλλὰ τὰ βέλτιστα διδάσκων). (*Acharnians* 655–8)

---

[47] I have not explored the comic aspects of the *Symposium* because this ground has been covered so thoroughly by others. See, e.g., Bacon 1959, Clay 1975, Patterson 1982.
[48] David 1984: 41–2 and Brock 1990 note a number of other Platonic allusions to comedy.

SOCRATES: I think that I am among the few Athenians (not to say the only one) who is engaged in the true political art and, of men today, that I am the only person practicing politics. For I do not say the things I do on each occasion in exchange for favor (πρὸς χάριν), but I aim at what is best, not at what is most pleasant. (521d–e)

As Henderson observes, the comic poets "claim to offer good advice of the sort not heard elsewhere: they, unlike others who appeal to the *dēmos*, are speaking only in the city's interests."[49] This is precisely the claim that Plato makes for his "philosopher" throughout the dialogues.[50]

But this simple comparison conceals a critical divergence. For, aside from the fact that the first passage is uttered in a humorous tone entirely lacking in the second, the positioning of each speaker/genre vis-à-vis the Athenian polis is completely different. As I suggested in chapter 1, Plato's philosopher is an outsider who is disembedded from the social and political economy of the city. The writers of Old Comedy, on the other hand, speak from within the Athenian democracy. As Henderson says of Aristophanes,

He never attacks the constitutional structure of the democracy or questions the inherent rightness of the *dēmos*' rule. This was after all an inheritance from the sacrosanct dead and therefore immune from comic or any other public criticism.[51]

The comic playwrights spoke as "a citizen before citizens"; as an authorized "voice" at the civic festivals, comedy "negotiated" both the "possibility of transgression" and the "limits of license."[52] It is precisely this negotiation with the *dēmos* that, in Plato's eyes, disqualified comedy from speaking the truth. For comedy does not occupy a position of disinterest: its desire to please the *dēmos* and to win first prize simply make this impossible. For Plato, there can be no limits to license when it comes to speaking the truth. To be sure, the comedians may at times hit the mark in their censure of the Athenians. But they lack both the requisite knowledge and the "outside" positioning that allow for free and truthful speech.

Consider one final – and, I believe, crucial – point of convergence between Old Comedy and the Platonic dialogue: the "mixed" or multi-generic form.[53] To put it more precisely, *both the comedians and Plato*

[49] J. Henderson 1990: 312.
[50] A detailed discussion of this claim is found in chapter 1.
[51] J. Henderson 1990: 310.
[52] Goldhill 1991: 188.
[53] Note also several other formal similarities between the two genres: the dramatic structure; the avoidance (or parodic inclusion) of "high" language; the focus on the contemporary world; and the dramatization of "real-life" individuals (rather than exalted characters from myth). Together with the multi-generic form, these are the very features that Bakh-

regularly incorporate "alien" genres of discourse into their dramas. In Old
Comedy and the Platonic dialogue, moreover, this inclusion of other
genres of discourse is always oriented towards the "contest of public
voices" that was a prominent feature of social and political life in democratic Athens.[54] Indeed, in both genres, the "contest" itself – together with
one or more of its competing "voices" – is regularly subjected to an
"honest" critique. For the discourse of poets, politicians, and other claimants to wisdom is "included" in the comedies/dialogues precisely so that
it may be ridiculed and criticized. I would argue, in fact, that it was Old
Comedy that offered Plato a model for dramatizing and criticizing the
"contest of public voices" in Athens and for enlisting a new and privileged
"voice" in the competition.[55] For this kind of polyphony is not found in
any other genre in this period.[56] To be sure, there is a good deal of interaction between writers within any single genre, but the incorporation of
different genres of discourse into an "alien" text is surprisingly uncommon. Considering that so many new prose genres were springing up in
just this period, this affiliation between the Platonic dialogue and comic
drama is even more remarkable.

It was the polyphony that characterized Old Comedy, I would urge,
which provided the paradigm for Plato's "mixed" texts. But Plato wrests
this formal structure away from its native genre as well as from the privileged position that the genre occupied within the Athenian democracy.
Plato's polyphony plays outside the boundaries of the social, political,
and cultural transactions of democratic Athens.

tin (1981: 21–6; 1984: 106–22) identifies as characteristic of the ancient (i.e. Greek and
Latin) "serio-comic" genres which were "the authentic precursors to the novel" (1981:
22). As scholars have noted, in spite of the fact that Bakhtin does not include Aristophanes in his list of "serio-comic" writers, his comedies meet all of Bakhtin's criteria for
the "serio-comic" genre (Suárez 1987, Platter 1993). For some recent discussions of Aristophanes' place in the Bakhtinian "carnavalesque" (a category which is not coextensive
with the "serio-comic" genre), see Edwards 1993 and Platter 1993.

[54] The notion of a "contest of public voices" is Goldhill's (1991: 167). See also Foley 1993:
130, who observes that "Aristophanes uses the contrast between genres to define his own
comedy; indeed, comedy's deliberate violation of tragic limits becomes the basis of its self-
defense, and of its claim to free speech, truth, and justice."

[55] It should be emphasized that, to a far greater extent than the comic poets, Plato tends to
privilege one "philosophic" voice over the others (although one hesitates to generalize in
this regard, since the dialogues differ in the degree to which they criticize or cooperate
with "alien" genres). This authoritative stance, however, is often attenuated by irony,
which undermines the privileged voice in a manner that is similar to comedy's dismantling
of its own claims to authority.

[56] A possible exception is Herodotus; but his inclusion of different "voices" is not oriented
towards the "contest of public voices" in Athens.

Conclusion

... Hang up philosophy!
Unless philosophy can make a Juliet,
Displant a town, reverse a prince's doom,
It helps not, it prevails not. Talk no more.

Shakespeare, Romeo and Juliet

As J. K. Davies has observed about ancient Greek thinkers,

> At first sight, the philosophers and intellectuals scarcely comprise a group. Quarrelsome and individualistic, they showed little sign of cohesion, and were socially diverse and geographically scattered. Yet they came to be denoted by labels such as "sophist" or "philosopher," which imputed some unity of role or status to them ...[1]]

But how exactly did these thinkers "come to be denoted" by these labels? As I have contended, the creation of "philosophy" was not simply a matter of giving a name to a new method of inquiry and argumentation. Rather, philosophy had to make a case for itself as a discipline that offered a unique kind of wisdom which rivaled the other brands on offer. This was by no means a simple enterprise, as Plato's frequent attempts to define and legitimize philosophy clearly attest. As we have seen, Plato defined philosophy at least in part by way of the rhetoric of invective and exclusion – rhetoric which had a specific valence in the context of the social and political structures of democratic Athens. But he did not rest content with explicit definitions and denunciations. For Plato also marked the boundaries of philosophy by scripting intertextual encounters with traditional genres of poetry and rhetoric. Although Plato is famous for his quarrels with "poetry" and "rhetoric" as supergenres, his parodic attacks invariably focus on individual genres of literature. As I have argued, Plato was concerned with the discourse and the dissemination of the poetic and rhetorical genres he interrogated: these genres are criticized both as literary forms and as discursive practices which played specific roles in the social and political life of Athens. It should come as no surprise, then,

---

[1] Davies [1978]/1983: 188.

that Plato introduces "philosophy" not just as an intellectual activity but as a new kind of social practice. For philosophy as Plato conceived it was not simply a distinctive mode of inquiry and argument, but rather a unique way of living based on specific ethical and political commitments.

It should go without saying that there are many aspects of Plato's effort to define philosophy which are not addressed in this study. A more comprehensive examination would have to deal, first of all, with all of the dialogues which define or investigate the nature of philosophy. In each dialogue, the interpreter would have to analyze both what Plato is *saying about* philosophy (whether explicitly or implicitly) and the various methods of inquiry used by the individuals who are *doing* philosophy. In such a study, considerations of dating and of development would also have to be addressed.[2] Finally, it would be necessary to examine Aristotle's conceptualization of philosophy (which differs from Plato's on a number of fundamental points), especially since it was Aristotle who composed the first and, indeed, the most influential account of the beginnings of philosophy in the West.[3] It is precisely because Aristotle's definitions and classifications of "philosophical" thinking have come to seem so natural, in fact, that the construction of these categories requires examination.

As Cascardi has argued, "The differentiation of 'literature' and 'philosophy' would indeed be absolute were it not for the fact that philosophy is itself unable to produce a coherent theory of the differences that separate it from literature."[4] My analysis of Plato's various attempts to define philosophy examines the "differentiation" between literature and philosophy in the very period when the boundaries of these disciplines were first demarcated in an explicit and systematic way. As I have argued, when Plato constructed the specialized discipline of philosophy, he defined it in opposition to other genres of discourse. But while Plato separated philosophy from its adversaries, he did not sequester it. Rather, he staged an ongoing dialogue between philosophy and its "others." To be sure, Plato's "conversations" with alien genres were not always friendly; parody, as we have seen, is the norm in the Platonic dialogues. But the parodies themselves, which offer painstaking and penetrating criticisms of the genres that they target, testify that Plato took "alien" genres very seriously indeed. The fact that Plato continued to compose "mixed" texts – texts in which poetic, rhetorical, and philosophical discourse are inter-

---

[2] The arrangement of the chapters in this book is not meant to indicate a chronological development in Plato's use of intertextuality or (correlatively) in his definition of philosophy.

[3] Mansfeld [1985]/1990: 10–12 suggests that, at least since the time of Hegel, Aristotle's history has been generally accepted by Western scholars and philosophers.

[4] Cascardi 1987: x. See also Mackey 1993, who deconstructs philosophy's claims to a "transcendence" that "sustains its authority as the definer of genres and the assessor of generic performances" (p. 13).

woven and/or juxtaposed – may indicate that he considered his many attempts to offer a "coherent theory of differences" insufficient. Alternatively, he may have sensed that a complete divorce from poetry and rhetoric was unnecessary or, indeed, undesirable.

Although this study deals with the original construction of the discipline of philosophy in the West, it addresses many of the same issues that are being discussed in contemporary dialogues about the present state of philosophy. What constitutes "true" philosophy in the 1990s? What is at stake when professional philosophers insist (in good Platonic fashion) that certain thinkers are *not* philosophers? Many scholars in recent decades have suggested that philosophy is either dead or in desperate need of transformation.[5] Not surprisingly, a number of contemporary philosophers are turning to literature in their attempts to stake out new ground for philosophy (e.g. Rorty, Cavell, Williams, Nussbaum). After effacing the boundaries that have traditionally separated philosophy from other discursive practices, of course, scholars must confront a new set of problems. In particular, we need to ask whether "the notion of argumentative reason [can] be loosened up enough to incorporate the rhetorical and figurative aspects of philosophical discourse, while being kept tight enough to allow for its demarcation from, say, literature or non-argumentative forms of persuasion."[6]

Plato does not proceed by "loosening up" the notion of argumentative reason. But his approach to literary discourse is in many ways instructive. For, though he defines philosophy in opposition to poetry and rhetoric, Plato deliberately violates the borders which he himself has drawn. The boundaries between philosophy and "alien" genres of discourse are created, disrupted, and created afresh. The ambivalence of this originary gesture is, perhaps, appropriate, since philosophy in the West has persisted by reinventing itself again and again. And this reinvention is surely necessary, since the discipline must respond to the socio-political practices as well as the intellectual developments of its respective culture. If one conceives of philosophy as a discipline whose boundaries are flexible rather than fixed, its present "crisis" may be but one more round in the ongoing (re)construction of this protean discipline.

[5] See, e.g., Baynes, Bohman, and McCarthy 1987 for a collection of essays announcing the "end" of philosophy as we know it. For a book of essays on the same theme written by philosophers working (for the most part) outside the boundaries of academic philosophy, see Ogilvie 1992.

[6] Baynes, Bohman, and McCarthy 1987: 17.

Bibliography

Adam, J. (1902) ed. and comm., *The Republic of Plato*. 2 vols. Cambridge.
Adkins, A. W. H. (1983) "Orality and philosophy," in K. Robb, ed., *Language and Thought in Early Greek Philosophy*, 207–27. La Salle, Illinois.
Annas, J. (1981) *An Introduction to Plato's Republic*. Oxford.
  (1982a) "Plato's myths of judgement," *Phronesis* 27: 119–43.
  (1982b) "Plato on the triviality of literature," in J. Moravcsik and P. Temko, edd., *Plato on Beauty, Wisdom, and the Arts*, 1–23. New Jersey.
Anton, J. P. (1974) "The secret of Plato's *Symposium*," *Southern Journal of Philosophy* 12: 277–93.
Appadurai, A. (1986) "Introduction: commodities and the politics of value," in A. Appadurai, ed., *The Social Life of Things: Commodities in Cultural Perspective*, 3–63. Cambridge.
Arieti, J. A. (1991) *Interpreting Plato. The Dialogues as Drama*. Savage, Maryland.
Arnott, G. (1972) "From Aristophanes to Menander," *G&R* 2nd ser. 19: 65–80.
Arrowsmith, W. (1973) "Aristophanes' *Birds*: the fantasy politics of *Eros*," *Arion* n.s. 1: 119–67.
Atkinson, J. E. (1992) "Curbing the comedians: Cleon versus Aristophanes and Syracosius' decree," *CQ* n.s. 42: 56–64.
Austin, J. L. (1962) *How to Do Things with Words*. Cambridge, Mass.
Austin, M. M. and P. Vidal-Naquet (1977) *Economic and Social History of Ancient Greece: An Introduction*, trans. and revised by M. M. Austin. Berkeley.
Bacon, H. (1959) "Socrates crowned," *Virginia Quarterly Review* 35: 415–30.
Bakhtin, M. M. (1981) *The Dialogic Imagination*, trans. C. Emerson and M. Holquist. Austin.
  (1984) *Problems of Dostoevsky's Poetics*, trans. C. Emerson. Minneapolis.
  (1986) *Speech Genres and Other Late Essays*, trans. V. W. McGee. Austin, Texas.
Bakhtin, M. M. / P. N. Medvedev (1985) *The Formal Method in Literary Scholarship. A Critical Introduction to Sociological Poetics*, trans. A. J. Wehrle. Repr. Cambridge, Mass.
Barker, E. (1918) *Greek Political Theory. Plato and his Predecessors*. London.
Barnes, J. (1983) "Aphorism and argument," in K. Robb, ed., *Language and Thought in Early Greek Philosophy*, 91–109. La Salle, Illinois.
Batstone, W. W. (1986) "Commentary on Cooper: oratory, philosophy, and the common world," *Proceedings of the Boston Area Colloquium in Ancient Philosophy* 1: 97–113.

Baynes, K., J. Bohman, and T. McCarthy (1987) edd., *After Philosophy. End or Transformation?* Cambridge, Mass.

Beck, F. A. G. (1964) *Greek Education 450–350 B.C.* New York.

Belfiore, E. (1983) "Plato's greatest accusation against poetry," in F. J. Pelletier and J. King-Farlow, edd., *New Essays on Plato* (*Canadian Journal of Philosophy* suppl. vol. 9) 39–62. Ontario.

(1984a) "Dialectic with the reader in Plato's *Symposium*," *Maia* 36: 137–49.

(1984b) "A theory of imitation in Plato's *Republic*," *TAPA* 114: 121–46.

Bell, J. M. (1978) "Κίμβιξ καὶ σοφός: Simonides in the anecdotal tradition," *QUCC* 28: 29–86.

Benardete, S. (1991) *The Rhetoric of Morality and Philosophy. Plato's Gorgias and Phaedrus.* Chicago.

(1993) *The Tragedy and Comedy of Life. Plato's Philebus.* Chicago.

Berger, H., Jr. (1990) "*Phaedrus* and the politics of inscription," in B. P. Dauenhauer, ed., *Textual Fidelity and Textual Disregard* (American University Studies, ser. 3, Comparative Literature 33) 81–103. New York.

Bergren, A. (1992) "Architecture, gender, philosophy," in R. Hexter and D. Selden, edd., *Innovations of Antiquity*, 253–305. New York.

Blank, D. L. (1985) "Socratics versus sophists on payment for teaching," *CA* 4: 1–49.

Blass, F. (1907) *Isocratis Orationes*, 2 vols. Teubner edition. Leipzig.

(1962) *Die Attische Beredsamkeit*³ vols. I–III.2. Hildesheim.

Bloom, A. (1968) *The Republic of Plato.* New York.

Blundell, M. W. (1989) *Helping Friends and Harming Enemies. A Study in Sophocles and Greek Ethics.* Cambridge.

Bolotin, D. (1979) *Plato's Dialogue on Friendship.* Ithaca.

Booth, W. C. (1974) *A Rhetoric of Irony.* Chicago.

Bourdieu, P. ([1972]/1989) *Outline of a Theory of Practice*, trans. R. Nice. Repr. Cambridge. First published as *Esquisse d'une théorie de la pratique* (Switzerland 1972).

([1979]/1984) *Distinction: A Social Critique of the Judgement of Taste*, trans. R. Nice. First published as *La Distinction: Critique sociale du jugement* (Paris 1979).

Bowie, A. (1982) "The parabasis in Aristophanes: prolegomena, *Acharnians*," *CQ* 32: 27–40.

(1993) *Aristophanes. Myth, Ritual and Comedy.* Cambridge.

Brickhouse, T. C. and N. D. Smith (1984) "Vlastos on the elenchus," *OSAPh* 2: 185–95.

(1989) *Socrates on Trial.* Princeton.

Brisson, L. (1982) *Platon, les mots et les mythes.* Paris.

Brock, R. (1990) "Plato and comedy," in E. M. Craik, ed., *Owls to Athens. Essays on Classical Subjects Presented to Sir Kenneth Dover*, 39–49. Oxford.

Brumbaugh, R. S. (1989) *Platonic Studies of Greek Philosophy: Form, Arts, Gadgets, and Hemlock.* New York.

Buchheit, V. (1960) *Untersuchungen zur Theorie des Genos Epideiktikon von Gorgias bis Aristoteles.* Munich.

Bundy, E. L. ([1962]/1986) *Studia Pindarica.* Berkeley. First published in 1962 as

198   Bibliography

vol. 18, nos. 1 and 2, of the University of California Publications in Classical Philology.

(1972) "The 'quarrel between Kallimachos and Apollonios.' Part I: The epilogue of Kallimachos's *Hymn to Apollo*," *CSCA* 5: 39–94.

Burford, A. (1972) *Craftsmen in Greek and Roman Society*. Ithaca.

(1993) *Land and Labor in the Greek World*. Baltimore.

Burge, E. L. (1969) "The irony of Socrates," *Antichthon* 3: 5–17.

Burger, R. (1980) *Plato's Phaedrus: A Defense of the Philosophic Art of Writing*. Alabama.

Burgess, T. C. (1902) "Epideictic literature," *The University of Chicago Studies in Classical Philology* 3: 89–261.

Burke, E. M. (1992) "The economy of Athens in the classical era: some adjustments to the primitivist model," *TAPA* 122: 199–226.

Burkert, W. (1960) "Plato oder Pythagoras? Zum Ursprung des Wortes 'Philosophie,'" *Hermes* 88: 159–77.

Burnyeat, M. F. (1977) "Socratic midwifery, Platonic inspiration," *BICS* 24: 7–16.

Bury, R. G. (1932) *The Symposium of Plato*. Cambridge.

Calhoun, G. M. (1919) "Oral and written pleading in Athenian courts," *TAPA* 50: 177–93.

Carrière, J. C. (1979) *Le carnaval et la politique*. Paris.

Carson, A. (1986) *Eros the Bittersweet. An Essay*. Princeton.

(1992) "How not to read a poem: unmixing Simonides from *Protagoras*," *CP* 87: 110–30.

Carter, L. B. (1986) *The Quiet Athenian*. Oxford.

Cascardi, A. J. (1987) ed., *Literature and the Question of Philosophy*. Baltimore.

Chance, T. H. (1992) *Plato's Euthydemus. Analysis of What Is and Is Not Philosophy*. Berkeley.

Charlton, W. (1985) "Greek philosophy and the concept of an academic discipline," in P. A. Cartledge and F. D. Harvey, edd., *Crux. Essays presented to G. E. M. de Ste. Croix on his 75th birthday*, 47–61. Exeter, England.

Cherniss, H. (1935) *Aristotle's Criticism of Presocratic Philosophy*. Baltimore.

(1944) *Aristotle's Criticism of Plato and the Academy*. Baltimore.

([1953]/1977) "The history of ideas and ancient Greek philosophy," in L. Tarán, ed., *Harold Cherniss. Selected Papers*, 36–61. Leiden. First published in *Studies in Intellectual History*, 22–47 (Baltimore 1953).

(1977) "Ancient forms of philosophic discourse," in L. Tarán, ed., *Harold Cherniss. Selected Papers*, 14–35. Leiden.

Christ, M. R. (1990) "Liturgy avoidance and *antidosis* in classical Athens," *TAPA* 120: 147–69.

Clay, D. (1975) "The tragic and comic poet of the *Symposium*," *Arion* 2: 238–61.

(1994) "The origins of the Socratic dialogue," in P. A. Vander Waerdt, ed., *The Socratic Movement*, 23–47. Ithaca.

Cohen, E. E. (1992) *Athenian Economy and Society. A Banking Perspective*. Princeton.

Cohen, R. (1989) "Do postmodern genres exist?" in M. Perloff, ed., *Postmodern Genres*, 11–27. Norman, Oklahoma.

Cole, T. (1991) *The Origins of Rhetoric in Ancient Greece*. Baltimore.

Colie, R. L. (1966) *Paradoxia Epidemica. The Renaissance Tradition of Paradox.* Princeton.

Collard, C. (1972) "The funeral oration in Euripides' *Supplices,*" *BICS* 19: 39–53.

Compton, T. (1990) "The trial of the satirist: poetic *vitae* (Aesop, Archilochus, Homer) as background for Plato's *Apology,*" *AJP* 111: 330–47.

Connor, W. R. ([1971]/1992) *The New Politicians of Fifth-Century Athens.* Repr. Indianapolis.

Conte, G. B. (1986) *The Rhetoric of Imitation. Genre and Poetic Memory in Virgil and Other Latin Poets,* trans. and ed. C. Segal. Ithaca.

([1991]/1994) *Genres and Readers,* trans. G. Most. Baltimore. First published as *Generi e lettori: Lucrezio, L'elegia d'amore, L'enciclopedia di Plinio* (Milan 1991).

Cooper, J. (1984) "Plato's theory of human motivation," *History of Philosophy Quarterly* 1: 3–21.

(1986) "Plato, Isocrates and Cicero on the independence of oratory from philosophy," *Proceedings of the Boston Area Colloquium in Ancient Philosophy* 1: 77–96.

Cooper, L. (1922) *An Aristotelian Theory of Comedy.* New York.

Cornford, F. M. (1907) *Thucydides Mythistoricus.* London.

(1971) "The doctrine of eros in Plato's *Symposium,*" in G. Vlastos, ed., *Plato* vol. II, 119–31. New York.

Coulter, J. A. (1964) "The relation of the *Apology of Socrates* to Gorgias' *Defense of Palamedes* and Plato's critique of Gorgianic rhetoric," *HSCP* 68: 269–303.

(1967) "*Phaedrus* 279a: The praise of Isocrates," *GRBS* 8 : 225–36.

Couvreur, P. (1971) ed., *In Platonis Phaedrum Scholia.* Hildesheim.

Dalfen, J. (1974) *Polis und Poiesis. Die Auseinandersetzung mit der Dichtung bei Platon und seinen Zeitgenossen.* Munich.

David, E. (1984) *Aristophanes and Athenian Society of the Early Fourth Century B.C.* Leiden.

Davies, J. K. (1971) *Athenian Propertied Families 600–300 B.C.* Oxford.

(1981) *Wealth and the Power of Wealth in Classical Athens.* New York.

([1978]/1983) *Democracy and Classical Greece.* Repr. Stanford.

Dawson, D. (1992) *Cities of the Gods. Communist Utopias in Greek Thought.* New York.

Derrida, J. ([1972]/1981) *Dissemination,* trans. B. Johnson. Chicago. First published as *La Dissémination* (Paris 1972).

Detienne, M. (1967) *Les maîtres de vérité dans la grèce archaïque.* Paris.

([1972]/1977) *The Gardens of Adonis. Spices in Greek Mythology,* trans. J. Lloyd. New Jersey. First published as *Les Jardins d'Adonis* (Paris 1972).

([1981]/1986) *The Creation of Mythology,* trans. M. Cook. Chicago. First published as *L'invention de la mythologie* (Paris 1981).

(1988) ed., *Les savoirs de l'écriture en Grèce ancienne.* Lille.

Detienne, M. and Vernant, J.-P. ([1974]/1978) *Cunning Intelligence in Greek Culture and Society,* trans. J. Lloyd. Chicago. First published as *Les ruses de l'intelligence: la Mètis des grecs* (Paris 1974).

De Vries, G. J. (1953) "Isocrates' reaction to the *Phaedrus,*" *Mnemosyne* 6: 39–45.

(1969) *A Commentary on the Phaedrus of Plato.* Amsterdam.

(1971) "Isocrates in the *Phaedrus*: a reply," *Mnemosyne* 24: 387–90.

(1985) "Laughter in Plato's writings," *Mnemosyne* 38: 378–81.

Diès, A. (1927) *Autour de Platon*, 2 vols. Paris.

Dittmar, H. (1912) "Aeschines von Sphettos," *Philologische Untersuchungen* 21.

Dodds, E. R. (1959) ed. and comm., *Plato: Gorgias*. Oxford.

Dover, K. J. (1964) "Eros and nomos (Plato, *Symposium* 182a–185c)," *BICS* 11: 31–42.

(1968a) *Aristophanes: Clouds*. Oxford.

(1968b) "Greek comedy," in *Fifty Years (and Twelve) of Classical Scholarship*, 123–56. New York.

(1972) *Aristophanic Comedy*. Berkeley.

(1974) *Greek Popular Morality in the Time of Plato and Aristotle*. Oxford.

([1976]/1988) "The freedom of the intellectual in Greek society," *Talanta* 7: 24–54; repr. in Dover 1988, 135–58.

(1980) *Plato: Symposium*. Cambridge.

([1986]/1988) "Ion of Chios: his place in the history of Greek literature," in *Chios: A Conference at the Homereion in Chios 1984*. Oxford; repr. in Dover 1988, 1–12.

(1988) *The Greeks and their Legacy. Collected Papers* vol. II: *Prose Literature, History, Society, Transmission, Influence*. Oxford.

([1978]/1989) *Greek Homosexuality*. Updated ed. Cambridge, Mass.

(1993) *Aristophanes' Frogs*. Oxford.

Easterling, P. E. (1993) "The end of an era? Tragedy in the early fourth century," in A. H. Sommerstein, S. Halliwell, J. Henderson, and B. Zimmermann, edd., *Tragedy, Comedy and the Polis*, 559–69. Bari.

Edwards, A. T. (1991) "Aristophanes' comic poetics: τρύξ, scatology, σκῶμμα," *TAPA* 121: 157–79.

(1993) "Historicizing the popular grotesque: Bakhtin's *Rabelais* and Attic Old Comedy," in R. Scodel, ed., *Theater and Society in the Classical World*, 89–118. Ann Arbor, Michigan.

Ehrenberg, V. (1962) *The People of Aristophanes. A Sociology of Old Attic Comedy*. 3rd ed. New York.

Einarson, B. (1936) "Aristotle's *Protrepticus* and the structure of the *Epinomis*," *TAPA* 67: 261–85.

Emerson, C. (1986) "The outer word and inner speech: Bakhtin, Vygotsky, and the internalization of language," in G. Morson, ed., *Bakhtin. Essays and Dialogues on His Work*, 21–40. Chicago.

England, E. B. (1921) ed. and comm., *The Laws of Plato*, 2 vols. Manchester.

Eucken, C. (1983) *Isokrates. Seine Positionen in der Auseinandersetzung mit den zeitgenössischen Philosophen*. Berlin.

Fantham, E. (1986) "ΖΗΛΟΤΥΠΙΑ: a brief excursion into sex, violence, and literary history," *Phoenix* 40: 45–57.

Feaver, D. D. and J. E. Hare (1981) "The *Apology* as an inverted parody of rhetoric," *Arethusa* 14: 205–16.

Ferrari, G. R. F. (1985) "The struggle in the soul," *Ancient Philosophy* 5: 1–10.

(1987) *Listening to the Cicadas. A Study of Plato's Phaedrus*. Cambridge.

(1989) "Plato and poetry," in G. A. Kennedy, ed., *The Cambridge History of Literary Criticism* vol. I, 92–148. Cambridge.

Field, G. C. (1930) *Plato and his Contemporaries*. London.

Finley, M. I. [Finkelstein] (1935) "Ἔμπορος, ναύκληρος, and κάπηλος: a prolegomena to the study of Athenian trade," *CP* 30: 320–36.

(1952) *Studies in Land and Credit in Ancient Athens, 500–200 B.C.* New Bruns-
wick, New Jersey.

(1962) "Athenian demagogues," *Past and Present* 21: 3–24.

(1970) "Aristotle and economic analysis," *Past and Present* 47: 3–25.

(1981) *Economy and Society in Ancient Greece*, edd. B. D. Shaw and R. P.
Saller. London.

(1985) *The Ancient Economy*². Berkeley.

Firth, R. ([1965]/1975) *Primitive Polynesian Economy*. Repr. New York.

Fisher, N. (1990) "The law of *hubris* in Athens," in P. Cartledge, P. Millett and S.
Todd, edd., *Nomos. Essays in Athenian Law, Politics and Society*, 123–38.
Cambridge.

Foley, H. (1985) *Ritual Irony: Poetry and Sacrifice in Euripides*. Ithaca.

(1993) "Tragedy and politics in Aristophanes' *Acharnians*," in R. Scodel, ed.,
Theater and Society in the Classical World, 119–38. Ann Arbor, Michigan.

Forbes, C. A. (1942) *Teachers' Pay in Ancient Greece* (Studies in the Humanities
no. 2). Lincoln, Nebraska.

Fortenbaugh, W. W. (1966) "Plato's *Phaedrus* 235c3," *CP* 61: 108–9.

Fraustadt, G. (1909) *Encomiorum in Litteris Graecis usque ad Romanam Aetatem
Historia*. Leipzig.

Frede, D. (1993) "Out of the cave: what Socrates learned from Diotima," in
R. M. Rosen and J. Farrell, edd., *Nomodeiktes. Greek Studies in Honor of
Martin Ostwald*, 397–422. Ann Arbor, Michigan.

Frede, M. (1992) "Plato's arguments and the dialogue form," *OSAPh* supplementary volume: 201–20.

Friedländer, P. ([1954]/1958) *Plato. An Introduction*, trans. H. Meyerhoff. New
York. First published as *Platon: Seinswahrheit und Lebenswirklichkeit*, 2nd
ed. (Berlin 1954).

([1957]/1964) *Plato II: The Dialogues, First Period*, trans. H. Meyerhoff. New
York. First published as *Platon, II: Die Platonischen Schriften, Erste Periode*
(Berlin 1957).

Gabrielsen, V. (1986) "Φανερά and ἀφανὴς οὐσία in classical Athens," *CM* 37: 99–
114.

(1987) "The *Antidosis* procedure in classical Athens," *CM* 38: 7–38.

Gadamer, H.-G. (1980) *Dialogue and Dialectic. Eight Hermeneutical Studies on
Plato*, trans. P. C. Smith. New Haven.

Gagarin, M. (1977) "Socrates' *hubris* and Alcibiades' failure," *Phoenix* 31: 22–37.

Gardiner, M. (1992) *The Dialogics of Critique. M. M. Bakhtin and the Theory of
Ideology*. London.

Genette, G. (1982) *Palimpsestes*. Paris.

Gentili, B. ([1985]/1988) *Poetry and Its Public in Ancient Greece*, trans. A. T.
Cole. Baltimore. First published as *Poesia e pubblico nella Grecia antica: da
Omero al V secolo* (Rome 1985).

Gera, D. L. (1993) *Xenophon's Cyropaedia: Style, Genre, and Literary Technique*.
Oxford.

Gernet, L. ([1945]/1981) "The origins of Greek philosophy," in Gernet [1968]/

1981, 352–64. Baltimore. First published as "Les origines de la philosophie," *Bulletin de l'Enseignement Public du Maroc* 183 (1945) 1–12.

([1968]/1981) *The Anthropology of Ancient Greece*, trans. J. Hamilton and B. Nagy. Baltimore. First published as *Anthropologie de la grèce antique* (Paris 1968).

Glotz, G. ([1926]/1987) *Ancient Greece at Work*. Repr. Hildesheim.

Gold, B. K. (1980) "A question of genre: Plato's *Symposium* as novel," *Modern Language Notes* 95: 1353–59.

Goldhill, S. (1986) *Reading Greek Tragedy*. Cambridge.

(1990) "The Great Dionysia and civic ideology," in J. J. Winkler and F. I. Zeitlin, edd., *Nothing to do with Dionysos? Athenian Drama in its Social Context*, 97–129. Princeton.

(1991) *The Poet's Voice. Essays on Poetics and Greek Literature*. Cambridge.

Gomme, A. W. (1938) "Aristophanes and politics," *CR* 52: 97–109.

Gooch, P. W. (1987) "Socratic irony and Aristotle's *eiron*: some puzzles," *Phoenix* 41: 95–104.

Goossens, R. (1962) *Euripide et Athènes*. Brussels.

Gould, T. (1990) *The Ancient Quarrel between Poetry and Philosophy*. Princeton.

Gourinat, M. (1986) "Socrate était-il un ironiste?" *Revue de Metaphysique et de Morale* 91: 339–53.

Goux, J.-J. (1990) *Symbolic Economies*, trans. J. C. Gage. Ithaca.

Greene, W. C. (1920) "The spirit of comedy in Plato," *HSCP* 31: 63–123.

Griffith, M. (1990) "Contest and contradiction in early Greek poetry," in M. Griffith and D. J. Mastronarde, edd., *Cabinet of the Muses*, 185–207. Atlanta.

Griswold, C. L., Jr. (1986) *Self-Knowledge in Plato's Phaedrus*. Yale.

(1987) "Irony and aesthetic language in Plato's dialogues," in D. Bollig, ed., *Philosophy and Literature*, 71–99. New York.

Guthrie, W. K. C. (1955) "Plato's view on the nature of the soul," *Fondation Hardt* 3: 2–22.

(1962) *A History of Greek Philosophy* vol. I: *The Earlier Presocratics and the Pythagoreans*. Cambridge.

(1971) *Socrates*. Cambridge.

(1975) *A History of Greek Philosophy* vol. IV: *Plato, the Man and His Dialogues: Earlier Period.* Cambridge.

Hackforth, R. (1936) "Plato's theism," *CQ* 30: 4–9.

(1952) *Plato's Phaedrus*. Cambridge.

Hahn, R. (1987) "What did Thales want to be when he grew up? or, Reappraising the roles of engineering and technology in the origin of early Greek philosophy/science," in B. P. Hendley, ed., *Plato, Time, and Education. Essays in Honor of Robert S. Brumbaugh*, 107–29. Albany.

Halliwell, S. (1984a) "Plato and Aristotle on the denial of tragedy," *PCPS* n.s. 30: 50–8.

(1984b) "Aristophanic satire," in C. Rawson (with J. Mezciems), ed., *English Satire and the Satiric Tradition*, 6–20. Oxford.

(1984c) "Ancient interpretations of ὀνομαστὶ κωμῳδεῖν in Aristophanes," *CQ* 34: 83–8.

(1988) *Plato: Republic 10*. Warminster, Wiltshire, England.

(1993) "Comedy and publicity in the society of the polis," in A.H. Sommerstein, S. Halliwell, J. Henderson, and B. Zimmermann, edd., *Tragedy, Comedy and the Polis*, 321–40. Bari.

(1994) "Philosophy and rhetoric," in I. Worthington, ed., *Persuasion. Greek Rhetoric in Action*, 222–43. London and New York.

Halperin, D. (1985) "Platonic *erōs* and what men call love," *Ancient Philosophy* 5: 161–204.

(1986) "Plato and erotic reciprocity," *CA* 5: 60–80.

(1990) *One Hundred Years of Homosexuality*. New York.

(1992) "Plato and the erotics of narrativity," *OSAPh* supplementary volume, 93–129.

Hamilton, E. and H. Cairns (1973) edd., *The Collected Dialogues of Plato*. Seventh printing. Princeton.

Hansen, M. H. (1991) *The Athenian Democracy in the Age of Demosthenes*. Oxford.

Harris, W. V. (1989) *Ancient Literacy*. Cambridge, Mass.

Harrison, S. (1992) "Ritual as intellectual property," *Man* n.s. 27: 225–44.

Harvey, A. E. (1955) "The classification of Greek lyric poetry," *CQ* n.s. 5: 157–75.

Hasebroek, J. (1933) *Trade and Politics in Ancient Greece*, trans. L. M. Fraser and D. C. MacGregor. London.

Hausmann, U. (1958[1962]) "Zur Antiope des Euripides. Ein hellenistischer Reliefbecher in Athen," *MDAI(A)* 73: 50–72.

Havelock, E. A. (1957) *The Liberal Temper in Greek Politics*. New Haven.

(1963) *Preface to Plato*. Cambridge, Mass.

(1983a) "The Socratic problem: some second thoughts," in J. P. Anton and A. Preus, edd., *Essays in Ancient Greek Philosophy* vol. II, 147–73. Albany.

(1983b) "The linguistic task of the Presocratics," in K. Robb, ed., *Language and Thought in Early Greek Philosophy*, 7–82. La Salle, Illinois.

Heath, M. (1987) *Political Comedy in Aristophanes (Hypomnemata* vol. 87). Göttingen.

(1989a) "The unity of Plato's *Phaedrus*," *OSAPh* 7: 151–73.

(1989b) "The unity of the *Phaedrus*: a postscript," *OSAPh* 7: 189–91.

Hegel, G. W. F. (1892) *Lectures on the History of Philosophy* vol. I, trans. E. S. Haldane. London.

Held, G. F. (1984) "ΣΠΟΥΔΑΙΟΣ and teleology in the *Poetics*," *TAPA* 114: 159–76.

Henderson, J. (1990) "The *dēmos* and comic competition," in J. J. Winkler and F. I. Zeitlin, edd., *Nothing to do with Dionysos? Athenian Drama in its Social Context*, 271–313. Princeton.

(1991) *The Maculate Muse: Obscene Language in Attic Comedy*. Repr. New York.

(1993) "Comic hero versus political élite," in A. H. Sommerstein, S. Halliwell, J. Henderson, and B. Zimmermann, edd., *Tragedy, Comedy and the Polis*, 307–20. Bari.

Henderson, M. M. (1975) "Plato's *Menexenus* and the distortion of history," *Acta Classica* 18: 25–46.

Herington, J. (1985) *Poetry into Drama: Early Tragedy and the Greek Poetic Tradition*. Berkeley.

Hirschkop, K. (1989) "Introduction: Bakhtin and cultural theory," in K. Hirschkop and D. Shepherd, edd., *Bakhtin and Cultural Theory*, 1–38. Manchester.

(1990) "On value and responsibility," in C. Thomson, ed., *Mikhail Bakhtin and the Epistemology of Discourse*, 13–27. Amsterdam–Atlanta.

Hirzel, R. (1895) *Der Dialog: Ein Literarhistorischer Versuch*, vol. I. Leipzig.

Hoerber, R. G. (1959) "Plato's *Lysis*," *Phronesis* 4: 15–28.

Holquist, M. (1990) *Dialogism. Bakhtin and his World*. London.

Howland, R. L. (1937) "The attack on Isocrates in the *Phaedrus*," *CQ* 31: 151–9.

Hubbard, Thomas K. (1991) *The Mask of Comedy. Aristophanes and the Intertextual Parabasis*. Ithaca.

Hudson-Williams, H. L. (1949) "Isocrates and recitations," *CQ* 43: 65–9.

Humphreys, S. C. (1978) *Anthropology and the Greeks*. London.

(1983) *The Family, Women, and Death: Comparative Studies*. London.

(1985) "Social relations on stage: witnesses in classical Athens," *History and Anthropology* 1: 313–69.

Hutcheon, L. (1985) *A Theory of Parody*. London.

(1989) "Modern parody and Bakhtin," in G. S. Morson and C. Emerson, edd., *Rethinking Bakhtin. Extensions and Challenges*, 87–103. Evanston, Illinois.

Irwin, T. (1979) trans. and comm., *Plato: Gorgias*. Oxford.

Isager, S. and M. H. Hansen (1975) *Aspects of Athenian Society in the Fourth Century B.C.*, trans. J. H. Rosenmeier. Odense.

Jacoby, F. (1949) *Atthis. The Local Chronicles of Ancient Athens*. Oxford.

Jaeger, W. (1944) *Paideia* vol. III, trans. G. Highet. Oxford.

(1948) *Aristotle*, trans. R. Robinson. 2nd ed. Oxford.

Jameson, F. (1981) *The Political Unconscious. Narrative as a Socially Symbolic Act*. Ithaca.

Janko, R. (1981) "The structure of the Homeric hymns: a study in genre," *Hermes* 109: 9–24.

Jebb, R. C. (1962) *The Attic Orators from Antiphon to Isaeos* vols. I and II. New York.

Joly, R. (1956) *Le thème philosophique des genres de vie dans l'antiquité classique*. Brussels.

Kahn, C. H. (1963) "Plato's funeral oration: the motive of the *Menexenus*," *CP* 58: 220–34.

(1979) *The Art and Thought of Heraclitus*. Cambridge.

(1981) "Did Plato write Socratic dialogues?" *CQ* 31: 305–20.

(1983) "Drama and dialectic in Plato's *Gorgias*," *OSAPh* 1:75–121.

(1994) "Aeschines on Socratic eros," in P. A. Vander Waerdt, ed., *The Socratic Movement*. Ithaca.

Kambitsis, J. (1972) ed. and comm., *L'Antiope d'Euripide*. Athens.

Kassel, R. and C. Austin (1983–?) edd., *Poetae Comici Graeci* vols. II, III.2, IV, V, VII. Berlin.

Kauffman, C. (1979) "Enactment as argument in the *Gorgias*," *Philosophy and Rhetoric* 12: 114–29.

Kennedy, G. (1958) "Isocrates' *Encomium of Helen*: a panhellenic document," *TAPA* 89: 77–83.

(1963) *The Art of Persuasion in Greece*. Princeton.

Kerferd, G. B. (1976) "The image of the wise man in Greece in the period before Plato," in *Images of Man in Ancient and Medieval Thought*, 17–28. Louvain.

(1981) *The Sophistic Movement*. Cambridge.

Klosko, G. (1984) "The refutation of Callicles in Plato's *Gorgias*," *G&R* 31: 126–39.

Knox, B. M. W. (1968) "Silent reading in antiquity," *GRBS* 9: 421–35.

Knox, D. (1989) *Ironia. Medieval and Renaissance Ideas on Irony*. Leiden.

Koster, S. (1980) *Die Invektive in der griechischen und römischen Literatur* (Beiträge zur klassischen Philologie vol. 99). Meisenheim am Glan.

Kraut, R. (1983) "Comments on Gregory Vlastos, 'The Socratic elenchus,'" *OSAPh* 1: 59–70.

(1992) "Introduction to the study of Plato," in R. Kraut, ed., *The Cambridge Companion to Plato*, 1–50. Cambridge.

Kristeva, J. (1980) *Desire in Language*, trans. T. Gora, A. Jardine, and L. S. Roudiez. New York.

Kuhn, H. (1941) "The true tragedy: on the relationship between Greek tragedy and Plato, I," *HSCP* 52: 1–40

(1942) "The true tragedy: on the relationship between Greek tragedy and Plato, II," *HSCP* 53: 37–88.

Kurke, L. (1990) "Pindar's sixth Pythian and the tradition of advice poetry," *TAPA* 120: 85–107.

(1991) *The Traffic in Praise. Pindar and the Poetics of Social Economy*. Ithaca.

Laistner, M. L. W. (1930) "The influence of Isocrates' political doctrines on some fourth century men of affairs," *Classical Weekly* 23: 129–31.

Leutsch, E. L. and F. G. Schneidewin (1965) edd., *Corpus Paroemiographorum Graecorum* vol. I. Hildesheim.

Lévy, E. (1979) "L'artisan dans la *Politique* d'Aristote," *Ktema* 4: 31–46.

Lewis, T. J. (1986) "Refutative rhetoric as true rhetoric in the *Gorgias*," *Interpretation* 14: 195–210.

Lloyd, G. E. R. (1966) *Polarity and Analogy*. Cambridge.

(1979) *Magic, Reason, and Experience: Studies in the Origins and Development of Early Greek Science*. Cambridge.

(1987) *The Revolutions of Wisdom. Studies in the Claims and Practice of Ancient Greek Science*. Berkeley.

(1990) *Demystifying Mentalities*. Cambridge.

Long, A. A. (1984) "Methods of Argument in Gorgias' *Palamedes*," in *The Sophistic Movement*, Papers of the Greek Philosophical Society, 233–41. Athens.

(1991) "Representation and the Stoic self," in S. Everson, ed., *Companions to Ancient Thought 2. Psychology*, 102–20. Cambridge.

(1992a) "Stoic readings of Homer," in R. Lamberton and J. J. Keaney, edd., *Homer's Ancient Readers. The Hermeneutics of Greek Epic's Earliest Exegetes*, 41–66. Princeton.

(1992b) "Finding oneself in Greek philosophy," *Tijdschrift voor Filosofie* 54: 257–79.

(1993) "Hellenistic ethics and philosophical power," in P. Green, ed., *Hellenistic History and Culture*, 138–56, 162–7. Berkeley.

Loraux, N. ([1981]/1986) *The Invention of Athens. The Funeral Oration in the Classical City*, trans. A. Sheridan. Cambridge, Mass. First published as *L'invention d' Athènes: Histoire de l'oraison funèbre dans la "cité classique"* (Paris 1981).

(1988) "Solon et la voix de l'écrit," in M. Detienne, ed., *Les savoirs de l'écriture en Grèce ancienne*, 95–129. Lille.

([1984]/1993) *The Children of Athena*, trans. C. Levine. Princeton. First published as *Les enfants d'Athéna: Idées athéniennes sur la citoyenneté et la division des sexes* (Paris 1984).

(1989) "Therefore, Socrates is immortal," in M. Feher with R. Naddaff and N. Tazi, edd., *Fragments for a History of the Human Body*, part 2, 12–45. New York.

Lowenstam, S. (1985) "Paradoxes in Plato's Symposium," *Ramus* 14: 85–104.

Lucas, D. W. (1972) ed. and comm., *Aristotle: Poetics*. Oxford.

Lynch, J. P. (1972) *Aristotle's School. A Study of a Greek Educational Institution*. Berkeley.

MacDowell, D. M. (1978) *The Law in Classical Athens*. Ithaca.

Mackey, L. (1993) "The philosophy of genre and the genre of philosophy," in T. R. Flynn and D. Judovitz, edd., *Dialectic and Narrative*, 5–19. Albany.

Mader, M. (1977) *Das Problem des Lachens und der Komödie bei Platon* (Tübinger Beiträge zur Altertumswissenschaft, vol. 47). Stuttgart.

Mansfeld, J. ([1983]/1990) "Cratylus 402a-c: Plato or Hippias?" in Mansfeld 1990: 84–96. First printed in L. Rossetti, ed., *Atti del Symposium Heracliteum 1983*, vol. I, *Studi*, 43–55 (Rome 1983).

([1985]/1990) "Myth, science, philosophy: a question of origins," in Mansfeld 1990: 1–21. First printed in W. M. Calder III, U. K. Goldsmith, and P. B. Kenevan, edd., *Hypatia*, 45–65 (Boulder 1985).

([1986]/1990) "Aristotle, Plato, and the preplatonic doxography and chronography," in Mansfeld 1990: 22–83. First printed in *Storiographia e dossografia nella filosofia antica*, 1–59 (Torino 1986).

(1990) *Studies in the Historiography of Greek Philosophy*. The Netherlands.

Maranhão, T. (1990) ed., *The Interpretation of Dialogue*. Chicago.

Marrou, H. I. ([1956]/1964) *A History of Education in Antiquity*, trans. G. Lamb. Repr. New York.

Martin, J. (1974) *Antike Rhetorik. Technik und Methode*. Munich.

Martin, R. (1989) *The Language of Heroes. Speech and Performance in the Iliad*. Ithaca.

(1992) "Hesiod's metanastic poetics," *Ramus* 21: 11–33.

(1993) "The seven sages as performers of wisdom," in C. Dougherty and L. Kurke, edd., *Cultural Poetics in Ancient Greece*, 108–28. Cambridge.

Mauss, M. (1990) *The Gift*, trans. W. D. Halls. New York.

McKechnie, P. (1989) *Outsiders in the Greek Cities in the Fourth Century BC*. London and New York.

McKim, R. (1988) "Shame and truth in Plato's *Gorgias*," in C. L. Griswold, ed., *Platonic Writings, Platonic Readings*, 34–48. New York.

Mecke, J. 1990. "Dialogue in narration (the narrative principle)," in T. Maranhão, ed., *The Interpretation of Dialogue*, 195–215. Chicago.

Meijer, F. and O. van Nijf (1992) *Trade, Transport and Society in the Ancient World: A Sourcebook*. London.

Meikle, S. (1979) "Aristotle and the political economy of the polis," *JHS* 99: 57–73.

Millett, P. (1983) "Maritime loans and the structure of credit in fourth-century

Athens," in P. Garnsey, K. Hopkins, and C. R. Whittaker, edd., *Trade in the Ancient Economy*, 36–52. London.

(1990) "Sale, credit and exchange in Athenian law and society," in P. Cartledge, P. Millet, and S. Todd, edd., *Nomos. Essays in Athenian law, politics and society*, 167–94. Cambridge.

(1991) *Lending and Borrowing in Ancient Athens*. Cambridge.

Moline, J. (1981) *Plato's Theory of Understanding*. Wisconsin.

Momigliano, A. ([1971]/1993) *The Development of Greek Biography*, expanded edition. Cambridge, Mass.

Montgomery, H. (1983) *The Way to Chaeronea: Foreign Policy, Decision Making and Political Influence in Demosthenes' Speeches*. Bergen.

Morgan, K. A. (1993) "Pindar the professional and the rhetoric of the ΚὠΜΟΣ," *CP* 88: 1–15.

(1994) "Socrates and Gorgias at Delphi and Olympia: *Phaedrus* 235d6–236b4," *CQ* 44: 1–12.

(forthcoming) *Mythological Philosophers*.

Morris, I. (1986) "Gift and commodity in archaic Greece," *Man* n.s. 21: 1–17.

(forthcoming) "The Athenian economy twenty years after *The Ancient Economy*."

Morrison, J. S. (1958) "The origins of Plato's philosopher-statesman," *CQ* n.s. 8: 198–218.

Morrow, G. R. (1960) *Plato's Cretan City. A Historical Interpretation of the Laws*. Princeton.

Morson, G. S. (1981) *The Boundaries of Genre. Dostoevsky's Diary of a Writer and the Traditions of Literary Utopia*. Austin.

(1986) ed., *Bakhtin. Essays and Dialogues on his Work*. Chicago.

(1989) "Parody, history and metaparody," in G. Morson and C. Emerson, edd., *Rethinking Bakhtin. Extensions and Challenges*, 63–86. Evanston, Illinois.

Morson, G. and C. Emerson (1990) *Mikhail Bakhtin. Creation of a Prosaics*. Stanford.

Mossé, C. ([1966]/1969) *The Ancient World at Work*, trans. J. Lloyd. New York. First published as *Le travail en Grèce et à Rome* (Paris 1966).

(1983) "The 'world of the *emporium*' in the private speeches of Demosthenes," in P. Garnsey, K. Hopkins, and C. R. Whittaker, edd., *Trade in the Ancient Economy*, 53–63. London.

Nagy, G. (1979) *The Best of the Achaeans*. Baltimore.

(1990a) *Pindar's Homer: The Lyric Possession of an Epic Past*. Baltimore.

(1990b) *Greek Mythology and Poetics*. Ithaca.

Natorp, P. (1921) *Platons Ideenlehre*. Leipzig.

Nauck, A. (1964) ed., *Tragicorum Graecorum Fragmenta*, with a supplement by B. Snell. Hildesheim.

Nehamas, A. (1982) "Plato on imitation and poetry in *Republic* 10," in J. Moravcsik and P. Temko, edd., *Plato on Beauty, Wisdom , and the Arts*, 47–78. New Jersey.

(1990) "Eristic, antilogic, sophistic, dialectic: Plato's demarcation of philosophy from sophistry," *History of Philosophy Quarterly* 7: 3–16.

Nightingale, A. W. (1992) "Plato's *Gorgias* and Euripides' *Antiope*: a study in generic transformation," *CA* 11: 121–41.

(1993a) "The folly of praise: Plato's critique of encomiastic discourse in the *Lysis* and *Symposium,*" *CQ* 43: 112–30.

(1993b) "Writing/reading a sacred text: a literary interpretation of Plato's *Laws,*" *CP* 88: 279–300.

Norlin, G. (1980) *Isocrates* vol. I (Loeb Classical Library). Repr. Cambridge, Mass.

Norwood, G. (1932) *Greek Comedy.* Boston.

Nussbaum, M. (1986) *The Fragility of Goodness. Luck and Ethics in Greek Tragedy and Philosophy.* Cambridge.

Ober, J. (1989) *Mass and Elite in Democratic Athens. Rhetoric, Ideology, and the Power of the People.* Princeton.

Ober, J. and B. Strauss (1990) "Drama, political rhetoric, and the discourse of the Athenian democracy," in J. J. Winkler and F. I. Zeitlin, edd., *Nothing to do with Dionysos? Athenian Drama in its Social Context,* 237–70. Princeton.

Ogilvie, J. (1992) ed., *Revisioning Philosophy.* Albany.

Ong, W. (1982) *Orality and Literacy. The Technologizing of the Word.* London.

Osborne, R. (1991) "Pride and prejudice, sense and subsistence: exchange and society in the Greek city," in J. Rich and A. Wallace-Hadrill, edd., *City and Country in the Ancient World,* 119–45. London.

(1993) "Competitive festivals and the polis: a context for dramatic festivals at Athens," in A. H. Sommerstein, S. Halliwell, J. Henderson, and B. Zimmermann, edd., *Tragedy, Comedy and the Polis,* 21–38. Bari.

Owen, G. E. L. (1983) "Philosophical invective," *OSAPh* 1: 1–25.

Patterson, R. (1982) "The Platonic art of comedy and tragedy," *Philosophy and Literature* 6: 76–93.

(1987) "Plato on philosophic character," *Journal of the History of Philosophy* 25: 325–50.

(1991) "The ascent in Plato's *Symposium,*" *Proceedings of the Boston Area Colloquium in Ancient Philosophy* 7: 193–214.

Patzer, A. (1986) *Der Sophist Hippias als Philosophiehistoriker.* Munich.

Pease, A. S. (1926) "Things without honor," *CP* 21: 27–42.

Pechey, G. (1989) "On the borders of Bakhtin: dialogization, decolonisation," in K. Hirschkop and D. Shepherd, edd., *Bakhtin and Cultural Theory,* 39–67. Manchester.

Peck, A. L. (1979) *Aristotle. Historia Animalium* vol. I (Loeb Classical Library). Repr. Cambridge, Mass.

Penner, T. (1992) "Socrates and the early dialogues," in R. Kraut, ed., *The Cambridge Companion to Plato,* 121–69. Cambridge.

Pickard-Cambridge, A. W. (1933) "The tragedy," in J. U. Powell, ed., *New Chapters in the History of Greek Literature,* 3rd series, 68–155. Oxford.

Platter, C. (1993) "The uninvited guest: Aristophanes in Bakhtin's 'History of Laughter'," *Arethusa* 26: 201–16.

Polansky, R. (1985) "Professor Vlastos's analysis of Socratic elenchus," *OSAPh* 3: 247–59.

Polanyi, K. (1957) "Aristotle discovers the economy," in K. Polanyi, C. M. Arensberg, and H. W. Pearson, edd., *Trade and Market in the Early Empires: Economies in History and Theory,* 64–94. New York.

Poulakos, T. (1987) "*Evagoras*: epideictic rhetoric and moral action," *Quarterly Journal of Speech* 73: 317–28.

Raaflaub, K. A. (1983) "Democracy, oligarchy, and the concept of the 'free citizen' in late fifth-century Athens," *Political Theory* 11: 517–44.
Race, W. H. (1982) "Aspects of rhetoric and form in Greek hymns," *GRBS* 23: 5–14.
(1987) "Pindaric encomium and Isokrates' *Evagoras*," *TAPA* 117: 131–55.
Radermacher, L. (1951) *Artium scriptores: Reste der voraristotelischen Rhetorik.* Vienna.
Radt, S. (1977) ed., *Tragicorum Graecorum Fragmenta* vol. IV. *Sophocles.* Göttingen.
Rau, P. (1967) *Paratragodia.* Munich.
Reckford, K. J. (1987) *Aristophanes' Old-and-New Comedy.* Chapel Hill.
Reeve, C. D. C. (1988) *Philosopher-Kings. The Argument of Plato's Republic.* Princeton.
(1989) *Socrates in the Apology.* Indianapolis.
(1992) "Telling the truth about love: Plato's *Symposium*," *Proceedings of the Boston Area Colloquium in Ancient Philosophy* 8: 89–114.
Rehm, R. (1994) *Marriage to Death. The Conflation of Wedding and Funeral Rituals in Greek Tragedy.* Princeton.
Ribbeck, O. (1876) "Über den Begriff des εἴρων," *Rheinisches Museum für Philologie* 31: 381–400.
Riffaterre, M. (1978) *Semiotics of Poetry.* Bloomington, Indiana.
([1979]/1983) *Text Production*, trans. T. Lyons. New York. First published as *La production du texte* (Paris 1979).
Riginos, A. S. (1976) *Platonica. The Anecdotes concerning the Life and Writings of Plato* (Columbia Studies in the Classical Tradition vol. III). Leiden.
Roberts, C. H. (1935) "Some new readings in Euripides," *CQ* 29: 164–7.
Robinson, R. (1941) *Plato's Earlier Dialectic.* Ithaca.
Robinson, T. M. (1984) *Contrasting Arguments. An Edition of the Dissoi Logoi.* Repr. Salem, New Hampshire.
Romilly, J. de (1975) *Magic and Rhetoric in Ancient Greece.* Cambridge, Mass.
Roochnik, D. L. (1987) "The erotics of philosophical discourse," *History of Philosophy Quarterly* 4: 117–30.
Rose, Margaret A. (1979) *Parody//Meta-fiction.* London.
Rose, P. (1992) *Sons of the Gods, Children of Earth. Ideology and Literary Form in Ancient Greece.* Ithaca.
Rosen, R. M. (1988) *Old Comedy and the Iambographic Tradition* (American Classical Studies vol. 19). Atlanta.
Rosen, S. (1993) *The Quarrel Between Philosophy and Poetry.* New York.
Rössler, D. (1981) "Handwerker," in E. C. Welskopf, ed., *Untersuchungen ausgewählter altgriechischer sozialer Typenbegriffe* (Soziale Typenbegriffe im alten Griechenland und ihr Fortleben in den Sprachen der Welt vol. 3), 193–268. Berlin.
Rostovtzeff, M. (1941) *The Social and Economic History of the Hellenistic World* vol. I. Oxford.
Rothwell, K. S., Jr. (1990) *Politics and Persuasion in Aristophanes' Ecclesiazusae.* Leiden.
Rowe, C. J. (1986a) "The argument and structure of Plato's *Phaedrus*," *PCPS* 32: 106–27.

(1986b) comm., *Plato: Phaedrus*. Wiltshire.

(1989) "The unity of the *Phaedrus*: a reply to Heath," *OSAPh* 7: 175–88.

Russell, D. A. and N. G. Wilson (1981) *Menander Rhetor*. Oxford.

Sahlins, M. (1972) *Stone Age Economics*. Chicago.

Ste. Croix, G. E. M. de (1972) *The Origins of the Peloponnesian War*. Ithaca.

(1981) *Class Struggle in the Ancient Greek World*. Cornell.

Santas, G. X. (1979) *Socrates: Philosophy in the Early Dialogues*. Boston.

Saxonhouse, A. W. (1978) "Comedy in Callipolis: animal imagery in the *Republic*," *American Political Science Review* 72: 888–901.

(1992) *Fear of Diversity. The Birth of Political Science in Ancient Greek Thought*. Chicago.

Schaal, H. (1914) ed. and comm., "De Euripidis *Antiopa*," diss. Berlin.

Schein, S. (1974) "Alcibiades and misguided love in Plato's *Symposium*," *Theta Pi* 3: 158–67.

Schenkeveld, D. M. (1992) "Prose usages of ἀκούειν 'to read'," *CQ* n.s. 1: 129–41.

Schiappa, E. (1991) *Protagoras and Logos. A Study in Greek Philosophy and Rhetoric*. Columbia, South Carolina.

Schroeder, O. (1914) *De laudibus Athenarum a poetis tragicis et ab oratoribus epidicticis excultis*. Göttingen.

Scodel, R. (1980) *The Trojan Trilogy of Euripides* (*Hypomnemata* vol. 60). Göttingen.

(1983) "Timocreon's encomium of Aristides," *CA* 2: 102–7.

Seeskin, K. (1982) "Is the *Apology of Socrates* a parody?" *Philosophy and Literature* 6: 94–105.

Segal, C. (1986) *Interpreting Greek Tragedy. Myth, Poetry, Text*. Cornell.

Shell, M. (1978) *The Economy of Literature*. Baltimore.

(1982) *Money, Language, and Thought*. Berkeley.

Sider, D. (1980a) "Plato's *Symposium* as dionysian festival," *QUCC* 33: 41–56.

(1980b) "Did Plato write dialogues before the death of Socrates?" *Apeiron* 14: 15–18.

Snell, B. ([1944]/1966) "Die Nachrichten über die Lehren des Thales und die Anfänge der griechischen Philosophie- und Literaturgeschichte," in *Gesammelte Schriften*, 119–28. Göttingen. First published in *Philologus* 96 (1944) 170–82.

(1964) *Scenes from Greek Drama*. Berkeley and Los Angeles.

Sommerstein, A. H. (1986) "The decree of Syrakosios," *CQ* 36: 101–8.

Spengel, L. (1853) *Rhetores Graeci*. Leipzig.

Spira, A. (1960) *Untersuchungen zum Deus ex machina bei Sophokles und Euripides*. Kallmünz.

Stewart, S. (1978) *Nonsense. Aspects of Intertextuality in Folklore and Literature*. Baltimore.

(1986) "Shouts on the street: Bakhtin's anti-linguistics," in G. S. Morson, ed., *Bakhtin. Essays and Dialogues on his Work*, 41–57. Chicago.

Stokes, M. (1992) "Socrates' mission," in B. S. Gower and M. C. Stokes, edd., *Socratic Questions. New Essays on the Philosophy of Socrates and its Significance*, 26–81. London and New York.

Strauss, B. S. (1986) *Athens after the Peloponnesian War. Class, Faction, and Policy 403–386 BC*. Ithaca.

Suárez, J. (1987) "Old Comedy within Bakhtinian theory: an unintentional omission,"*CB* 63: 105–11.

Taplin, O. (1978) *Greek Tragedy in Action*. Berkeley.

(1983) "Tragedy and trugedy," *CQ* 33: 331–3.

(1986) "Fifth-century tragedy and comedy: a *synkrisis*," *JHS* 106: 163–74.

(1993) *Comic Angels and other Approaches to Greek Drama through Vase-Paintings*. Oxford.

Taylor, A. E. (1934) "Aeschines of Sphettos," in *Philosophical Studies* , 1–27. London.

(1949) *Plato. The Man and his Work*. Sixth ed. London.

Taylor, C. (1989) *Sources of the Self. The Making of Modern Identity*. Harvard.

Tecuşan, M. (1990) "*Logos sympotikos*: patterns of the irrational in philosophical drinking: Plato outside the *Symposium*," in O. Murray, ed., *Sympotica. A Symposium on the Symposion*, 238–60. Oxford.

Thomas, R. (1989) *Oral Tradition and Written Record in Classical Athens*. Cambridge.

(1992) *Literacy and Orality in Ancient Greece*. Cambridge.

Thompson, W. E. (1982) "The Athenian entrepreneur," *L'Antiquité Classique* 51: 53–85.

Thomson, C. (1990) ed., *Mikhail Bakhtin and the Epistemology of Discourse*. Amsterdam.

Tigerstedt, E. N. (1977) *Interpreting Plato*. Stockholm, Sweden.

Todorov, T. ([1981]/1984) *Mikhail Bakhtin. The Dialogical Principle*, trans. W. Godzich. Minneapolis. First printed as *Mikhaïl Bakhtine: le principe dialogique suivi de Ecrits du Cercle de Bakhtine* (Paris 1981).

([1978]/1990) *Genres in Discourse*, trans. C. Porter. Cambridge, England. First printed as *Les genres du discours* (Paris 1978).

Turner, E. G. (1952) *Athenian Books in the Fifth and Fourth Centuries B.C.* London.

Überweg, F. (1871) *History of Philosophy* vol. I, trans. from the 4th German edition by G. S. Morris. New York.

Ussher, R. G. (1973) *Aristophanes. Ecclesiazusae.* Oxford.

Vegetti, M. (1988) "Dans l'ombre de Thoth. Dynamiques de l'écriture chez Platon," in M. Detienne, ed., *Les savoirs de l'écriture en Grèce ancienne*, 387–419. Lille.

Vernant, J.-P. ([1962]/1982) *The Origins of Greek Thought*. Ithaca. First published as *Les origines de la pensée grecque* (Paris 1962).

([1965]/1983) *Myth and Thought among the Greeks*. London. First published as *Mythe et pensée chez les Grecs* (Paris 1965).

Vernant, J.-P. and Vidal-Naquet, P. (1988) *Myth and Tragedy in Ancient Greece*, trans. J. Lloyd. New York.

Vickers, B. (1983) "Epideictic and epic in the renaissance," *New Literary History* 14: 497–537.

(1988) *In Defense of Rhetoric*. Oxford.

Vidal-Naquet, P. ([1967]/1986) "Greek rationality and the city," in Vidal-Naquet [1981]/1986: ch. 12. First published as "La raison grecque et la cité," *Raison présente* 2 (1967) 51–61.

([1981]/1986) *The Black Hunter. Forms of Thought and Forms of Society in the Greek World*, trans. A. Szegedy-Maszak. Baltimore. First published as *Le chasseur noir: Formes de pensées et formes de société dans le monde grec* (Paris 1981).

Vlastos, G. ([1941]/1981) "Slavery in Plato's political theory," in G. Vlastos, *Platonic Studies*[2], 147–63. Princeton. First published in *PhR* 50 (1941) 289–304.

([1964]/1981) "ΙΣΟΝΟΜΙΑ ΠΟΛΙΤΙΚΗ" in G. Vlastos, *Platonic Studies*[2], 164–203. Princeton. First published in J. Mau and E. G. Schmidt, edd., *Isonomia: Studien zur Gleichheitsvorstellung im griechischen Denken*, 1–35. Berlin.

(1967) "Was Polus refuted?" *AJP* 88: 454–60.

(1983a) "The Socratic elenchus," *OSAPh* 1: 27–58.

(1983b) "Afterthoughts on the Socratic elenchus," *OSAPh* 1: 71–4.

([1987]/1991) "Socratic irony," *CQ* 37: 79–96; reprinted in Vlastos 1991: ch. 1.

(1991) *Socrates, Ironist and Moral Philosopher*. Cornell.

Wallace, R. W. (1989) *The Areopagos Council, to 307 B.C.* Baltimore.

(1994) "Private lives and public enemies: freedom of thought in classical Athens," in A. L. Boegehold and A. C. Scafuro, edd., *Athenian Identity and Civic Ideology*, 127–55. Baltimore.

Webster, T. B. L. (1954) "Fourth Century Tragedy and the *Poetics*," *Hermes* 82: 294–308.

(1956) *Art and Literature in Fourth Century Athens*. London.

(1970) *Studies in Later Greek Comedy*, 2nd ed. New York.

Wecklein, N. (1923) "Die Antiope des Euripides," *Philologus* 79: 51–69.

Westerink, L. G. (1970) ed., *Olympiodori in Platonis Gorgiam Commentaria*. Leipzig.

Whitehead, D. (1977) *The Ideology of the Athenian Metic*. Cambridge.

(1983) "Competitive outlay and community profit: φιλοτιμία in democratic Athens," *CM* 34: 55–74.

Wilamowitz-Moellendorff, U. von. (1920) *Platon*, 2 vols. Berlin.

Wilcox, S. (1943) "Criticisms of Isocrates and his φιλοσοφία," *TAPA* 74: 113–33.

(1945) "Isocrates' fellow rhetoricians," *AJP* 66: 171–86.

Winkler, J. J. (1985) "The ephebes' song: *Tragōdia* and *Polis*," *Representations* 11: 26–62.

(1990) *The Constraints of Desire. The Anthropology of Sex and Gender in Ancient Greece*. New York.

Wood, E. M. ([1988]/1989) *Peasant-Citizen and Slave. The Foundations of Athenian Democracy*. Corrected paperback ed. London.

Wood, E. M. and N. Wood (1978) *Class Ideology and Ancient Political Theory: Socrates, Plato, and Aristotle in Social Context*. Oxford.

Woodruff, P. (1982a) *Plato. Hippias Major*. Indianapolis.

(1982b) "What could go wrong with inspiration? Why Plato's poets fail," in J. Moravcsik and P. Temko, edd., *Plato on Beauty, Wisdom, and the Arts*, 137–50. New Jersey.

Yunis, H. (1990) "Rhetoric as instruction: a response to Vickers on rhetoric in the *Laws*," *Philosophy and Rhetoric* 23: 125–35.

Zeitlin, F. I. (1990) "Thebes: theater of self and society in Athenian drama," in J. J. Winkler and F. I. Zeitlin, edd., *Nothing to do with Dionysos?*, 130–67. Princeton.

Ziolkowski, J. E. (1981) *Thucydides and the Tradition of Funeral Speeches at Athens*. New York.

General index

abuse, 173n, 174, 183, 185, 187; *see also* blame, invective
Academy of Plato, 14n
active/passive roles of lovers, 149n, 154n, 160; *see also* lover and beloved
Adonis, gardens of, 166–7
Adrastus, 103n
advice, 174, 181, 183n, 191
Aeschines, 4, 44n, 56n, 109n
Aeschylus, 63, 149
afterlife, 78, 86
Agathon, 173
Agesilaus, 103n
agōn (verbal), 54, 73, 77, 111, 127
Ajax, 151n
akouein and its cognates, 136, 139n, 141–2, 145; *see also* hearsay
Alcibiades, 46–7, 71, 91, 99n, 110, 113–16, 119–27
Alcidamas, 100; *On the Sophists*, 27n, 72n
alien discourse, 134–8, 142, 144–6, 162, 165–6, 170, 192, 194
alien voices, 12, 135n, 138, 145, 148–9, 154
allegory of the cave, 18, 178–9
allusion, 6, 8, 78n
Ameipsias, 61–2
Amphion, 69–70, 73–80, 84, 86, 90–1
amplification, 103, 112
Anacharsis, 66
Anacreon, 137, 158, 161
analogy, 167, 190
Anaxagoras, 150
Andocides, 56n
antidosis, 28, 30; *see also* exchange, property
Antiope, 69, 73, 79
Antiphon, 16n
Antisthenes, 97, 177n
apologia, 29
apragmōn, 75, 78n
apragmosunē, 77n
Archidamas, 99n
Archilochus, 64

Archippus, 63
aretē, 34, 45, 49–50, 92; *see also* virtue
Aristippus, 23
Aristophanes, 15, 52, 83n, 104n, 113, 172n, 173, 181–2, 184n; *Acharnians*, 181, 190–1; *Birds*, 61–2; *Clouds*, 15n, 61–3; *Ecclesiazusae*, 15n, 56n, 62, 177–8; *Frogs*, 61–3, 174; *Knights*, 56n, 187–9; *Lysistrata*, 167n; *Peace*, 63; *Thesmophoriazusae*, 62, 149–50; *Wasps*, 62
Aristotle, 4, 24n, 174; on *banausia*, 56–7; on comedy, 183; his concept of philosophy, 18n, 194; on epideictic speech, 97; on epitaphs and encomia, 99; and history of ideas, 19; on life of *theōria*, 51n; *History of Animals* 146n; *Nicomachean Ethics*, 57, 173n; *Parts of Animals*, 146n; *Poetics*, 91n; *Politics*, 35n, 57; *Rhetoric*, 94–5, 101, 103–4, 117; *Sophistici Elenchi*, 100–1; on tragedy, 88n
arrangement (*diathesis*), 139–40
assembly, 25, 51, 53, 72, 136, 181
astronomers and astronomy, 15, 27, 61
Athenaeus, 100; *Deipnosophistae*, 119–20
Athens, political ideology, 104, 106; social and political life, 9, 14, 20–1, 24, 35, 38, 40–1, 94, 126, 162, 174, 184, 191, 193
atimia, 45
Attic orators, 104n; *see also* orators
audience, 6, 26, 38, 53–4, 68, 96–8, 102, 138, 139n, 142; *see also* readers
authentic discourse, 146, 163, 168–70
authenticity, 134, 138n, 142, 145
authority, 2, 7, 49, 64, 138, 142, 146, 162, 166, 168–9, 190, 192n
authorship, 137, 142, 165–6, 171
auxēsis, 103; *see also* amplification

Bacchylides, 62n
Bakhtin, M. M., 3n, 6–7, 148, 149n, 169–70, 191–2n

213

214   General index

banausia/banausoi, 55–9, 132; *see also* craft,
   technē
beauty, 47, 130
Belfiore, E., 130n
beloved, *see* lover and beloved
benefactors of the city, 33, 37–8, 41–2; *see
   also* civic good
binary logic, 155–6
binary oppositions, 139, 157
biography, 4
blame, 94, 139, 154n, 155, 157, 174, 185n;
   see also abuse, invective
Blank, D. L., 47–8
Boreas, 159
boundaries, generic, 2, 12, 133, 155, 157,
   161, 194–5, *see also* genre; psychic, 145,
   see also soul
Bowie, A., 182
Brock, R., 61n, 66

Callias, 16, 186
Capaneus, 103n
Carson, A., 158–9, 161
Carter, L. B., 51n, 76–7n
Cascardi, A. J., 194
censure, 98, 101, 105, 117, 119n, 126,
   155, 184, 187, 191; *see also* blame,
   invective
Cephalus, 100
Chaerephon, 61, 63
charis, 39, 41–2, 50, 54, 187–8; *see also*
   gratification
Charondas, 66
Chimaera, 134, 144
Cicero, 74, 101
Cimon, 99n, 189
Cinesias, 62
citizens, 24n, 25, 35, 45, 78, 105, 125, 175,
   185–6, 191
city, 23, 25, 33, 37–9, 76, 105, 131; *see also*
   polis
civic good, 37, 40, 78–80, 89, 125; *see also*
   benefactors of the city
civic life, 22–3, 25, 36, 43, 45, 51, 70,
   191; *see also* Athens
Clay, D., 4, 172
Cleon, 56n, 181, 187–8
Clytemnestra, 100
Cohen, E., 126n
Cohen, R., 2
Colie, R., 102
comedy, 2, 4, 6, 12, 22n, 56, 61, 66, 68, 82n,
   88–9, 96n, 158, 172–6, 181–5, 187;
   politicization of, 183–4; *see also* New
   Comedy, Old Comedy

comic, 87–9; characters, 180, 186; joking,
   183; persona, 90; poets, 62–3, 178, 180,
   184, 190–1; subtext, 177, 179–80, 186
commonplaces of genre, 138–40, 142
comparison (*sunkrisis*), 69, 103, 119n, 132
competition, 118, 127–8, 184
Connus, 62
Conte, G. B., 3, 8n
contest of public voices, 192
contemplative life, 79
corruption, 28–9, 45, 175
courtesans, 100
craft and craftsmen, 57–9; *see also technē,*
   banausia
Cratinus, 61
credit, 40n
Critias, 16n
Cronus, 86
Cyrus, 99n, 150

daemonic man, 55
daimōn, 55
Damon, 22, 62
decree of Syrocosius, 181n
deliberative rhetoric, 94
demagogues, 52, 184
dēmiourgos, 48
democracy, 1, 9, 11, 18, 20, 26, 28, 38, 40n,
   41–2, 48, 68, 71–2, 99, 116, 126, 173, 180,
   186, 189, 193
dēmos, 21–2, 38, 40n, 50, 52–3, 62, 68, 96,
   116, 174, 180–4, 187–9, 191
Demosthenes, 24n, 184n; *Against Leptines,*
   95n
desire, 109, 118–19n, 143, 160–1, 187, 188;
   see also erōs
Detienne, M., 54
deus ex machina, 73, 80, 85–7
dialectic, 3, 81–3, 134, 146, 148, 163, 167n,
   168
dialogism, 7; *see also* double-voiced
   discourse, intertextuality, parody
dialogue, 83, 162, 169, 171
Dio Chrysostomos, 74n
Diomedes, 46–7
Dionysus, 183
Diotima, 55n, 116n, 121, 127, 128n, 130
Dirce, 73
discovery (*heuresis*), 139–40, 142, 145, 167–
   9
disenfranchisement, 45
disinterest, 52, 59
display-pieces, 101, 104, 111
Dissoi Logoi, 15n
divided self, 158n

Index of passages from Plato

220